COM+ and the Battle for the Middle Tier

Roger Sessions

Wiley Computer Publishing

John Wiley & Sons, Inc.

NEW YORK · CHICHESTER · WEINHEIM · BRISBANE · SINGAPORE · TORONTO

Publisher: Robert Ipsen
Editor: Theresa Hudson
Associate Developmental Editor: Kathryn A. Malm
Managing Editor: Micheline Frederick
Text Design & Composition: Benchmark Productions, Inc.

Library of Congress Cataloging-in-Publication Data:

ISBN 0-471-31717-9

Printed in the United States of America.

10 9 8 7 6 5 4 3 2

CONTENTS

I am very grateful to all the people who made this book possible.

First is my family. My wife, Alice Sessions, has supported and encouraged me for project after project. I can't imagine the last 25 years without her. My son, Michael, puts up with me working away on Baby at the strangest times and in the most ridiculous places (Disney World, malls, while waiting for movies to begin, the ubiquitous Starbucks, you get the idea). And my daughter, Emily. Austin lost a little bit of its sparkle the day she left for college at Brandeis. And finally, my mother, Vivian, who has finally gotten over the shock of my leaving IBM, and now won't rest easy until I have personally met Bill Gates. Bill, if you happen to be reading this, please drop her a note. It would mean so much to her.

I have had some great reviewers to help me with this book.

The Microsoft chapters have benefited greatly from the many suggestions made by Mary Kirtland (an excellent writer on Microsoft technologies) and Dan McLain (a Microsoft middle tier field specialist). Microsoft is lucky to have such dedicated employees on their side.

Chapter 10, "Enterprise JavaBeans" has greatly benefited from suggestions made by my reviewers: Bob Orfali and Dan Harkey (two of my favorite authors on distributed components), Ed Roman (who has recently written an excellent book on EJB), Anne Thomas (a highly regarded analyst with Patricia Seybold), Dan Burke, and the many other readers who responded to an early version of this chapter published in the ObjectWatch Newsletter. I appreciate all of their help, and the chapter has been improved by their input. However, this chapter should in no way be interpreted as reflecting any of their opinions.

Chapter 11, "CORBA" has greatly benefited from suggestions made by Ed Cobb (the top technical person at BEA Systems and the editor of the CORBA Component Specification) and Jon Siegel (on staff with the OMG). I appreciate their help, and this chapter has been improved by their input. However, this chapter should in no way be interpreted as reflecting either of their opinions.

The case studies could not have been done without cooperation from the companies about which I wrote. For the Silknet case study I am indebted to Mike O'Brien and Eric Carlson (both of Silknet). For the Dell case study I am indebted to Dave Dix and Michael Dunn (both of Dell). For the Acentris case study I am indebted to Darin Lang (of Acentris) and Ryan Donovan (of Microsoft).

And finally, thanks to the others who have supported this book. The staff at John Wiley & Sons, Inc. has been unbelievably helpful. Terri Hudson, Kathryn Malm, and Gerrie Cho have been very involved in the development of this book and have given a great deal of helpful feedback. Thanks to Janet Van Sickler, the ObjectWatch Executive Administrator, has helped with a million little details that hold my professional life together.

Thanks to all of you.

Roger Sessions is one of the world's leading experts in distributed component technology. He has extensive experience with Microsoft's COM/DCOM/MTS/COM+, OMG's CORBA, and Sun's EJB. He has written four books, dozens of articles, and is a popular keynote speaker at conferences on Component Oriented Middleware. He writes and publishes the ObjectWatch Newsletter, a widely read, highly regarded, and often hotly debated newsletter on Distributed Component Technologies. Past issues are available at www.objectwatch.com.

From 1990–1995 Roger Sessions worked at IBM on the CORBA effort. He spent a year as a lead architect for the CORBA persistence service and four years as the lead architect for the object persistence portion of the IBM implementation of CORBA. His third book, *Object Persistence, Beyond Object-Oriented Databases* (Prentice Hall, 1996), was about the CORBA Persistence Service.

Roger Sessions left IBM in 1995 to start ObjectWatch, Inc., a company dedicated to offering training and consulting services in the field of distributed components. Roger soon turned his attention to Microsoft's middle tier technologies, including COM, DCOM, MTS, MSMQ, and MSCS. His last book was *COM and DCOM: Microsoft's Vision for Distributed Objects* (John Wiley & Sons, Inc., 1997), which, for the first time, articulated Microsoft's middle tier architectural vision.

His depth of experience with CORBA, EJB, and Microsoft makes him uniquely qualified to compare and contrast these important Component Oriented Middleware visions.

Welcome to the Battle for the Middle Tier. I hope you like excitement and maybe even a little bloodshed. This is serious stuff. The company that wins control of the middle tier will become a dominant force in the future of corporate computing, and, not incidentally, will take home some rather large bucks. In this book, I am going to tell you about the technology on which Microsoft is betting its future in this high-stakes race. I will also tell you how its technology compares to its competitors. And if you think you don't care about the middle tier, I am going to tell you why you are wrong.

This book is for people seeking a conceptual understanding of middle tier component issues, how those issues are addressed by Microsoft's middle tier architecture (COM+ and related products) and how Microsoft's solution compares with the competition. If your primary interest is in how to save five microseconds by using an optimized C++ in-line call, then you need another book. If your primary interest is in how to design your commerce systems so that your company will still be in business five years after that optimized in-line call returns, then you are in the right place.

Not only do I tell you how to design your next-generation systems, but I use such simple explanations that if you have a basic understanding of object-oriented programming, you will have no trouble understanding everything I say. How do I pull off this neat trick? I focus on the unifying concepts, not the details. I make the programming examples as easy to understand as possible. I use everyday analogies to explain things, rather than convoluted technobabble.

Microsoft helps with this simple explanation business. They have designed their middle tier architecture to be easy to use. They are making you a reasonable proposition: You worry about the business logic and Microsoft will worry about the rocket science. This is a good deal. It means that with a basic understanding of component technology, a general grasp of the instance management algorithms, and a reasonable overview of transactions, you too can build applications that can work well in the unforgiving world of online commerce, in which only the strong survive.

COMWare

This book is about Component-Oriented Middleware (COMWare). COMWare is the new technology that is revolutionizing the field of electronic commerce. It is the software architecture that governs the middle tier, which allows business logic to run efficiently, especially when that business logic is written in the form of reusable components, and especially when those components involve electronic commerce.

The COMWare industry started when Microsoft introduced MTS (Microsoft Transaction Server), the first product to bring together the up-until-then disparate technologies of components and transaction processing monitors. In my last book, *COM and DCOM: Microsoft's Vision for Distributed Objects* (John Wiley & Sons, Inc., 1997), I predicted that MTS would shake the computer industry to its core. I said that MTS was the first of a new generation of technologies that would allow small, inexpensive server machines to take over the work of large, expensive mainframes. I believe that prediction has come true.

Although MTS was not widely recognized by the general public for its important contributions, within the industry, MTS was a wake-up call. Companies like IBM, Sun, and Oracle saw MTS for what it was: a challenge to the mainframes for control of commerce on the Web. These companies had to respond to MTS or become extinct.

The first response was from Sun. Sun released its first Enterprise JavaBeans (EJB) specification as a rather uninspired rewrite of MTS for Java. As EJB has matured, Sun has tried to branch off from MTS and introduce some new, original ideas.

The second response was from the OMG (Object Management Group), an industry consortium led by IBM, Sun, Oracle, and BEA. This response was the CORBA Component Specification, which, as of press time, is in the process of completion. This specification is largely based on EJB, with a few new tricks of its own.

Now Microsoft is preparing to release COM+. COM+ is the next generation of its COMWare technology. You can think of it as the next release of MTS: The packaging is new, much of the interior is rewritten, and there are a few new features thrown in. But COM+ continues the challenge started by MTS.

This book gives a general overview of COMWare, describes COM+ and the related Microsoft COMWare technologies, and compares COM+ to Enterprise JavaBeans and the CORBA Component Specification.

Who Should Read This Book

This book is for people who are trying to get an overview of the COMWare industry, what Microsoft offers in this important area, and how its offerings compare to the competition. This book is for technical officers, managers, system designers, programmers, and others who need to understand COMWare. This book does not go into a lot of technical depth, so it won't appeal to programmers who just want to know how to get their programs to work. It is intended more for those trying to make decisions about which technical direction their companies should move in with respect to COMWare.

In this book, I present material you will see nowhere else, such as some of the problems with newer Enterprise JavaBeans technology. But I am equally quick to point out problems in the Microsoft technologies. I do my best to be fair to all technologies. I like the Microsoft COMWare technologies, but nothing is perfect, and every technology has its own unique set of advantages and disadvantages.

I have included three case studies, so you can see some of the ways your peers are using Microsoft's COMWare technologies. I discuss the advantages and disadvantages of the choices they have made. My hope is that these case studies will give you some good ideas that you can incorporate into your own products.

It is definitely not my goal to convince you to turn over your operation to COM+. I am not affiliated with Microsoft. My goal is to help you better understand the good and bad points of all technologies, so that you can make the best possible choices between competing technologies. If you end up feeling this book helped you make intelligent choices, then I will feel that this book has been successful.

How This Book Is Organized

Let's take a look at the organization of this book, which I have split into four parts.

Part One   Introduction to Component-Oriented Middleware

Part One introduces Component-Oriented Middleware (COMWare). This section is applicable to all of the COMWare technologies. It discusses what problems we need to solve to create Web-based commerce systems, how component architectures came about, the first middle tier infrastructures introduced by transaction processing monitors, and how these components and transaction processing monitors came together to form the new field of COMWare. This section includes the following chapters:

Chapter 1. The Problems of Commerce. When evaluating COMWare technologies, you need to start with a definition of a problem. This chapter describes the problems involved in Web-based commerce, because it is within the context of these problems that I will be evaluating and discussing COMWare.

Chapter 2. Components. What do we mean by a component? How does it relate to an object? In this chapter I look at traditional component technologies and the distributed architectures that are common to both COM/DCOM, CORBA, and Java RMI.

Chapter 3. Transaction Processing Monitors. This chapter describes another technology that was developed independently of components. TPM was the first technology to attempt to deal with large distributed commerce systems, and was extremely influential in the development of COMWare.

Chapter 4. COMWare. This chapter defines Component-Oriented Middleware, the infrastructure that combines components and TPMs, and comes up with a new technology that is a little of each, but quite different than either. This new technology will be driving our commerce systems for many years to come.

Part Two   COM+

Part Two delves into the Microsoft COMWare technologies. It describes the different functions of COM+, and how COM+ addresses the various issues raised in Part One. It covers the basic COM+ component model, the closely related middle tier technologies, and the runtime environment COM+ offers to support scalability, security, and transactional integrity. Part Two includes these chapters:

Chapter 5. COM+ and Friends. COM+ is an important technology, but it isn't enough to develop large commerce systems. This chapter introduces some of the other closely related Microsoft technologies, some of which will be used in conjunction with COM+, and some of which will provide important layers upon which COM+ builds.

Chapter 6. COM+ Components. This chapter introduces the basic component model of COM+. I talk about how we take business logic, hide it behind an interface, and package it into reusable components that will be managed by the COM+ runtime environment.

Chapter 7. COM+ Runtime Environment. Speaking of the COM+ runtime, here is where I discuss how COM+ manages components, the decisions you must make about your components' runtime characteristics, and how COM+ makes it possible to develop large complex applications without having to get involved with the difficult issues of security, transaction boundary management, and scalability.

Chapter 8. The COM+ Services. COM+ offers two important services that extend the capability of the runtime. This chapter discusses asynchronous components and the COM+ event model, as well as some related topics.

Chapter 9. COM+ Interoperability. Microsoft is serious about interoperability, and in this chapter I discuss some of the ways you can build COM+ components that interact with non-Microsoft technologies.

Part Three   The Competition

Part Three looks at the competition. Microsoft, of course, is not the only organization trying to win the hearts and minds of middle tier programmers. This section discusses the alternatives to COM+ being proposed by the OMG and Sun. This section includes these chapters:

Chapter 10. Enterprise JavaBeans. Enterprise JavaBeans (EJB) is the Java COMWare technology that is heavily influenced by MTS, which is the official name of the first generation of COM+. In this chapter I discuss how EJB compares to COM+. There are some great features of EJB, but also some serious problems that have generally been overlooked by the press. I'll discuss both the good and the bad features of EJB here.

Chapter 11. CORBA. The OMG is in the process of releasing their COMWare technology, which is called the CORBA Component Specification (CCS). CCS has important characteristics of both EJB and COM+. Here I take a critical look at this just-off-the-press technology.

Part Four   Case Studies

The proof is in the pudding, so in Part Four I look at some actual systems that have been built with Microsoft first- and second-generation COMWare technologies. I have chosen three companies, which represent many of the important requirements of serious commerce systems. I suspect that every company can find something to relate to in one or more of these case studies.

In this section, I have had to make some choices. I could have focused only on COM+ applications, which would have limited me to applications that have not yet been released and proven in the market, since COM+ is, as of press time, still in beta. But I think nonproven applications are of limited value. So I have chosen to include two case studies of market-tested applications built using MTS. MTS is the first generation of COM+, and from the perspective of these applications, there is very little difference between MTS and COM+. However I have also included a pure COM+ application that is very close to being released, and which has already completed a series of important benchmarks. This section includes these chapters:

Chapter 12. Silknet: Treating Customers as People. Silknet is built on MTS, the first generation of COM+. This is an excellent case study that shows how to build a well-designed application from COM+-style components. This case study focuses mostly on the design issues.

Chapter 13. Dell: Commerce on the Cheap. Dell has built a huge commerce application MTS; again, the first generation of COM+. This case study focuses on an important feature of COM+, the cost of processing a transaction.

Chapter 14. Acentris: Transactional Gusto. Acentris is a pure COM+ case study. This case study focuses on the transactional throughput attainable with COM+. You will be surprised at some of the results Acentris found.

Part Five   Wrap-Up

I'll leave you with information that I think will help you make sense out of the confusing area of COMWare. First, I'll tell you how to choose between the different technologies, then give you some common definitions that can be used with any COMWare technology. I'll also give you directions for future reading.

Chapter 15. Considering COMWare Technologies. I am often called upon to help companies make decisions about COMWare technology. Over the years, I have found a few issues that seem to stand out in the decision making process. I will point out some of the most important issues that I think you should consider when choosing between COMWare technologies.

Glossary. This contains my recommendations for terminology relevant to COMWare.

Additional Resources. I'll tell you about some of my favorite COMWare books, which you can use to further your understanding. I recommend books on general COMWare, COM+, CORBA, EJB, and a few that fit into none of these categories.

And now, without further ado, we will begin the show.

Introduction to Component-Oriented Middleware

W hat is Component-Oriented Middleware (COMWare)? Why do we need it? Where does it come from? These are some of the questions I will tackle in the first part of this book. COMWare is the marriage of two technologies: Transaction Processing Monitors (TPMs) and Components. COMWare is both of these and neither of these. It is really a whole new technology, but a new technology with deep roots. Part I is a general overview to this exciting technology that so many agree has so much promise. By all accounts, COMWare will enable commerce on the Web. Later, I will discuss the specific COMWare platforms: COM+, Enterprise JavaBeans (EJB), and CORBA. Let me start by telling you what is common to all the COMWare platforms and exactly what this technology is all about.

The Problems of Commerce

You can pretty much learn everything you need to know about commerce systems by sitting in Starbucks for two hours. I do this frequently, especially the one on Route 183 and Lake Line Parkway in the northwest suburbs of Austin, Texas. I think of this particular Starbucks as being the worldwide headquarters of ObjectWatch, Inc. I have my business meetings here. I do my writing here. This is where Janet, the ObjectWatch Executive Administrator, and I plan our classes, and in general develop our strategy for worldwide conquest.

Today is a typical day at Starbucks. Brian and Mark are behind the counter, as usual, working the polished La Marzotco espresso machine like a finely tuned musical instrument. Mark is taking money. A dozen people are sitting around working, reading the newspaper, or greeting friends. Ella Fitzgerald is singing "Let's Fall in Love" in the background. I am sipping my Doppio Macchiato, one sugar, extra foam. If I am lucky, I have managed to grab one of the two easy chairs; if not, I am at the polished wood table. Baby, my laptop, has four hours of battery life left, more than enough for me to put in a couple of hours working on my next book, hoping against hope that for once in my life I can look Terri in the face (or actually, look her e-mail in the face) when she asks, "Is the next chapter finished yet?". Yes, a typical day at Starbucks.

I usually arrive at Starbucks around 7:30 A.M., a particularly good time to observe commerce at work—at least at Starbucks. The line waiting to conduct commerce is often to the door, and in the next two hours perhaps three hundred people will conduct their business, culminating in their ritualistic first sip of coffee that, for many, marks the official beginning of the new day.

Rules of Commerce

As I sit here starting my business day, these are some of the important commerce rules I see played out in front of me.

Rule 1. Companies Need Profit

It doesn't take very many Doppio Macchiatos at Starbucks to figure out that Starbucks is not a nonprofit institution. I can hardly blame them for this—after all, neither is ObjectWatch. This is fine with me. I have become dependent on my local Starbucks, and I don't like to have dependencies on companies that are not making a profit. I figure if they aren't making a profit, they probably won't be around very long.

Rule 2. Individual Clients Don't Spend Much

Starbucks doesn't make much money on any one client. This is sometimes difficult to believe as I add up my daily bill for Doppio Macchiatos, but the fact is that even my fully addicted intact rate of approximately 350 Doppio Macchiatos per year brings in only about $626 to the worldwide Starbucks corporation. Even assuming that 50 percent of this is profit, the money Starbucks makes on me per year would not fund the Starbucks worldwide operations for more than about 30 seconds. So if Starbucks is going to survive, they need a lot of people like me.

Rule 3. Clients Spend Money Slowly

Not only do clients not spend very much money (see Rule 2), they spend it very slowly. A full 24 hours may elapse between my Starbucks transactions. If Starbucks were to plot my daily activity, it would look something like the graph shown in Figure 1.1. Notice that there is a peak of Doppio activity at about 8:00 A.M., and sometimes a second peak

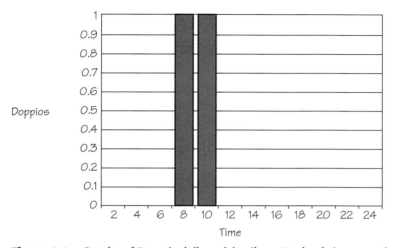

Figure 1.1 Graphs of Roger's daily activity (from Starbucks' perspective).

around 10:00 A.M. But that is it. Any more peaks than that and you have to pry me off the walls. Starbucks cannot tie up a lot of resources waiting for me to decide to buy my next Doppio.

Since I spend most of my day *not* buying Doppios at Starbucks, Starbucks can't afford to tie up a lot of resources on me except during that short period of time when I am actually buying Doppios. If Starbucks were to dedicate Brian to me for the whole time I am sitting there, Brian would be doing nothing for most of the day. Sure, Brian would have 30 seconds of work to do for me at 8:00 A.M., and again at 10:00 A.M., but for the rest of the time, Brian would be twiddling his thumbs. If Starbucks were to dedicate a Brian to every customer sitting around at Starbucks, there would be a lot of people behind the counter twiddling their thumbs. Assuming each Brian makes $8.00 an hour, Starbucks could easily turn into a very expensive thumb-twiddling operation.

So Starbucks doesn't dedicate a Brian to me. Starbucks trains Brian to work for me only during those short periods of time when I am actually ordering. While I am sitting around staring at the unforgiving screen of Baby, Brian is busy processing some other customer's order.

Rule 4. You Need A Lot of Clients

How do you make a living in this crazy world? What do you do with a bunch of clients that do not spend very much money, and what little they do spend, they spend at a snail's pace? You have two options: You can either drive yourself crazy trying to get your clients to spend more and spend it faster. Or you can go for a large number of clients. Starbucks has gone the second route. Starbucks can survive quite well on my measly 600 odd dollars per year, as long as there are a lot more of me where I came from. You take one million of me, each one spending $600 per year, and suddenly we are looking at some serious money. So the answer is not in trying to squeeze more money out of each client. The ultimate answer is in trying to have a whole lot of clients.

Rule 5. You Need A Lot of Starbucks

If you want to make a lot of money, you need a lot of clients. But there is a limit to how many clients one Starbucks can service. You could build a super-Starbucks the size of a football field, and it wouldn't make significantly more money than a cozy Starbucks the size of a swimming pool. Ten cozy Starbucks, each costing $100,000 to build will yield much more profit per dollar of investment than one super-Starbucks costing $1,000,000.

Having multiple Starbucks has two other advantages as well: *load balancing* and *redundancy*.

Let's start with load balancing. Many customers drive past two or more Starbucks between their home and work each day. Some people probably drive past three or four. If I drive past one Starbucks that is overly crowded, I can just go to the other Starbucks. If one super-Starbucks gets overly crowded and it is the only game in town, then Starbucks loses my business. I go next door to the competition.

Now consider redundancy. The United Confederation of Starbucks can easily lose one or two isolated Starbucks, here or there. If, for example, my local Starbucks gets flooded out, I will just move on down the street to my "almost" local Starbucks. Starbucks probably won't even lose any business. However if the United Confederation has spent its entire Austin building allotment on one super-Starbucks that gets flooded out, then business is finished. No more Austin customers.

Starbucks is one business where a lot of small units is better than a few large units. Small units better meet the needs of a geographically dispersed client base, do a better job distributing workload, and are better able to handle unexpected store closings.

In the background, as I sip my Doppio Macchiato, Ella Fitzgerald sings, "Don't put all your eggs in one basket." It seems appropriate.

Rule 6. Starbucks Needs to Be Easy to Build

If we are going to be building a lot of Starbucks, then Starbucks needs to be easy to build. One of the reasons Starbucks can be built so easily is the Starbucks Corporation does not worry much about infrastructure. They use existing roads, existing sewage systems, existing electrical supplies, existing phone lines. They limit their attention to the business they understand: building coffee houses and serving coffee products to a severely addicted population.

Rule 7. Starbucks Needs to Be Easy to Modify

Starbucks are not all the same. The Starbucks at the Austin airport bears only a superficial resemblance to the Starbucks at Route 183 and Lake Line. The airport Starbucks has no seats, no parking, few amenities, and workers less willing to work with you on any individual parameters you like passed to your coffee request. Nevertheless, it is clearly a Starbucks. I can order my Doppio Macchiato, and get a drink that closely resembles what I get when I order a Doppio Macchiato from my usual Starbucks. So the Starbucks Corporation has build in variability to the Starbucks formula. They can adapt the Starbucks plan to local requirements.

Rule 8. Starbucks Needs to Support Many Client Types

A lot of different types of people come into Starbucks each morning: IBMers stopping for coffee on their way to work; Westwood High School students on their way to school; office-less workers looking for a quiet place to work for a few hours; lovers meeting for a quick rendezvous; teachers on break; retirees relaxing over the newspaper.

We know (by Rule 4) that Starbucks needs a lot of clients to make a lot of money. To service a lot of clients, Starbucks can't be limited to only one type of client. It must appeal to technologists, students, vagabonds, paramours, intellectuals, and the leisure class without prejudice.

Rule 9. Starbucks Must Be Dependable

I count on Starbucks: I count on it for my morning Doppio and I count on it for a place to work for a few hours each morning. If I come in one morning and find Starbucks closed, I will not be happy. If I come in a second morning, and still find it closed, I will start looking for alternatives. Even if Starbucks opens again the following day, I will never know it. I will be history. It will be weeks, perhaps months before I will trust my delicate morning routine to Starbucks again.

Closing for two days is much more expensive to Starbucks than the actual business lost during those two days. The real cost is the long-term loss of good will. Customers are willing to put up with a lot. They will put up with waiting on line, untrained staff, and occasional order mistakes. But they will not put up with not knowing if they can get their critical business needs (a.k.a. caffeine fix) met when they need it.

Rule 10. Starbucks Is a Database-Updating Company

Not to shatter any illusions, but Starbucks actually has little interest in selling coffee. Selling coffee is an ends to a means. What Starbucks really cares about is making profit. If Starbucks ever discovers that selling coffee does not equate to making profit, I assure you, they will have as much interest in selling coffee as Computer City has in selling OS/2 operating systems. Ultimately, Starbucks is a technology for moving money from one place (my bank account) to another place (their bank account).

Given this, you may be surprised at how often the following scene plays out in front of me each day. Somebody comes into Starbucks. They pick a bunch of stuff and bring it over to the counter. Brian looks over the merchandise. Some conversation ensues. Eventually the customer happily leaves Starbucks, merchandise in tow, *without leaving a penny in payment*. Not only does Brian not call the police, but he cheerfully invites the customer to return again.

I myself often work this way. I come in and start a tab. Janet comes in and between us we run up an $8–10 tab. Then I leave without ever giving anybody any money. I'm well known for doing this, yet nobody minds. How can this be?

The fact of the matter is that many of the transactions at Starbucks do not involve cash at all. Many people pay the way I do, with a credit card. No money changes hands, at least in the literal sense. Starbucks could probably start a cashless policy and lose very little business.

Starbucks could survive quite happily doing nothing more than updating databases. That, of course, is what a credit card transaction is—a series of database updates. Starbucks updates the database containing my American Express account, adding a debit to my account. It then updates the database containing its bank accounts, adding a credit.

A series of database updates that are logically connected are what we call a *transaction*. So you can see that Starbucks is ultimately nothing more than an excuse for processing transactions.

Rule 11. Starbucks Needs Security

Money is funny. It brings out the worst in people. Some people would like to steal Starbucks' hard-earned profit. If enough people are successful at this, Starbucks will go out of business, regardless of how much profit they make. Therefore Starbucks needs to worry about security, and worry about it a lot.

There are all kinds of opportunities for people to make off with Starbucks' hard-earned profit. Customers can pass off counterfeit money or give bad credit cards. Employees can take from the till. Deposits can be lost. Suppliers can make up phony invoices. Accounts receivable clerks can set up phony accounts. If there is a single hole in the Starbucks security system, somebody will figure out how to exploit it. And Starbucks will be no more.

Rule 12. Starbucks Depends on a Middle Tier

Since Starbucks wants to make a profit (see Rule 1), you might expect that the simplest Starbucks organization would be for me to come in, walk over to the espresso machine, make my Doppio, walk over to the cash register, open it, and put in my money. Believe it or not, this is not how Starbucks operates.

Starbucks has a whole middle tier architecture between their client tier (me) and their money storage tier (the cash register). This middle tier is made up of a series of cooperating components, usually a Brian component and a Mark component. The Brian component looks at me and says, "The Usual?" Upon my confirmation he yells out to the Mark component, "One Doppio Macchiato, one brown sugar, extra foam!" Then the Mark component either creates my Doppio directly, or sometimes batches up the order for as-soon-as-possible processing. Meanwhile, the Brian component tells me the cost. I hand the Brian component some money. He calculates my change, places my money in the cash register, takes my change out of the cash register, and hands me my change. I go back to my table. Eventually the Mark component calls out, "One Doppio Macchiato, one brown sugar, extra foam." I get my drink, and the day has officially begun. Even Baby seems somehow more relaxed when the Doppio ritual has been completed successfully.

Wouldn't things be much simpler if we just eliminated this whole middle tier? After all, Brian and Mark are fairly expensive components, with regular ongoing maintenance costs. Why doesn't Starbucks just tell me to make my own Doppio and take care of my own money transaction?

The fact is, there are a whole series of advantages to this middle tier that more than outweigh its costs. Let's consider a few.

The middle tier provides security. Starbucks worries about security (see Rule 11). It needs to limit the number of people with access to its money. The Brian component is trusted to put money in and out of the cash register. I am not. Starbucks is not alone in this opinion. My wife, Alice, is equally suspicious of my ability to manage money.

The middle tier makes the whole system easy to modify. Starbucks needs to modify its technology to meet local demand (see Rule 7). The middle tier consolidates business logic. Starbucks doesn't have to train hundreds of thousands of customers to understand the subtle differences between the northwest Austin Starbucks and the Airport Starbucks. Instead, it can rely on a few well-trained employees. Customers are taught only how to interact with Starbucks employees to get their coffee. Thus customers can successfully get their coffee from either of these Starbucks, even though those two Starbucks are quite different.

The middle tier provides efficiency. Without a middle tier, customers would line up at the espresso machine and then line up again at the cash register. With a middle tier, customers just line up once to place an order and pay. Since this operation is quite fast, customers are freed to work on their next book chapter while the time consuming operation (making the drinks) is occurring in the background.

The middle tier allows the system to support many more customers. Let's say Starbucks has 10 keys to its cash register. With no middle tier, each customer is responsible for his or her own money transfers. Each customer, therefore, needs a key to the cash register. I, as a regular Starbucks customer, need my key to the cash register. Janet, who often meets me at Starbucks, needs her own key. Besides Janet and me, Starbucks is limited to only eight more customers before its key supply is used up.

But we know Starbucks needs a lot more than 10 customers to make money (see Rule 4). So dedicating a cash register key to each customer is not practical. Starbucks needs some other way for customers to get money into the cash register.

That other way is Brian. He is the middle tier component that will access the cash register. Because customers will only access the cash register indirectly, through Brian, only Brian (and the Brian equivalents at other shifts) needs keys to the cash register. This allows a very large number of customers to deposit money into the cash register even though Starbucks has only a very small number of keys to that cash register available.

So we can immediately see four advantages to the Starbucks middle-tier architecture. The middle tier adds security. The middle tier makes the whole system easy to modify. The middle tier allows customers to be processed more efficiently (with less waiting time). And the middle tier allows a much larger number of customers to be processed with limited resources.

Rule 13. Portability Is Not a Major Issue

Recently I went into a great Austin coffee house called Ruta Maya. It looks nothing like Starbucks. I was just about to open my mouth and utter my usual words, "One Doppio Macchiato, please" when I happened to glance up at the menu. Prominently displayed was a large red sign with the dire warning: "No Starbuckese spoken here!" I went into a panic. Is "Doppio Macchiato" a universal concept, or is it "Starbuckese"? Am I about to be recognized for the coffee cognoscenti that I have always believed myself to be, or am I about to announce to the world that I am a witless pawn of The Slimeball Enemy? I frantically read the Ruta Maya menu. No Doppios! No Macchiatos of any kind! Now what?

I am happy to report I survived the experience. I forced myself to relax. I took a few deep breaths. I figured out that what Starbucks calls a "Doppio," Ruta Maya calls a "Double." What Starbucks calls a "Macchiato," Ruta Maya calls an "Espresso with Foam."

This scary experience could have been avoided if only we had a world-wide standard for ordering from coffee shops. Let's imagine all the coffee shops in the world form a consortium whose purpose is to define an absolute standard to define what coffee shops can sell and how customers are expected to order. The consortium might call this standard the Coffee Or Related Beverage Activity standard, or just CORBA for short.

The advantage of this is clear. I can walk into any coffee shop in the world that claims to supports CORBA and know exactly what I can order and how to order it before I even enter. I don't have to look at the menu. I don't have to worry about whether or not my favorite beverage is sold. My order is portable, in that it can be freely moved from any one coffee shop to any other.

Unfortunately, there are many disadvantages to CORBA.

As a consumer, my first concern is whether or not my particular beverage is going to be available when and where I want it. After all, I am not exactly open minded about my morning caffeine. I want one Doppio Macchiato, one sugar, extra foam. Period. I don't want a Solo Macchiato. I don't want a Doppio Mochachino. It is much more important to me that when I walk into Starbucks, I can get my Doppio Macchiato, than it is that Starbucks support some arbitrary (from my perspective) standard. I spend on average 15 hours a week at Starbucks. I spend on average 15 minutes a week in all other coffee shops in the world combined. I want my Starbucks time optimized. When I am visiting foreign territory, I will make do.

From the perspective of the coffee shop proprietors, the standard is also questionable. If all coffee shops support only the CORBA standard, how can coffee shops distinguish themselves? Obviously, by extending the standard. Even though coffee shops will claim to support CORBA, each will add on their own proprietary extensions. So Ruta Maya will sell CORBA plus its own Four Shot Special.

Unfortunately, from the consumers' perspective, these proprietary extensions rapidly dilute whatever value the standard had in the first place. If I am a Ruta Maya regular, how do I know whether the Four Shot Special is specific to Ruta Maya or is part of CORBA? The only way to find out is to walk into another CORBA coffee shop and see what their reaction is when I order the Four Shot Special.

The biggest coffee shop, namely Starbucks, has little reason to support the standard anyway. From Starbucks perspective, there is already a *de facto* standard: the Starbucks menu. The standard is freely available and anybody that wants to support it is free to do so. The little shops might argue that Starbucks will manipulate the menu, constantly trying to put them at a disadvantage. But Starbucks just sees itself as constantly striving to improve its own products.

So if the CORBA standard is not going to be supported by the world's biggest coffee shop, and if those coffee shops that do support it will be extending it, and if the standard provides little if any benefit to the consumers in any case, why have it? Those of us who have been jaded might suspect that the real reason for CORBA has little to do with making anyone's life easier. What it really is about is all the little coffee shops trying to figure out how to stop Starbucks from taking over the world.

The little coffee shops might care if Starbucks takes over the world, but frankly, I don't. I want my Doppio Macchiato. I want it in northwest Austin. I want it in downtown Austin. I want it in Paris. I want it in Sweden. I ask for so little, after all.

Rule 14. Interoperability *Is* a Major Issue

We should not confuse portability with interoperability. Portability means that my coffee order can be recognized by any coffee shop in the world. Interoperability means that my Starbucks Doppio Macchiato can be drunk while typing on my COMPAQ Armada 7800, while talking to Janet on my Nokia Digital telephone, or while reading Michael Ventura's latest column in the Austin Chronicle. After all, Starbucks is only one part of my world. The value of my Doppio Macchiato comes from its ability to fit into a world that is much larger than just Starbucks.

Not only do I need interoperability for my Doppio, Starbucks' entire organization depends on interoperability. As I sit here, I am staring at a recent delivery awaiting transport to the back room. I see boxes of hot cups from the Solo Cup Company, cold cups from the Sweetheart cup company, plastic wrap from the Purity, even a new mop head from the Pollock Corporation. And this is just the tip of the iceberg. Starbucks depends on hundreds of vendors circling the globe, and each of those vendors depends on hundreds of others. There must be a million people contributing in one way or another to my humble

Doppio. I would like to let each and every one of you know how much I appreciate your efforts.

Who Cares About Starbucks?

By now you may be wondering what this book has to do with COM+ and modern software development. We are going to focus on a particular facet of modern software development: those systems intended to support commerce. We will call these systems *commerce systems*. It turns out that commerce systems have to solve many of the same problems as does Starbucks.

Like Starbucks, commerce systems are there to support the profitability of some company (Rule 1). So the delicate balance between income and expenses is always very much on the mind of those creating commerce systems. COM+ allows commerce systems to be developed at low cost, and allows those systems to run on commodity hardware.

Like Starbucks, most commerce systems have to deal with transactions that individually do not make much money (Rule 2). When you spend $40 to buy a book from barnesandnoble.com, the actual profit (after all expenses) from that book is probably under $1. That $1 doesn't go very far in supporting the barnesandnoble.com corporation. You cannot dedicate many resources to an individual sale when profit margin from that sale is so slim. COM+ minimizes the expense of dealing with individual customers by making very efficient use of resources, by making the underlying infrastructure itself very inexpensive, and by allowing the whole middle tier to be run on an inexpensive class machines.

Like Starbucks, most commerce systems have to deal with clients that spend money slowly (Rule 3). The typical customer at barnesandnoble.com may stay on their web site for one hour before they finally click the button that will eventually result in the generation of $1 in profit. Clients cannot be tying up middle-tier resources during the entire time they are working with the commerce system. Middle-tier resources include database connections, TCP/IP connections, message queue handles, and other expensive resources. COM+ addresses this problem by minimizing the time an individual client uses the middle tier. Resources are allocated at the last possible moment and reclaimed as early as possible. You can get a sense of this from Figure 1.2.

Like Starbucks, most commerce systems need to be able to process a large number of clients at the same time to make money (Rule 4). If barnesandnoble.com can service only one customer at a time, and if that customer takes one hour to make a purchase that generates $1 in profit, barnesandnoble.com won't be in business very long. So commerce systems must be able to handle not one, but many clients at the same time. If barnesandnoble.com can process 100,000 customers at a time, then it can still generate reasonable profits even if each one of those customers takes an hour to complete an order. COM+, as shown in Figure 1.3, addresses this issue by providing a rich, middle-tier infrastructure that is focused primarily on support for a large number of clients.

Figure 1.2 Last moment resource allocation.

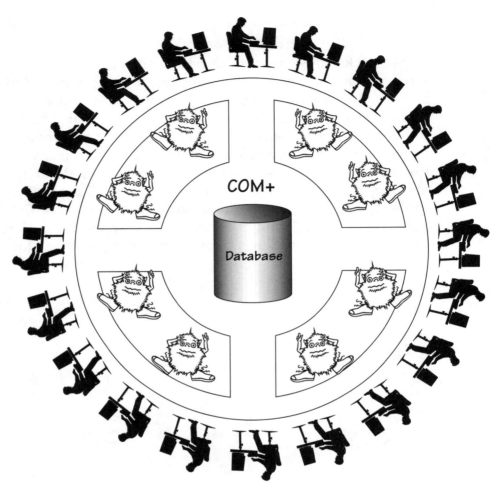

Figure 1.3 COM+: A rich, middle-tier infrastructure.

Like Starbucks, most commerce systems need redundancy (Rule 5). If barnesandnoble.com builds one large system to deal with all its customers, it is taking a large risk on that system going down or getting overloaded with work. A customer deals with commerce systems when it is convenient to the customer, not when it is convenient to the system. It is much safer to develop a commerce system that is distributed over a series of machines than to develop one that runs only on one large, mammoth computer. The distributed system provides better load balancing and better fault tolerance. COM+ has very good support for system redundancy.

Like Starbucks, most commerce systems must be easy to build (Rule 6). This easily could be in conflict with Rule 3, which dictates mechanisms to minimize per client cost; Rule 4, which dictates support for large numbers of clients; and Rule 5, which dictates the use of collections of machines and systems that are distributed. Systems that support all of these needs are quite sophisticated and difficult to build. COM+ addresses this issue by providing a rich runtime environment for the middle tier that *automatically* provides client efficiency, scalability, and redundancy without any work on the behalf of the business logic programmer.

Like Starbucks, most commerce systems must be easy to modify (Rule 7). Today's commerce systems must be readily adaptable to meet new competitive challenges. The Web itself is constantly changing and offering new opportunities for technologically savvy companies. Customers have greater expectations every year. Yesterday's state-of-the-art interfaces are today's anachronisms. Commerce systems need the ability to adapt almost instantaneously to new market pressures. COM+ addresses this issue through its embrace of component technology, the most adaptable software technology known for defining and implementing business logic.

Like Starbucks, most commerce systems need to be able to relate to all types of clients (Rule 8). Commerce systems today have all kinds of clients, and need to be adaptable to new clients that today we aren't even thinking about. The basic business logic for a bank, for example, may have to serve clients accessing the systems through phone-in tellers, drive-in tellers, automatic teller machines, web browsers, or dial-in menus. Nobody knows how tomorrow's clients will be accessing these systems. If the bank down the street doubles its business by allowing clients to do banking through Palm Pilots, you can be sure the bank up the street will be offering Palm Pilot service as well in the immediate future. COM+ business components can work efficiently with a wide diversity of client needs, as shown in Figure 1.4.

Like Starbucks, most commerce systems need excellent dependability (Rule 9). When I need my money, I need my money. I don't want to hear explanations from the bank about why their system is down. It takes very few such explanations before I move to another bank. When I want to buy something, I want to buy something. If the store can't take my credit card because the credit card system is down, the store loses a sale. It doesn't take many lost sales before that store finds

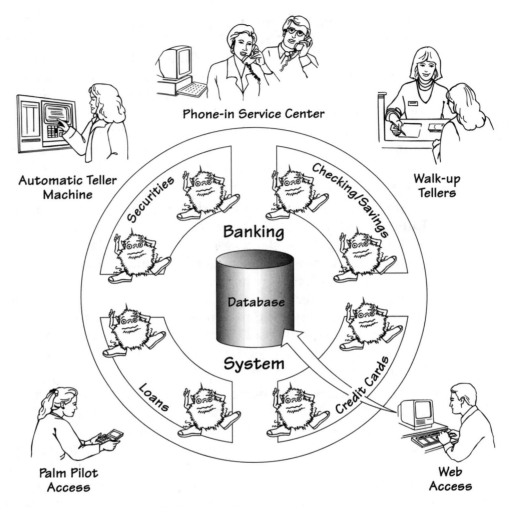

Figure 1.4 One business logic, many clients.

another credit card system. COM+ uses cluster-like technology to ensure that systems have high reliability.

Like Starbucks, most commerce systems are database updating systems (Rule 10). In today's electronic world, "moving money" is most often a matter of updating databases. When I buy a shirt from Eddie Bauer's, very rarely does any cash change hands. Usually the purchase involves a cascade of database updates, flowing from my credit card to the Eddie Bauer's bank accounts and to the suppliers' accounts. We might even say that the ultimate purpose of commerce systems is to update databases. COM+ ties in well with all popular database products.

Like Starbucks, most commerce systems are very worried about security (Rule 11). Where there is money, there is greed. Any company that depends on the good nature of the human species is not going to be with us very long. Of course, 99 percent of the people are trustworthy, but it only takes one dishonest person to do a lot of damage. COM+ has a reliable and simple security model that is well integrated with the security of the underlying operating system.

Like Starbucks, most commerce systems depend on a middle tier (Rule 12). Most modern electronic commerce systems are organized in at least three tiers. The back end is the database tier. This includes a confederation of machines that are involved with managing databases. The front end is the client tier. This includes machines that are hooked up to living, breathing human beings. Frequently the client tier is closely associated with a Web tier that processes HTTP requests on behalf of client machines and returns Web pages. Between the client/Web tier and the database tier is a series of cooperating machines that contain the business logic. This is the middle tier. The relationship between these tiers is shown in Figure 1.5.

The middle tier is critical to commerce systems. This is where the action is. There are two compelling reasons why we need a middle tier: manageability and scalability. It is impossible to build a manageable commerce system without consolidating the business logic onto a small number of well-controlled middle tier machines. It is also impossible to scale a commerce system to a large number of users without depending on a middle tier infrastructure. We will discuss the dual issues of manageability and scalability in the next chapter.

Like Starbucks, most commerce systems do not need to be portable (Rule 13). When I speak at conferences, I often ask how many people consider portability important for the middle tier. Invariably, 80 percent of the people raise their hands. Then I ask how many people have ever ported a middle tier application. Ironically, only 1 to 2 percent of those people who believe portability is important have ever actually made use of portability. In my experience, it is much more important for a middle tier application to run well on the platform on which it will run than it is for that application to be hypothetically

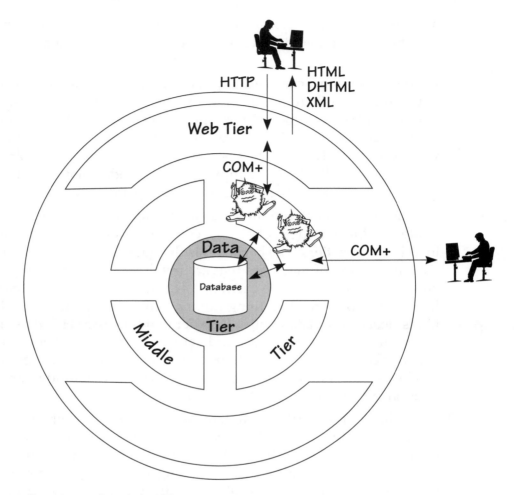

Figure 1.5 Tier relationships.

portable to some other middle tier platform on which it will almost certainly never run. COM+ is not portable. COM+ takes every possible advantage of Windows 2000, which has been designed from the ground up to support COM+. COM+ works so well precisely because of its tight coupling to the operating system. It uses every conceivable operating system trick to improve performance, scalability, and reliability. Where the operating system did not provide adequate support, it was not COM+ that changed, it was the operating system. Had COM+ been designed primarily for portability (like Enterprise JavaBeans or CORBA), it could not have these close ties to the operating system. Efficiency and portability are natural enemies. You get one or the other (if you are lucky), but you never get both. COM+ has chosen to give you the former.

Like Starbucks, most commerce systems need excellent interoperability (Rule 14). In fact, when most people say they need portability, what they really mean is that they need interoperability. People confuse portability with interoperability. On the middle tier, interoperability is critical. Our commerce systems must be able to work with a hugely diverse collection of databases, other commerce systems, and client technologies. Many people attack COM+ saying that it works only in a complete Microsoft environment. This is unfair. I am not aware of any middle-tier technology that comes even close to COM+ in its support for interoperability. COM+ interoperates with both Microsoft and non-Microsoft clients, with non-Microsoft middle-tier systems, and with virtually every important back-end database in the market.

So you can see why sitting for long periods of time at Starbucks is important. A few sips of Doppio, and the secrets of the business world unfold before you like a flower in spring. All that, and Ella Fitzgerald too. What more can one ask? And after having our first shot of caffeine for the day, we are ready to dive into the world of COM+ components. You may now turn this page.

Components

L
ife seems terribly unfair. When I want my next Doppio Macchiato I have to drop everything I am doing. I have to put down Baby, get up, walk over to the counter, and wait on line. Eventually, when Brian sees me, he calls out, "one Doppio Macchiato, one brown sugar, extra foam," so I don't actually have to disturb my delicate vocal chords. But all this getting up and walking over stuff (not to mention standing on line with the riffraff of society) is for the birds.

This is how I think it should work. I am sitting in a wicker chair, on the expansive lawn of my English estate. A grape arbor provides a hint of shade; honeysuckle scents waft over the landscape. A single butterfly joyfully lands on my cup reminding me that my Doppio Macchiato is empty. I reach down and, with a barely perceptible wrist movement, ring a tiny brass bell. An ethereal song rings out, one so clear and subtle that it could only come from one whose heart is pure and whose soul is filled with the poetry of life. Brian materializes out of the flowers, and places a cup at my side. It is of the purest bone china, white as clouds, and filled with the perfect mixture of dark, pungent espresso and billows of light-as-air foam. I take a sip, and words flow like honey onto the waiting screen of Baby, her keys literally dancing with joy at the timeless wisdom that so effortlessly pours forth from my finger tips. Yes, I'm quite sure this is how it is supposed to work.

Unfortunately, life just won't cooperate. So here I sit in the Starbucks at Route 183 and Lake Line, my half drunk Doppio cold, the line at the counter growing, Baby sulkily waiting for my next sentence, and outside the door, a napkin blows by, heading for the uncaring traffic whizzing past.

But in one way I can live at least part of my fantasy—through software components. They may not know how to deliver the perfect Doppio Macchiato, but they do know how to perform a lot of other very useful functions. All you need to know is how to ask.

History of Components: Objects

There are a lot of things you might ask a software component to do: You might ask it to validate a credit card purchase or transfer funds from one account to another. You might ask it to find the lowest fare for flying from Austin, Texas to Orlando, Florida. A software component is just a blob of software that can do something for you.

Historically, the idea of a blob of software that can do something for you goes back to the late 1980s. Back then we had this idea of building software systems as objects. We used object-oriented programming languages to create these objects. We built complex systems as hierarchies of objects. For example, we might have an object that knows how to calculate a sales tax; that object could be designed to use a dictionary object, which could use a hash table object. The hash table object could make use of entry objects, which could be composed of a sales-tax object and a state object. The state object could have a string object. And so on.

Back then, this seemed like a good way to develop software. We thought that we would end up with a lot of building blocks that could be developed independently, tested thoroughly, and recycled in future projects. The same dictionary that would be used to build today's sales-tax-calculator could be used to build tomorrow's spelling-checker. It seemed that in no time, we would end up with mountains of reusable code, and be able to build new complex systems by just choosing from catalogs of ready-to-use objects.

We started to formalize our idea of objects. An object was believed to be something that contained behavior and state. When you asked an object to perform one of its behaviors, it did so, with the result that its internal state was modified. The changes to an object's internal state could never be seen directly, but they could be implicitly seen in how the object responded to future behavior requests.

Let's look at a simple example: an object that represents an employee. Such an object might support the following behaviors:

- updateYourName, which takes a string representing the new name.
- tellMeYourName, which takes a string representing the name of the person asking the question.

Although we don't know how the object stores its name, we can assume that somehow the updateYourName behavior changes something inside the object that is being used to represent the name. So we expect to be able to have code like the following:

```
emp = create Employee()
tell emp to updateYourName("Roger Sessions");
ask emp to set name = tellMeYourName("Alice Sessions");
```

At the end of this code segment, we expect the variable name to have the value "Roger Sessions," demonstrating behaviorally, the state change induced by the request to updateYourName. We can think of this code segment as a conversation between a *client*, the one making requests of the employee, and the *object*, the blob of software receiving and acting on the requests. This segment of code works very much like the conversation shown in Figure 2.1.

We can also have multiple objects all supporting the same behavior, but having different states; for example, the following code segment:

```
emp1 = create Employee()
emp2 = create Employee()
tell emp1 to updateYourName("Roger Sessions");
tell emp2 to updateYourName("Emily Sessions");
. . .
ask emp1 to set name1 = tellMeYourName("Alice Sessions");
ask emp2 to set name2 = tellMeYourName("Alice Sessions");
```

At the end of this code segment, we expect to see name1 with the value "Roger Sessions" and name2 with the value "Emily Sessions".

It is also possible to have the exact same behavior description implemented two different ways. We can agree, for example, that all

Figure 2.1 Conversation between client and object blob.

Employees support the behaviors updateYourName and tellMeYour-Name. But some Employees will tellMeYourName to anybody, and some Employees will tellMeYourName only to someone who is at least a manager. Let's say the first type of Employee is LaidBackEmployee and the second type of Employee is ParanoidEmployee. Both Laid-BackEmployee and ParanoidEmployee are Employees, in the sense that they both support the Employee behaviors. But they support that behavior quite differently. The implementation of ParanoidEmployee's tellMeYourName might look like this:

```
tellMeYourName(string whoWantsToKnow)
{
  if isAManager(whoWantsToKnow) return myName
  else return "None of Your Business"
}
```

and the implementation of LaidBackEmployee's tellMeYourName might look like this:

```
tellMeYourName(string whoWantsToKnow)
{
  if not(null(whoWantsToKnow)) return myName
  else return "May I ask who wants to know?"
}
```

Now suppose I tell you that "Dilbert" is not a manager. Try to predict what the following code segment will do:

```
tell empX to updateYourName("Roger Sessions");
...
ask empX to set name = tellMeYourName("Dilbert");
```

The fact is that we can't tell what this will do. It depends on whether empX is a LaidBackEmployee or a ParanoidEmployee. If the former, then name will get set to "Roger Sessions." If the latter, then the name will get set to "None of Your Business." Even knowing that empX is an Employee doesn't do us any good. That just promises that we can ask empX to tellMeYourName. It doesn't promise us which implementation of that behavior we will get.

So how do we know? Obviously, we must get some implementation of tellMeYourName, and somebody has to make the decision as to which.

The answer is partially that it is up to empX to make the decision. If empX is a LaidBackEmployee, then he will give us the laid-back answer. If he is a ParanoidEmployee, then he will give us the paranoid answer. But this doesn't fully resolve the issue. We have merely put off the inevitable. How does empX know if he is a LaidBackEmployee or a ParanoidEmployee?

The answer to this question occurs at the *point of instantiation*; that is, the point at which an actual Employee blob is created. At exactly one point in the program, the point of instantiation, empX actually comes into existence. There will be some line of code equivalent to either

```
Employee empX = create ParanoidEmployee()
```

or

```
Employee empX = create LaidBackEmployee()
```

Notice that there are two purposes to these lines of code:

- To declare that empX is an Employee. Knowing that empX is an Employee guarantees us that empX supports some implementation of tellMeYourName.

- To create one of possibly many specific Employees. For the first line, that specific Employee is a ParanoidEmployee. For the second line, that specific Employee is a LaidBackEmployee.

The point of instantiation is typically the one and only time we care exactly what kind of an Employee empX really is. From now on, our code can deal with either ParanoidEmployees or LaidBackEmployees equivalently, knowing nothing more about them other than that they are some implementation of an Employee.

I often describe this behavior as *callee makes right*, because it is the callee (the Employee) that is responsible for choosing the correct behavior. In a non-object-oriented system, the caller makes right; that is, it is the client code that is responsible for choosing which of several code paths to take. This whole idea of never knowing exactly what code will be invoked in a callee makes right system may strike you as a little weird. But in fact, it actually simplifies our coding quite a bit.

Consider what a program might look like that is written with *caller* makes right; that is, non-object-oriented technology. Since the caller now needs to distinguish all the possible code paths, we need to have unique names for each code path. Let's say we call the paranoid code path *paranoidTellMeYourName* and the nonparanoid code path *normalTellMeYourName*. If the caller makes right, we are going to see code like this scattered throughout our system:

```
tell empX to updateYourName("Roger Sessions");
...
if (paranoid) then
  ask empX to set name = paranoidTellMeYourName("Dilbert");
else if (normal) then
  ask empX to set name = normalTellMeYourName("Dilbert");
```

Compare this to the greatly simplified code when the callee makes right:

```
tell empX to updateYourName("Roger Sessions");
...
ask empX to set name = tellMeYourName("Dilbert");
```

Keep in mind that these code segments may occur hundreds of times throughout our system. This has many problems. First, we need a lot more code to get the same amount of work done—four lines instead of one. Second, these if/else statements are easy to mess up and difficult to debug. Third, the code is very difficult to modify. Imagine we need to add a new security level, one that allows nonmanagers to access an employee's name, but only during working hours. This new implementation, for SemiParanoidEmployee, might look like this:

```
tellMeYourName(string whoWantsToKnow)
{
  if (isAManager(whoWantsToKnow)or(duringWorkingHours))
    return myName
  else return "None of Your Business"
}
```

How much work would it take me to integrate SemiParanoidEmployee into either a caller makes right or callee makes right system? The callee makes right requires one small segment to be modified, the point of instantiation. This might be three lines of code out of a multi-thousand line of code system. If the original point of instantiation originally looked like this:

```
if (paranoid mode)
  Employee empX = create ParanoidEmployee()
else
  Employee empX = create NormalEmployee();
```

now it will look like this:

```
if (paranoid mode)
  Employee empX = create ParanoidEmployee()
else if (semiParanoid mode)
  Employee empX = create SemiParanoidEmployee()
else Employee empX = create NormalEmployee();
```

This may look more complicated, and it is a bit, but the complexity is located to one very small segment of the entire system, the point of instantiation. This area is easy to find, relatively easy to modify, and extremely easy to test to make sure the right type of Employee has been instantiated.

In contrast, a callee makes right system requires a huge number of changes, scattered throughout the code. Every single place where we need a name, we need a modification. If we started with this:

```
if (paranoid) then
   ask empX to set name = paranoidTellMeYourName("Dilbert");
else if (normal) then
   ask empX to set name = normalTellMeYourName("Dilbert");
```

now we need this:

```
if (paranoid) then
   ask empX to set name = paranoidTellMeYourName("Dilbert")
else if (semiParanoid) then
   ask empX to set name = semiParanoidTellMeYourName("Dilbert")
else if (normal) then
   ask empX to set name = normalTellMeYourName("Dilbert");
```

So not only are the caller makes right changes more complicated, much more important, they are scattered throughout the entire system. And to make matters worse, they are almost impossible to test.

Object technology was where this callee makes right idea was first introduced. Object gurus use a much more complicated name for this idea: *polymorphism*. Polymorphism just means that there are many possible implementations of a behavior, and it is the responsibility of the callee to figure out which one should be used.

The idea of callee makes right was one of the three general ideas introduced by object technology. The others were *encapsulation* and *inheritance*. Encapsulation meant that you made behavioral requests of an object (software blob) without any idea of how that behavior would be implemented. Inheritance was never well defined, but meant to most people that you could reuse behaviors implemented in one type of object in another.

Both encapsulation and inheritance largely failed in having a major impact on the industry. Encapsulation failed not because it was a bad idea, but because no object-oriented programming languages actually supported it. C++ was particularly bad at this, generally defining and implementing the behaviors of an object in the same file. Java did a much better job than C++, and allows programmers to separate the *definition* of a behavior, called an *interface*, from the *implementation* of that behavior. But even Java forced the client programmer to work in the same language as the object programmer, a most fundamental violation of the notion of encapsulation.

Inheritance failed for a much simpler reason. Nobody could figure out how to use it successfully, even in those limited cases when they could agree on what it was.

The language dependency between the object and client programmer caused two very serious problems for object-oriented programming.

- It made it very difficult to reuse objects developed for one system (say, a C++ system) in another system (say, a Java system).

- To get any of the advantages of objects, companies had to retrain their entire staffs in object-oriented programming.

For object programmers, this second point arguably couldn't be avoided. But most programmers are client programmers. They are familiar with languages like Visual Basic, and have no reason to learn object-oriented programming languages. But the object-oriented programming languages were quite rigid on this point. If you want to use a Java object, you will learn Java, like it or lump it.

Enter Components

Component technology was originally introduced as an attempt to solve some of the problems with objects. Like objects, components were viewed as blobs of software that could do things for you. And like objects, they supported the important notion of callee makes right. However components were different than objects in the following important ways.

Components were always seen as a *packaging* technology. Component technology was a way of packaging a blob of software so that it could be used by a client. It was not an *implementation* technology. Object-oriented programming languages were possible implementation technologies, but not the only ones. Component technologies are perfectly happy to let you implement the components with Visual Basic or COBOL, should you so choose.

Components are seen as *language neutral.* There is no expectation that the component programmer and the client programmer are using the same language. Indeed, there is no expectation that the client programmer has any idea what language was even used to implement the component.

Components are *encapsulated* **in a much stronger way than were objects.** Component technologies typically had a way of describing the collection of behaviors to which the component could respond. Usually this was through an *interface definition language* (IDL). But unlike the object-oriented languages, the interface definition language described *only* behaviors, and had no syntax to describe implementations of those behaviors.

This notion of *components* (a package of software) as distinct from *objects* (an implementation of software, maybe or maybe not packaged as a component) was fairly rigorous throughout most of the 1990s. The two dominant component models throughout that period were the CORBA (Common Object Request Broker Architecture) from the Object Management Group (OMG) and the COM/DCOM from Microsoft. Both of these models were language neutral and very well encapsulated. We will discuss the CORBA model in greater detail in Chapter 11, "CORBA," and, of course, the Microsoft model in detail throughout this book.

In 1998, some of these ideas began to regress due to the increasing influence of Sun's Java technology. Sun also supported the idea of large blobs of software, and often described these blobs as components. But Sun's components are completely tied to the Java programming language. For Sun, Java is the component implementation language, the client programming language, the underlying operating system platform, and the interface definition language. It is Java, in whole, and indivisible. We will discuss the Sun model for components in greater detail in Chapter 10, "Enterprise JavaBeans."

For our purposes, we are going to consider a component to be in its purest form. It is a language-neutral, encapsulated package of software that supports the notion of callee makes right. It may or may not be implemented in an object-oriented programming language. It may or may not be used from an object-oriented client.

Some Terminology

Before we go too far, we should agree on some terminology. If you forget any of this, refer to the Glossary at the end of this book. Most people use the term *method* to describe one of the behaviors a component can support. We also use the verb *invoke* to describe the requesting of a method by a client on a component. A collection of methods are called an *interface*. To distinguish one interface from another, we name the interfaces. So the *employee* interface, for example, could be the interface that supports the following methods:

- updateYourName, which takes a string representing the new name.

- tellMeYourName, which takes a string representing the name of the person asking the question and returns a string with the name of the employee.

- updateYourSocialSecurityNumber, which takes a string representing a new social security number.

- tellMeYourSocialSecurityNumber, which takes a string representing the name of the person asking the question, and returns a string with the social security number.

Of course, this is just one of many possible employee interfaces.

An interface is the main contract between the software component and the client. In an ideal world, it would be the only contract between the component and the client. In reality, there are various understandings that are not captured by the interface definition, such as the fact that the client must invoke updateYourName before invoking tellMeYour-Name. If we had better techniques for specifying interfaces, these informal understandings would be captured as well, but with the current state of the art, this is not yet possible.

A blob of software can support more than one interface. The same blob could, for example, support both an *employee* interface and a *manager* interface. Therefore we can think of a component as being a collection of interfaces supported by some blob of software. We will call the collection of interfaces supported by some blob the *component type*. As we have already seen, we can have multiple implementations of a component, such as the ParanoidEmployee and LaidBackEmployee. We will call one of these implementations a *component implementation*. Strictly speaking, it is an implementation of a component type, but we will usually be less formal where we can get away with it.

Instances

We have seen that Employee is a component type and ParanoidEmployee is one possible implementation of that type. What is empX, as in the following code segment?

```
Employee empX = create ParanoidEmployee()
```

We have indicated that empX is in instance of a ParanoidEmployee. An instance is a blob of memory that can do something for you. But what do we mean by that?

Perhaps we mean that empX is a DLL that contains the compiled code that implements the ParanoidEmployee implementation. This might seem reasonable, until you realize that we can have many instances (blobs of memory) that can do ParanoidEmployee-type things for us, as shown here:

```
Employee empX = create ParanoidEmployee()
Employee empY = create ParanoidEmployee()
Employee empZ = create ParanoidEmployee()
```

Surely we don't want to duplicate the DLL for each instance of Paranoid-Employee. Most component systems share the DLL (or DLL equivalent) between all the instances of ParanoidEmployee. They need some way to map between methods and offsets in the DLL. Typically, there is another blob of memory (much smaller than the DLL blob) that is used to translate between methods and DLL offsets.

You might expect that this mapping blob would constitute the real instance. But most component systems optimize this even further. They allow the mapping blob to be shared by all instances of the same implementation. The blob of memory that actually constitutes an instance is then nothing but a reference to the mapping blob and some way of locating yet another blob of memory that contains any state needed by the instance. Confusing? Then take a look at Figure 2.2, which brings all these blobs of memory together.

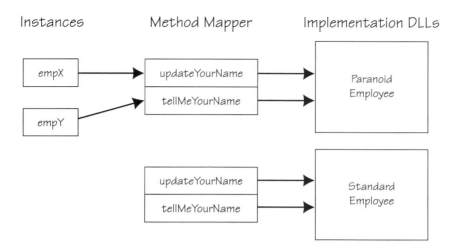

Figure 2.2 Mapping methods to DLLs.

Notice we just slipped in a new concept: *instance state*. What is this all about? Instance state is any specific information an instance needs to track. An example of this could be the Employee's name. In order for the tellMeYourName method to return the correct information, the name string must be stored someplace when the updateYourName method is invoked. The string can't be stored in the mapping blob or the DLL, or each instance would overwrite each other instance's name, and code such as the following wouldn't work:

```
tell empX to updateYourName("Roger Sessions");
tell empY to updateYourName("Kate Van Sickler")
ask empX to set name = tellMeYourName("Dilbert");
```

So the name must be stored in some area that is completely owned by one and only one instance. Contrast Figure 2.3, which demonstrates the collision that would occur if this instance state was stored in a shared area to Figure 2.4, which shows the correct functioning of nonshared instance state.

It turns out that instance state is a bit of a red herring. It will actual be a rare business component that will store any important information in instance state. Most business components store their important information in one or more databases, as shown in Figure 2.5. But this is getting a bit ahead of ourselves. We will return to this when we are in a

Figure 2.3   One state storage per system.

better position to understand the infrastructure requirements of the middle tier.

The Interface Boundary

The component interface serves two critical roles in component architectures. The first is to protect the client from the implementation of the component. The second is to protect the component from the implementation of the client.

Think of the component interface as a brick wall separating the client from the component instance. Think of the methods as small, well-defined holes in that brick wall through which the client and the instance can communicate. Neither the client nor the instance can see through to the other side of the wall. The client knows only that when requests are made through the holes in the wall, somebody answers.

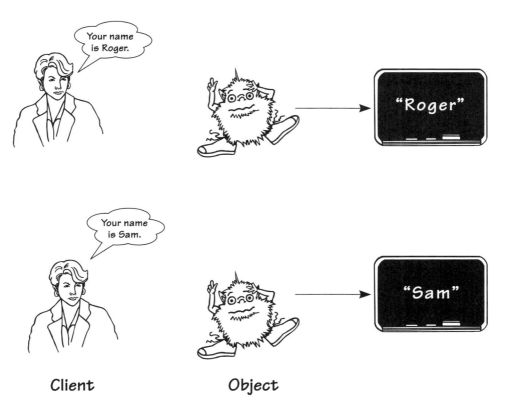

Figure 2.4   One state storage per instance.

The instance knows only that requests come through the holes in the wall, and that whatever is the source of these requests seems interested in the getting the results. Figure 2.6 shows what this looks like.

This hole in the wall architecture makes it easy to swap out one component implementation with another. The only requirement is that the new implementation must be the same component type as the original, meaning that the two implementations support the same interface(s). In other words, instances of the new implementation can speak through the same holes in the wall as instances of the original implementation. As long as they can do that, the client will be none the wiser.

The idea of a component interface provides the first real solution to a problem identified, but not solved, by the object-oriented programming languages: encapsulation. The component interface is serious encapsulation. The client knows nothing about the other side of the wall,

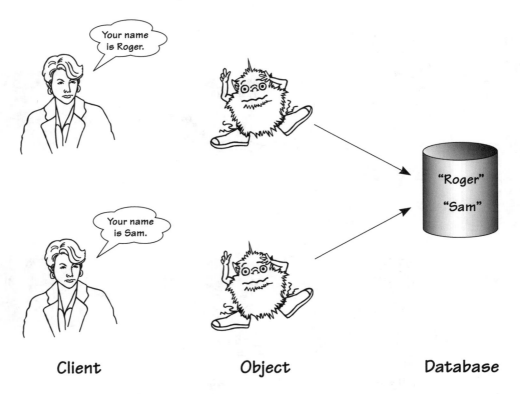

Figure 2.5   State storage in databases.

nothing about the implementation, nothing about the programming language—not even if there really is a component on the other side, or if the appearance of a component instance is naught but an elaborate illusion provided by the programming environment. This brings us to the next topic.

Distributed Components

The strength of the interface wall provided an unexpected solution to a seemingly unrelated problem that had been vexing systems developers for years: how to better manage the distribution of complex business logic. As desktop class machines became more and more powerful, newer applications placed more and more of the business logic on those desktop machines. This freed up the large back-end machines to focus on data management, and began the era of client/server programming. The

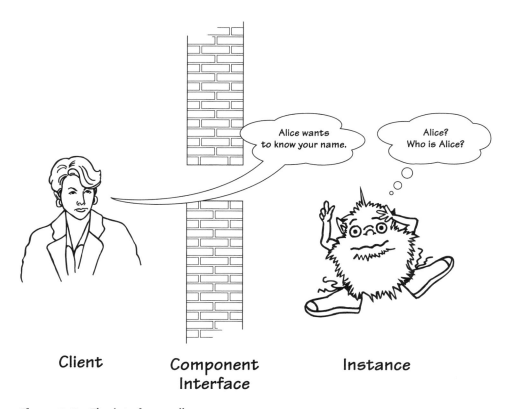

Client   Component   Instance
                Interface

Figure 2.6 The interface wall.

client machines contained the user interfaces and much of the business logic. The back-end machines acted as data servers, which made much more efficient use of resources, but it created two problems:

- It created a logistical nightmare: How do you update the business logic when it is spread over tens of thousands of small machines?

- It encouraged the development of systems in which the user interface logic was hopelessly intermingled with the business logic. Changes to either the user interface or the business logic were very difficult to make without impacting the other.

For the component world, the solution to these two problems seemed fairly obvious, and indeed, was integrated very early on into component technology. The solution was to separate the client and the component instance into separate processes, and to move those processes onto different machines. The client process moves onto machines that are specialized for working with human beings (desktop machines). The component process moves onto machines that are specialized for sharing business logic, and that are centrally located where they can be administered easily.

But what does all of this have to do with the interface wall? Well, it turns out that the strong notion of business logic encapsulated into a component implementation extends very nicely to a distributed component architecture.

This extension of the basic nondistributed component architecture to distributed component architecture occurs as follows.

We start with the notion of a single process containing both the client and the component instance. This is shown in Figure 2.7. As usual, the client communicates with the component instance on the other side of the wall (the interface). The communication occurs through the holes

Process

Figure 2.7 Client and instance in one process.

Client Process   Component Process

Figure 2.8   Moving the instance.

in the wall (the methods). The client has no idea what is happening on the other side of the wall, as long as information is returned eventually through the methods. Similarly, the component instance has no idea what is happening on the client's side of the wall, as long as somehow, somebody is feeding method requests to the instance.

Since the client doesn't know what is on the other side of the wall, we can create another process and move the component instance to that process. We will call the process in which the component instance lives the *component process*. The only thing we need to do is leave the wall back in the client process and create a new wall in the component process. This is shown in Figure 2.8.

Everything looks normal to the client code. It still sees a wall and has no idea that the instance that had so recently lived behind the wall has been moved to another process on another machine. At least everything looks normal, until the client tries to communicate through the wall with a method request. Now the client has a problem. There is nobody on the other side of the wall listening.

To give somebody for the client to talk to (in the client process) and for the component instance to talk to (in the component process) we add surrogates to both processes. In the client process, we add a surrogate for the component instance, which we will call the *instance surrogate*. In the component process, we add a surrogate for the client, which we will call the *client surrogate*. This is shown in Figure 2.9.

Client Process   **Component Process**

Figure 2.9   Adding surrogates.

This works, almost. The client has somebody behind the wall with whom to communicate, the instance surrogate. The instance has somebody on the other side of its wall with whom to communicate, the client surrogate. The only remaining problem is that the instance surrogate has no real business logic. Nor does the client surrogate have any real user interface logic. So when the client makes a method request to its instance surrogate, all it gets in return is a blank stare (which, of course, the client can't even see, being on the other side of the wall).

So we need to hook the two surrogates together through some communications network. With this in place, we have a fully functional distributed component system, as shown in Figure 2.10. The client makes requests through a hole in the wall (step a). That request is accepted by the instance surrogate (step b). The surrogate packages up the request and sends it over the communications network to the client surrogate living in the component process (step c). The client surrogate passes the request through its wall to the actual component instance (step d). The instance, having no idea of where the method originated, simply responds through a hole in its wall (step e). The response is picked up by the client surrogate and packaged up for a return trip over the network to the instance surrogate living in the client process (step f). The instance surrogate replies to the client back through the hole in the wall (step g). And everybody is happy.

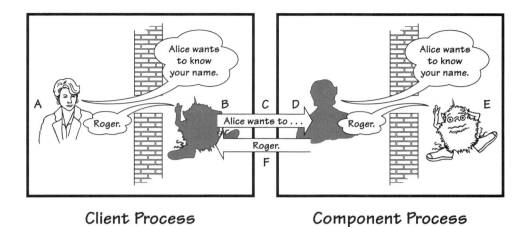

Client Process   Component Process

Figure 2.10   Method flow.

The nice thing about this is that none of the programmers involved need understand anything about building distributed systems. In fact, there is no distribution. The client code simply talks through the holes in the wall, just like it did in a nondistributed system. The component code simply accepts work requests through the holes in its wall, just like it always did. The distribution is handled automatically by the surrogates and the underlying network.

This basic distribution architecture is used by all of the main component systems available today. This includes Microsoft's COM/DCOM/MTS, the OMG's CORBA, and Sun's EJB. They don't all implement the surrogates the same, and they use different terminology to describe what is happening. But at an architectural level, there is surprisingly little deviation from this model. And the idea that makes it all possible is this strict notion of an interface logically separating the client and component instance.

Naive Three-Tier Architectures

Using distributed components, we can build three-tier applications. These applications will be a bit naive, as we will see when we start looking at some of their limitations. But they still represent a significant advance in the state of the art. Let's consider some of the benefits of building three-tier applications using this technology.

First, we have a clean separation of user interface from business logic. Our business logic sits on a dedicated tier of machines and our user interface sits on a different tier of machines. They are separated physically by machine boundaries and logically by interface boundaries. It is impossible to put any user interface code on the middle tier, because any output it produced would go to a screen not connected to a human being. And if we choose carefully between the user interface technologies, it is difficult to put business logic on the client machines.

This separation of user interface from business logic gives us considerable flexibility in designing user interfaces and reusing our business logic. For example, imagine a component that processes credit cards. That same component can be used by dial-up swipe machines, Web-based commerce pages, PC authorization machines, banks that process hand-written credit card forms, and customer service representatives at call centers.

The second advantage of building three-tier systems is the speed to build. Since you are using business logic that is well tested, new user interfaces can be slapped together very quickly. Even new business logic can be constructed out of well-tested middle-tier components. Remember, easy to build systems was one of the requirements we identified in the last chapter. By the same token, changes to business logic can be made without impacting existing user interfaces, and changes to user interfaces can be made with impact on the business logic. So not only are these systems easier to build, but they are easier to modify, another key requirement.

The third advantage of the three-tier approach is system manageability. It is much easier to manage business components on a central middle tier than on a highly dispersed client platform. Many companies consider the manageability of three-tier systems sufficient reason in and of itself for moving to this technology.

So if three-tier systems are so great, why do I call the systems we can build with distributed component technology naive? The problem is that although we have solved several important problems, there are many others left unsolved.

We have not made our systems secure. We have added two surrogates and a network. The client is sending out requests through its hole in the wall. How does it know that the instance at the other end is a Really-Do-A-Credit-Card-Authorization component, and not a Steal-Credit-Card-Numbers-And-Sell-To-The-Highest-Bidder component (both of which are valid implementations of Authorize-Credit-Card)? The component instance is accepting credit card authorization requests through its hole in the wall. How does it know those requests are coming from an authorized store and not from an off-shore money laundering operation? Requests and responses must travel over a communications wire as they move between the client and the component instance. How can anybody be sure that nobody is listening on the wire? How do they know that information, as it crosses the wire, is not being modified by some society misfit?

We have not added transactions. Commerce depends on transactions to keep things consistent. Transactions make sure my credit card is not debited if the airline has no tickets for the flight I want. Transactions make sure you have money in your savings account to cover the transfer to your checking account. Transactions prevent your stock from being sold to Sally after you have promised it to Mary. All database systems have transactional capability, but only as long as you are using only one database and one process to make the request. Distributed component-based systems often have multiple databases involved and many cooperating processes (two, at least: client and component).

The most important thing we have not added is scalability. In our simple distributed component architecture, every client is represented by a paired surrogate and component instance in the component process. These component instances are typically great resource hogs. They probably are using database connections and message queue connections, and are processing large amounts of data. There will be a very limited number (perhaps hundreds) of these instances we can support on a given component-tier machine. If each client needs a dedicated instance, then we can also support a very limited number of clients. But hundreds don't cut it anymore. If you are doing business on the Web, every PC in the world is a potential client. You need to be able to scale to hundreds of thousands of clients.

So components are great. Distributed components are even better. But we need a little more than just this if we are going to build the next generation of commerce systems—and if I am going to realize my dream of sitting on my wicker chair and ordering my Doppio Macchiato by pushing a button on the Web browser running on my laptop connected to my cell phone. In the next chapter, we will look to see where we can find the missing pieces.

3

Transaction Processing Monitors

My wife, Alice, and I are flying back from a week of vacation on the Monterey Peninsula. Baby is on my lap, her screen an empty canvas. I am staring blankly as I prepare to start my next chapter. I call this "deep in a contemplative mind meld with the universal life force." Alice calls this "writer's block." She assumes that merely because no physical words have appeared on Baby for the last hour, that I am making no progress. She looks over at Baby. She thinks she sees the problem. "Your screen is dusty," she says. "Would you like a Kleenex to wipe it off?" In this relationship, it is obvious who's who. Alice is Felix. I am Oscar.

Only Felix would think that the world's problems could be solved by wiping the dust off a computer screen. The Oscars of the world know better. True creativity comes from within. The great words of literature shine through any amount of dust and even the stains of yesteryear's Doppio Macchiatos. Would Shakespeare's sonnets be any less moving if they were coffee stained? Of course not.

On the other hand, I must admit that we did get though this vacation without losing a single item, without getting lost once, and without ever having to spend hours searching for the last place the rented car was parked; events that I usually take for granted as a natural element of any travel adventure. So I admit to a certain grudging respect for the Felix mindset.

I think all great relationships have a bit of *The Odd Couple* in them. A Felix by himself would be nauseatingly predictable. An Oscar by himself would be nauseating, period. It is the constant tension between Oscar and Felix, and the ability to resolve that tension creatively that makes the relationship between the two great.

Components

Components are the Oscars of the software world. They are the rugged individuals. They can do anything—they have no rules. As we have seen in the last chapter, we can build complex, distributed commerce systems from these blobs of software we call *components*. But as we have seen in the last chapter, components by themselves lack the social graces that allow them to function in an orderly society.

The three most important social graces components by themselves lack are:

- Security
- Transactions
- Scalability

Security is important. Without it, a component instance can't trust its client, a client can't trust its instance, and neither can be sure that messages are being neither monitored nor altered by unscrupulous third parties. Transactions are important. Without it, we can't guarantee that complex, distributed business logic is executed both *nolo booboo* and *in toto* or, if that isn't possible, then as a second best choice, *in nihilo*. Scalability is important. Without it, our commerce systems can't support the large number of clients needed to feed a profitable enterprise.

Introducing Transaction Processing Monitors (TPMs)

Where do we look to find the social graces needed to allow components to function in polite society? It turns out that there is another technology that has been developed more or less in parallel with the development of components. This other technology is called *Transaction Processing Monitors*, often referred to as TPMs.

TPMs are the Felixes of the software world. They don't worry about how we go about doing our business. But they do worry about how we interact with the rest of society. TPMs were a major advance in the civilization of software, a history that up until then had been dominated by a kind of frontier mentality in which only an Oscar would find himself at home. TPMs taught the world that it is only through a formal set of social conventions that we can obtain the big three requirements of distributed commerce systems: security, transactions, and scalability. To appreciate the achievement of TPMs, we need to go back in time and trace through their history.

In the bad old days, there were no terminals. At least there were no terminals on which human beings worked. Commerce was conducted totally off-line. People filled out paper forms and other people transformed these paper forms into punch cards. Computers read the punch cards. Five years ago, when I worked at IBM, you could still find closets full of old punch cards. Of course, they weren't used for anything and hadn't been for years. But apparently nobody could find the right forms to fill out to get approval for their disposal. So there they sat, a silent testimonial to a bygone era when mainframes were King and PCs were toys.

Then terminals came along. At first terminals were pretty dumb and could do nothing more than display and read characters. All of the processing was still done by expensive big computers. A single computer, even a mainframe, couldn't support many terminals, so cost-effective online processing was still prohibitively expensive, except for certain specialized applications.

Then terminals got smarter. Now they were capable of managing fairly sophisticated user interfaces. Human input could be collected on the terminal and then sent down as complete records to the back-end computer. The back-end computer could then focus its mental energies on managing business logic and data rather than having to deal with human beings. This was the era of the client/server two-tier model. The client tier machine collected and displayed data. The back-end server tier computer ran business logic and organized the data.

Then terminals got even smarter. Soon they not only had their very own CPUs, they even had their own disk drives and operating systems. In fact, the terminals had *become* computers. But they were not the big expensive computers in the back room. The back-room computers were very good at moving data on and off shared disk drives and very bad at moving data between the CPU and the display consoles. The new breed of terminal/computers were exactly the opposite. They were very slow at moving data on and off disk drives, and the disk drives, such as they were, were not sharable. But what they lacked in data storage capability, they made up for in their incredible speed at moving information between the CPU and the display consoles. They were thus very good intermediaries between the human beings and the workhorse computers. We usually call these terminal/computers *workstations*.

A typical commerce configuration now consisted of a relatively large number (say, dozens) of smart terminal/computers hooked up through communication lines to a single back-room, large, expensive computer. New applications were developed to take maximum advantage of this configuration. More and more business logic moved from the back-room computer to the smart terminals where it could interact closely with the user interface logic. The data management all stayed on the back-room computer, where it could be managed centrally and shared between workstations. For the back-end computers, this was an incredible relief. Freed from the tedium of managing business logic, they could dedicate themselves fully to the work they did best: getting data on and off disk drives.

The database vendors were paying close attention to these hardware developments. As terminals evolved into workstations, database systems evolved from batch-oriented technologies that required the business logic to coreside with the database to distributed systems that allowed business logic to run on one machine (the workstations) and the data to be managed on another (the database machine).

If you were to look at the workstation programming logic for a typical order entry system of this era, you would see code something like the following:

```
DisplayUserLoginScreen;
myName = readNameFromScreen;
myPassword = readPasswordFromScreen;
dbc = getDatabaseConnection(myName, myPassword);
exitSystem = false;
repeat until (exitSystem == true)
{
  displayOrderEntryScreen;
```

```
    data = readDataFromScreen;
    action = readDesiredAction;
    if (action == processOrder) {
      updateDatabase(dbc, data);
    }
    if (action == requestToExit) exitSystem = true;
  }
  closeDatabaseConnection(dbc);
  exit();
```

This program would be the only thing that would ever run on a typical workstation. It would start as soon as the workstation was turned on and would continue running until the workstation was turned off.

Notice that there are three parts of the program:

- All the stuff before the repeat loop (We will call this the *loop prelude.*)
- All the stuff in the repeat loop (We will call this the *loop proper.)*
- All the stuff after the repeat loop (We will call this the *loop postlude.*)

The loop prelude executes only when the machine is turned on. The loop postlude executes only when the machine is turned off. The loop proper, on the other hand, executes many times per day. Each iteration of the loop proper represents one sale occurring at the workstation, so we want to encourage iterations of the loop proper. The more iterations of the loop proper, the happier our stockholders are. The frequency of loop proper iterations is governed by two factors: how fast customers come to the salesperson and how fast the salesperson can process an individual customer. Let's say that on average, the salesperson processes one customer every five minutes, and therefore the average workstation iterates through the loop proper once every five minutes.

Now the database computer has some maximum workload it can perform. Let's say the database computer can handle 10 database updates per second (this was the old days, after all).

Here is the $64 million question. If you have a back-end database machine that can perform ten database updates per second, how many workstations can you attach to that machine if each workstation requests one database update per five minutes?

You might think that this is a simple calculation. Each workstation requests, on average, one database update per five minutes, or one database update per 600 seconds. Thus every workstation requests, on average, .00167 database updates per second. Since our database machine can support 10 updates per second, we should be able to support 10/.00167 work stations, or approximately 6000 workstations.

As you add more and more workstations to the database, you will find something interesting. The database machine will die long before you reach 6000. In fact, you will be lucky to attach even dozens of workstations, let alone thousands.

What's the problem? It turns out that database connections are very expensive resources. Most database systems support a very limited number of connections. Our database machine is not dying because it has run out of available updates per second. It is dying because it has run out of database connections.

Why has it run out of database connections? Look back at our code. We acquire the database connection in the loop prelude and don't release it until the loop postlude.

But why is that a problem? After all, if we need the connection, we need the connection. But consider the execution time of the loop proper. Let's look again at the code of the loop proper:

```
repeat until (exitSystem == true)
{
  displayOrderEntryScreen;
  data = readDataFromScreen;
  action = readDesiredAction;
  if (action == processOrder) {
    updateDatabase(dbc, data);
  }
  if (action == requestToExit) exitSystem = true;
}
```

The vast bulk of the elapsed time for this code is not in the updateDatabase request; it is in the waiting for the user to finish entering the data so that the readDataFromScreen can be executed. In fact, if we can execute 10 database updates in a second, then the updateDatabase request can't be accounting for more than 0.1 second of the 5 minutes elapsed time. For that 0.1 second, we are making good use of our database connection. For the other 299.9 seconds, we are wasting a very scarce resource.

"Aha!" you might think. I'll move the acquisition of the database connection from the loop prelude to the loop proper and the release of the database connection from the loop postlude to the loop proper. "That will surely solve the problem." This new code, with moved code shown in bold, looks like this:

```
DisplayUserLoginScreen;
myName = readNameFromScreen;
myPassword = readPasswordFromScreen;
exitSystem = false;
repeat until (exitSystem == true)
{
  displayOrderEntryScreen;
  data = readDataFromScreen;
  action = readDesiredAction;
  if (action == processOrder) {
    dbc = getDatabaseConnection(myName, myPassword);
    updateDatabase(dbc, data);
    closeDatabaseConnection(dbc);
  }
  if (action == requestToExit) exitSystem = true;
}
exit();
```

This new code indeed makes very efficient use of database connections. But it has a new problem. The acquisition of a database connection is unbelievably expensive, on the order of hundreds of times more expensive than a database update. On a machine for which updateDatabase requires 0.1 second, getDatabaseConnection will likely require at least 20 seconds.

The movement of the acquisition of the database connection to the loop proper has two ramifications:

- The salesperson will have an annoying delay (20 seconds) while waiting for the database to update.
- The theoretical maximum number of workstations that can be supported is now drastically reduced.

When the acquisition of the database connection was in the loop prelude, the theoretical number of workstations we could support was given by

```
(10 updates per second) / (.00167 updates per second per workstation)
= 5988 workstations
```

With the acquisition of the database connection in the loop proper, the theoretical number of workstations we can support is given by

```
(.050 updates/second) / (.00161 updates per second per workstation)
= 31 workstations
```

So you can see that we are darned if we do, darned if we don't. If we keep the database connection acquisition in the loop prelude, we are limited to a few dozen workstations by the number of database connections our system can support. If we move the acquisition to the loop proper, we are limited to a few dozen workstations by the increased work demand on the database machine. *And this on a database system that theoretically should be able to support almost 6,000 workstations.* No matter what we do, we can't win!

There is only one way we can get ahead, and that is to figure out a more efficient way to use our database connections. Suppose we don't have our workstations update our database. Suppose we move the database updating code onto another machine. We will need a special process in which to run this code. Let's call this process the update process, and use a procedure called *request* to request an update.

With this new architecture, we don't need any database connections in our workstation. We can rewrite our workstation order entry code to look like this:

```
exitSystem = false;
repeat until (exitSystem == true)
{
  displayOrderEntryScreen;
  data = readDataFromScreen;
  action = readDesiredAction;
  if (action == processOrder) {
    request(update, data);
  }
  if (action == requestToExit) exitSystem = true;
}
exit();
```

Now the *request* procedure could be quite complicated, since it has to do interprocess communications; but assume for the moment that this has been supplied by the system vendor who has cleverly figured out how to hide its complexity from us. Notice two things about this code. First, it appears much simpler, since we have been able to remove the login code, which was only needed to acquire the database connection. Second, we have removed any reference to the database connection. Since our workstation code has no need for a database connection, we are no longer limited in the number of workstations we can support by the number of available database connections.

But hold on a moment! Somebody has to update the database, and whomever does that is going to need a database connection. What about the code that actually does the update? And what about the limitations of the process in which it is running?

Let's consider how we might write the update process. We could imagine creating this code to have three procedures.

- An *initialize* procedure could be called when the update process is first started. Its purpose is to acquire the needed database connection and to store it in a global variable available to the other procedures of the process.

- An *update* procedure could contain the code that actually requests the database update. It is called repeatedly, once for each iteration of the loop process in the workstation.

- A *shutdown* procedure could be called when the update process is ready to be taken down. Its purpose is to release the database connection. The code for the update process could look like this:

```
databaseConnection dbc;
initialize()
{
  dbc = getDatabaseConnection("Roger", "ObjectWatch");
}
update(data)
{
  updateDatabase(dbc, data);
}
shutdown()
{
  closeDatabaseConnection(dbc);
  exit();
}
```

Keep in mind that we have divided the code that used to reside in one process on one machine into two processes on two machines, as shown in Figure 3.1. And every request to update the database now requires some sort of intermachine communication. Let's consider the timing sequence of a typical interaction between the two processes.

T0. The update process on the update machine starts up. Our initialize procedure is invoked. A connection to the database is created and stored in the global variable.

T1. The workstation is started up and the order entry program starts up.

T2. A salesperson starts entering data on the workstation.

T3. The salesperson completes the data entry, and the code inside the loop proper executes the request procedure.

T4. This results in an intermachine request to the update process passing across the data to be updated. The workstation blocks until the update process has completed the request.

T5. The request is received by the update process and the update procedure is called with the data passed in as a parameter.

T6. The update procedure updates the database.

T7. The update procedure returns, and the update process waits for the next update request.

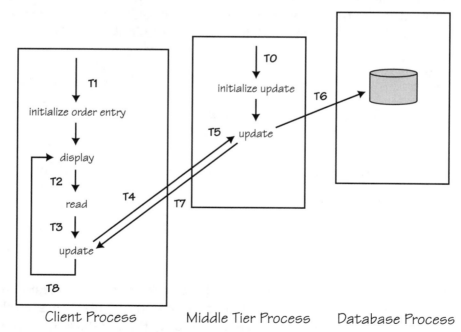

Figure 3.1 Division of code.

T8. The workstation is allowed to continue with the next iteration of the loop.

What has all this brought us? On the face of it, nothing. Our workstations may not be limited by the number of database connections, but our update machines are now limited, since each one requires its own database connection. And if each workstation needs a dedicated update machine, we haven't gained much.

But suppose that the update process is not limited to getting requests from only one workstation. Suppose it can accept update requests from *any* workstation. Now during all the time that the salesperson is entering data (T2), that update process is free to accept requests from other workstations. And since we have already calculated that the time needed for collecting data (5 minutes) is 3,000 times as long as the time needed to update the database (0.1 seconds), this means that a single update process can theoretically manage the updates for 3,000 workstations. And even if we assume the intermachine communication triples the cost of the database update, driving it up to 0.3 seconds, we can still have our update process handling 1,000 different workstations.

The huge concentration of workstations onto update machines is very significant. The important point is not that workstations are sharing update machines. The important point is that by workstations sharing update machines, they are effectively sharing database connections. And this means we do not have expensive database connections hanging around waiting for slow human beings to finish their data entry.

How many update machines can we support? If we have one update process running on each, we can have as many update machines as we have available database connections. If we have 36 available database connections, that means we can have 36 update machines. If each can service 1000 workstations, we can now have 36,000 workstations. That's a lot of workstations. Of course, we need to add into the cost of our system 36 update machines, but that is a very small price to pay for going from a system that supports 36 workstations to a system that supports 36,000 workstations. And in fact, we don't really need 36 update machines, just enough machines to effectively run 36 update processes. And in fact, we don't really even need that. All we really need is enough machines to support however many users we plan to be working at any one time. Even one machine running one update process increases the number of users we can support from a few dozen to one thousand, with plenty of room left over for future scalability should we need to add more users.

There is a lot of magic needed to make this whole thing work. We need something that makes the update request from the workstation to the update machine very easy to use, both for the workstation programmer and for the update programmer. We need a process that runs on the update machine that can make sure the initialize, update, and shutdown procedures are called in the proper order. We need something that queues requests, so that if an update request arrives while the update machine is busy, that request is saved until the update machine *is* available. We might even want something that makes sure our update request doesn't go to just any update machine, but to the one that has the fewest requests in its queue.

If we don't have all of this magic in place, then we are in trouble. Our 36 database connections will support only 36 workstations. Our 36 workstations will support only 36 sales people. And our 36 sales people will have a lot of angry customers waiting on 36 very long lines to pay. And those 36 lines don't even include the steady exodus of even angrier customers who left the store in frustration, never to return. So magic we need, and magic we must get. But where do we find magic like this?

This sharing magic is what you get from Transaction Processing Monitors (TPMs). TPMs provide all the support needed to concentrate our workstations onto update machines and thereby share database connections. TPMs provide transparent communications that shield both the workstation programmer and the update programmer from having to know the hideously ugly details about interprocess communications. TPMs provide frameworks to ensure the initialize, update, and shutdown procedures are called properly on the update machines. TPMs provide queues, so that requests are not lost. And TPMs provide load balancing, so that workstation requests do not wait for one overworked update process while there are other update processes hanging around bored out of their little minds.

There is an interesting side effect of using TPMs. We have gone from a two-tier system to a three-tier system. We have one logical tier that is responsible for collecting the data, another that is responsible for executing the business logic, and another that manages the database.

By now you may be wondering why TPMs are called TPMs. After all, they seem to have little to do with transaction processing, and they don't seem to be monitors in any traditional sense of the word. And, in fact, when TPMs first came on the scene, they weren't called Transaction Processing Monitors. According to the Grand Master of TPMs, Jim Gray, TPMs originally stood for Tele-Processing Monitors, a name that seems more descriptive of their role in supporting large numbers of what were then teleprocessing terminals.[1] However the idea of teleprocessing soon seemed anachronistic, and people looked for another description. Loath to abandon the now familiar acronym, they merely redefined the acronym to be Transaction Processing Monitors. So the term TPM seems more a historical accident than a well thought out description of a technology.

TPMs provide us with benefits. They enable a shared middle tier. And a shared middle tier enables us to increase greatly the number of clients our systems can support. And believe it or not, this is not all TPMs do for us. Let's look at some of their other important functions.

Transactions Across Databases

If the software industry awarded Academy Awards for lifetime achievement, databases would definitely be in line for their one contribution that dramatically changed the way we think about business logic. That contribution had nothing to do with data models, as you might think. Had the world never seen relational databases or object-oriented databases, the world would be little changed. The one contribution made by the database industry that completely changed the software industry was the concept of a *transaction*.

Why are transactions important? What are they? Before we answer these questions, imagine a world without transactions. What would it take to create commerce applications? Take a simple problem, like withdrawing money from a savings account. Assume that savings accounts consist of three sets of records in a database:

- Savings account records, which contains fields for accountIDs, ownerIDs, and current balances.

---

[1] *Transaction Processing: Concepts and Techniques.* Jim Gray and Andreas Reuter. San Mateo, CA: Morgan Kaufmann Publishers. 1993.

- Owner records, which contain fields for ownerIDs, names, and addresses.

- Logs, which contain fields for accountID, date, time, and update amount.

A subset of the records in this database is shown in Figure 3.2.

What is involved with something as simple as withdrawing money from a savings account? When Bill Gates walks into the bank to withdraw some money, he presents two things. First, he presents a withdrawal slip that has his account number and the amount he wants to withdraw. Second, he presents some picture ID that proves he is really Bill Gates. The teller then runs a program that authorizes the withdrawal, and hands Bill his cash.

If we are not going to worry about errors, the teller's program is fairly simple. It must do two things: It must update Bill's balance and it must

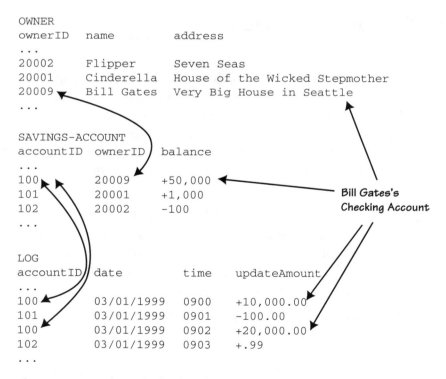

Figure 3.2 A subset of a banking database.

add a new record to the log to reflect the new withdrawal. Pseudocode for this program could look like this:

```
account = getAccountIDFromTeller();
amount = getAmountFromTeller();

accountRec = getSavingsAccountRecordFromDB(account);
ownerRec = getOwnerRecordFromDB(account.ownerID);
name = getNameFromTeller();

log = createNewLogRecord();
log.accountID = account;
log.date = TODAY;
log.time = NOW;
log.amount = amount;
accountRec.balance = accountRec.balance + amount;

replaceSavingsAccountRecordInDB(accountRec);
addLogRecordToDB(update);
```

This seems simple enough, doesn't it? Now let's consider some of the things that can go wrong. Here is a partial list:

- The account ID given may not really be Bill Gates's account.
- There may not be enough money in the account to cover the withdrawal.
- We may get an error upon reading the savings account record.
- We may get an error upon creating a new log record.
- We may get an error upon replacing the savings account record in the database, or upon adding the log record, or both.
- The system (including our program) may go down after replacing the account record but before adding the log record.
- The system may go down after our program has completed, but before the database IO buffers have been written out to disk.
- The system may go down after our program has completed, and after some of the database IO buffers have been written out to disk, but before others have been written to disk, resulting in an update to either the account record or the log table, but not both.
- In between the time you have read Bill's saving account record but before you updated and replaced the record, another teller could have closed out Bill's account, allowed Bill's wife to withdraw some

money, or allowed Bill's wife to deposit some money, any of which would invalidate what your program believes is Bill's correct balance.

- The disk drives containing the database could crash after Bill had gotten his money.

And this is just a few of the things that can go wrong. With a little thought, you can probably add another dozen items to this list.

Do we need to worry about any of these things? At least 99 percent of the time none of these errors will occur and our program will work correctly as written. But are you going to put your money in a bank that loses one deposit out of a hundred because of random system errors? Not likely.

Try to imagine how much code you would need to guard this system against all of these errors. Some of these errors are so complex, you probably can't even figure out what code could protect your system. To guard your system against every possible error (if you could even think of every possible error), you would need hundreds, perhaps thousands of additional lines of code to ensure that the withdrawal works perfectly, every single time it is done, regardless of what else is happening (or not happening) in the system. Not only would there be a huge amount of this error checking code, that code would be very complex, very difficult to test, and virtually impossible to debug. In a word, it is simply not practical to protect your system from everything that can go wrong.

But despair not! The database vendors have given you a wonderful tool. This tool allows you to write simple business logic without having to worry about any of these problems! This tool is called *transactions*.

The deal goes like this. We can include a line of code that marks the beginning of a transaction. We can also include a line that marks the end of a transaction. At the end of the transaction, we can tell the system we want all of the code within the transaction executed, or we can tell the system we want none of the code within the transaction executed. If we choose to execute the code, then the system logically submits the changes to the database. The database is responsible for deciding if all the changes can be made (*in toto*) without any error occurring. If the database decides that all of the changes can be done without any possibility of error (*nolo booboo*), it accepts the changes. If the database decides that there is even the teensiest weensiest chance that some error might occur if it attempted to make all the requested changes, it accepts none of the changes (*in nihilo*). The database must accept or reject the changes *in toto*. It may not accept some and reject others.

Let's look at the pseudocode again, with transactional logic added and shown in bold:

```
beginTransaction();
account = getAccountIDFromTeller();
amount = getAmountFromTeller();
name = getNameFromTeller();

accountRec = getSavingsAccountRecordFromDB(account);
ownerRec = getOwnerRecordFromDB(account.ownerID);

update = createNewUpdateRecord();
update.accountID = account;
update.date = TODAY;
update.time = NOW;
update.amount = amount;
accountRec.balance = accountRec.balance + amount;

replaceSavingsAccountRecordInDB(accountRec);
addUpdateRecordToDB(update);

error = FALSE;
if (noMatch(ownerRec.name, name)) error = TRUE;
if (accountRec.balance < 0) error = TRUE;

if (error) endTransaction (DontDoIt);
else endTransaction (DoIt);
```

Ending a transaction with a request to "do it" is usually referred to as a *commit*. Ending a transaction with a request to "don't do it" is usually referred to as a *rollback*. So it would be more accurate to show the final two lines of pseudocode as:

```
if (error) rollback();
else commit();
```

Keep in mind that just because *you* want to commit doesn't mean the *database* will want to commit. It will accept the commit only if it can successfully do every single database update issued from the beginning of the transaction until this point without any possibility of an error occurring. If it cannot do every update, or if it isn't sure if it can do every update, it will reject the commit *en masse*. And if it does this, it rejects all of the updates, without exception. For our example, this means it will either replace the savings account record and add the log record, or it will do neither. Which, in case you haven't noticed, is exactly what you want.

This ability to bunch business logic together into a single transaction that will be done or not done *en masse* is a cornerstone of modern commerce systems. It would be impossible to write such systems without the unifying concept of a transaction. And transactions are brought to you courtesy of the database vendors.

This is all very bully for the database vendors. What does this have to do with Transaction Processing Monitors? We don't need Transaction Processing Monitors to support transactions. Databases have this built in.

But what databases can't do is convince two or more of their brethren to cooperate in a single transaction. Suppose in our example the savings account records were stored in an Oracle database and the log records were stored in a SQL Server database. Sure, the Oracle database can tell you it is willing to commit the savings account changes, and the SQL Server database can tell you it is willing to commit the new log record. But neither can speak for the other. Suppose the Oracle database accepts the saving account change, and the SQL Server database rejects the log record? Suddenly our system is in an inconsistent mess, and we need a bunch of ugly code to try to patch things together again.

To solve this problem, TPMs took it upon themselves to coordinate transactions across database systems. To do this, the TPMs invented a new algorithm, called the *two-phase commit protocol*, a rather odd name since it is really has three phases. The three phases of the two-phase commit protocol are shown in Figure 3.3. As you can see in that figure, phase 0 is all the time in between the beginning of the transaction and the commit point. Phases 1 and 2 both occur when (and if) the commit is issued. If a rollback is issued instead of a commit, then the algorithm

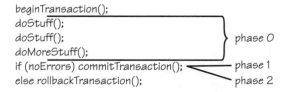

Figure 3.3   The three phases of the two-phase commit protocol.

is not needed. The part of the TPM that coordinates the two-phase commit protocol is often called the *Distributed Transaction Coordinator* (DTC).

Phase 0 is the contemplative phase. During the contemplative phase, DTC is participating only as an observer. It sees everything that is happening and monitors all database updates. When it sees a database updated, it makes a mental note of the transaction and the database. By the time the commit point is reached, it has a mental list of every database that was updated during phase 0.

Phase 1 is the voting phase. Remember that although phase 1 begins when the commit has been issued, the commit does not complete until the end of phase 2. In the voting phase, DTC goes back through its list of databases that were updated during phase 0. It asks each in turn if it is willing to commit the updates it has received during phase 0. "Excuse me, Mr. Database. You know all the updates you have been getting as part of this transaction? Let me ask you this hypothetical question. Let's say I were to ask you to commit those changes. *Now don't get excited and do anything!* I'm not asking you to really commit those changes, I'm just saying *if* I were to ask you, would you be willing to do the commit?" Each database gets to answer yes or no. If it says yes, then it is saying, "OK. *If* you were to ask me to commit the transaction, yes, I would be willing to do that." If the database says no, then it is saying, "Nope, I'm sorry. *If* you were to ask me to commit this transaction, I would have to say no. I just don't feel right about this transaction at this time."

Phase 2 is the final phase. At the beginning of this phase, DTC looks over the result of the voting in phase 1. DTC asks itself this question: Did every single phase 0 database vote to do the commit? If the answer to this question is yes, then in phase 2 DTC goes back to each database and says, "Remember when I just asked you if you would be willing to commit the transaction? Well, good news. We are going to go for it. Do it. Commit that baby." However if even one database said it would not be willing to commit, then in phase 2 DTC tells each database, "Remember I asked if you would be willing to commit that transaction? Well, I appreciate your willingness, and this is no reflection of my feelings for you, but I have changed my mind. I'm sorry to have bothered you, but we have decided to do a rollback. Please make it so."

This may seem a bit unfair. What if all 100 databases on the wall are more than willing to commit the transaction, and one obstinate database way over in the corner is giving us a hard time? Should all 100 databases be forced to do a rollback just because one database woke up on the wrong side of the bed that morning? But that's life in the database world. It's everybody or nobody.

What happens if a database changes its mind? Suppose during phase 1, a database agreed to commit. But between phase 1 and 2, a few more people added some records, the electricity went off a few times, and now the database no longer wants to accept the commit. So even though it agreed to accept the commit in phase 1, come phase 2 it says no go.

Agreeing to commit in phase 1 and then backing out in phase 2 is the ultimate sin for a database. There are no excuses. You are kicked out of the database union for this. You become a database pariah. They rip the epaulets off your shoulder, break your disks in half, and you are forced to crawl back to the file system slime from whence you came. No self-respecting TPM will ever associate with you again.

So you can see that TPMs through their relationship with DTCs do have *something* to do with transaction. It's not exactly the major portion of their business, and certainly is less important than the scalability they provide. It hardly warrants the top billing it gets in the TPM acronym. But, for those applications that need to update multiple databases, two-phase commit is a critical piece of the three-tier puzzle. And, that ain't all TPMs do.

Security

TPMs not only do everything they can to get your data safely to disk, they protect it once it's there. This annoys the databases a little, who think that protecting the data is their job. And it was, back in the days of two-tier architectures. Once three-tier architectures displaced two-tier architectures, the database model for data protection no longer worked. To see why, let's take a closer look at a typical database security model.

All databases organize data into records, and records into some type of collections. For relational databases, these collections take the form of tables. A table consists of rows and columns. A row corresponds to a record, a column corresponds to a field in a record, and a table corresponds to a collection of records. This is shown in Figure 3.4.

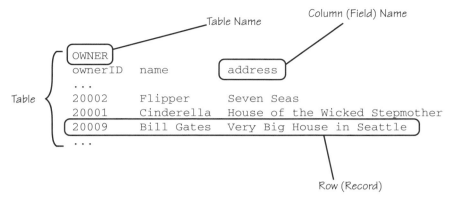

Figure 3.4 The organization of a relational database.

All databases allow administrators to determine which user IDs can access which collections of records. In a relational database, this translates to determining which user IDs can access which tables. Sometimes the database even allows access to be determined on a column (field) level.

As we discussed back in the section on scalability, in a two-tier architecture a database provides some reasonably small number of database connections. Processes running remotely from the database machine need to acquire a database connection before they can access the database. When they update data in the database, they do so through the database connection. If you recall, it was these database connections that became a roadblock to scalability in a two-tier architecture.

When the database connection is first created it is associated with a user ID. When a remote process updates a database, you can think of the following events occurring:

- The database looks at the user ID of the database connection being used by the remote process.
- The database looks at the access rights of the table being updated.
- If the user ID of the database connection has update rights to the table being updated, the database allows the update to proceed. If not, it doesn't.

Although we think of table protection as based on user ID, in fact, it is really based on the ID associated with the database connection. Let's look again at the two-tier pseudocode for our order entry system:

```
DisplayUserLoginScreen;
myName = readNameFromScreen;
myPassword = readPasswordFromScreen;
dbc = getDatabaseConnection(myName, myPassword);
exitSystem = false;
repeat until (exitSystem == true)
{
  displayOrderEntryScreen;
  data = readDataFromScreen;
  action = readDesiredAction;
  if (action == processOrder) {
    updateDatabase(dbc, data);
  }
  if (action == requestToExit) exitSystem = true;
}
closeDatabaseConnection(dbc);
exit();
```

You can see that a name and password are read from the screen and used to acquire the database connection. This database connection is used for all further database updates. The security associated with this database connection is the security defined inside the database for the name and password used to create the database connection. If the connection was established using the name "Donald" and the password "Duck," then updating through that connection will only be allowed if the Donald whose password is Duck has update access to the tables being updated.

This is all well and fine for two tiers. But what happens when we move to three tiers? Now the database connection is no longer owned by the process attached to the human being. It is owned by a process working in the middle tier. This process is not attached to any one client-tier process. In fact, our ability to scale the system is based entirely on the willingness of the middle-tier processes to allow themselves to be shared by many client-tier processes. Let's look again at database updating pseudocode as it is found in the middle tier process:

```
databaseConnection dbc;
initialize()
{
  dbc = getDatabaseConnection("Roger", "ObjectWatch");
}
update(data)
```

```
{
  updateDatabase(dbc, data);
}
shutdown()
{
  closeDatabaseConnection(dbc);
  exit();
}
```

Remember that the initialize method is invoked when this process starts up. We can choose whatever user ID and password we want at process initialization time to acquire our database connection, but we are stuck with whatever we choose. You can see this in Figure 3.5, which shows two clients making use of the same middle tier update process.

The important point is that the middle tier update process gets its database connection long before it gets the update request from the client tier. And it is that existing database connection that controls the security of the database. So there is no way the database can base its security on the client. It has no idea who the client is. All the database knows is the user ID of the database connection being used by the middle-tier process, and that never changes.

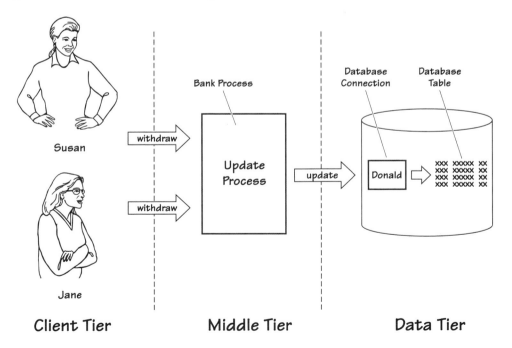

Figure 3.5 Ownership of database connections.

You might think that moving the database connection acquisition code into the middle-tier update routine could solve this problem. If we did this, the new middle-tier code would look like this:

```
initialize()
{
}
update(userID, password, data)
{
  databaseConnection dbc;
  dbc = getDatabaseConnection(userID, password);
  updateDatabase(dbc, data);
  closeDatabaseConnection(dbc);
}
shutdown()
{
}
```

This code does solve the problem. It receives the user ID and password from the client tier and uses this ID and password to get a new database connection with every update request. With this code, we can keep our security in our database.

Unfortunately, this code will not work. Not because of security problems, but for another reason—it is much too slow. Acquiring database connections is slow, painfully slow. Getting a new connection for every update is like trying to run a hundred-yard dash on a track covered with molasses. This middle-tier process will be totally exhausted just getting and releasing database connections, and will have no mental energy left to service more than a very small handful of clients.

So the acquisition of the connection *must* go in the process initialization, where it is done only once and it doesn't really matter how long it takes. But, as we have already shown, placing the connection acquisition in the process initialization means the database has no way to control security. So if we are going to use TPMs and three-tier architectures, we need a new security model.

The TPM Security Model

The TPM security model is quite simple. It says we don't check authorization upon updating the database. We check authorization upon making a request to the middle-tier process. In other words, we move security from the middle-tier/data-tier boundary to the client-tier/ middle-tier boundary, as shown in Figure 3.6. We no longer have the database checking requests upon arrival to see if their originator (the client) has update authority to specific tables. Now we have the TPM check requests as they arrive to the middle-tier process to see if their originator (the client) has the right to request the specified operation. Once the request has been accepted by the TPM, we no longer worry about requests going into the database as long as those requests are coming from the middle-tier process. We assume the TPM and the middle-tier process it controls are trusted.

It is still possible that a client will access the database directly, bypassing the TPM authorization scheme. So we will probably still configure the database security. If we have a client, say Susan, that is allowed to

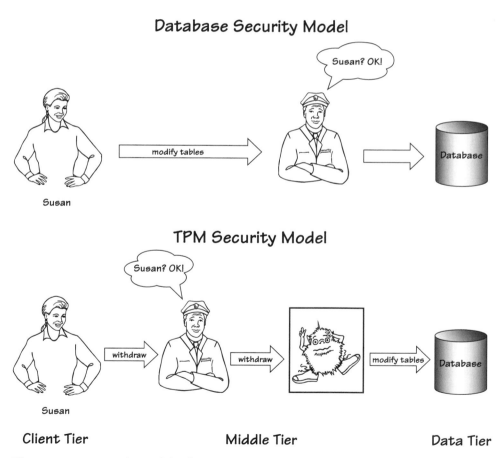

Figure 3.6 Comparison of database security model and TPM security model.

make requests to a middle-tier process running as Fred, but not allowed to access the database directly, we would configure our TPM and database security as shown in Figure 3.7. If she was allowed to access the database directly in addition to her indirect access through Fred, then we would configure the database so that she had whatever access she needs.

It's worth noting that, from the database's perspective, the middle-tier process, say Fred, ends up with a lot of access. Fred may support dozens of different types of requests, each of which could require access to many tables. As new requests are added to the middle-tier process, Fred's access needs to the database will increase further. Since Fred is trusted anyway, many systems may simply configure the database to let Fred do anything he wants, except, perhaps, administrative functions.

This new security model forces us to rethink not only the point of authorization, but also the nature of authorization. In the database world, we grant users specific types of access to specific tables. Referring back to Figure 3.2, we might, for example, grant Susan *update* access to the owner table, *read* access to the savings account table, and *write* access to the log table. This would allow her to write updates, read owners, and either read or write logs.

When we move security to the TPM, we no longer have concepts such as read, write, and update. You can either make a request, say a withdrawal,

Figure 3.7 Typical database security configuration used with TPM.

or you can't. If that request results in an update to some table, then you need to update the table. It doesn't make much sense to say that Susan *can* make a withdrawal request, but that her request *cannot* result in an update to the account balance in the database.

What's Wrong with TPMs?

Obviously, TPMs are the best thing since chocolate pudding. They give us scalability, database coordination, and a brand new security model. Who needs components? This is a reasonable question that many customers are asking. TPMs are well understood, well tested, and well proven in the demanding world of high-throughput commerce.

As good as TPMs are, they have one serious problem. They are difficult to program, at least by today's standards of build-it-fast-and-whup-it-out software. They come from a different era. Time moved much slower back then. Planning on five or more elapsed years to build a commerce system was the norm. We can't live with those time scales anymore. If the bank across the street offers its customers a total Web-based banking solution, your bank doesn't have five years to respond. In five years, you will be a donut shop! If you want to remain in the banking business, you had better respond in six months and you had better respond with a knocks-your-socks-off system with all the bells and whistles, and some bells and whistles that the bank across the street hasn't even thought of yet.

Does this sound scary? It is! You need all the help you can get. TPMs were designed back when *the Web* was something you swept out of the corners of dusty cabins. Today's Web is redefining our notions of commerce. The Web has already had an immeasurable impact on commerce systems. Over the next five years the Web will revolutionize commerce in a way unseen since the introduction of computers, perhaps unseen since the replacement of barter by cash!

There are many reasons TPMs are difficult to program. They require a specialized API and an understanding of the TPM architecture. And perhaps the most important reason is their archaic (by today's standards) programming model, one based on the *Remote Procedure Call* (RPC). With RPC systems, the unit of distribution is a procedure. A client invokes a procedure. The procedure on the client side is really nothing but a stub for the real procedure living in a remote process. The client's stub takes the procedure request and moves it across a lower level distribution mechanism to the remote process. The process accepts the request and turns it back into a procedure request that is delivered to the actual code bearing procedure.

Although this process sounds similar to the distributed component architecture we outlined in the last chapter, there is one important difference. The RPC architecture, unlike the distributed component architecture, does not support polymorphism. This can make a real difference in the design of systems. It means that every possible code path must be defined on the *calling side*, which, for typical TPM systems, would mean on the client side. And every new introduction of a code path means major modifications to the client code.

Suppose we have a banking system that supports three types of accounts: savings accounts, checking accounts, and early retirement accounts. Every action you might want to take with an account requires three code paths, one for each possible account. The *deposit* action is representative. The following pseudocode shows what you might expect to find controlling your *deposit* logic:

```
if (action = DEPOSIT) {
  type = getAccountType(accountID);
  if (type = SAVINGS) then savingsDeposit(accountID, amount);
  else if (type = CHECKING) then checkingDeposit(accountID, amount);
  else if (type = ERA) then eraDeposit(accountID, amount);
  else handleError(accountID);
}
```

This is quite different from the code you would expect to find in a component system. The analogous *deposit* pseudocode for a component system is as follows:

```
if (action = DEPOSIT) then account.deposit(accountID, amount);
```

Quite a difference. Not only does the component code have fewer lines of code (one instead of seven), but we have eliminated four of our five branch statements. Branch statements are notoriously hard to write, test, and debug, so any that can be eliminated will result in a considerable reduction in time of delivery. You can see this intuitively by looking at the two code samples. One looks complicated; the other looks trivial.

The time to write the code is only part of the problem. The other is the time cost in modifying the code. Consider the changes needed to the two systems when the bank across the street comes up with a new account type, say a money market account. With the RPC code, you must modify the deposit code as shown here:

```
if (action = DEPOSIT) {
  type = getAccountType(accountID);
  if (type = SAVINGS) then savingsDeposit(accountID, amount);
  else if (type = CHECKING) then checkingDeposit(accountID, amount);
  else if (type = ERA) then eraDeposit(accountID, amount);
  else if (type = MONEY_MARKET)
    then moneyMarketDeposit(accountID, amount);
  else handleError(accountID);
}
```

The new component-based code doesn't need to change in the slightest. The line

```
if (action = DEPOSIT) then account.deposit(accountID, amount);
```

works just as well for money market accounts as it does for savings accounts.

If you have a *deposit* and a *withdrawal* action, you will have two sections of RPC code to modify when you introduce the new account type. In general, for each action you have a corresponding section of RPC code to modify. As you add new account types trying to keep up with the bank across the street, each of these sections grows in length and complexity. The component code never changes. It looks just as simple and elegant with three types of accounts as it does for one hundred. It is easy to modify precisely because it requires no modification.

So you can see that perhaps the component approach to software development *does* have something to offer. Neither components nor TPMs by themselves can do the job. Components are the Oscars of the software world. They know how to get things done. TPMs are the Felixes of the software world. They know how to keep order. We need both. In the next chapter, we will see how this Odd Couple manages to live together.

Another Voice Heard From

Alice still can't come to grips with my computer's screen. This clearly is bothering her. She will not sleep well tonight thinking about all those dust particles on Baby. In an attempt to make her feel better, I have promised her the last word in this chapter. Here it is, direct from Alice:

"I find it astounding that someone can create with a dirty computer screen. The distraction of the dirt keeps me from concentrating on what to say. How can neat thoughts come from a dirty world? In addition, the process of ordering the physical things around me helps to order the ideas as well. Felix is right: Order is essential in our world."

I suspect that the old TPM programmers are nodding their heads in agreement. They know exactly how Alice feels.

CHAPTER 4

COMWare

M aybe it's the Alps. It's hard to argue in the midst of such beauty. Maybe it's the history of peace. Switzerland, after all, has long been considered a refuge for reason.

Still, the whole thing was a set up for a debate. Jeri Edwards was invited to give an overview of the middle tier from the perspective of BEA, a company specializing then in middle tier architectures based on CORBA technology. Jeri is a vice president of BEA, and a well known, articulate, and very convincing spokesperson for their technology. I was invited to give an overview of the middle tier from the perspective of Microsoft. Although I have never worked for Microsoft, I was the reigning expert in their middle-tier strategy. The debate was to be held in Lucerne, Switzerland, at one of the most prestigious technical universities in one of the most beautiful countries on earth. What a place for a debate.

It's hard to imagine two speakers more poised for a slug fest: Jeri Edwards and Roger Sessions, representing the honor of BEA and Microsoft, respectively. Two companies that have bet their future on the middle tier and on The Odd Couple relationship between Components and Transaction Processing Monitors (TPMs). And two companies that seem to disagree on almost everything, including how to build components; how to define the interfaces to components; what components should look like; how to manage data going in and out of components; what the role of industry standards should be; how to incorporate TPM algorithms into the middle-tier infrastructure; what communications protocols to use; what programming languages to support (and how to support them); how to interoperate with databases, client programs, and other middle-tier applications; how to plug into the Web; what the relationship should be between the middle tier architecture and the operating system; whether caffeinated or decaffeinated coffee is best for your heart, and a host of other issues that could fuel enough religious wars to satisfy even the most diehard of fanatics.

When Jeri finished her presentation on the brilliance of BEA's middle-tier vision, Bob Orfali turned to me. "Roger," he said, "you probably don't agree with some of Jeri's presentation. Would you like to offer a different perspective?" Bob is one of the best CORBA writers in the business. He has a sharp mind and is very flamboyant. Between these two traits you can assume that if Bob is there, Bob is the center of attention. When Bob Orfali asks a question and turns to wait for your reply, the whole world turns and waits with him.

"Wow," I thought to myself. "What a setup!" I cracked my knuckles and slowly stood up. I gave my sternest, most scholarly look, the one I had practiced in the mirror for weeks and weeks just waiting for this very opportunity. I was Atticus in *To Kill a Mockingbird*, Clarence Darrow in *Inherit the Wind*, and Yoda in *Star Wars* together in one impeccable package. Jeri would wither under my brilliant and penetrating attack. I knew she would. I had visualized it in my mind dozens of times.

But I guess I was overcome by the moment. Peace and tranquillity flooded my heart. It was repulsive to be sure, but I couldn't avoid it. Here I was presented with a golden opportunity for an argument, and all I could see was The Common Ground. Maybe that's what happens to you after living for a week in a Riccola commercial.

So instead of debating the differences in Microsoft and BEA's middle-tier vision, I began instead to articulate the similarities. And I was struck by how many similarities there were, how deeply embedded those similarities were in the product designs, and how relatively superficial were the differences in the two products.

Since that day, Enterprise JavaBeans (EJB) has become a serious middle-tier competitor. Another attempt to define a middle-tier vision; another attempt to tame The Odd Couple; and another glimpse at how much these seemingly divergent middle-tier technologies really have in common.

That day in Lucerne, Switzerland, was the beginning of this chapter, my first attempt to define a consistent perspective on the middle-tier component-oriented technologies I call COMWare. This includes COM+, EJB, and CORBA. I will have plenty of time in this book to describe the differences between these major COMWare technologies. In this chapter, I am going to tell you what they all have in common.

The similarity between all of these technologies is not entirely coincidental. After all, Microsoft was the first company to try to convince components and TPMs to reside together in one big happy family. This was the concept behind Microsoft Transaction Server (MTS), which created a TPM-like environment for COM components. MTS was released in 1996, well ahead of BEA's M3 technology (then called *Iceberg*) which was the first of the CORBA COMWare technologies. It was even further ahead of EJB, which was not even released as a specification until 1998. MTS was highly influential in the design of all these follow-on COMWare technologies and was the standard against which all COMWare products would be measured for the next three years. Now, Microsoft has released COM+. COM+ is the next generation of COM and MTS. Like MTS before it, COM+ will almost certainly set the standard for the next generation of COMWare technologies.

Components + TPMs = COMWare

Components are great technology. As I discussed in Chapter 2, "Components," components allows us to create binary, distributable little blobs of software than can act as our loyal servants and fulfill our every wish.

But these little blobs, as good as they are, lack the social skills needed to cooperate in civilized society. Apparently these little blobs never attended kindergarten. They never learned to work together (act as a transaction). They can't hold hands (act securely). And worst of all, they are unwilling to share (act in a scalable manner). They can do simple tasks, drink beer, and burp. In short they are the Oscars of the software world. But nobody can survive (or would want to survive) in a world full of only Oscars.

On the other hand, we have the straight-laced world of the Transaction Processing Monitors (TPMs). As I discussed in Chapter 3, "Transaction Processing Monitors," TPMs are the organizers of the world. They can get people to work together, to hold hands, to share, to speak only when spoken to. But they are boring beyond belief. No flexibility. No adaptability. No imagination. In a word, they are the Felixes of our industry. And the Felixes will drive you crazy with their air sprays, their little hand-written notes, their perfectly balanced meals three times a day.

So we need a new technology—a hybrid technology that takes the organizational capabilities of TPMs and the flexibility of components, gives both a great middle-tier infrastructure *and* a great programming model, can both scale across the Web *and* be built quickly and cheaply, and that supports both commerce in the large *and* programming in the small.

This technology is the technology that I call Component-Oriented Middleware (COMWare). It would be tempting to use a different acronym for Component-Oriented Middleware. The acronym of choice is COM. Unfortunately, Microsoft is already using that acronym to describe their basic component architecture. And rather than introduce confusion about when I was talking about Component-Oriented Middleware and when I was talking about Microsoft's Component Object Model, I have decided instead to introduce a new acronym. Thus we have COMWare. I hope you like it.

There is widespread agreement in the industry that COMWare is the way to go. Unfortunately, there is no consensus on what terms we should use to describe COMWare. What I call *components*, some call *objects*. What I call *COMWare*, some call *Object Transaction Monitors (OTMs)*. I think that the terms *objects* and *OTMs* have serious problems when used in this context.

The term *objects* is confusing because it seems to imply a specific implementation technology, namely, object-oriented programming. As I discussed in Chapter 2, object-oriented programming languages are only one possible implementation strategy for components. Many companies will build components from traditional, non-object-oriented languages.

Using the term *objects* to mean *components* has another problem. It gives people the dangerous illusion that you can create components by taking existing objects and just renaming them to be components. Nothing could be further from the truth. True, you can create a component by renaming an existing object, but it will be a pretty pathetic excuse for a component. It will have highly inefficient methods, it will be much too fine grained, and it will have none of the support needed for survival in the middle tier. Renaming an object to be a component is like hiding a sheep in wolf's clothing and expecting it to live the rest of its life in a wolf pack. Yes, it will live the rest of its life in the wolf pack. But that life is going to be pretty darn short.

The term *OTM* is also a problem. To start, it uses the horrid word *object*, one that I have hopefully already convinced you to abandon. Then it moves on to *T* for Transactions. True, COMWare does have something to do with transactions, but this is a relatively small part of its responsibilities. COMWare's first three responsibilities are scalability, scalability, and scalability. Finally, we come to the *M* in *OTM* for Monitors. Monitors?!? What do monitors have to do with anything? This is about component runtime environments, not monitors!

About the only good thing you can say for the term *OTM* is that it is faintly reminiscent of the term *TPM*, much like a whiff of freshly baked bread might remind you of old family traditions. But we need better terminology, and the terms *components* and *Component-Oriented Middleware* (COMWare) are much more descriptive and accurate.

So COMWare is the convergence of two important technologies: components and TPMs. The Odd Couple. And like The Odd Couple, both will be stronger for the relationship. And also like The Odd Couple, both will have to make significant readjustments in how each approaches life to make the relationship work.

The COMWare Subtechnologies

All COMWare platforms, including COM+, can be divided into five subsystems:

- Component System
- Component Runtime Environment
- Administrative Tools
- Interoperability Services
- Component Services

None of the COMWare platforms describe themselves as using these subsystems, and all use their own terminology to describe exactly what they do. So I have developed my own common COMWare classification system to demonstrate their similarities. Although each of the COMWare platforms tries to trumpet its own uniqueness, the fact is that all of the COMWare platforms are described very well by this common classification.

The first of the COMWare subsystems is the *component system*, which we described in Chapter 2. The component system includes the tools needed to package a bunch of possibly ugly code into a hopefully beautiful component. The code itself could include legacy code, procedural code, objects, scripts, stored procedures, TPM services, or what have you. The component system allows you to define a neat, well understood, and easy to use interface around that whole mish-mash, so that people don't have to worry about all the ugliness inside. Component systems do not worry about *eliminating* ugliness. That may or may not be the domain of object-oriented programming languages. Component systems are concerned with *encapsulating* ugliness.

The component system defines how clients make use of the components. Clients have a way to create instances of a component that can act as dedicated well-behaved servants. The component system also provides the naive distribution capability that allows component instances to live in one process and component clients to live in another, without providing a middle-tier infrastructure to support the ongoing interactions between the components and the clients.

With the exception of Enterprise JavaBeans, all COMWare component systems also support the notion of language neutrality, meaning that most popular languages can be used equally well to develop both the components and the clients, and that neither the client programmer nor the component programmer has any dependency on the language choice of the other.

The second of the COMWare subsystems is the *component runtime environment*. The component runtime environment is the sheltered environment in which all component instances run. The notion of a sheltered component runtime environment is probably the single most important difference between the first generation component systems and the technology we know today as COMWare. Every COMWare platform today supports the notion of a component runtime environment, and there is remarkably little difference in how the different COMWare platforms have implemented the component runtime environment. We will be discussing the common notion of a component runtime environment in detail in this chapter.

The third of the COMWare subsystems is the *administrative tools*, used to manage the overall system and to configure components to run in the system. These tools store information in some kind of a *shared COMWare administrative database*. The relationship between the component system, runtime environment, administrative tools, and the shared database pieces is shown in Figure 4.1.

The fourth of the COMWare subsystems are the *interoperability services*. The interoperability services allow the COMWare platform to interoperate with other critical, but external technologies, such as database systems. One of the most important of the interoperability services is the *distributed transaction coordinator*, which allows a variety of databases to work together and coordinate their activities. We will discuss the distributed transaction coordinator later in this chapter.

The fifth of the COMWare subsystems are the *component services*. The component services provide miscellaneous facilities for adding value to components. This area is the most difficult of all the five COMWare subsystems to describe in a common way, since the various COMWare platforms differ widely in what component services they support and how they provide that support. This is also an area in which we are seeing

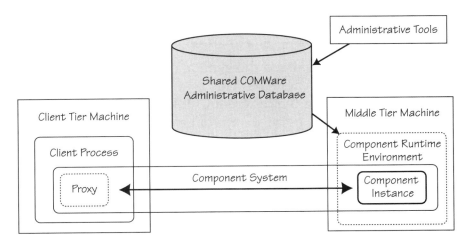

Figure 4.1 The major COMWare subsystems.

rapid evolution. Historically, many of the component services, such as asynchronous communications, have been poorly integrated into the overall COMWare platforms. Vendors are fiercely competing to improve this situation. We will save most of the discussion on component services to the platform-specific chapters in this book.

The distinction between the *component services* and the *interoperability services* is a bit arbitrary. A database API is clearly in the interoperability category, since it has no value without the involvement of a back-end database. However messaging is a little less clear. It can either be used within the component system itself, as when one COM+ component instance makes an asynchronous request to another COM+ component instance, or it can be used to interoperate with an outside system, such as when a system built of COM+ components uses messages to interoperate with a system built of CORBA components. In the COM+/COM+ case, messaging best falls in the component services category, but in the COM+/CORBA case, it best falls in the interoperability services category.

The three main COMWare platforms with which we are concerned are the Microsoft, Java, and CORBA platforms. I will describe the Microsoft platform in more detail throughout this book, and later chapters will contrast the Java and CORBA platforms. Of all the COMWare subsystems, by far the greatest agreement is about the Component Runtime Environment, the process in which the component instance resides. Therefore we will focus on this subsystem in this chapter.

The Component Runtime Environment

We have already discussed the general notion of components, the first of the COMWare subsystems. This is an area in which there is serious disagreement among the different COMWare platforms. But once you have gotten past the fights over what a component is, there is relative tranquillity over the issue of the environment in which that component should run. And this is encouraging, because it is the runtime environment that is the single most important feature distinguishing the naive distributed components we looked at in Chapter 2 from the much more sophisticated COMWare technologies we are considering here.

Technically, the component runtime environment is the process in which the component instances live. Since the only purpose for that process is to provide a living space for homeless component instances, I usually describe that process as the *component process*. Some people refer to this process as a *server process*, a much overused term that is meant to imply the fact that it services requests.

All component instances live in some component process, even in the naive (pre-COMWare) model. You can't run anything inside a computer that is not inside some process, and this includes component instances. But the component process is very different in a naive distributed component system than it is in the COMWare system.

In a naive distributed component system, the component process is very simplistic. It basically serves as a receiver for remote method requests and a transmitter of information back to the client. The code for the process is so minimal that it is often considered the responsibility of the component programmer to provide that code.

In a COMWare system, the component process is very complicated. It still has the receiving and transmitting functions. But in addition it provides an entire milieu for the component instance. I often think of the component process as a fishbowl, in which the component instances are living. The fishbowl provides the nourishment, the air, and the medium of life. The component instances are as dependent on the component process as fish are on the fishbowl.

From the perspective of a component instance, living in a COMWare system is like working for a large bureaucracy. When I worked for IBM, I was given my work orders by my manager. Of course, being a highly independent component instance I usually ignored these orders and did what I felt like, but, at least in theory, the system was highly efficient. When a work request came in from the outside world, it went to my manager, who had about a dozen people reporting to him. (At IBM, my managers were always "hims.") Depending on from whom the request originated, he decided to accept or ignore the work order. If he accepted it, he then next decided who, among his reports, could handle the order, and who, among those that could handle the order, were not involved in any other critical work at the moment, and then who, among those relatively available, would whine the least about getting the work order (which usually left me out). Only after processing the work order through this highly complex algorithm would the work actually be assigned.

For a component instance, living in a naive distributed component environment (in other words, a non-COMWare environment) is like working for a very small company, say ObjectWatch. At ObjectWatch, there are no managers. There are no buffers between the originator of work requests and the component instance that will process the work request. It's hard to have managers when you only have two employees. I suppose Janet and I could take turns managing each other. It would be a funny system. If somebody called Janet to book a class seat, she would say, "Wait, I'll check with Roger." Then when she checked with me, I would say to her, "Wait, I'll check with Janet." And then she would say to me, "Wait, I'll check with Roger." And then I would say to her . . ., well, you get the picture. A lot of time managing and not much time doing work.

There are advantages to both the ObjectWatch (non-COMWare) and the IBM (COMWare) systems. The ObjectWatch system is highly efficient and cost effective. Janet and I have no office and we work when and where we need to. Our computers are portable laptops. We contact each other by e-mail or cell phone. When we need to meet, we do so at Starbucks, using a table only for as long as we need it and then giving it up to the next highly efficient non-COMWare enterprise. The IBM system, on the other hand, scales well. It can process a huge number of clients that I cannot even imagine. It does so by adding a level of bureaucracy (or, in IBM's case, several levels of bureaucracy) that acts as an intermediary between the clients and worker bees.

Which is the best system? It depends on what you want. If you want astronomical scaling then you must make sure that every component instance is enveloped in a protective environment and you must be prepared to pay for that protective environment. If you want lean and mean then you must make sure that every component instance is free to act on its own and you must be prepared to limit the number of clients your system can support. Each system works well for its problem space.

All of the COMWare platforms agree on the tradeoff between lean and mean and scalability. When you buy into COMWare, you buy into scalability at the cost of lean and mean. If you don't need scalability, you don't need COMWare. The only difference between the various platforms is the details: what that cost will be, exactly what the nature of the protective environment is, how well the COMWare environment works with the underlying component model, and the relationship between the COMWare platform and the underlying operating system.

From the client's perspective, COMWare is invisible. It isn't there. The primary directives of all COMWare platforms is to preserve the illusion that there is a simple relationship between a client and a component instance. A client asks an instance to do some task. The instance does it and returns the result. COMWare clients get the best of both worlds. The client sees none of the bureaucracy that makes the whole system scale nicely, but still gets the scalability benefits that the bureaucracy provides.

The COMWare Environment

All COMWare platforms start out with the supportive, protective COMWare environment. From the component instance's perspective, this environment is the warm and fuzzy process in which the component instance runs. The component instance and the component process need an understanding on how to work together. This understanding is embodied in a *COMWare contract* between the environment and the component instance. The contract is defined through a hopefully small set of interfaces defined by the COMWare environment and implemented by the component programmer and/or vendor-supplied tools.

Before we look at the purpose of the COMWare environment, let's review briefly the basic naive distributed component architecture first presented in Chapter 2. Figure 4.2 shows a distributed component without COMWare. Every component supports one interface, say a Credit-Card interface. It can support more, but let's assume one for simplicity. Consider a CreditCard interface supporting two methods, as follows:

- Charge, which takes a credit card number, a merchant number, a name, an expiration date, and an amount, and which bills the credit card for that amount.

- Refund, which takes the same information, but refunds the amount to the credit card.

Any blob of software that can respond to these two requests can legitimately call itself a component that supports the CreditCard interface. We could have an AmexCreditCard component and a VisaCreditCard component both of which support the same CreditCard interface. If *charge* is invoked on an AmexCreditCard, then the amount is charged against the customer's American Express card. If *charge* is invoked on a VisaCreditCard. . .well, you get the picture.

Figure 4.2   Plain component without COMWare.

The client system will have a line of code someplace that instantiates either an AmexCreditCard or a VisaCreditCard. Since both components support the same interface, it doesn't matter to subsequent code which component was actually created. At the point of instantiation, an instance of the appropriate component is created in a remote component process. If we are not using COMWare, that component process is a very simple process. At the same time that the component instance is created in the remote process, an instance of a proxy is created in the client process.

That client side proxy will also support the CreditCard interface. It implements the two methods by packaging up the method request and shipping it over to the component process. In a non-COMWare architecture, that component process receives the request, unpackages the request, and invokes the appropriate method on the actual instance.

Point of Interception Algorithms

The COMWare component process starts out looking similar to the non-COMWare component process. Like its Neanderthal cousin, the COMWare component process also receives, unpackages, and invokes the method request. However, the COMWare process does one additional important function. It *intercepts* the method before it is actually delivered to the component instance. That interception is critical to the workings of the COMWare environment, because it is at the *point of interception* that a variety of algorithms can be incorporated into the delivery of that method. All COMWare platforms rely on these *point of interception algorithms* to allow the instances to work well in a middle-

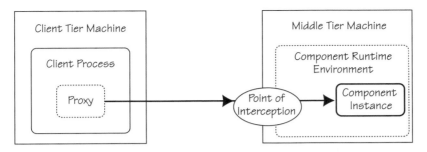

Figure 4.3 Client, component, and point of interception.

tier world. Figure 4.3 shows the relationship between the client, the component instance, and the point of interception.

There are four general categories of point of interception algorithms, all of which we will discuss in detail in this chapter.

Instance management algorithms. Allow sharing of component instance resources among multiple clients.

Load balancing algorithms. Allow workload to be spread across machines.

Security algorithms. Ensure that clients using the component instances are qualified to do so.

Transactional boundary algorithms. Define transactional envelopes for business logic.

Not only is there remarkably little difference between how the three COMWare platforms incorporate these algorithms (at the point of interception), there is relatively little difference in the algorithms themselves. Thus it makes sense to look at these algorithms en masse in this overview chapter.

Typical COMWare Problem

Let's consider a typical problem that might be solved using COMWare. Consider setting up a banking system. Our bank wants to allow customers to deposit into accounts, withdraw from accounts, and transfer money from one account to another. The bank wants to allow customers to do this three different ways:

- Customers can come into the bank and work with a teller.

- Customers can use an ATM machine.

- Customers can access accounts through the Web.

The basic approach the bank will use to solve this problem will be similar regardless of which COMWare platform the bank chooses. There are three basic questions the bank must ask. First, will this problem benefit from a component-based solution? Second, will this problem benefit from a three-tier plus solution, where we have at least three tiers, with at least one tier dedicated to hosting components? Third, will this problem benefit from using a COMWare technology? Only if the answer to all three questions is "yes" should our bank look at one of the COMWare platforms for a solution. Let's consider each of these questions.

Will this problem benefit from a component-based solution? The answer to this question is almost always yes. Components are easy to build, modify, and reuse. In some cases, you can even buy the components already built. About the only reason I can think of for not using components is if you are forced to build for some operating system that has no component support, and these days, that would be a rare operating system indeed.

The most common reason companies shy away from component technology is because of an unwillingness to retrain staff in object-oriented programming languages. This has validity if we are looking at a Java component solution, since that particular platform does tightly couple the notion of objects and components. However, neither CORBA nor COM+ has any built-in language expectation. Although there is widespread confusion in the industry as to the difference between components and objects, the fact is that these two ideas are completely independent of each other.

Programmers can just as easily implement components in a procedural language as they can in an object-oriented language. In many cases, the procedural programmers will end up with better components. Procedural programmers are less likely to make many of the common component design errors that seem to plague object-oriented programmers, such as making methods too fine-grained and doing a poor job of managing data.

Since our bank wants to build its systems quickly and be able to respond quickly to market changes, it will definitely want to use components.

Will this problem benefit from a three-tier plus solution? In a three-tier plus solution the business logic is, by definition, completely compartmentalized. The compartmentalization means that the business logic is independent of the user interface logic. This is a benefit if we want to either run the business logic on different machines from those running the user interface or have multiple user interfaces to the same business logic.

Our bank absolutely needs to support multiple user interfaces for its business logic. It doesn't want to have one implementation of business logic for an account transfer that comes over the Web and another implementation for a transfer that comes through an ATM machine. These two transfers differ only in how the user makes the request.

Our bank also needs to run the business logic on machines other than those running the user interfaces. It is at least theoretically possible to include the business logic on the ATM machines and the machines used by tellers, although in a practical sense, this is extremely unwieldy. However there is no way to run the business logic on the machine used by the customer coming in from the Web. We do not want a nonsecure client machine deciding whether or not to make an account transfer. We want the client machine to ask nicely to make an account transfer, and we will have a machine we trust decide whether or not to allow that transfer to occur.

Since our bank wants both to support multiple interfaces and run business logic on its own central, trusted machines, it will definitely want to use a three-tier plus solution.

Will this problem benefit from using a COMWare technology? We can certainly build three-tier plus component solutions without COMWare technology. However, as we have pointed out, these solutions will have limited capability. The primary push into COMWare comes from a need to support a large number of users, in other words, scalability. If you expect a lot of users to be accessing your system, then use COMWare. If you don't have this expectation, then you have other options.

You may choose to use COMWare even if you don't care about scalability. There may be enough other benefits from COMWare to justify the cost even if you don't expect a large number of users, such as simplified system configuration and an easy to use threading model. But when you are expecting a lot of users to come knocking at your component-based three-tier plus door, then COMWare is a no-brainer. You can't support them any other way.

Our bank wants to be successful. It hopes people like its Web interface and will beat a path to its door. It needs COMWare.

Banking Pseudocode

So our bank has made the wise decision to base its new technology on COMWare. The first thing it needs to do is define its components. The different COMWare platforms have different ways of defining components, but all have some mechanism for defining an interface and then specifying that a component supports one or more of those interfaces. For our bank, I will define an *account* interface supported by both *checkingAccount* and *savingsAccount* components and an *accountTransfer* interface supported by a *standardAccountTransfer* component.

Since we are talking about all COMWare platforms, we will just use pseudocode to create our banking system. Here is a pseudocode definition of our bank's interfaces and components:

```
interface account {
  withdraw (accountID, amount);
  deposit (accountID, amount);
  money balance(accountID);
}
interface accountTransfer {
  transfer(fromAccountID, toAccountID, amount);
}
component checkingAccount supports account;
component savingsAccount supports account;
component standardAccountTransfer supports accountTransfer;
```

Of course, it isn't enough just to define interfaces and components. We must also implement these in some language. We will use a hypothetical procedural language that maps component methods to simple procedures, just to reinforce the idea that you do not need objects to use components. By the way, we won't deal with errors right now. We'll come back to them when we discuss transactions.

There are two conventions our hypothetical language will use. First, the name of the procedure will be a concatenation of the component name and the method name. Thus the standardAccountTransfer's transfer method will map to the procedure standardAccountTransfer_transfer procedure. Second, the instance state (as described in Chapter 2) will be passed through to the procedure as a structure-type gizmo as the first parameter of the procedure. We are not actually going to use the state in this implementation, but the language is set up just in case it does. The state will be followed by those parameters defined by the interface.

The following pseudocode implements the checking account component:

```
checkingAccount_withdraw(state, accountID, amount)
{
  dbc = getDatabaseConnection("Groucho", "Marx");
  balance = readCheckingAccount(dbc, accountID);
  balance = balance - amount;
  updateCheckingAccount(dbc, accountID, balance);
  releaseDatabaseConnection(dbc);
}

checkingAccount_deposit(state, accountID, amount)
{
  dbc = getDatabaseConnection("Groucho", "Marx");
  balance = readCheckingAccount(dbc, accountID);
  balance = balance + amount;
  updateCheckingAccount(dbc, accountID, balance);
  releaseDatabaseConnection(dbc);
}

checkingAccount_balance(state, fromAccountID, toAccountID, amount)
{
  dbc = getDatabaseConnection("Groucho", "Marx");
  balance = readCheckingAccount(dbc, accountID);
  releaseDatabaseConnection(dbc);
  return (balance);
}
```

You can probably figure out the pseudocode that implements the savings account, which is virtually identical to this.

The following pseudocode implements standardAccountTransfer:

```
standardAccountTransfer_transfer(
state, fromAccountID, toAccountID, amount)
{
  dbc = getDatabaseConnection("Groucho", "Marx");
```

```
    type = readAccountType(dbc, fromAccountID);
    if (type = "Checking") fromAccount = create ("checkingAccount");
    if (type = "Savings") fromAccount = create ("savingsAccount");

    type = readAccountType(dbc, toAccountID);
    if (type = "Checking") toAccount = create ("checkingAccount");
    if (type = "Savings") toAccount = create ("savingsAccount");
    releaseDatabaseConnection(dbc);

    fromAccount.withdraw(fromAccountID, amount);
    toAccount.deposit(toAccountId, amount);

    destroy(fromAccount);
    destroy(toAccount);
}
```

Let's go through the preceding transfer code, just to make sure we are in sync. We start out by getting a database connection. This connection will be needed for the code that looks up the account ID in the database and returns information as to the type of the account, which can be either "Checking" or "Savings." We need to know the account types so that we can instantiate the proper account types. Once we have the proper accounts instantiated, we can release the database connection and complete our withdrawal. The code responsible for the transfer doesn't even know which account is which; the code will work equally well for a transfer from a savings account to a checking account as it will from a checking account to a savings account. Finally, we destroy the two account instances, since we no longer need them.

This code is interesting in that the account component could be used either by a real client process, as in when a real person wants to make an account deposit, or by another component instance, such as a *transfer* instance that can coordinate this activity for the person.

As you look through the preceding code, you can see considerable inefficiency in the management of database connections. Every request to transfer money requires the creation and destruction of three database connections. One connection is used by the transfer method to determine the type of the accounts, one is used by the withdraw method, and one is used by the deposit method.

In Chapter 3, I discussed the high cost of creating and destroying database connections. These components as written will also perform very poorly. Most of the runtime will be spent acquiring database connections.

I can make the database connection acquisition much more efficient by moving the database connection acquisition to the point of instantiation. This solves the problem for the standardAccountTransfer component, but not for the savingsAccount and checkingAccount components. For those components, even moving the database connection acquisition to the point of instantiation doesn't completely solve the problem because they are being instantiated and deinstantiated so frequently. So we also need to move their instantiation to the instantiation of the standardAccountTransfer component.

But if we move the database connection acquisition to the standardAccountTransfer instantiation, how do we let the transfer method know where to find the database connection? The most straightforward way to do this is by putting the information in the state information, which, for our hypothetical programming language, is passed as the first parameter to each method invocation.

Every COMWare platform has a way of adding code both to the point of instantiation and to the point of deinstantiation. The instantiation code is added to some method that is guaranteed to be called when a component instance is first created, and the deinstantiation code to a method that is guaranteed to be called when that instance is destroyed. The platforms do not agree on what these methods are named. To keep this discussion general, let's call these two methods *instantiate* and *deinstantiate*.

Here is a new version of the checkingAccount component showing the instantiate and deinstantiate methods, and the revised deposit method. The withdraw and balance methods are not shown, since their changes are very similar to deposit:

```
checkingAccount_deposit(state, accountID, amount)
{
  balance = readCheckingAccount(state.dbc, accountID);
  balance = balance + amount;
  updateCheckingAccount(state.dbc, accountID, balance);
}
checkingAccount_instantiate(state)
{
  state.dbc = getDatabaseConnection("Groucho", "Marx");
}
checkingAccount_deinstantiate(state)
{
  releaseDatabaseConnection(state.dbc);
}
```

Here is a new version of standardAccountTransfer with its changes:

```
standardAccountTransfer_transfer(
state, fromAccountID, toAccountID, amount)
{
  type = readAccountType(state.dbc, fromAccountID);
  if (type = "Checking") fromAccount = state.checkingAccount;
  if (type = "Savings") fromAccount = state.savingsAccount;

  type = readAccountType(state.dbc, toAccountID);
  if (type = "Checking") toAccount = state.checkingAccount;
  if (type = "Savings") toAccount = state.savingsAccount;

  fromAccount.withdraw(fromAccountID, amount);
  toAccount.deposit(toAccountId, amount);
}
standardAccountTransfer_instantiate(state)
{
  state.dbc = getDatabaseConnection("Groucho", "Marx");
  state.savingsAccount = create ("savingsAccount");
  state.checkingAccount = create ("checkingAccount");
}
standardAccountTransfer_deinstantiate(state)
{
  releaseDatabaseConnection(state.dbc);
  destroy (state.savingsAccount);
  destroy (state.checkingAccount);
}
```

Are these new component versions any better than the earlier versions? It depends on how clients make use of these components. If a client creates a remote standardAccountTransfer instance and then uses it over and over, then this code is much more efficient than the first version. If the client creates a remote instance, uses it once, and then immediately discards it, then this code is about the same as the previous version. So let's take a look at some typical client scenarios.

Client Scenarios

Clients come in many shapes and sizes. They come in Visual Basic, Java Applets, DHTML, Server Scripts, and many other forms. From the perspective of the middle tier, however, we can separate clients into one of two categories:

- Those that hold proxies to the component instance directly.
- Those whose proxies are held by a surrogate process.

These two categories are contrasted in Figure 4.4.

When a client holds a proxy directly, it creates the proxy early on and holds onto it as long as possible, to avoid the significant cost of instantiating a remote instance any more than necessary. This is typical of rich clients (sometimes called "fat clients"), such as those written in Visual Basic. Rich clients give the best possible performance and the richest possible user experience, because they use interfaces defined and implemented in programming languages. However they require an *a priori* knowledge of the configuration of the client machine. Since this is usually only possible in an *intranet* situation, we typically see rich clients used only for intranet applications. And since only rich clients have the ability to hold proxies directly, again, we see this also as typical of an intranet application. A rich client application will look something like this:

```
create instances
loop (many times)
{
  get input;
  use instances to process data;
}
destroy instances
```

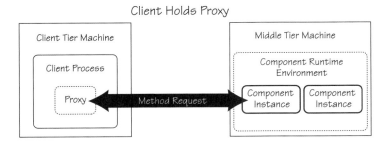

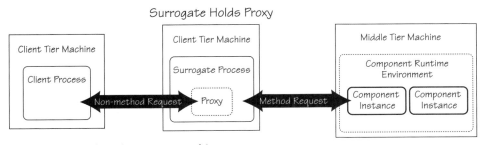

Figure 4.4 Styles of proxy ownership.

When the proxy is held not by the client process, but by a surrogate process, we typically see a very short term use of the instances. The surrogate process processes a request from the client, with no knowledge of whether or not it will see another request from that client ever again. So it typically creates the necessary instances on an as-needed basis and destroys them as soon as possible. The major advantage of this system is that you need make no assumptions about the client machine other than that it is running a standard browser, so it is well suited for *Internet* applications. These types of applications are often called *thin clients*, and are usually written in something like DHTML making use of server side scripts. These scripts run on the surrogate process that lives in the Web processing machine, as shown in Figure 4.5. The thin client surrogate will look something like this:

```
receive input from client;
create instances;
use instances to process data;
destroy instances;
return information to client;
```

It would seem that the rich client applications are the most sensitive to how the components they use are implemented, since they get the most benefit from moving the expensive database acquisition into the point of instantiation. However, many of the Web processing systems have been built in close association with the COMWare platforms, and many will optimize the remote instantiation by saving old proxies under the

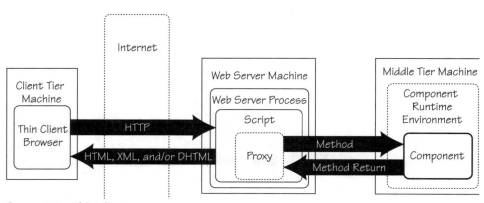

Figure 4.5 Thin clients.

covers. So it may be that although the thin clients appear to get no benefit from our modified components, in fact, they too can see significant cost savings.

Instance Management Algorithms

So for most rich clients and some thin clients, moving costly initialization code, such as database acquisition code, to the point of instantiation makes for much more efficient middle-tier components. But there is a serious problem with this. It is the *lazy client problem*.

The lazy client problem states that for a certain class of clients (primarily rich clients), the amount of time the component is being used is a small fraction of the time the proxy is being held. In other words, the client is lazy in that it spends most of its time doing nothing, at least as far as the instance is concerned. This causes a problem with our newly modified components. Remember, proxies and instances are in a one-to-one relationship in a naive distributed component environment. This means that the component instance is also being used a small fraction of the time, and the underlying resources (including database connections) are also being used a small fraction of the time. As I discussed in Chapter 3, database connections and other similar system resources are in scarce supply. We cannot afford to leave them lying around unused.

So for the same reasons that TPMs had to come up with techniques for sharing middle-tier processes, COMWare technologies have had to come up with techniques for sharing component instances. If we can't share these instances, we can't share our system resources, and just like our TPM ancestors discovered before us, if we can't share system resources, we can't support but a handful of clients. And a handful of clients just doesn't cut it in the world of Web commerce.

All of the COMWare platforms use a category of algorithms to deal with the lazy client problem that I call *instance management algorithms*. Instance management algorithms are intended to preserve the illusion of a one-to-one relationship between a proxy and an instance, while under the covers managing that relationship so that unused instances are not lying around tying up resources.

There are two common instance management algorithms used by most COMWare platforms:

- Instance pooling algorithm
- Just-in-time instantiation algorithm

Both algorithms are introduced at the point of interception as the method request moves from the client proxy through the COMWare component process. Conceptually, there is an *instance manager* that is responsible for administering the appropriate instance management algorithm at the point of interception. Exactly what that instance manager does depends on which of the instance management algorithms that particular COMWare platform is using, or, if it supports both algorithms (as does COM+), then on how that particular component has been configured.

Both instance management algorithms are similar in that client-side proxies are effectively decoupled from component process instances. When the client creates a remote instance, a proxy is created in the client process space, but in the component process, no instance is assigned to receive work from the client's proxy. Note that this is quite unlike the pre-COMWare component architecture, in which proxy creation always occurs concurrently with instance creation. In the COMWare architecture, the assignment of a component process instance to a client-side proxy is deferred until the time of method invocation.

When the client-side method is invoked, it is intercepted in the COMWare component process and handed off to the instance manager, who is responsible for finding an instance to service that method request. How the instance manager finds an instance depends on which of the two instance management algorithms is being used.

Instance Pooling Algorithm

In the instance pooling algorithm, the instance manager is managing a pool of ready and willing instances, much like my manager at IBM managed his eight or so direct reports. When a method invocation is intercepted by component process, the instance manager arbitrarily chooses one of the instances from the pool to process that method invocation. As long as that method is being processed, that instance is dedicated to that proxy. As soon as the method has been completed, the instance is returned to the pool to await another assignment from the instance manager (shown in Figure 4.6). The instance pooling algorithm has historically been favored by Enterprise JavaBeans.

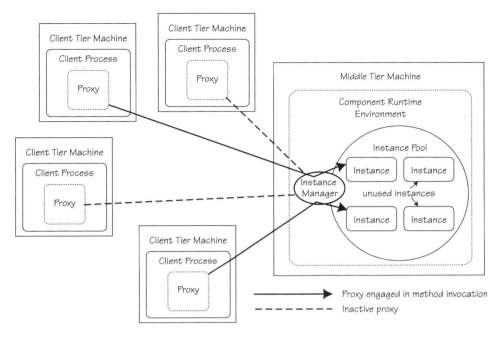

Figure 4.6 Instance pooling.

Just-in-Time Instantiation Algorithm

In the just-in-time instantiation algorithm, the instance manager is not managing a pool of instances, but is instead presiding over empty space. When a method invocation is intercepted by the component process, the instance manager creates a new instance to process that request. As in the instance pooling algorithm, as long as that method is being processed, that instance is dedicated to that proxy. Unlike the instance pooling algorithm, when the method has been completed, the instance is destroyed (shown in Figure 4.7). The just-in-time instantiation algorithm was the standard instance management algorithm of Microsoft's middle-tier architecture until the arrival of COM+. Even now, just-in-time instantiation is probably favored in COM+.

Resource Management

You might expect a great deal of inefficiency in the just-in-time instantiation algorithm due to the constant instantiation and deinstantiation of

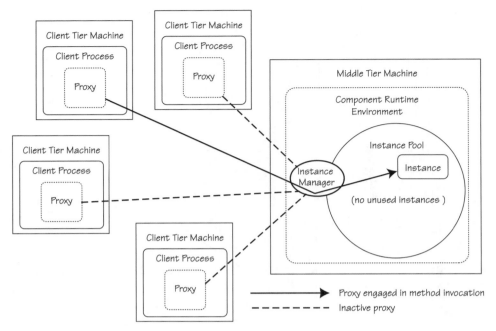

Figure 4.7   Just-in-time instantiation.

remote instances. However, because the instantiation is not impacting the client's proxies, the instantiation does not need to involve any remote communication. From the client's perspective, there is no remote instantiation. Therefore the cost of instantiation is not the cost of a remote instantiation, it is the cost of a local instantiation by the instance manager. Local instantiation is a relatively low-cost item.

Unfortunately, it's not quite this simple. Although the cost of the local instantiation is low, there are actually two costs associated with the creation of a new component instance. One is the cost of the instantiation itself, which is indeed low. However, the other is the cost of the initialization of that instance.

Initialization costs are often quite high. Take our savingsAccount component, for example. It needs to acquire database connections. We already know that database connections are extremely expensive to create. If our instance needs to create a new database connection each time it is instantiated, it will never be able to run under the just-in-time instantiation algorithm with any degree of efficiency. So COMWare platforms that rely on just-in-time instantiation for instance management also depend on something else to minimize the cost of initialization. In most cases, that something else is *resource pooling*.

Resource pooling is the ability to pool resources, so that when a resource such as a database connection is needed, it doesn't need to be created from scratch, it can be borrowed from a resource pool. And then when it is no longer needed, it can be returned to the pool. Pool management is not without its own cost, but that cost is negligible compared to the cost of creating a new resource. It is certainly negligible when that resource is a database connection.

The ability to pool resources is not the responsibility of the COMWare component process *per se*. Rather it is part of what I think of as the interoperability services. Since resource pooling is always associated with the use of something outside the COMWare environment (such as a database), it is part of the solution COMWare platforms offer to interoperate with outside systems. In the case of Java, the database connection pooling is part of JDBC 2.0. In the case of COM+, it is part of ODBC. In the case of CORBA, this is not directly addressed by the current draft of the Component Specification, but is assumed to be part of the implementation of the component process.

Although resource pools are critical to just-in-time instantiation, they can even be useful for systems using instance pooling for their instance management algorithm. Instance pools are partitioned by component. A client needing a savingsAccount instance can only make use of the savingsAccount pool and not the checkingAccount pool, even though both of these components share the same interface. If a system has enough different components (not instances, but actual different components) it is possible to start having a significant number of resources tied up in pools that are not being heavily used. For such a system, scalability could be improved by having the components grab a resource from the resource pool just before it is needed, and then released as soon as it is no longer needed, as shown in Figure 4.8.

Who Needs Instance Management Algorithms?

Resource pools are so useful that some people wonder if instance management algorithms are even needed in a system that has good resource pools. This is a reasonable question. Remember that we started the dis-

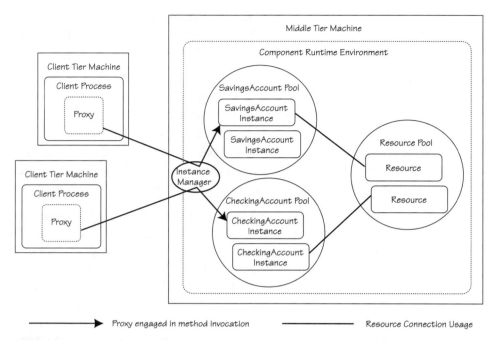

Proxy engaged in method invocation   Resource Connection Usage

Figure 4.8 Resource pools.

cussion of instance management with an observation that it takes a long time to acquire database connections. But if we have a good pooling mechanism, then it doesn't take long to acquire database connections (or at least, no place near as long).

I believe that instance management algorithms are important, regardless of resource pooling, for three reasons. First, components may make use of resources that do not support pooling. Not even all databases support pooling. For components that require such resources, resource pooling is not an option. The only way they can share resources is indirectly by sharing instances.

Second, middle-tier component instances (which are the ones we are concerned with in this book) tend to have large amounts of data. As we add more and more clients to our system, we start placing heavy demands on the virtual memory management of our system. We can quickly get into a situation in which most of our disk activity is going toward managing virtual memory, and this can be a huge drain on our throughput. Instance management algorithms solve this problem by preventing bulky, but unused instances from accumulating in our system.

Third, every instance potentially takes up a thread, a little piece of a process that can be split off for concurrent processing. We will discuss this shortly, but for now just realize the implications of this. Threads are valuable resources. Even if our instance is not using any other system resources, it is probably tying up a thread. Since we need only as many threads as we have active instances, instance management algorithms are also effectively thread management algorithms.

Some people wonder if the trend toward thin client technology will ultimately eliminate the need for instance management. This, also, is a reasonable question. As we pointed out earlier, thin clients, such as those found in Internet applications, do not hold their own proxies, but depend on a surrogate process running in the Web server to hold their proxies. But because of the nature of the interaction between the thin client and the surrogate process, remote instances (and the surrogate side proxies) tend to be created just before they are needed and then destroyed as soon as possible. But doesn't this seem very similar to the just-in-time instantiation algorithm? Why do we need both?

There are two reasons why I believe instance management algorithms are here to stay, even in the face of increased thin client popularity. First, even though thin clients are the clients of choice for the Internet, rich clients are still the clients of choice for the intranet. And rich clients, as I pointed out earlier, do not follow the thin client profile for instantiation. They do their instantiation early on and hold their proxies as long as possible. This will be the kiss of death to a system that does not support instance management. When we design components, we want them to be independent of client-side technology, and this means designing them to support both thin and rich clients efficiently. And this means using instance management.

Second, even though the surrogate thin client process tends to instantiate and deinstantiate with little time in between, it is likely that as the surrogate process becomes better and better integrated into the COMWare platform, that it will find ways to optimize the use of proxies. I discussed this earlier in the context of rich and thin client comparisons. So even if the server script code thinks it is destroying a remote instance and therefore also destroying a local proxy, the surrogate process in which that script is running may well be smarter than that.

Performance versus Throughput

You can see that the overall process of invoking a method, which looks so simple from the client perspective, can get quite complicated. As shown in Figure 4.9, first the client invokes the method on the proxy. The proxy packages the request and sends it over to the component process. The component process unpackages the request and invokes the method on the component instance. Before that method is delivered, it is intercepted. At the incoming point of interception, the instance manager jumps into action and, in the case of just-in-time instantiation, creates a component instance to process the request. The instance gets its necessary resources from the resource pools. It then executes the business logic, returns the resource to the resource pool, and then returns from the method call. The return is also intercepted and the instance manager once again jumps into action, destroying the no longer needed instance. And finally, the day is done.

No matter how efficient we make our COMWare component process, this has to take longer than a simple client method invocation on a remote instance without the involvement of COMWare. When you add COMWare, you add point of interception, instance management, and resource pooling. All of these things take time. So what is COMWare buying us?

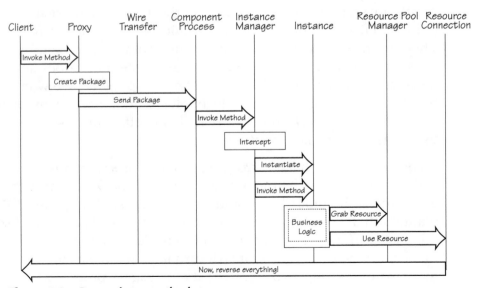

Figure 4.9 Processing a method.

Surprisingly, COMWare is *not* buying us performance. At least not performance in the traditional meaning of the word. We usually think of performance as being measured from the perspective of client response time. COMWare adds a lot of algorithms between the client and the instance. Somebody has to pay for all these algorithms, and the one who will pay is the client, in the form of degraded response time.

What COMWare *does* buy us is *system throughput*. It buys us the ability to increase the number of transactions we can push through our middle tier dramatically. And this translates to a huge increase in the number of clients we can support—which is exactly what we need, if we are in the Web commerce business.

The fact is that the degradation of client response time, although significant, is probably not measurable. After all, how many people can tell the difference between a system that responds to a request in 0.1 seconds and one that responds in 0.2 seconds? But I assure you that you *can* tell the difference between a system that can process 10 transactions per second (for a pre-COM+ COM/DCOM system) and one that can process 800 transactions per second (a COM+ system).

Threading

If you are a pre-COMWare middle-tier component programmer, you are painfully aware of threads. If your component process is going to be able to service more than one client at a time, you must build threads into your process. When a client creates an instance, the main component process (for which, I remind you, you are responsible) accepts the creation request. The main process then typically starts up a thread. That thread creates the instance and returns a proxy to the client. From then on, when the client makes requests through that proxy, the request is routed to that instance living on that thread. In the meantime, the main process is free to listen for more creation requests. This is how you get the component process to service multiple clients.

The design of an efficient and robust threading system is not easy. You need to make sure that threads are managed properly, that multi-user access to variables is coordinated, and that you don't end up with deadlocked threads. Many people do not fully understand threading issues and end up with component processes that fail in unexplained, unpredictable, and nonreproducible ways.

COMWare component programmers don't have to worry about threads. Threads are the responsibility of the component process, and guess what?—the component process is not your problem! When the COMWare component process does its magical instance management algorithm, it automatically makes sure that each instance is properly started on its own thread, that threads start and stop properly, and that they don't interfere with each other. Many COMWare component programmers have never even heard of threads!

Life Cycle

You would think that something as simple as the life and death of a component instance would not be a big deal in a pre-COMWare environment. After all, this is one of the few things for which the component process is not responsible. It is the *client* that says when an instance is created and when it is destroyed. But that is exactly the problem. Of all the unreliable scum in the universe, the worst is client programmers.

Client programmers make every mistake imaginable. They create remote instances and then forget to destroy them. They crash in the middle of their programs. They go into loops creating remote instances as if there is no tomorrow. In a pre-COMWare environment, every one of these mistakes leaves lost proxies on the client side. Every one of these lost proxies is attached to similarly lost instances in the component process. Each of these lost instances is tying up resources, threads, and virtual memory as they spend eternity sniffling their way through the world with no direction, no future, no hope.

For humanitarian reasons, if no other, we should adopt a COMWare environment and the instance management algorithms. Instance management algorithms can't do much about lost proxies on the client side, but that's the client's own fault for hiring trashy programmers. What the instance management algorithms can do is make sure that those lost proxies are not tying up any component instances and are therefore not tying up any middle-tier resources. The instance management algorithms do this as a natural consequence of the fact that nobody asks lost proxies to do any work. It's hard to ask them to do any work if they're lost, right? (This was one of the rules of life I discovered at IBM.) As long as the proxy is not actively being asked to accomplish work, the instance manager will not assign any component instance to process that work. If no instance has been assigned to the proxy, no resources are tied up. Viola! Automatic garbage collection!

State Management

Okay. I have been putting this off as long as possible. There's no sunshine without a little rain. No laughter without a little tears. No light without. . . well, you get the idea. I hate to be the bearer of bad news, but after all, that's why they pay me the big bucks. So sit back. Take a deep breath. This won't take long, and someday you'll thank me. Actually, you will thank me before the end of this chapter although you may not believe that right now.

Here goes: Instance management is not totally free. There is just a little programming cost to using instance management algorithms. You need to do just one itsy bitsy little thing: You just need to make your components stateless.

WHAT?! I HAVE TO MAKE MY COMPONENT STATELESS!??!. Yes. Somehow I knew that was going to be your reaction. It always is.

I can understand why the COMWare vendors hate to mention this point. We seem to have a whole generation of programmers that think they are vastly superior to the rest of the world because they have learned to say the mantra, "objects are behavior plus state. . .objects are behavior plus state. . ." and here we are to tell them that they're only half right. Behavior, yes. State, no.

Actually, it's not quite as bad as this. In fact, there is nothing wrong with having state in objects. The real problem comes in when people continue to confuse *objects* with *components*. You can put all the state you want in your *objects*. It's your *components* that must be stateless.

What exactly does it mean to say that a component must be stateless? It basically means I lied to you in Chapter 2 when I showed you code snippets like this:

```
emp1 = create Employee()
tell emp1 to updateYourName("Roger Sessions");
ask emp1 to set name1 = tellMeYourName();
```

For this code snippet to work, the Employee component instance known as *emp1* must store the information about its name long enough to be able to reply intelligently when asked for its name. The only obvious place to store that information is in the instance state. Going back to the hypothetical language we used earlier in this chapter, we might expect an implementation of Employee to look like this:

```
Employee_updateYourName(state, name)
{
  state.name = name;
}
Employee_tellMeYourName(state)
{
  return state.name;
}
```

If you are wondering why the method implementations have one more parameter (the *state* parameter) than do the method invocations, remember that that is how we defined the hypothetical language bindings. Since this hypothetical language is non-object-oriented, it automatically passes in the state structure through to each method invocation.

There is only one problem with this implementation of Employee component. It doesn't work. Or at least, it doesn't work very well. The problem is that this implementation is incompatible with either of the two instance management algorithms.

It is incompatible with instance pooling because in that algorithm, instances are randomly assigned from the instance pool to service requests. If there are N instances in the pool, the chances of the instance that accepted the updateYourName request being the same as the one that responds to the tellMeYourName request is approximately $1/N$. In other words, this double method invocation will fail N times as often as it will succeed. Obviously not very good odds.

This implementation does even worse with the just-in-time instantiation algorithm. Because the instance is destroyed after every method invocation, the chances of the same instance getting both method invocations is zilch. So with just-in-time instantiation, this implementation *never* succeeds. Of course, *never* succeeding is not much worse than *almost* never succeeding, which is what this implementation does with instance pooling. Neither is acceptable.

So how do we deal with this problem? Are we forced to create boring components that have no state? Not really. All we need to do is find someplace else for that state to live.

Moving the State Out of the Instance

The different COMWare platforms all agree that if you keep state in the component instance, you will end up with components that are incompatible with instance management algorithms. And this is a bad thing. A very bad thing. No instance management, no scalability, no Web access. So where do you move the state?

The most common place to hold state is going to be the back-end database. Remember the back-end database? As we pointed out in Chapter 1, "The Problems of Commerce," commerce has very little to do with moving money and a lot to do with updating databases. Database may not be good at much, but they do happen to be good at storing data efficiently, adjudicating between competing needs for that data, and making sure that data is never lost. So databases are the obvious place to store the state for the component instance.

This requires a different implementation of Employee. The new implementation will look like this:

```
Employee_updateYourName(state, name)
{
  read employee's name from database;
  write employee's name to database;
}
Employee_tellMeYourName(state)
{
  read employee's name from database;
  return name;
}
```

This particular implementation is simplistic, because there is no business logic except for the setting and getting of the Employee name. The general form of an implementation designed for instance management looks like this:

```
method(parameters)
{
  read state from database;
  do business stuff;
  write state out to database;
}
```

I find it remarkable that every COMWare platform agrees on the basic form of this algorithm. There are many details on which they disagree, but on these three critical points, there is complete agreement:

- The state *must* be moved out of the instance in order to be compatible with instance management.

- The most logical place to move that state is to a back-end database.

- All method implementations must follow the basic pattern of *read* state, *process* business logic, *update* database.

Instance management, and therefore scalability, is possible if and only if the state is moved out of the instance, probably into a database. I will not go into the details of how the database read/write logic is physically coordinated with the business logic, since this differs for each COMWare platform. I will cover that in the platform-specific chapters. For now, you might take a moment to meditate on how incredible it is that all COMWare platforms agree on this fundamental relationship between *instance management* and *state management*.

Some readers might wonder about the value of instance management. After all, I am saying you must add two database accesses to each method in order to get the whole thing to work. Database accesses may not be as expensive as the acquisition of a database connection, but still, they ain't hay. Is it really worth it? I would like to tell you that there are some cute tricks you can use to avoid the database access, and indeed, all of the COMWare vendors have added platform-specific features intended to give you this illusion. But ultimately, it is an illusion. There is just no way around the ugly fact of life that instance management requires two extra database accesses.

There is one piece of good news: those two extra database accesses happened to be required whether you make use of instance management algorithms or not. They are needed for reasons completely unrelated to instance management. Looking at things in this light, there is really *no* extra cost for instance management. But before I can convince you of this, I will need to convince you that those database accesses really are unavoidable. And for that story, we are going to have to wait until just a little further in this chapter.

What, No State?

Before you get in a tizzy about your instances not being able to have state, let me point out a few exceptions.

Exception one: Your instances can have state, as long as that state is not specific to a particular client/proxy. Actually, this is only half true. It is true for instance pooling, but not for just-in-time instantiation (at least, not without secondary support). There are many examples of state that is *not* proxy-specific, and therefore acceptable. One common example is one in which the state consists of resource connections. I discussed one such case earlier in this chapter: the reimplementation of checkingAccount with the acquisition of the database connection moved to the instantiate and deinstantiate methods. Another example would be an inventory component that contains regional sales tax information. Sales tax is not specific to any one client. Sales tax is sales tax. Any instance a client happens to pick up at the point of interception will work equally well.

Exception two: Your *object* instances can have state, just not your *component* instances. So if you are using an object-oriented programming language, you may have a component-level method that is implemented with hundreds of objects, all calling each other in a mad feeding frenzy, each packed with more state than sardines in a can. As long as the last object has flushed the last bit of its state by the time the component method is ready to return, you can still use our beloved instance management algorithms.

Exception three: You can put all the state you want in your components. You just can't use the instance management algorithms. All of the COMWare platforms support this. It is called a *conversational mode*. In a conversational mode, your proxy hogs a component instance all to itself. Even when your proxy is not using the instance, nobody else can get their hands on it.

There is really only one reason I can think of for using a conversational mode in a large commerce system, and that is when you can be absolutely positive the conversation isn't going to last very long. Take this code:

```
emp1 = create Employee()
tell emp1 to updateYourName("Roger Sessions");
ask emp1 to set name1 = tellMeYourName();
```

If you can positively guarantee that tellMeYourName will be called milliseconds after updateYourName, then you can convince me to allow the use of the conversational mode in this specific case. However, this guarantee is very difficult to make. In almost all cases the use of conversations is a design flaw that represents laziness and/or a lack of understanding on the part of the programmer.

Load Balancing Algorithms

I hope we all agree that instance management is a good thing, and that it is well worth the cost of figuring out how to manage your component's state to make it all work. The payoff to instance management is scalability: commerce systems that will support every potential client in the world. Or will they?

Let's say we have a system that can support 200 database connections, that each component instance requires one database connection, and that, on average, a client uses a component instance about 1/100th of the time. Without COMWare, this system is limited to 200 clients, one for each database connection. With COMWare, the number of clients can potentially jump to 20,000, one hundred for each database connection. Not too shabby, but also not enough to support hundreds of thousands of concurrent clients. What do we need to jump from tens of thousands to hundreds of thousands of clients? We need *load balancing* algorithms.

I think of load balancing algorithms as a subset of *blob algorithms*. Blob algorithms are algorithms that allow a bunch of computers to act as a single blob. Instead of asking a particular machine to do work, you ask the blob to do work, and the load balancing algorithms coordinate the distribution of workload among the machines in the blob. If one machine in the blob gets overworked, the rest of the machines in the blob take on some of its work load. Figure 4.10 shows you this blob mentality.

Conceptually, the blob as a whole is controlled by what I call a *blob manager*. The blob manager is always monitoring the health of the blob. It knows which machines are part of the blob, which of those machines are currently running, and how much work each machine has been assigned.

The blob manager lives in its own process with its own point of interception, which differs from the process and point of interception used by the instance management algorithms. In general, as a method invo-

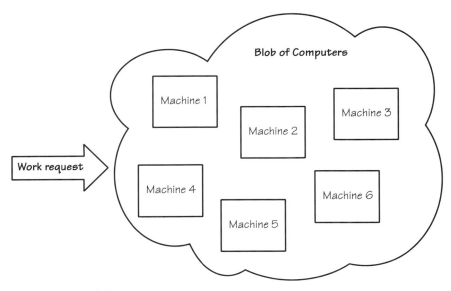

Figure 4.10 Blobs.

cation comes in from a client, that method invocation is first intercepted by the blob manager. The blob manager then decides which component process running on which machine should get the method request. It makes this decision based on the overall state of the blob. Once that decision has been made, the method is forwarded to the appropriate component process living in the chosen machine. At that point, the interception algorithms kick in (as shown in Figure 4.11).

Not all COMWare platforms use this exact algorithm. COM+, for example, uses an algorithm that is very similar, but not identical, to this generic description. I will discuss the COM+ load balancing algorithm in Chapter 8, "The COM+ Services." The similarities between COM+ and this generic algorithm are close enough so that this discussion is completely relevant.

The mathematics of load balancing are reasonably simple. Let's say we have an application whose clients use components an average of 1 millisecond out of N (or $1/N$th of the time), running on middle-tier machines that can support approximately M component instances, using a blob of B machines. Without instance management we can support M clients. With instance management, we can support $N \times M$ clients. With load balancing and instance management we can support $N \times M \times B$ clients. The nice thing about B is that whereas N and M are relatively fixed, B is not.

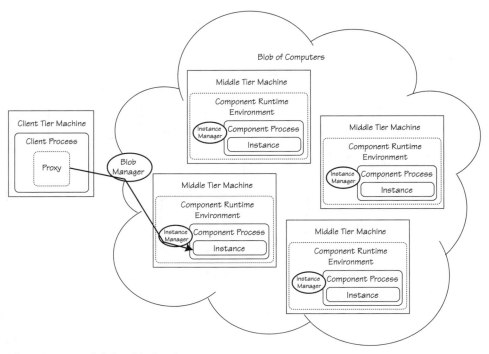

Figure 4.11 Blob load balancing.

N is fixed by the speed at which a client works. M is fixed by the amount of resources consumed by a typical component and the amount of those resources available on one machine. But B is bounded only by the size of the blob. And there is no theoretical maximum to the size of the blob. It is limited only by the implementation of a particular COMWare platform.

Blob management is closely related to instance management. As I'm sure you remember, the instance management algorithms are based on the ability of the instance manager to assign client method requests to randomly chosen (or randomly created) component instances. You can think of the blob manager as an extension to instance management allowing not only *instances* to be chosen randomly, but also *processes* and *machines*.

When talking about state management with regard to instance management, I suggested that the most common place to place component state will be in a back-end database. This is especially true for components that will run on a blob. The fact that the state is in a shared database means it can be accessed by any machine in the blob. This is what allows the instances to roam freely, so to speak. You can see this is Figure 4.12.

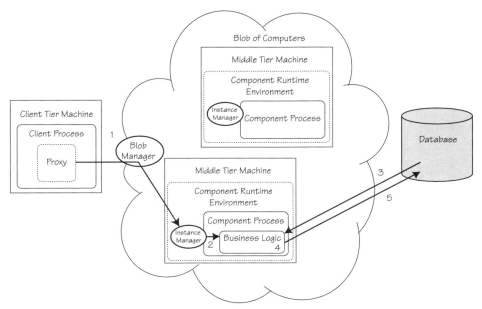

Figure 4.12   Relationship between state and blob management.

Blob management has another important function besides load balancing, and this is *failover*. Failover refers to the ability of the blob to withstand outages of individual machines in the blob. When one machine dies, the other machines take over its workload. Just as the blob manager is monitoring the workload of each machine in the blob, it is also monitoring whether or not those machines are functioning. If any machines aren't working, then the blob managers reassigns their work elsewhere in the blob.

The mathematics governing blob reliability is very interesting, and assumes only that the chances of any machine in the blob dying are both random and independent of the chances of any other machine in the blob dying. This makes the two events independent, and independent events are easy to predict. Like dice.

Let's review dice briefly. Say we have thrown D numbers of six-sided dice. What are the chances of all D dice coming up as 1? Since the chances of any one die coming up as 1 is random and independent of the chances of any other die coming up as 1, then the chances of all die coming up as 1 is $1/6 \times 1/6 \times$, up to the D, or just $(1/6)^D$. If D is 2, then the chances of all D dice coming up as 1 is $(1/6)^2$, or 1/36.

So if we have B similar machines in our blob, and the chances of any one failing is F on any given day, what are the chances of the blob as a whole failing on any given day? Perhaps a better way to ask this question is if we need *Bmin* machines to give us the necessary scalability, how many more machines (say, *Btotal*) do we need to guarantee us scalability even in the face of machine failure?

Essentially, the blob as a whole fails when one machine more than the minimum number of machines fails. If there are three machines and the minimum is two, then the blob fails when more than one machine of the three total fails. We can express this as saying failure occurs when ($Btotal - Bmin + 1$) out of all the *Bmax* machines that have failed. If, like the dice, the chances of machine failure are random and independent, then the chances of two machines failing is F^2, and of ($Btotal - Bmin + 1$) machines failing is $F^{(Btotal - Bmin + 1)}$.

Let's consider some possible numbers. Let's say our application needs a blob of 10 machines to provide us our desired scalability. Let's say we measure the machine reliability at 1/10, meaning that a machine fails, on average, one day in 10. Let's say we need our application as a whole to fail one day in 10,000, or no more than one day every 25 years. How many machines do we need in the blob to achieve this reliability?

This becomes fairly simple to work out. We get the following numbers:

```
F = 1/10
Bmin = 10


Btotal    F(Btotal-Bmin+1)
10        (1/10) (10-10+1))  = 1/10
11        (1/10) 11-10+1  = 1/100
12        (1/10) 12-10+1  = 1/1000
13        (1/10) 13-10+1  = 1/10000
14        (1/10) 14-10+1  = 1/100000
```

And there is our answer. If we want a blob of machines that will fail approximately one day in 10,000, where failure is defined as inadequate scalability to meet our expected client load, we need a blob of 13 machines. Of these 13 machines, 10 are required for scalability and 3 are required for redundancy.

What is particularly interesting about blob mathematics is that the cost of the blob goes up much slower than the reliability of the blob. If a given machine costs $10,000, then we need 10 machines for a total cost of $100,000 to achieve the necessary scalability. By increasing the over-all system cost a minuscule 30 percent, we increase the overall reliability of the system by 100,000 percent!

Of course, every application will come up with different results. The important point is not to convince you to buy blobs of 13 machines, but to show you how to calculate your needed blob size based on your own easily measured application numbers. All you need to know is the number of expected concurrent clients, the fraction of time a given client uses a component, the number of instances you can run on a given machine, and the measured reliability of one machine.

The final function that is often associated with the blob is system maintainability. In general, we mean the ability to run a system 24 hours a day, 7 days a week, 52 weeks per year. Plus a little extra for leap years. The most difficult problem to solve is system upgrade. In general, you must take down a system in order to upgrade it. But while the system is down, it isn't running. And yet, you can't go forever with upgrading. How do you do this?

The blob comes to the rescue. Since there are plenty of other machines ready to take over at a moment's notice, you can bring any machine down for system upgrade, and nobody outside the blob will know the difference. The other machines in the blob may whine a bit, but they will get over it as soon as this machine comes back on line. Once this machine is upgraded, you bring it back on line, and nobody is the wiser.

You should be able to see that if your components are not compatible with instance management, they also will not be compatible with blob management. The converse is not necessarily true. You can have instances that are instance-manager compatible, but not blob-manager compatible, although it would take a fair amount of effort to achieve this. If you follow my recommendations, components will be both instance-manager compatible and blob-manager compatible. For large commerce systems, blob compatibility, like instance-manager compatibility, is critical. If your component is not blob compatible, it cannot take advantage of blob scalability, blob failover, or blob maintainability.

The term *blob* is much too intuitive to have any chance of becoming official. So the fancy-shmancy COMWare vendors generally use the much more boring term *cluster*. But what the heck, a blob by any other name smells as sweet.

Transaction Boundary Management

In the last chapter, I discussed the importance of transactions in the context of Transaction Processing Monitors (TPMs). Transactions, I said, can best be thought of as a framework for error management. Transactions guarantee that a bunch of business logic will be processed only if it all can be processed without any chance of errors occurring. This is no less true for business logic packaged as components as it is for business logic packaged as remote procedure calls (the typical packaging of TPMs), so I don't need to repeat this discussion in this chapter. And, like our remote procedures before them, our components are using databases for storing information, and databases are quite good at transactions.

Though databases are good at transactions, they are not good at cooperating among themselves. That is why we needed our TPM system to provide a distributed transaction coordinator. Since COMWare is to components what TPMs are to remote procedures, any self-respecting COMWare platform must provide functionality similar to the distributed transaction coordination found in the TPM systems.

All COMWare platforms provide a mechanism for coordinating distributed transactions, and they do so using exactly the same algorithm used by the TPM systems. This algorithm (the *two-phase commit* protocol) was described in detail in Chapter 3, so we won't repeat that discussion, as fascinating as it was. However I will do just the *briefest* of reviews, so that we see how that algorithm relates to components and COMWare.

The first thing to remember about the two-phase commit protocol is that it is really a three-phase commit protocol. It was named the two-phase commit protocol by people who are trying to confuse you. They are not your friends. I am your friend, so you should believe me, not them. The three phases are as follows.

Contemplative phase. Starts when the transaction begins. During this phase, the distributed transaction coordinator is monitoring all database updates, and keeping track of which databases were updated during this transaction.

Consensus phase. Begins when and if a commit request is made by the initiator of the transaction. During this phase, the distributed transaction coordinator asks all of the databases that were updated during the transaction how they would feel about committing the work.

Final phase. Begins when the distributed transaction coordinator has finished collecting the opinions of all the databases in the consensus phase. During the final phase, the distributed transaction coordinator tells each of the updated databases whether to commit or to rollback the transaction. Every database gets the same instructions. The decision as to whether to issue a commit or rollback is based on whether any of the databases poo-pooed the commit during the consensus phase.

The COMWare distributed transaction coordinator is perfectly happy to take care of the two-phase commit, as long as it knows when the contemplative phase and the consensus phase should begin. It can figure out for itself when the final phase begins, but it has no way to know when the transaction should begin (and therefore when the contemplative phase should begin) and when the commit should be issued (and when therefore the consensus phase should begin). It depends on somebody else to make these decisions.

In the TPM environment, it is the client code that makes that decision. In Chapter 3, we showed client code that followed this outline:

```
beginTransaction();
do a bunch of business logic;
error = FALSE;
if (any errors occured) error = TRUE;
if (error) rollback();
else commit();
```

The client's beginTransaction() signals to the distributed transaction coordinator that it is time for the contemplative phase to begin. The client's commit() signals that it is time for the consensus phase to begin, and then when that phase has completed, to begin the final phase.

In component systems, the business logic is going to be encapsulated into a component method. Translating the preceding pseudocode to a component system, we would get something like:

```
myInstance = create GreatComponent();
beginTransaction();
ask myInstance to doSomething();
error = FALSE;
if (any errors occured) error = TRUE;
if (error) rollback();
else commit();
destroy (myInstance);
```

However this code assumes that the doSomething method of GreatComponent has a transactional requirement. How can we know this, if the business logic inside GreatComponent has really been encapsulated? And how do we know that a new implementation of GreatComponent won't come along that doesn't have a transactional requirement. And if that happens, how do we know that the new implementation won't need to invoke a method on some other component that *does* have a transactional requirement? And what if that component changes someday?

The point is that depending on the client to decide when the transaction begins and ends (or rolls back) has two problems. First, it breaks encapsulation, and second, it is very fragile code.

So the COMWare products, led by the granddaddy of all COMWare products, Microsoft Transaction Server, have all come to the same conclusion. Clients can't be trusted to decide when transactions begin and end. We need to leave that to somebody we do trust. And whom do we trust in the world, above everybody else? The COMWare runtime environment of course, in the form of the component process.

The different COMWare technologies provide administrative tools to configure components. One of the things they allow you to configure is the transactional requirements of those components. If the component requires a transaction, say because it plans on updating a database, then it will be documented as *requiring* a transaction, and it will be so configured by the system administrator. Should a new implementation of that component come on board that does not require a transaction, because it has figured out how to implement its methods without using a database, then it will be configured as *not requiring* a transaction. And when the new implementation is configured into the system, the system administrator will configure it according to its needs.

The nice thing about all this is that the client code need have no knowledge of whether the component is transactional or not. The preceding client code becomes simplified to:

```
myInstance = create GreatComponent();
ask myInstance to doSomething();
destroy (myInstance);
```

Nice, isn't it?

When does the component process decide to kick off a transaction? It does it at the same time it does everything else—at the point of interception.

The general algorithm for managing the transaction boundaries, which I call, oddly enough, a *transactional boundary algorithm*, comes in two parts. The first part occurs with the incoming point of interception and the second part occurs with the outgoing point of interception.

On the incoming side, when a method is invoked on an instance, it is intercepted, of course. At the point of interception, we can think of a *transaction boundary manager* as jumping into the fray, much like the instance manager. The transaction boundary manager looks at the target of the invocation, and asks whether or not this particular method on that particular component requires a transaction. If the answer is no, then the transaction boundary manager goes back to sleep. If the answer is yes, then the transaction boundary manager asks another question: Is there already a transaction running on behalf of the original client? If the answer to this question is yes, then the transaction boundary manager decides that no further action is warranted, and goes back to sleep. If the answer to this question is no, then the transaction boundary manager kicks off a brand new transaction on behalf of this client.

On the outgoing side, as each method makes the return trip back to the client, and again goes through the point of interception, the transaction boundary manager asks another question: at the incoming point of interception, did we kick off a new transaction? If the answer is yes, then it now concludes the transaction. If the answer is no, it does nothing.

Let's follow this through with a simplified version of the standardAccountTransfer component I discussed earlier in this chapter. Now I will modify the code so that an account interface can deal with information for either a savings or checking account. This eliminates the need for a database access in the standardAccountTransfer implementation. The new version looks like this:

```
standardAccountTransfer_transfer(
state, fromAccountID, toAccountID, amount)
{
  fromAccount = create ("genericAccount");
  toAccount   = create ("GenericAccount");

  fromAccount.withdraw(fromAccountID, amount);
  toAccount.deposit(toAccountId, amount);
```

```
    destroy(fromAccount);
    destroy(toAccount);
}
```

The new genericAccount will, of course, require database accesses, and therefore definitely needs to be configured as requiring a transaction. How should we configure the standardAccountTransfer? We might logically expect to configure standardAccountTransfer as not requiring a transaction; however, this will not work. Let's see why.

Here is some client code for this component:

```
newTransfer = create ("standardAccountTransfer");
get fromAccount, toAccount, amount;
ask newTransfer to transfer(fromAccount, toAccount, amount);
destroy (newTransfer);
```

Follow the flow of control, as shown in Figure 4.13. On the incoming transfer method, the transactional boundary manager sees no need for a transaction, so does nothing. On the incoming withdraw method, the transactional boundary manager does see a need for a transaction, so starts one. On the outgoing withdraw, the transactional boundary manager sees that this method began a transaction, so terminates it. On the next incoming deposit method, the transactional boundary manager sees another need for a transaction, so starts another one. On the outgoing deposit, it terminates that transaction.

The problem with this configuration is that the withdraw and deposit are in separate transactions. This effectively means that one can succeed

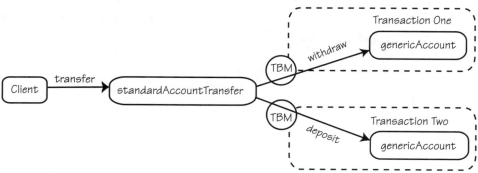

Figure 4.13   Transaction boundary management.

while the other fails. This is not good. We want them to either *both* succeed or *both* fail.

The way to solve this problem is to configure the standardAccount-Transfer to require a transaction. This gives us an entirely different flow of control, as shown in Figure 4.14. With this configuration, the incoming transfer kicks off a transaction. On the first incoming withdraw, the transaction boundary manager sees a need for a transaction, but sees that one is already in progress so it doesn't start a new one. On the outgoing withdraw, the transaction boundary manager knows that it didn't start the transaction on this incoming interception so it doesn't terminate the transaction. On the next incoming deposit, the transaction boundary again sees a need for a transaction, but again sees that one is still in progress, so it doesn't start a new one. On the outgoing interception, it knows that the incoming interception did not trigger a new transaction so it doesn't end the transaction. Now we have finished the transfer method, and we intercept its return. Now the transactional boundary manager says, "Aha! On the incoming interception of this transfer method, I started a new transaction. So the time has come to bring this ceremony to a conclusion." The transaction terminates.

This gives the distributed transaction coordinator all the information it needs to decide when to kick off the three phases of the two-phase commit. It kicks off the contemplative phases when the transaction boundary manager decides to start a new transaction. It kicks off the consensus phase when the transaction boundary manager decides to terminate the transaction. And, of course, it can figure out for itself when to kick off the final phase. Isn't it nice how everybody works together?

This whole process does a great job of managing the transactional boundaries and providing the distributed transaction coordinator with

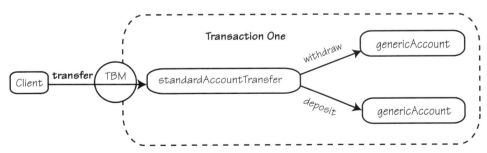

Figure 4.14 Alternative transaction boundary management.

the information it needs to do its job. But there is one more issue that must be dealt with. Once we reach the termination of the transaction, should it commit or rollback? This is not something that can be configured. Only the business logic can know the answer to this, and the answer changes depending on the success or failure of a particular invocation.

The COMWare platforms all provide some API for the business logic to voice an opinion on whether or not it is happy with the way things are going. We would expect to see this API used, for example, in the genericAccount implementation, perhaps like this:

```
genericAccount_deposit(state, accountID, amount)
{
  balance = readAccount(state.dbc, accountID);
  if readError then
  {
    I am unhappy;
    return;
  }
  balance = balance + amount;
  if balance < 0 then
  {
    I am unhappy;
    return;
  }
  updateCheckingAccount(state.dbc, accountID, balance);
  I am happy;
}
```

The final decision as to whether to commit or roll back on the end transaction boundary then becomes a consensus on whether or not all the business logic was happy. If everybody was happy, then we issue a commit and the databases makes it so. If anybody was unhappy, then we issue a rollback and the databases makes it not so. Since ultimately the only state we care about is the state of the databases, rolling back the databases effectively brings the system back to its original state before this transaction ever saw the light of day.

This whole scheme makes the client code unbelievably easy to write. Not only does the client not need code to mark the transaction boundary, it also doesn't need to worry about whether the business logic was successful or not. Yes, life is great for clients in the COMWare world. Charles, another Doppio Macchiato please!

Transactions Equal Methods

There is one interesting side effect of all this. If are going to make use of all this wonderful COMWare-provided transactional boundary management, we need to have at least one method someplace where the method boundary corresponds to a transactional boundary. In the case of our transaction component, that natural transaction/method boundary occurred on the transfer method. We either wanted everything encompassed by the method to succeed, or we wanted none of it to succeed.

We can even go further than this. Since a component never knows when it is going to be used directly by a client, or indirectly by some other client, we can say that *every* method boundary should be a reasonable transaction boundary. In the case, for example, of our genericAccount deposit method, we have a method that could be a reasonable transaction in its own right (as in the case of a client depositing money into an account), or it could be part of a larger transaction (as in the case of a transfer from one account to another). Since the genericAccount component will be configured to require a transaction, it will have an associated transaction one way or the other, and since the method boundary makes sense on its own or as part of a larger transaction, the component can be used very flexibly.

What is an example of bad component design? Suppose instead of defining our account interface like this:

```
interface account {
  withdraw (accountID, amount);
  deposit (accountID, amount);
  money balance(accountID);
}
```

we instead used this interface:

```
interface account {
  setFromAccount(accountID);
  setToAccount(accountID);
  deposit (amount);
  withdraw (amount);
  money balance();
}
```

This new interface has no logical transaction boundary. If, for example, you were to deposit money into an account with this, you would have to invoke two methods (setFromAccount and setToAccount), and you would need all of them somehow encompassed in one transaction. There is no way the automatic transaction boundary management algorithm can be used to manage this transaction boundary, unless this component is used *only* within a larger component. And this would be a bad design assumption. If, after all, the component is *only* going to be used within a larger component, then why not just make it *part* of the larger component? That will surely be more efficient. The *only* reason for making something a component in the first place is so that it *can* be used independently!

The net result of all this is that if you are using COMWare to manage your components, you need to design your methods to be natural transaction boundaries. Think of this simple but important rule: *methods = transactions*. If you violate this rule, I guarantee you, there will be no Doppio Macchiatos for you tonight.

Law of Transactional Integrity

When you are working with transactions, you need to be aware of a general law of programming that I call the law of transactional *integrity*. The law of transactional integrity says that transactions must be programmed as follows:

```
begin transaction;
read state from database;
do business stuff;
write state back to database;
end transaction;
```

This law has nothing to do with components, or even three-tier systems. It applies equally well to a large, looping program, such as this:

```
repeat until (the cows come home) {
  see what they want to do;
  if (not done) {
    begin transaction;
    read state from database;
    do business stuff;
    write state back to database;
  }
}
```

Now think about this program a moment. Doesn't this seem a bit silly to reread the state from the database every time we go through the loop? After all, it's not like our program went out for coffee or anything. Our program state hasn't changed since we last did the write. Why add the extra burden of rereading all that stuff again?

The problem is that our program is not the only program running in the universe. There may be thousands of other people running exactly the same program, and there is absolutely no way to be sure one of those slimy devils didn't update the database since our transaction last completed. So even if our program thinks it knows what the database looks like, it must do a reread to be sure.

If we extend the law of transactional integrity to the component world, what does this mean? Since we have just agreed that method boundaries are going to be transactional boundaries, it means that we must code every method like this:

```
method(parameters)
{
  read state from database;
  do business stuff;
  write state back to database;
}
```

You really have no choice but to code like this. It is a natural consequence of the law of transactional integrity and the algorithm(s) used for transactional boundary management by every COMWare platform in existence.

But hold everything! This code looks hauntingly familiar. In fact, it is *exactly* the same code that I showed earlier in this chapter as the code that was required to make components stateless. We need components to be stateless for instance management. Remember how you complained so bitterly about the "unnecessary database accesses"? Remember I told you that you were going to have to do those database accesses anyway, whether or not you used instance management? Now you see why. You need those database accesses so that you can have transactional integrity. And transactional integrity is *not* something that is open to debate.

It turns out that there is a great technical convergence around the notion of transactions and methods. Once you accept the rule that *methods = transactions*, the world starts to make sense in an almost mystical way.

Transactional Flow

We are almost finished with transactions, but not quite. There is one more piece of transaction-related functionality provided by your friendly COMWare vendors. This is *transactional flow*. Transactional flow refers to the ability to flow a transaction through to other transactional environments.

The simplest example of transactional flow is to a database. Databases are transactional, and all COMWare platforms have mechanisms in place to involve databases in the COMWare transaction. When the commit occurs in the COMWare distributed transaction coordinator, the databases participate in that commit. We say that the transaction *flows* through to the database.

There are various other transactional environments that may or may not participate in the transactional flow—for example, other COMWare environments. At this point, we have no generally accepted standards on how to flow a transaction from one COMWare environment to another. So if my COM+ component has the audacity to make a request of an EJB component, when the COM+ distributed transaction coordinator commits, that commit is not propagated to the EJB component, even though both are COMWare platforms and both recognize the importance of transactional flow. They just happen to be competing COMWare technologies with different ideas on how to propagate the flow and on who should be in charge.

All the COMWare vendors recognize the importance of transactional flow, and all support it at least at the database level. Beyond that, there is very little agreement about how to manage transactional flow. So we mention it here, but won't spend any time on it.

Security

We have finally finished with transactions, but not yet with all the major functionality of the COMWare component process. The last remaining item on which all COMWare vendors agree is security. I have good news and bad news on the security front. First the bad news. Security is a major issue and needs a significant discussion. I know it's been a long chapter and you really aren't up for another major discussion. The good news is that we have already been through most of the security discussion, and there is very little that needs to be added here.

The major point about security is that in a COMWare environment, responsibility for security needs to move from the database to the COMWare component process. The reasons for this move are exactly the same reasons as those we discussed in Chapter 3, those that forced security to move from the database to the TPM systems, namely compatibility with middle-tier scalability . If you have forgotten the implications of security on middle-tier scalability, then grab yourself another Doppio and reread Chapter 3.

The only thing we need to add here is *how* security is done in the COMWare environment. This is another of those areas in which there is widespread agreement among all COMWare platforms. In general, the assumption is that security is configured on either a component or an interface basis using the COMWare administrative tools. These tools allow the system administrator to configure exactly which clients are allowed to invoke which methods on which components.

The actual security is handled at the point of interception, where we add in yet another conceptual manager into the fray. This one is a *security manager*. Its responsibility is to look at the originating client and target of each method invocation. If the client has appropriate access to that method, then the method is allowed to go through. If not, the method is zapped in mid-air. The instance never even sees it.

The COMWare Proposal

Why COMWare? Why not just use components? The various COMWare platforms are all offering you a basic deal. Package your business logic as components. Build them based on simple COMWare rules, most of which are generic to all COMWare platforms and a few of which are specific to particular platforms. Turn your life over to one COMWare vendor or another. And in return, they will take care of all the difficult problems involved with large, multitier, commerce systems. They will take care of scalability, transaction management, and security issues that will otherwise devour a huge amount of your time, turn much of your hair gray, and leave you a mere husk of your former self.

A COMWare Compatible Component

If you are going to build large commerce systems, you need to use COMWare. If you are going to use COMWare, you must follow the rules. You can't take run-of-the-mill, ignorant, unenlightened components and expect them to function in a COMWare world. In my experience, the most common failure of COMWare applications occurs because the application designers do not understand the expectations the COMWare environment has of the components it will be managing. By now you should have a good idea of these rules, but let's review them here, just to wrap up this chapter.

Keep in mind that all of the COMWare platforms allow any or all of these rules to be violated. But once you violate these rules, you lose the advantages of COMWare. You might as well go back to simple naive distributed components, for all the benefit you will get.

Rule 1: Move the state out of the instance. All COMWare platforms agree on this rule, for a very good reason. There is no known algorithm for doing instance management that is compatible with stateful components. The details on how the state should be removed are to a large extent platform specific, but all have this fundamental requirement if you are going to use the COMWare platforms efficiently. By far the most common place to store the instance's state will be in a back-end database. If you *are* using a database, then start each method by reading the state from the database, perform your business logic, and then write your state back out to the database. Different COMWare platforms have different ways of coordinating this activity.

Stateless components have the following benefits:

- They can be managed by instance management algorithms, allowing them to be used very efficiently.

- They automatically get thread management, through the instance management algorithms.

- They can take advantage of load balancing algorithms, which allows systems to be designed that can support huge numbers of clients.

Rule 2: Use resource pools. This is really more of a suggestion. There are many situations where resource pools, such as database connection pools, can significantly improve performance. For the just-in-time instantiation algorithm, resource pools are an absolute necessity. When you are using resource pools, the standard advice is to acquire the resource as late as possible and release it as soon as possible.

Rule 3: Make methods a transactional boundary. This has three main benefits. First, it enables the transaction boundary management algorithms, which makes it much easier for clients to use your components. Second, it greatly reduces the fragility of the client code. Third, it means that the code you write for transactional integrity will be exactly the same as the code you write for statelessness.

Rule 4: Move security to the component process. Even if you make your components completely stateless, you will not be able to scale your systems if you do not move security to middle tier. If you are using the just-in-time instantiation algorithm, you won't be able to use resource pools. If you are using instance pooling, you will not be able to share your instance pools. Either way, you have a system that supports very few clients.

That's about it. If you keep these four rules in mind, you will probably have reasonably good middle-tier components. Notice, though, that these rules cannot be applied retrospectively to components. Several have direct and important implications on the design of interfaces. These rules must be kept prominently in mind from the earliest moments of your project inception.

Components that are designed and built without regard to the four COMWare rules will be virtually impossible to retrofit into any COMWare environments. Such systems may run great in the lab, but they will fall flat on their faces as soon as they are deployed in any large scale environment such as the Web. By then, it will be too late.

As you can see, there is a lot of material on which all the COMWare platforms agree. But there is still plenty to fight over. That will be the topics of the remaining chapters. Let the battle begin.

PART TWO

COM+

Microsoft introduced the first COMWare environment in 1995. It was the oddly named Microsoft Transaction Server. Now Microsoft is releasing the next generation of COMWare: COM+. COM+ combines the traditional COM, DCOM, and MTS, and introduces some new capabilities in the form of COM+ services. If you are developing for Microsoft, you must understand their COM+ and related technologies. If you are trying to plan your company's future, you must understand the Microsoft infrastructure, which will define the Microsoft middle tier. This section gives an overview of Microsoft's COM+ and the related technologies.

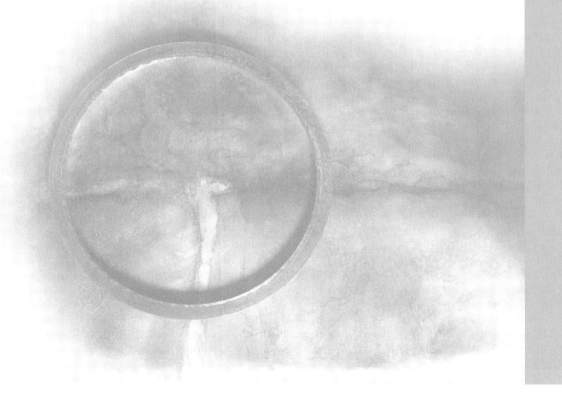

CHAPTER 5

COM+ and Friends

W hat, exactly, is Microsoft's middle-tier architecture? This is not as easy to answer as you might expect. Microsoft does not have a term to describe those technologies that, taken as a whole, make up a coherent middle-tier vision. This is rather odd, considering that Microsoft is a company that normally comes up with three new acronyms before breakfast each morning.

In my last book, *COM and DCOM* (Wiley 1996), I coined the term *Microsoft Distributed Component Architecture* (MDCA) to describe a collection of middle-tier technologies that, taken together, make up what I see as a unified middle-tier vision. That was back in 1996. I fully expected Microsoft to come up with a competing term the day my book hit the shelves, and to be immediately out of date. But here it is 1999, and nothing has changed. Microsoft still has no formal term to describe its middle-tier technologies. So MDCA seems as good a term to use today as it was back in 1996.

Microsoft frequently uses the term *Distributed interNet Applications* (DNA). Many people think DNA describes Microsoft's middle tier, but this is not so. Microsoft uses the term DNA to describe its entire three-tier architecture. It includes in DNA any product that runs on any tier and that has anything to do with support for distributed applications. At one point, it seemed that Microsoft used this term to describe any product that ran on any tier, period, whether or not it had any thing to do with developing distributed applications. There were times that I half expected Microsoft's encyclopedia *Encarta* to show up in a DNA slide.

Over the last year, Microsoft's description of DNA has tightened up a bit. Now when Microsoft shows pictures of its DNA vision, it shows a client tier with Visual Basic or XML/DTHML/HTML pages interacting with Internet Information Server (IIS), a middle tier with COM+, and a data tier with SQL Server. This picture, although simplistic, makes sense on both the client side and the data side. But on the middle tier, the idea that COM+ alone provides a fully functional environment is misleading.

COM+, of course, plays a critical role in the Windows 2000 middle tier. It provides the component model, the distribution technology, and the component runtime environment. It wraps together in one neat package technologies that in NT 4.0 seemed to be arbitrarily split between COM (the original component model), DCOM (the original distribution technology), and Microsoft Transaction Server (MTS, the original component runtime environment).

But to build a full middle-tier solution with Windows 2000, COM+ isn't enough. In this chapter, we look at some of COM+'s closest allies: the rest of the Windows 2000 MDCA. These are those other Microsoft products that you will use, directly or indirectly, to build and support middle-tier applications that can support commerce in the large. It is these additional MDCA technologies that allow our systems to be robust, our distributed transactions to be coordinated, and our middle-tier components to work effectively with foreign systems.

Looking at MDCA as a whole, rather than at COM+ in isolation, is actually rather reassuring. Nobody wants to be on the bleeding edge of new technology, not in the world of commerce. We all want to use technology that is established and proven. We want to see large companies that have bet their future on the technology we are considering and we want to see that those companies have won their bets.

Whereas COM+ at first appears to be new and revolutionary, taken in the overall context of MDCA, it is neither new nor revolutionary. MDCA has evolved between NT 4.0 and Windows 2000, but less than you might think. There are new features, as you would expect with any new release. However, most of Windows 2000 MDCA is either just a new façade on old NT 4.0 MDCA functionality, a logical reorganization of old functionality, or the inclusion into MDCA of well understood algorithms that, in NT 4.0, customers had to implement for themselves. Windows 2000 MDCA, including almost everything in COM+, is well established, extensively tested, and proven in many of the world's largest commerce applications.

So what, exactly, is meant by this unofficial term MDCA? For NT 4.0, I included six products in MDCA:

- COM
- DCOM
- MTS
- Microsoft Distributed Transaction Coordinator (MS-DTC)
- Microsoft Message Queue Server (MSMQ)
- Microsoft Cluster Server (MSCS).

In Windows 2000, with the repackaging of COM, DCOM, and MTS into COM+, I include:

- COM+
- MS-DTC
- MSMQ
- MSCS

There are some other important products that focus more on interoperability, such as COM-Transaction Integrator (COM-TI), but I usually think of MDCA as those products that specifically target the Microsoft middle tier. Many also include IIS in the middle-tier technologies, but I see this as more oriented toward client interaction.

In this chapter, I focus on the MDCA helper technologies. I discuss COM+ in the next three chapters, and the interoperability products in Chapter 9, "COM+ Interoperability." To give you a sense of the strong continuity of MDCA between NT 4.0 and Windows 2000, let me take you through a brief history of Microsoft's middle tier architecture as that history enfolded for me.

The History of Microsoft's Middle Tier

Between 1990 and 1996, if you had asked me if I would ever be writing a book describing the value of Microsoft technologies, I would have thought you were crazy. For most of that time I was working on IBM's implementation of the Common Object Request Broker Architecture (CORBA, a technology I will describe in Chapter 11, "CORBA"). This was an early component architecture developed by the Object Management Group (OMG). In 1992 I represented IBM at the OMG for the Object Persistence Specification, a subpiece of CORBA, and worked closely on many other OMG specifications. The OMG was (and still is) a consortium of hundreds of companies trying to define a common architecture for distributed components. Much of the work done by the OMG between those years defined the components industry for years to come. Those were the glory years for the OMG.

Microsoft was not then considered a factor in distributed components technologies. Its only component technology was COM, first released in 1993. At that time, COM was a language-neutral model for components. It had no distribution capability, and therefore was not in the same league with the work of the OMG.

Microsoft's first foray into *distributed* components occurred in mid-1995 with its introduction of DCOM. DCOM was a technology that allowed COM components to be separated from the clients that used them. DCOM turned COM's components into distributed components. Distributed components? Now wait just one minute. Distributed components were the domain of the OMG!

I remember very well my first serious introduction to COM and DCOM. It was in 1996, barely a year after the introduction of DCOM. I had left IBM to do consulting in the CORBA area. Terri Hudson of John Wiley & Sons asked me to consider writing a book about COM and DCOM. I had written three books at that point, the third about the CORBA Persistence Specification. My immediate reaction to Terri was one of dismissal. COM and DCOM, if you were involved with the OMG, was The Enemy. It represented everything we were against. Not only a competing technology, but a blatant attempt by one company to ignore what we in the OMG believed was the will of the industry. But I agreed to at least consider the idea. Perhaps I was curious about what, exactly, the big bad wolf had up its sleeves.

I read every paper, book, and technical document I could find about COM and DCOM. At the end of this analysis, I decided that the OMG had nothing to fear from COM and DCOM. They represented a relatively rudimentary distributed component technology. Microsoft lacked many of the object services the OMG had defined for CORBA. The Microsoft technologies, I thought, were not worth worrying about, and were certainly not worth writing a book about.

As I prepared to dismiss the book project, I stumbled on a paper about a curious product called the Microsoft Transaction Server (MTS). At first, I assumed that MTS was Microsoft's answer to the CORBA Object Transaction Service, an API for performing distributed transaction coordination. But as I read through the paper, I realized the Microsoft Transaction Server had very little to do with transactions. Instead, MTS was a runtime environment for middle-tier components.

The idea of a runtime environment for middle-tier components intrigued me. As I learned more about MTS, I recognized many ideas from Transaction Processing Monitors (TPMs), the only technology that up until then attempted to offer a middle-tier infrastructure for distributed applications of any type. I began to realize that MTS was far more than just an add-on technology for distributed components. It was the foundation of an architectural vision, and one that seemed to me to challenge the mainframe computer's hold on the middle tier. It was still true that COM and DCOM were not worth a book. But COM, DCOM, and MTS—that was an entirely different kettle of fish.

The MTS Vision

Most of the members of OMG came from a traditional object-oriented programming background, and the CORBA model was strongly influenced by our existing notions of objects. MTS was influenced more by Transaction Processing Monitors than by objects. Microsoft did not worry a lot about the academic arguments of what, exactly, constituted an object, and whether MTS components were or were not objects. Microsoft worried instead about the pragmatic details of making things work in the real world.

With MTS, Microsoft challenged many of CORBA's most firmly held assumptions.

CORBA took it for granted that component instances had data, or state, associated with them. This was a natural extension of the idea of objects, and most people back then were thinking of components as objects that can move around a network. Microsoft claimed that component instances were not the correct place to store state. Databases, Microsoft said, were the correct place to store shared data of any type, including state. Figure 5.1 shows the difference between these two perspectives.

The CORBA model assumed not only that component instances had state, but that the proper way to share information between clients was to share instances, and, indirectly, the state they contained. There were many techniques for doing this. The most common was to associate an instance with a well known name, register that name and instance with a well known name service, and allow that name service to return proxies to any client that wanted access to that instance and the state it contained.

Microsoft said that clients should share information not through proxies that share instances, but through instances that share back-end databases. Microsoft claimed this model was much better for at least two reasons. First, it is simpler, since databases already knew how to share data and you didn't need to invent new locking mechanisms for component instances. Second, it is more robust, since if any one component tier machine went down, the component instance state that is stored in robust databases was not lost. Figure 5.2 shows the difference between the CORBA model and the MTS model for sharing state between clients.

The CORBA model assumed that an extensive API was required for programmers to control nonbusiness-related logic, such as the begin-

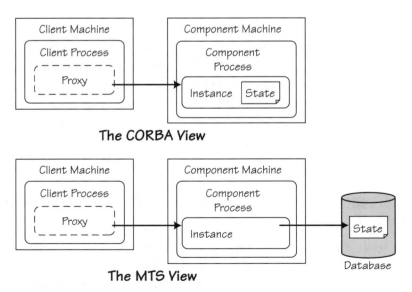

Figure 5.1 The difference between the CORBA and MTS views of state.

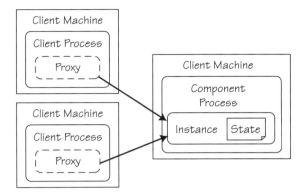

The CORBA View

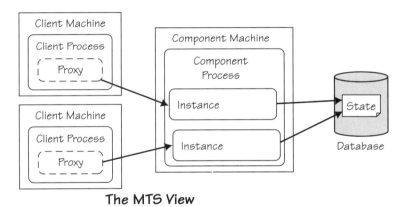

The MTS View

Figure 5.2 The difference between the CORBA and MTS views of sharing state.

ning and end of transactions, security, and locating specific component instances. The OMG focus was on enriching the CORBA API through defining and including new object services. One of those object services was the one I had helped to define, the *Persistence Object Service*.

Microsoft focused not on agreeing on a new API, but on eliminating the API altogether. Instead of programmer APIs, MTS introduced interceptors between the client-side proxy and the component instance. These interceptors read component configuration parameters and automatically made environment adjustments (such as starting new transactions) as necessary. Clients never saw the invisible, but powerful environment that controlled almost every aspect of the relationship between themselves and their back-end component instance. Figure 5.3 shows the difference between the CORBA and the Microsoft views on API versus interceptors.

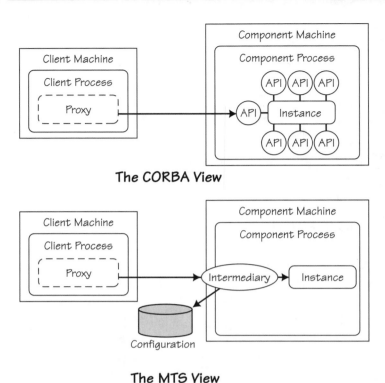

The CORBA View

The MTS View

Figure 5.3 CORBA and Microsoft views on API versus interceptors.

The CORBA model assumed that the relationship between the client-side proxy and the component instance was long term, begun at the time of client instantiation and continuing until the time of client deinstantiation. Microsoft said that this model would not scale. To support the number of clients we expect for Web commerce, middle-tier instances had to be used very efficiently. They should be assigned on an as-needed basis to client proxies and only for as long as necessary to complete a work request. I have discussed this idea in Chapter 4, "COMWare." Suffice it to say that this concept was first introduced by MTS.

It was soon clear to me that Microsoft had gone beyond the issue we have been debating in the OMG. We had been concerned with relatively simple applications represented by clients working directly with component instances. Microsoft, in contrast, had been focusing on sophisticated component infrastructures to support commerce in the large. And MTS was a critical piece of that overall infrastructure.

In retrospect, MTS was much more important than I realized at the time. It did much more than introduce a new infrastructure. It really defined a whole new industry—what I now call Component-Oriented Middleware (COMWare).

Although MTS was the technology that first sparked my interest in the Microsoft architecture, it was soon clear to me that three other products (besides COM and DCOM) also played a critical role. These three players were Microsoft Distributed Transaction Coordinator (MS-DTC), Microsoft Message Queue (MSMQ), and Microsoft Cluster Server (MSCS). In Windows 2000, these three technologies continue to play equally important (and in some cases, more important) roles in supporting COM+. It is therefore worthwhile to look at each of these technologies, how they work together, and what their overall part is in the Microsoft middle-tier drama that I call MDCA.

COM+ is, of course, the central figurehead in MDCA. I will be looking at the many facets of COM+ in the next four chapters. Because COM+ builds on and depends on these other MDCA technologies, I begin in this chapter with an introduction to MS-DTC, MSMQ, and MSCS.

MS-DTC

MS-DTC is responsible for coordinating the two-phase commit protocol that I described in Chapter 3, "Transaction Processing Monitors." This protocol allows multiple databases, or multiple database connections, to work together in a coordinated transaction. Consider a bank money transfer involving a transfer component, a savingsAccount component, and a checking account component. The transfer component can coordinate the activity between the savingsAccount and the checkingAccount. But since it is likely that the savingsAccount and checkingAccount were developed independently, they probably have their own database connections, and possibly even different databases. The transfer component can coordinate the business logic, but somebody needs to coordinate the database activity. This somebody needs to ensure that either both the savings account and checking account databases update their data (i.e., they both commit), or that neither of them update their data (i.e., they both rollback). This somebody is MS-DTC.

MS-DTC ensures that everything involved with a transaction either commits or rolls back, even when different products that know nothing about each other are involved. MS-DTC is the common glue between these products. They all know how to cooperate with MS-DTC, and MS-DTC knows how to coordinate their activity with each other.

MS-DTC can coordinate the overall transaction only if it knows when the transaction has begun and ended. This is where the COM+ runtime environment (which, in this chapter, I refer to as COM+) comes into the picture. I discuss the COM+ runtime environment in Chapter 7, "The COM+ Runtime Environment," but for now, realize that COM+ is responsible for coordinating the transaction boundaries much like its predecessor, MTS.

Once COM+ notifies MS-DTC that the transaction has begun, MS-DTC coordinates the various databases in the two-phase commit protocol. I described this process for COMWare in general in Chapter 4. COM+ follows the general COMWare transactional boundary interception algorithm. This is not too surprising, since MTS first invented these algorithms, which were then widely adopted by the other COMWare platforms. I'll review transactional boundary management briefly here, for those who of you who weren't paying attention (and you know who you are!) back in Chapter 4.

The general flow, shown in Figure 5.4, is as follows: The method leaves the client proxy and heads for the component instance. Before reaching the instance, it is intercepted by the COM+ runtime environment. Assuming this component has been configured to require a transaction, the interceptor fires off a message to MS-DTC saying that a new transaction has started. MS-DTC starts the contemplative phase of the two-phase commit protocol, as described in Chapter 3. The business logic of the method then executes, resulting in some number of databases being updated. MS-DTC, which never misses anything, keeps track of which databases were updated for future reference.

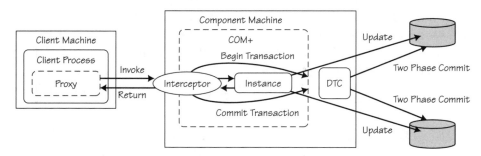

Figure 5.4 Relationship between COM+ and MS-DTC.

When the business logic completes, the method returns, heading back to the proxy. As it passes through the return interception, COM+ realizes that the method is returning from the method that initiated the transaction, and thus terminates the transaction. If all the business logic was happy, then the termination becomes a commit request to MS-DTC, and MS-DTC starts the consensus phase of the two-phase commit protocol. If any of the business logic was not happy, then the termination becomes a rollback request to MS-DTC.

Since COM+ is responsible for starting and ending the transaction, the business programmer does not need to explicitly write code to do this. This is a good thing. As I discussed in Chapter 4, transactional boundary code is very fragile. The reason it is so fragile is that it is highly dependent on both the implementation of the component method (does it or doesn't it use a transactional database?) and exactly how that method will be invoked (inside or not inside a higher level transaction).

Consider, for example, a banking system in which we have a savingsAccount component with a withdraw method. If we must code the transactional boundaries, how do we do so? Do we code the transactional boundary management, as shown here:

```
savingsAccount::withdraw(accountID, amount)
{
  startTransaction;
  withdrawFromDataBase(accountID, amount);
  endTransaction;
}
or do we leave it out, as shown here:
savingsAccount::withdraw(accountID, amount)
{
  withdrawFromDataBase(accountID, amount);
}
```

There is no way to know which of these is correct. It depends on how the method is invoked. If the withdraw method is invoked as part of an overall transfer from savings to checking, then the higher level transfer will have its own transaction. In this case, the withdraw method should be included in that transaction and the second version is correct. But if withdraw is invoked as a simple withdrawal, then there is no larger transaction. In this case, the first version is correct. What if our client is another component with its own transactional expectations? This rapidly becomes a complex problem with numerous dependencies and many opportunities for new component implementations to break existing systems. It is much better to let the COM+ runtime environment decide for itself through interception when the transaction starts and ends. We discuss this some more in Chapter 7.

MSMQ

Before 1998, the only way for a client to communicate with a component, or for one component to communicate with another, was through standard COM/DCOM method invocations. Back then, standard COM/DCOM method invocations were always synchronous. Synchronous method invocations are like a dance between the client and the component instance. This dance has the following characteristics:

Both dance partners must be synchronized. The client can't move ahead until the component instance has completed its last step. If a banking client requests a withdrawal, that client is blocked until the withdrawal is processed.

It takes two to Tango. Both the client and the component instance must be on the dance floor at the same time. If the component instance shows up late, for example, because its machine is down, then the client either waits for the instance to show up, or performs a mighty peculiar Tango all by itself.

Let's consider one such synchronous dance. Here is a dance between a client and a Purchase component (shown, as usual, in pseudocode). The client leads off:

```
get customerID;
get itemID;
cost = lookupCost(itemID);
thisPurchase = create("Purchase");
thisPurchase.processPurchase(customerID, itemID, cost);
destroy thisPurchase;
```

The Purchase component follows the customer's lead. Notice that the Purchase code is itself wrapped up in a dance with two other components (you can see where component instances received their well-deserved reputation as party animals):

```
Purchase::processPurchase(customerID, itemID, cost)
```

```
{
  charge = create ("Charge");
  shipment = create ("Shipment");
  if (charge->authorized(customerID, cost))
  {
    shipment->deliver(customerID, itemID);
  }
  destroy charge;
  destroy shipment;
}
```

In this example, the client asks the Purchase instance to process the purchase and then waits for the processing to complete. The Purchase instance asks a Charge instance to deduct the cost of the item and waits for that deduction to complete. Once that has completed, the Purchase instance asks a Shipment instance to deliver the item and waits for that delivery to be processed. So in effect, the client is blocked until the Purchase, Charge, and Shipment instances all have completed their work. If it takes five seconds both to process the charge and process the shipment, then the client is sitting looking at a frozen screen for at least ten seconds.

The alternative to the synchronous method is the *asynchronous message*. An asynchronous message is, like a synchronous method, a work request, but it is a work request that can be completed at a future time, and one for which the client will not wait. Asynchronous messages are the realm of the Microsoft Message Queue Server (MSMQ). MSMQ is Microsoft's version of IBM's MQSeries, a well established message queuing product primarily used on mainframe systems. Microsoft's MSMQ was first introduced in 1998 in the NT 4.0 Option Pack, along with MTS 2.0. It gave NT 4.0 MDCA the ability to have reliable asynchronous communications. It still plays the same role in Windows 2000 MDCA.

An MSMQ message looks nothing like a COM+ method invocation. An MSMQ work request is not formally represented by an interface definition, it merely represents an informal agreement by the sender(s) and the receiver(s). An MSMQ client does not invoke a method and pass in method parameters; it creates a string and sends that string to a particular message queue. Whomever has *write* rights to a queue can send messages to that queue and whomever has *read* rights to that queue can receive those messages. In this version, our purchase system has been rewritten to use both asynchronous charge authorization and shipping systems:

```
Purchase::coordinatePurchase(customerID, itemID, cost)
{
```

```
chargeQueue = getHandleToQueue ("Charge");
shipmentQueue = getHandleToQueue ("Shipment");
message = createChargeMessage(customerID, cost);
sendMessage(chargeQueue, message);

message = createDeliveryMessage(customerID, itemID);
sendMessage(shipmentQueue, message);

releaseQueue(chargeQueue);
releaseQueue(shipmentQueue);
}
```

Notice that the Purchase client is unaffected by these changes. It still looks like this:

```
get customerID;
get itemID;
cost = lookupCost(itemID);
thisPurchase = create("Purchase");
thisPurchase.processPurchase(customerID, itemID, cost);
destroy thisPurchase;
```

Let's consider both the synchronous and the asynchronous versions of the Shipment code. The synchronous code is a simple method invocation. Because it is synchronous, by definition it is only invoked when the next order is ready for shipping. It looks like this:

```
Shipment::deliver(customerID, itemID)
{
  processDelivery(customerID, itemID);
}
```

The asynchronous version is a bit more complicated. It will wait for the next message, process it, and then wait again. It looks like this:

```
Shipment::deliver()
{
  shipmentQueue = getHandleToQueue ("Shipment");
  repeat (forever) {
    waitForNextMessage(shipmentQueue);
    message = getMessage(shipmentQueue);
    extractDataFromMessage(customerID, itemID, message);
    processDelivery(customerID, itemID);
  }
  releaseQueue(shipmentQueue);
}
```

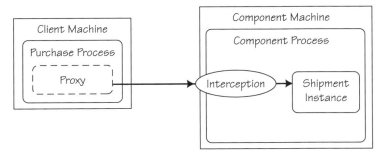

Figure 5.5 Synchronized system setup.

Not only is the asynchronous version more complicated than the synchronous version, but it requires a more complicated computer configuration. The synchronous version requires the usual two computers:

- One to send the method invocation.
- One to receive it.

This configuration is shown in Figure 5.5. The asynchronous version requires three computers:

- One to send the message.
- One to hold the message.
- One to receive the message and complete the work request.

This is the logical configuration. Physically, the holding machine can be the same as one of the others, but the most flexible configuration occurs when each logical machine is also a physical machine. This system is shown in Figure 5.6.

The extra middle machine (the "Queue Machine") provides the asynchronicity. When the purchase process is ready to send a message to the shipping process, it sends a message to its local queue. If the purchase machine is connected, that message is immediately transferred to the holding queue. If the purchase machine is not connected, that message can sit on the local queue until the next connection is made, and can be transferred at that time. Once the message has made it to the holding queue, it can wait indefinitely until the shipping machine decides to connect. At that time the message is transferred to the shipping machine where it can be reconstructed and processed.

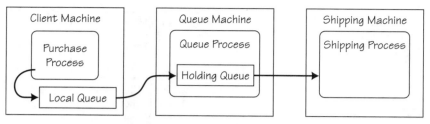

Figure 5.6 Asynchronized system setup.

Work Flow Issues

Many people think that synchronous systems can be turned into asynchronous systems by simply replacing synchronous method invocations by asynchronous message requests, as we did in the preceding code samples. But unfortunately, the reality is usually more complicated. Consider the difference between the synchronous and the asynchronous code. Here is the relevant extract from the synchronous system, the flow of which is shown in Figure 5.7:

```
if (charge->authorized(customerID, cost))
{
  shipment->deliver(customerID, itemID);
}
```

Here is the analogous extract from the asynchronous system:

```
message = createChargeMessage(customerID, cost);
sendMessage(chargeQueue, message);
message = createDeliveryMessage(customerID, itemID);
sendMessage(shipmentQueue, message);
```

Notice that the synchronous and asynchronous segments of code are not equivalent in functionality. The synchronous code prevents a shipment from being delivered until the charge has been authorized. The shipment is *dependent* on the charge authorization. Because the code is synchronous, we do not continue with the deliver until the authorization has returned and has been accepted.

The asynchronous version does not preserve this dependency. In fact, there is no way to introduce dependencies between two consecutive segments of asynchronous code. You can see this from the asynchronous

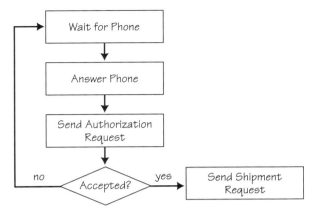

Figure 5.7. Synchronous processing.

flow, shown in Figure 5.8. True, we are blocked from *sending the message* to ship the purchase until after we have sent the message to charge the credit card, but the actual processing of these two requests is no longer chronologically related, or in anyway dependent. The credit card authorization could occur long before the shipment, long after the shipment, or at the exact same time. There is no way to tell.

The way we introduce dependent behavior into an asynchronous system is to use *work flow processing*. In this technique, the queue receiver (the credit charge system) moves the message onto the next queue (the shipment queue). This allows us to have a fully asynchronous system

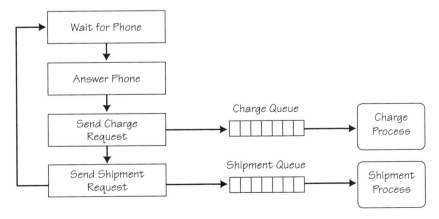

Figure 5.8 Asynchronous processing.

while still maintaining behavioral dependencies. Our rewritten purchasing system looks like this:

```
Purchase::coordinatePurchase(customerID, itemID, cost)
{
  chargeQueue = getHandleToQueue ("Charge");
  message = createChargeMessage(customerID, itemID, cost);
  sendMessage(chargeQueue, message);
  releaseQueue(chargeQueue);
}
```

Our charge authorization system looks like this:

```
Charge::authorize()
{
  ShipmentQueue = getHandleToQueue ("Shipment");
  ChargeQueue = getHandleToQueue ("Charge");
  repeat (forever) {
    waitForNextMessage(chargeQueue);
    message = getMessage(chargeQueue);
    extractDataFromMessage(customerID, itemID, cost, message);
    if (chargeAuthorized(customerID, cost)) {
        message = createDeliveryMessage(customerID, itemID);
        sendMessage(shipmentQueue, message);
    }
  }
  releaseQueue(ShipmentQueue);
  releaseQueue(ChargeQueue);
}
```

Notice that none of this rewrite is visible to our client code, which still looks like this:

```
get customerID;
get itemID;
cost = lookupCost(itemID);
thisPurchase = create("Purchase");
thisPurchase.processPurchase(customerID, itemID, cost);
destroy thisPurchase;
```

You can see how this rewritten processPurchase method gives us our desired behavior, while still preserving our asynchronous (from the client's perspective) behavior. This is a standard technique for work flow processing. Figure 5.9 diagrams the behavior of this asynchronous system with behavior dependencies.

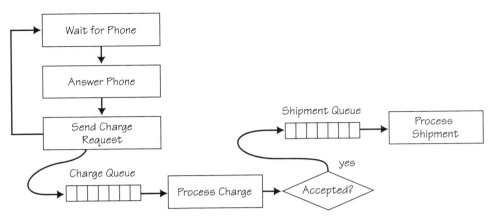

Figure 5.9   Asynchronous work flow processing.

Why Use Queues?

Asynchronous processing is more complicated than synchronous processing. It requires the use of a whole new message queue API (which I have minimized by showing only pseudocode). It often requires a significant restructuring of program logic. And it requires additional processes to daisy chain work flow.

It is also more demanding of system resource utilization. The queues make use of databases. The insertion and removal of messages requires transactions. Remote communications are necessary to the intermediary computers that serve as queue holders.

Why would we want to add this complexity and performance overhead to our code? Let's consider a few situations in which asynchronous functionality pays off.

Disconnected Work

The great thing about writing books is that I get to do what I want. I can go to sleep at 3:00 A.M., wake up at noon, and spend the day waiting for inspiration while slowly building up my blood caffeine levels sipping Doppio Macchiatos. I can work wherever I want. As long as there is room for Baby on the table and a cell phone tower nearby, I am as happy as a clam.

If I decide to go into the retail business, I certainly don't want to change my shiftless ways. Baby doesn't care if she is taking retail orders or storing the next great work of computer literature. My cell phone is as happy to take phone orders as it is to transmit pleas and/or threats from my editor.

But how can I get my purchasing system to run on Baby, without a network, so that I can continue to wile away the hours at Starbucks while still earning a living? This will be difficult if my local purchasing system requires synchronous communications with the credit card processing and shipping systems. Starbucks doesn't yet have networks installed, or at least, any networks into which I can plug Baby. I certainly can install the purchasing system on Baby (it's all local processing), but unless she also runs both the credit and shipping systems (unlikely, since both probably require the cooperation of remote systems), my little cell phone can ring its brains out, I'm not taking any orders.

The use of asynchronous communications makes it possible to continue the lifestyle to which I have become accustomed. Disconnected. Carefree. I take orders on my cell phone and enter them on Baby. They are stored on local message queues. When I get home I log onto the network and the messages are transferred to the holding queues. Either then or at some future point, the messages are picked up by the remote credit card system for processing. After the credit card has been processed, the order moves over to the shipping queue. By then, I won't care. I'll be long gone, sipping my next Doppio.

Buffering

Message queues also allow us to buffer workload. We can defer some of the processing of workloads that have peaked beyond our system capability to times when the workload is less.

Let's say I am a sword manufacturer and I have my asynchronous purchasing system hooked up to the Web. My system will likely get orders at a nonuniform rate. While *Xena, Warrior Princess* is on the air, for example, most of my potential buyers are totally engrossed in watching Xena fight off some two-headed monster. As soon as *Xena* is over, everybody thinks, "Wow! pretty cool sword Xena was using, I need one of those." Suddenly I have 1000 people at my Web site trying to make purchases. Two hours later, I am down to 150 people at my Web site, and then down to a trickle until next week's *Xena* episode when she uses her brand new jewel-encrusted saber, and then that becomes the latest rage for the two-headed monster killer wannabes.*

If each purchase takes ten seconds to process, then I can process six orders per minute, or 360 orders per hour. If I use synchronous method invocation for processing the purchase, the first few people will be able to purchase their swords without waiting. But once I have people entering orders faster than six per minute, the system will no longer be able to keep up. Customers will be forced to wait, staring at frozen screens, and wondering what is happening. The wait time will get worse and worse as more and more people enter the system. *Xena* watchers are not known for their long-term mental focusing abilities. Being one myself, I can attest to this. So before too long, people will give up, and I start losing business.

This loss of business seems unfair. After all, for most of the day, my system is sitting around twiddling its thumbs. Only for one hour a day is the system too swamped to keep up with orders. It just happens to be the same hour in which I get most of my orders, by an odd coincidence.

There are three ways I can deal with this:

- I can increase my system's peak throughput by buying a bigger computer. This is the solution my hardware vendors like.

- I can nicely ask my customers if they wouldn't mind returning another day, when I am not so swamped. This is the solution my competitors like.

- I can figure out how to buffer the workload, putting off the processing of some of the purchases until my system has had a chance to catch up.

This workload buffering is exactly what message queues allow. Customers don't have to wait for the processing to occur, they just have to wait until their purchase request has been dropped in the queue. Dropping a message in a queue takes very little time. Then when the system has a free moment, it can process the next purchase request. If my sys-

---

*When I wrote this chapter, I chose the most ridiculous example of Web commerce I could think of. Nobody, I thought, would ever seriously consider actually selling Xena paraphernalia on the Web, so I couldn't possibly offend anybody. Little did I know. a week after I wrote this, my son Michael came running over to me. "Dad," he said, "I found this really cool Web site where you can buy Xena's sword!" If you don't believe this, go check out www.atlantacutlery.com for yourself, where not only can you buy Xena's Sword ($245.00) "the only sword fit for a princess," but for an additional $53.94, they will throw in her Chakram.

tem is capable of 360 orders per hour, it can handle more than 8000 per day, as long as it is allowed to process them at its own pace.

Interestingly, the use of message queues will degrade the *peak* throughput of my system because of the overhead associated with the queues themselves. But this is more than compensated for by the increase in the *net* throughput of my system because of the queues' buffering effect. Message queues work smarter, not harder.

Of course, this buffering effect occurs only in systems for which workload arrives in peaks and valleys. The use of queues in systems for which workload arrives at a constant rate will see only the degradation. But in the world of commerce, constant rate systems are the exception, not the rule.

Heterogenous Glue

The final use for message queues is in tying together a world in which nobody seems to be able to agree on anything. What do you do when you have some systems written in Enterprise JavaBeans (EJB), others in CORBA, others in COM+, and yet more in old legacy systems? It turns out that although there are many distributed software technologies, there are relatively few message queue systems. And for those that exist, we have reasonable bridges available to translate between them. Figuring out how to convince a highly architected COM+ method invocation to work on an Enterprise JavaBean is a difficult problem. Figuring out how to get a relatively unarchitected MSMQ message queue to interoperate with a message queue product that runs on your EJB system is probably much easier. I discuss this much more in Chapter 9, "COM+ Interoperability."

MSMQ and MS-DTC

Asynchronous message queues are funny beasts. Unlike synchronous method invocations, we don't really care when the message is processed. But we do care that at some point, someday, somehow, the message eventually is processed. Consider, for example, a banking system that tracks all account transfers in a central log. There is no reason to delay the transfer until we can process the log request. The log request can occur anytime, as long as it is sometime. Our code for this system could look as follows:

```
transfer::accountTransfer(fromAccountID, toAccountID, amount)
{
  account = create ("Account");
  logQueue = getHandleToQueue ("logQueue");
  account.withdraw(fromAccountID, amount);
  account.deposit(toAccountID, amount);
  message = createTransferMessage(fromAccountID, toAccountID, amount);
  sendMessage(logQueue, message);
  releaseQueue(logQueue);
  destroy account;
}
```

We can reasonably assume that both the withdraw and deposit methods are going to involve database updates. We can also assume that the transfer component would have been configured to require a transaction, which means that COM+ will start a new transaction automatically if one was not already running at the point of interception for this method. This transactional boundary configuration will ensure that either the withdraw and the deposit methods will both succeed or they will both fail. We also know that COM+ will end the new transaction at the return point of interception. And when the transaction finally ends, MS-DTC will join the party by starting the consensus phase of the so-called two phase commit, as described in Chapter 3.

During the consensus phase, each database is asked whether or not it is willing to commit. If both agree, then in the final phase, each database is actually told to commit. And if they promised to commit in the consensus phase, then commit they will in the final phase. If they don't, they will be in big trouble with the database union.

But if, during the consensus phase, one or both databases rejected the commit (either has that right), then during the final phase a rollback will be issued. But if we issue a rollback, we don't want to log the transfer to the central logging system. That will just confuse the poor little brains of the clerks in the central bank, who will now have a message telling them about a transfer that never really occurred.

So if the net result of the two-phase commit is a rollback, somehow we want to get the message out of the message queue. But how do we do this? Look again at the code:

```
transfer::accountTransfer(fromAccountID, toAccountID, amount)
{
  account = create ( "Account" );
  logQueue = getHandleToQueue ( "logQueue" );
```

```
        account.withdraw(fromAccountID, amount);
        account.deposit(toAccountID, amount);
        message = createTransferMessage(fromAccountID, toAccountID, amount);
        sendMessage(logQueue, message);
        releaseQueue(logQueue);
        destroy account;
    }
```

We don't even know, at the time we place the message in the queue, whether the result of all this will be a commit or a rollback. That won't be determined until we hit the return point of interception, at which time MS-DTC will start processing the two-phase commit. But by then it will be too late! We will have already placed the log message in the queue!

Fortunately, we are saved by a very tight relationship between MSMQ and MS-DTC. It turns out that MSMQ is a transactional resource that participates in the two-phase commit protocol orchestrated by MS-DTC. So when MS-DTC is in the contemplative phase, observing every speck of dust that happens to float by, it notices not only that the database has been updated in this transaction, but also that the message queue has been given a message.

In the consensus phase, MS-DTC then includes the message queue in the list of those resources that are allowed to have an opinion on the eventual fate of the transaction. And in the final stage, the message queue is included in the list of those resources that are told the outcome of the transaction. This means that even though the message is *handed* to the message queue at send time, the message is not *accepted* by the message queue until it hears the results of the two-phase commit. If the result of the two phase commit is rollback, then that message is ejected from the message queue as if it was never sent. Which makes life much easier for the clerks in the logging center. No log, no transfer. No transfer, no log.

This relationship with MS-DTC also holds true on the receiving end. So if the logging system fails to process the log message properly, it will be sucked right back into the logging queue for another try on another day.

MSCS

The final piece of the Windows 2000 MDCA is the Microsoft Cluster Server (MSCS). MSCS is a Microsoft technology that allows two identically configured machines to back each other up. If one fails, the other automatically takes over the work load. This becomes very important in designing systems that never (well, almost never) go down. In Windows 2000 MDCA, the major function of MSCS in the middle tier is to support the future COM+ load balancing, one of the topics of Chapter 8, "The COM+ Services," so I will defer this discussion until then.

Windows 2000 MDCA: The Next Generation

In the beginning of this chapter, I said that Windows 2000 MDCA, including COM+, is just an evolution of NT 4.0 MDCA. This is really true. Of course, COM+ itself is primarily a repackaging of NT 4.0's COM, DCOM, and MTS. The remaining Windows 2000 MDCA technologies are largely unchanged from NT 4.0. In later chapters I discuss the additional features of COM+ in detail, but briefly, the most important new features are these:

Queued Components. Queued components are components that accept asynchronous method invocations. As I discuss in Chapter 8, this is implemented in COM+ as a veneer on top of MSMQ, a technology that was part of the NT 4.0 MDCA line.

Loosely Coupled Events. Loosely coupled events is a *publish and subscribe* technology. The new event model, as I discuss in Chapter 8, is, at least in its asynchronous usage, also a veneer on top of MSMQ.

This should give you a sense of the MDCA evolution. Table 5.1 summarizes the relationship between NT 4.0 and Windows 2000 MDCA features and technologies. All in all, not a lot of differences. So rest assured, you are using tried and true technology with only a few new bells and whistles.

Now let's move on to the most important part of Windows 2000 MDCA, the star of the show: COM+.

Table 5.1 NT 4.0 MDCA and Windows 2000 MDCA Compared

MAJOR MDCA FEATURE	NT 4.0	W2000
Component Model	COM	COM+
Basic Component Distribution	DCOM	COM+
Component Host Process	MTS	COM+
Method Interception	MTS	COM+
Instance Management	MTS	COM+
Transaction Boundary Management	MTS	COM+
Distributed Transaction Coordination	MS-DTC	MS-DTC
Component Security	MTS	COM+
Attribute Administration	MTS	COM+
Failover	MSCS	MSCS
Asynchronous Messages	MSMQ	MSMQ
Asynchronous Method Invocation	—	COM+/MSMQ
Loosely Coupled Events	—	COM+/MSMQ

CHAPTER 6

COM+ Components

Exactly what is a COM+ component? That is not an easy question to answer. Part of the reason is that Microsoft component technology has a history going back to 1993, when COM was first introduced. Over the last six years, this technology has been used to solve many different types of problems ranging from single application graphical user interface applications to single machine, multiprocess coordination applications to true multimachine, multiprocess, distributed applications. Also, part of the reason it is difficult to pin down COM+ is that Microsoft has frequently abandoned and redefined its terminology. First, Microsoft talked about OLE objects. Then OLE transformed into ActiveX controls. Suddenly, ActiveX was as passé as yesterday's top rock band, and Microsoft informed us that all along, it had been talking about COM components. OOPS, make that COM components that run in MTS. Did I say MTS? I meant COM+.

Even now Microsoft is not entirely consistent. Sometimes COM+ refers to a component model and sometimes to a component runtime environment. Five years ago, we didn't even have a component runtime environment. Today, it's difficult to figure out where the component ends and runtime environment begins. It's a wonder these poor little blobs of software aren't in a perpetual identity crisis.

To some extent, this mirrors the confusion of the software industry as it tries to sort out the differences between objects and components, local and remote instances, and shared and unshared state. These are just a few of the issues plaguing the component industry, at least those in the industry who admit that these are difficult issues.

In this chapter I lead you gently through the Microsoft component model and introduce the many choices you must make in deciding how your components will work. I also give you some simplifying rules about component design that can turn what appears at first to be confusing array of choices into an easily comprehended system for developing distributed commerce systems.

Review

In Chapter 2, "Components," I talked about the idea of components, and how they can be viewed as blobs of software whose behavior is defined by interfaces. I discussed the distribution model of components, using a surrogate in the client process for a back-end instance, and a surrogate in the component process for the front-end client. I also discussed the naiveté of this model, and all the important issues it does not address for large-scale distributed commerce systems.

In Chapter 4, "COMWare," I talked about Component-Oriented Middleware (COMWare) as the next generation of middle-tier infrastructure, borrowing many middle-tier ideas from the Transaction Processing Monitors. I talked about the Component Runtime Environment that provided a warm and nurturing home for component instances that could otherwise never survive in the cold, cruel world of high transactional throughput commerce. I introduced some new ideas that will impact the way you develop components, the most important being:

- Components must be stateless, to take full advantage of the new COMWare algorithms.
- Developers need to think of methods as being transactions.
- Security needs to move to the boundary between the client and the middle tier.

In Chapter 5, "COM+ and Friends," I said that COM+ is the next generation of Microsoft's COMWare technology. COM+'s lineage goes back to the days of COM and DCOM, and then MTS (Microsoft Transaction Server). So what exactly is COM+? Is it the basic component model? Is it the distribution capability? Is it the runtime environment? Is it the COMWare algorithms? The best answer to this is just yes—it is all of these things.

Microsoft positions COM+ as more than just a middle-tier COMWare architecture. They would tell you it is a good platform for client and database development as well. Since these are not my fields of expertise, I will defer to those who specialize in these areas. I am a bit skeptical, if for no other reason than that the availability of COM+ is limited to Windows 2000. But for a COMWare architecture, COM+ is clearly a strong technology that will set new standards for the middle tier.

I have tried to focus this chapter on the component technology itself and the next chapter on the runtime environment, but in most areas this separation is fairly arbitrary. Almost all aspects of the runtime environment have implications for the component implementation, and the choices we make in component implementation often have serious ramifications at runtime. Nevertheless, I am going to do my best to follow this division, if for no other reason than to keep the two chapters manageable.

The Distribution Model

The basic distribution model of COM+ is unchanged since the days of COM and DCOM. It follows the distributed component architecture I described in Chapter 2. The client lives in one process and the component in another. In the distributed commerce systems of interest to us, these processes are usually, but not always, on entirely different machines. The exception to this rule is Web-based commerce, where sometimes we see systems in which the client (from the component perspective) is actually a Web server, and runs on the same machine as the business logic.

COM+ calls a client's surrogate for the back-end instance a *proxy,* and the instance's surrogate for the front-end client a *stub.* The wire format defined by DCOM connecting these two surrogates remains unchanged since DCOM's introduction. Some people will still refer to this distribution architecture as DCOM, which does make some sense, since client systems may, in fact, run COM and DCOM rather than COM+. I expect it to be common to have COM+ only on the component tier. For the purpose of this discussion, it is easier just to lump the component and distribution capabilities into COM+.

The Basic Component Model

The most obvious benefit we get from COM+ is the ability to use remote components. What is a COM+ component? At the most superficial level, a COM+ component is a blob of software that adheres to the following rules:

- The blob hides behind one or more interfaces.

- The interface(s) defines the methods the blob supports.

- Every interface the blob supports must be derived from an interface called IUnknown.

- At most, one of the interfaces the blob supports may be (but is not required to be) derived from an interface called IDispatch. Since IDispatch is itself derived from IUnknown, this does not violate the previous rule. This rule is more pragmatic than technical. Though there is nothing preventing you from having multiple interfaces derived from IDispatch, the subsystems, such as Active Server Pages (ASP) that depend on IDispatch will be able to make use of only one of these interfaces (the default interface). Since Web access typically goes through ASP, this effectively means that only one interface can be used from Web pages.

- The interface(s) a particular blob supports are fully described by a file called the component's type library. Type libraries are for highly sophisticated computer programs. You, as a sniveling human being, are incapable of working with a type library.

- The blob lives in one or more processes on one or more systems.

As you can probably see, things are already starting to get a little confusing. Several immediate questions jump to mind. Why would a developer want to define more than one interface for a component? If there is more than one interface, how do you decide whether or not that interface should be derived from IDispatch? If you cannot work directly with a type library, how are you supposed to define, discuss, or even look at the interface?

Working with the Interface

Let's start with the interface. It would be helpful in our discussions of the rest of the issues if we had a common way to describe interfaces. There are several ways of "looking" at an interface. The COM+ runtime and programming languages care only about the type library. We humans will generally view the interface either through a program that interprets the type library for us or through a text file in a language called the *Microsoft Interface Definition Language* (MIDL).

Originally, programmers wrote MIDL themselves, and some still do. Programmers used MIDL to define the methods, interfaces, and components, and then compiled MIDL to create the type libraries. Today, most programmers work with one of the COM+ friendly programming languages, and let the language tools generate either the type library directly or the MIDL description, which can then be compiled into a type library.

Language tools can make it very easy to define and implement components. COM+ itself is completely language neutral. Any language can be used to implement COM+ components, but it is up to a particular language vendor to make it easy to do so. Not surprisingly, all of the Microsoft programming languages, including their version of Java, are very easy to use for implementing COM+ components. Also not surprisingly, Sun's Java is particularly difficult to use for implementing COM+ components.

Perhaps the easiest of all COM+ component implementation languages is Microsoft Visual Basic. With the release of version 6.0, Visual Basic becomes an attractive choice for the implementation of COM+ components. The process is quite easy. Visual Basic includes a class builder utility that steps you through the process of designing a component complete with methods and parameters. The tool queries you for the name of the component/class, the name of the methods, and the names and types of each parameter for each method. It's pretty hard to mess up anything with the class builder utility. Notice that in this context, what I call a component Microsoft calls a *class*.

Once you have defined your component, the class builder utility creates an empty template of code, which you can then fill in with your component implementation code. I used the class builder utility to define a Customer component with two methods:

- GetCustomerBalance
- GetCustomerInfo

Figure 6.1 Generated Visual Basic customer code.

GetCustomerBalance took two parameters, an input CustomerID and an output Balance. GetCustomerInfo took three parameters, an input CustomerID, and an output CustomerName and CustomerCity. The class builder utility created the Visual Basic code for me, shown in Figure 6.1.

At this point I can implement each of these methods. The GetCustomerBalance would open the database, query for account records matching the CustomerID, total them up, and return the result as Balance. Since I am just focusing on the interface, I won't bother with this, I'll just ask Visual Basic to create a DLL and save it. Visual Basic will automatically create a type library for me, compile my Visual Basic code, and put the whole mess in the DLL that is ready to drop into the COM+ runtime environment. Everything COM+ needs to run the component is neatly packaged together in one DLL.

Once I have my DLL containing the type library, I can use another tool (OLE/COM Object Viewer) that displays a type library and generates an equivalent MIDL file. Notice that what I call a component and what Microsoft until moments ago had been calling a class, has suddenly been turned into an *object*. You can start to see why I don't feel compelled to follow the Microsoft terminology. Microsoft has great software, but lousy terminology. The MIDL file created by the OLE/COM Object Viewer is shown in Figure 6.2.

The MIDL is strictly for my benefit; COM+ isn't going to make any use of it. COM+ will use the equivalent type library. But if I need to discuss my component with some other programmer, the MIDL can be a convenient lingua franca. Although I'm not going to discuss MIDL in depth, let's take a cursory look at the generated MIDL file, just to give you a sense of how COM+ will interpret this component.

A component has a name; this component's name is Customer. Referring to Figure 6.2, this is shown as the name of the coclass (a), the name Microsoft uses in this context to refer to a component.

A component supports one or more interfaces. The Customer supports one interface called _Customer (b). This interface was created for us by Visual Basic. If Customer supported more than one interface, they would

```
//Generated .IDL file (by the OLE/COM Object Viewer)
//
//typelib filename: Project1.dll

[
  uuid(205079F0-2C2F-11D3-8E51-000000000000),
  version(2.0)
]
library Project1
{
  //TLib : //TLib : OLE Automation :{00020430-0000-0000-C000-000000000046}
  importlib("STDOLE2.TLB");

  //Forward declare all types defined in this typelib
  interface_Customer;

  [
    odl,
    uuid(6BE7A1E5-2CE1-11D3-8E52-000000000000),
    version(1.0),
    hidden,
    dual,
    nonextensible,
    oleautomation
  ]
  interface _Customer : IDispatch {
      [id(0x60030000)]
      HRESULT GetCBalance(
          [in] short CID,
          [in, out] short* CBalance);
      [id0x60030001)]
      HRESULT GetCInfo(
          [in] short CID,
          [in, out] BSTR* CName,
          [in, out] BSTR* CCity;
  };

  [
    uuid(205079F2-2C2F-11D3-8E51-000000000000),
    version(1.0)
  ]
  coclass Customer {
    [default] interface _Customer;
  };
};
```

Figure 6.2 Customer code interpreted as MIDL.

be listed here. Although in theory a COM+ component can support multiple interfaces, many of the COM+ related tools, such as asynchronous components (a topic I will discuss in Chapter 8, "The COM+ Services") can work with only one interface (the one derived from IDispatch). Therefore I think it is a good rule of thumb to use only one interface in COM+ components (and to have that interface derived from IDispatch).

An interface supports zero or more methods. I had defined two methods, GetCBalance and GetCInfo. They are shown as the two methods (c) on the _Customer interface.

A method has zero or more parameters. Parameters can be either *in* or *in/out*. An in parameter is one that is not changed by the method. If the method does modify the input value, that modification is made locally only. An in/out parameter is one that is changed and returned to the caller by the method. The GetCBalance has two parameters. The first, CID, is the CustomerID, and is input only. The second, CBalance, is the Customer Balance. The purpose of this method is to look up a particular customer's balance. Therefore this parameter will be returned. In Visual Basic, a parameter can be either *byVal* or *byRef* (the default). A byVal parameter is one whose modifications are made locally and not returned to the caller. A byRef parameter is one whose modifications are returned to the caller. In MIDL, a Visual Basic byVal parameter becomes an in, and a byRef (or default) becomes an in/out. Thus CID (d) is declared in and CBalance (e) is declared in/out in the MIDL file.

Notice that there is not an exact match between parameter type names in Visual Basic and parameter type names in MIDL. The Visual Basic *integer* becomes a *short* in MIDL. An example of this is the CID parameter (e). In general, different programming languages use different parameter type names. What Visual Basic calls an integer, for example, C calls a short int. MIDL can't make everybody happy, so it does the best it can by using type names that are, at minimum, understood by everybody.

There are some features of the component in MIDL that had no corresponding feature in Visual Basic. Notice, for example, that the _Customer interface is declared as derived from IDispatch. There is no IDispatch in my Visual Basic code; where did that come from and what does it do?

We can learn a little about IDispatch by looking at its interface. One way to do this is with OLE/COM Object Viewer, the program that can give us a view into the Customer type library. Figure 6.3 shows the OLE/COM Object Viewer looking at the type library I created with my Customer Visual Basic code. I have fully expanded the _Customer interface to include all the inherited methods.

You can see that IDispatch consists of four methods:

- GetTypeInfoCount
- GetTypeInfo
- GetIDsofNames
- Invoke

You can also see that IDispatch is itself derived from IUnknown, which supports three additional methods:

- QueryInterface
- AddRef
- Release

If you follow my advice and make every interface derived from IDispatch, then every interface will also support these seven methods.

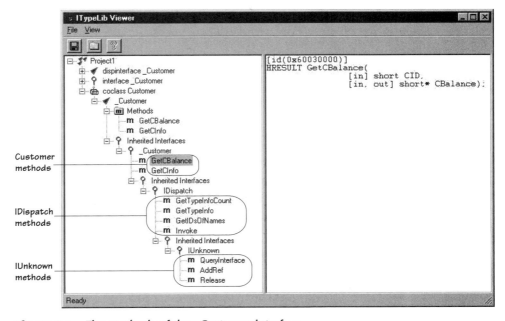

Figure 6.3   The methods of the _Customer interface.

The Methods of IDispatch

I'm not going to spend a great deal of time describing the IDispatch interface, namely because you will never use it directly. But because some systems like ASP use this interface under the covers, it is worth understanding what it does. The main thing to understand is that IDispatch provides a dynamic interface for discovering and invoking methods on instances at runtime. This is great for interpreted systems that often don't know until runtime exactly what they will be doing with a component instance. These systems need a flexible conversational mode for invoking methods. When ASP, for example, wants to ask an instance to do something for it, the conversation (using the IDispatch interface) goes something like this:

ASP: Excuse me, Ma'am. I was thinking of invoking a method named "GetCBalance" on you. Could I trouble you to tell me if you support such a method?

Instance: Why, yes, I do. "GetCBalance" is the method I know by the ID of 0x60030000.

ASP: Alright! By the way, (slight pause) what parameters do you like for that method?

Instance (in a deep, sexy voice): Just give me a short int and I will return to you a long int. You do know how to create a long int, don't you? You just put your lips together and blow!

ASP: Great! Do 0x60030000! Here is a short int, and here is a place to put that long int you will be giving me back.

Instance: You've got it.

So you can see that although you will never use IDispatch directly, it is important that your component support its functionality. The bad news is that IDispatch can be rather nasty to implement. The good news is that the COM+ friendly languages will implement the IDispatch methods for you. You get the advantages of runtime binding without any of the work.

Although invoking methods through IDispatch is the ultimate in flexibility, it is also time consuming. Many programs, like most compiled programs, do not need this flexibility. They use a much faster technique for invoking methods, one based on an in-memory data structure called a *VTable*. I will discuss VTables later in this chapter when I talk about component memory layout.

The Methods of IUnknown

The IUnknown interface is an even more basic interface than IDispatch. IUnknown must be supported by all interfaces of all components. If the interface supports IDispatch, then it will automatically support IUnknown, since IDispatch is derived from IUnknown. Again, very few programmers (except for C++ clients) will use the IUnknown interface, but it will be used by the underlying system. The methods of IUnknown have two purposes:

- Interface management
- Life cycle management

Let's start with interface management. COM+ components are allowed to support multiple interfaces. Back in Microsoft Windows NT 4.0, this was more important, because in MTS the interface represented the smallest division for security declarations. I will discuss security later in this chapter and in Chapter 7, "The COM+ Runtime Environment," but as a heads up, COM+ now allows security declaration at the method level. Given this and the various restrictions on the use of multiple interfaces (such as poor support by queued components), I no longer see any reason to recommend the use of multiple interfaces. I now recommend one interface per component. However if you have legacy components that already use multiple interfaces, I also see no reason to rush out and change them. If, for one reason or another, you do have a component that supports more than one interface, the IUnknown QueryInterface method is how you get from one interface to another.

The QueryInterface allows the client to say, in effect, "You know, Mr. Instance, I've really enjoyed using this particular interface to you, but now I need to ask you to do some work that is defined by another interface. So, could you please hand me a reference to this other interface, if by chance you happen to support it?"

Every interface supports QueryInterface (because every interface is derived from IUnknown) and every QueryInterface implementation knows about every interface the component supports. Thus QueryInterface becomes a useful tool for moving from one interface of a component instance to another. You as a client will probably never see this method, unless you have the misfortune to be writing in C++. Most languages will shield you from QueryInterface by giving you a more natural way to move from one interface to another, typically by the equivalent of a cast operation. But underneath it all, QueryInterface is doing the actual work.

Up until recently, you, as the component implementor, were responsible for implementing QueryInterface. It wasn't hugely complicated, certainly not as difficult as the IDispatch methods, but those days are pretty much behind us. The more COM+ friendly your language is, the less you have to worry about. Visual Basic completely implements QueryInterface and you can be happily ignorant of its existence.

The remaining two methods of IUnknown are AddRef and Release. These methods are somewhat anachronistic. Historically their use goes back before COM+ and even before MTS, back when COM and DCOM were all a poor programmer had to manage components and their instances. These were the dark ages for software development.

Back in the COM/DCOM days, people did not think about stateless components. Before instance management algorithms (i.e., before MTS) there was no particular incentive to use stateless components. So most people followed the standard object-oriented strategy of storing state with the instances.

One of the side effects of storing state with instances is a strong temptation to allow multiple clients to have proxies pointing to the same instance. This technique of having multiple proxies point to a single instance is often still used in component systems such as CORBA that do not yet have component runtime environments that provide instance management. Because they do not have instance management, most of the currently developed components use stateful instances. I discussed this topic back in Chapter 4. Because of the preponderance of stateful instances, we would frequently see references to component instances (or, more accurately, references to specific interfaces of component instances) passed around with relative abandon. We might, for example, have two manufacturing machines communicate about their progress by each having a proxy to the same instance of a process component. Or a manager might monitor a telephone support system by having a proxy to each of the work station instances.

The net result of all this was that you never really knew who had proxies to what instances, and the relationship between proxies and instances was often many to one, as shown in Figure 6.4. This made it very difficult to figure out when the component instance was no longer needed. None of the clients could take responsibility for making this decision, since nobody really knew who else happened to be using that same instance through some other proxy. If Sam decided to delete the instance just because he was finished with his proxy, Sally would get a nasty surprise the next time she asked her proxy, which was connected to the same instance, to invoke a method.

Microsoft designed the AddRef and Release methods of IUnknown to solve this problem. The convention was that anybody creating a proxy would immediately invoke AddRef, and anybody releasing their proxy would, just before the release, invoke Release. Like all methods, these requests would pass through to the back-end component instance. The component implementor was responsible for keeping count of how many references (proxies) were outstanding at any given time. When the count reached zero, meaning that all proxies to this instance have been released, the component instance itself was responsible for committing hari-kari.

In the world of stateless commerce components, life cycle is much less of a problem. I am assuming, of course, that you are following my admonition to make your components stateless. Please keep in mind that this admonition, like all the advice in this book, is geared toward the development of distributed, multitier, high-transactional through-

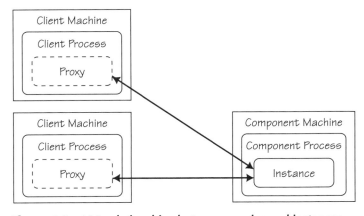

Figure 6.4 M:1 relationships between proxies and instances.

put commerce systems. If that's not your game, then this advice may not be germane. There are many other possible applications for COM+; they just aren't relevant to this discussion.

So what does state have to do with life cycle? The fact is, if there is no state in the instance, there is no reason for you to pass out references to that instance to your friends and neighbors. Such a practice accomplishes nothing and severely compromises the scalability of the system by defeating the instance management algorithms described in Chapter 4. Two clients that want to share state should not do so by having proxies point to the same instance, but by having two instances share a database ID to the same state storage, as shown in Figure 6.5.

However, COM+ still allows the sharing of instances among proxies (whether or not it is a good idea is a different issue), so this AddRef/ Release convention is still used. Like the rest of the IUnknown and IDispatch methods, this, too, is implemented on your behalf by your COM+ friendly language and the methods are automatically invoked for you at the appropriate time by the underlying language system. Unless, of course, you are a C++ programmer. Are you starting to get the idea that maybe life isn't so grand for the C++ programmer?

In Visual Basic, Release is invoked automatically at the time you reset your proxy to null, as in this code:

```
set Customer = Nothing
```

This line tells Visual Basic that you are finished with this particular proxy (or what you think of as an instance), and allows the system to clean up any resources associated with that proxy.

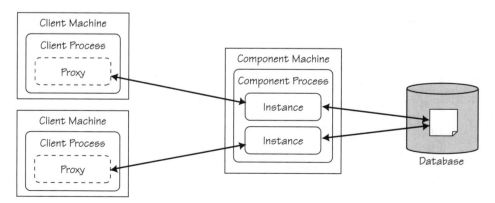

Figure 6.5 M:1 relationship between instances and state.

MIDL, Type Libraries, and Implementations

You can see that the use of the OLE/COM Object Viewer gives us some interesting insights into the hidden life of our Visual Basic component. You can also see close relationships between the implementation of a component (say, in Visual Basic), the MIDL file giving a human description of a component, and the type library giving a software description of a component. Given any one of these, the other two can be generated. If we have a MIDL file, we can create either a type library or a skeleton implementation (assuming the programming language is COM+ friendly). If we have a type library, we can create a MIDL description. If we have a language implementation, we can generate a type library. This relationship is shown in Figure 6.6.

You might ask why bother with the MIDL definition and type library if we already have a language implementation? The main advantage of the MIDL and type library is that they are language neutral. They are tools that can be used to develop client code in any programming language. The client programmer, say Clarence, can use a component without having to worry about the language the component programmer, say Colette, used to implement that component. Clarence can use C++, Visual Basic, or even JavaScript to make requests of the component. Colette can use her favorite language without being concerned with what language Clarence will use. Just as MIDL becomes the point of agreement between Clarence and Colette, the type library becomes the point of agreement between their software. MIDL and type libraries are therefore the crucial pieces that provide language neutrality. Language neutrality is one of the key features that separate COM+ from some other COMWare platforms, particularly Enterprise JavaBeans (EJB).

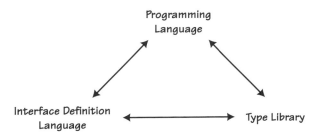

Figure 6.6   Interface relationships.

GUIDs and Uniqueness

Every once in a while, a really ugly character string appears in conjunction with some aspect of a COM+ component. A good example of this character string can be seen back in Figure 6.2, in the sixth line of the IDL, where we see this odd creature pop up its head:

```
uuid(205079F0-2C2F-11D3-8E51-000000000000)
```

This is an example of a string known as a *Globally Unique ID* (GUID). This is usually pronounced "guid" to rhyme with "fluid." A GUID is an identifier that is generated using an algorithm that promises never to generate the same string twice, even when the algorithm is run on two identical machines at the exact same instant in time. COM+ uses these GUIDs to unequivocally refer to things that might otherwise have name conflicts. For example, if you try to merge two banking systems together, you could end up with two account components. This would confuse poor COM+. When you ask COM+ to create an instance of an account, it wouldn't know which one you were asking for. So COM+ keeps track of things by GUIDs, which are always unique. But COM+ recognizes that it is dealing with less than perfect human beings who have trouble relating to component names like 205079F2-2C2F-11D3-8E51-000000000000 (the official name of the component shown in Figure 6.2). For your sake, most COM+ friendly languages allow you to refer to things by their human nicknames, such as "Customer" (the human nickname for component 205079F2-2C2F-11D3-8E51-000000000000 in Figure 6.2) or by their GUIDs. We will use only the human nicknames in this book, but it is useful to know that GUIDs often play an important role behind the scenes.

Memory Layout

Although we think of MIDL files and type libraries as being the fundamental building blocks of COM+, at a more primitive level, even they aren't required. You can think of MIDL and type libraries as being tools used to describe memory layout. It doesn't really matter if a tool uses MIDL or a type library, or an Ouija board. If that tool can figure out some way to lay out memory in the same way as COM+, it will be compatible with COM+. Let me take a moment to describe the memory layout of

COM+ components. If this is interesting to you, feel free to read this section. If not, or if you find this material too difficult, feel free to skip this section. You don't need to understand this material to use COM+.

Let's go back to the Visual Basic component I introduced earlier in this chapter. It had two methods of its own:

- GetCBalance
- GetCInfo

It had four methods it inherited from IDispatch:

- GetTypeInfoCount
- GetTypeInfo
- GetIDsOfNames
- Invoke

And it had three methods it inherited from IUnknown:

- QueryInterface
- AddRef
- Release

This is a total of nine methods, for those of you who haven't had your second Doppio yet.

Suppose that a client, Clarence, wants to invoke a method, GetCInfo on an instance of a Customer component. Remember, Clarence doesn't have the instance in his process space; it lives in the remote component process. What Clarence has in his process space is a proxy to that remote instance. When Clarence invokes GetCInfo, he really invokes GetCInfo on his proxy. The proxy is then responsible for marshaling the parameters and passing them over the wire to the remote process. On the remote process, a surrogate for Clarence picks up the requests and invokes the method on Clarence's behalf on the actual instance. The instance returns any information to the surrogate who passes it back to the proxy, who then returns the information to Clarence. This was all described in Chapter 2.

The code for the component is loaded into a DLL in the component process. This DLL has one entry point for each method, each representing the business logic corresponding to that method. The code for the proxy is loaded into a DLL in Clarence's process. This DLL also has one entry point for each method, but these entry points are for marshaling code, not business logic. Here are a few questions we need to answer to get a grip on the memory layout:

- In the simplest possible scenario, when Clarence invokes GetCInfo, how does it get mapped to the appropriate marshaling entry point?

- When the request is transmitted to the remote component process, how does the system map the request to the appropriate component-side entry point?

- When the request is transmitted to the remote component process, how does the system know which of possibly many instantiated Customer instances (not to mention non-Customer instances) is to receive the request?

- Where, exactly, is any instance-specific state stored?

- How does all this change when the IDispatch Invoke method is used to make the request?

Let's take a tour through the actual memory layout (as shown in Figure 6.7) of the client's process. The easiest way to discuss the memory layout is to follow an actual method as it is transferred from Clarence to his back-end instance.

This whole mess begins with Clarence saying to his proxy, "Please invoke GetCInfo for me. Here are the parameters. Return the result when you are done." But what, exactly, is a proxy? Good question.

Clarence's proxy is shown as (a) in Figure 6.7. It consists of a blob of memory divided into two sections. The first section just consists of an address. This is the address of the VTable, shown as (b), to which we will come back in a moment. The second section of the memory blob is a little larger and contains a small amount of data. This data consists of whatever is necessary to identify the machine, process, and instance to which this proxy considers itself hooked up. The actual instance is shown as (g) in Figure 6.8. We will come back to the instance later as well.

When COM+ "sends a message to an instance," what it really does is follow the VTable address in the proxy to the actual VTable. The term *VTable* comes from C++, which used this same table to contain addresses of what are called, in C++, *virtual methods*. The VTable consists of a table of addresses, where the *n*th address in the VTable is the

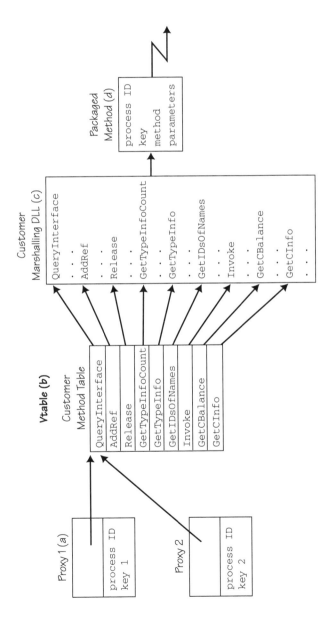

Figure 6.7 COM+ client process memory layout.

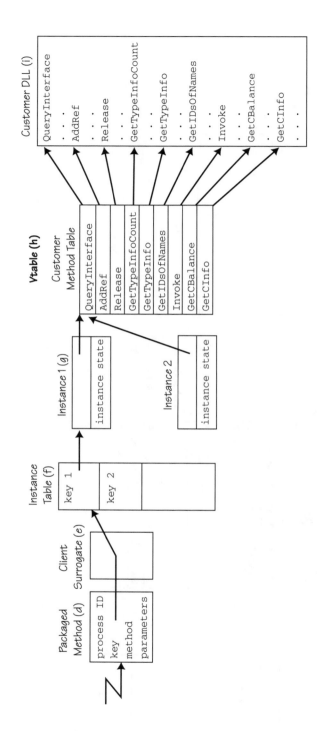

Figure 6.8 COM+ component process memory layout.

address of the entry point of the nth method supported by an interface. Clarence is invoking GetCInfo, which is the 9th method supported by Customer.

How do we know GetCInfo is the 9th method, and not the 8th? We start counting with the most derived interface, which is always IUnknown. Its three methods are 1 through 3. We then go to the next most derived interface, which, in this case, is IDispatch. Its four methods are 4 through 7. We then go to the next (and in this case, last) interface, Customer. It has two methods defined, and they occupy slots 8 and 9. According to the IDL we looked at earlier, the first of the defined methods is GetCBalance, so it is assigned slot 8. GetCInfo goes in the next available slot, number 9.

On the client side, each slot in the VTable is the address of the entry point in the DLL (d) that contains the marshaling code for that method. So COM+ now invokes the code at that entry point in the DLL, passing in two things. The first thing passed in to the entry point is the address of the proxy on which the method was invoked. This is needed so that the executed code can work with the second region of the proxy blob, the region containing the information about the machine, process, and instance to which this method is being directed. The second thing passed in to the entry point is the parameters that Clarence originally included with the method invocation.

We are now at the correct marshaling entry point within the DLL (c) for the GetCInfo method. The marshaling code has access to three important pieces of information. The method invoked can be deduced from which entry point we are at. The instance identification information can be located from the address of the proxy. And the parameters that need to be passed through are the same parameters as were passed into this entry point.

The marshaling code creates a package consisting of the method name, instance information, and parameters. This package is shown as (d) in Figure 6.7. This package now is sent over the wire to the component process. Let's switch over to Figure 6.8, which shows memory layout in the component process side. The package (d) is received by the client surrogate (e) that lives in the component process. The client surrogate, usually called a stub in COM+, pulls apart the package, getting the key, method ID, and parameters.

In the component process, we have a possibly large number of instances running. Each of these instances has an entry in a running instance table (f). An entry in the instance table consists, conceptually, of two values:

- A key that uniquely identifies an instance.
- An address of the instance itself.

The client surrogate requests the address of the instance matching the key it was passed in via the package.

The instance address is actually the address of a blob of memory that represents the Customer instance. The blob is divided into two regions. The first region consists of an address of another VTable (h). This VTable looks very similar to the VTable on the client side in that it has nine entries, one for each method supported by Customer, and is laid out in the same order as the client side VTable. They are also addresses to entry points in a DLL (i). However, this DLL is quite different from the DLL on the client side. This DLL actually contains the business logic that implements the method.

Given the correct offset in the VTable, the client surrogate can pass control over to the correct DLL entry point, passing in both a pointer to the instance itself and the parameters it found in the package. The pointer to the instance is needed to get to any state information associated with the instance. The parameters, of course, are needed to process the method.

Once the DLL has finished processing the business logic, it returns any results to the client surrogate who creates a package headed back to the marshaling DLL on the client side. The marshaling DLL unpackages the information and returns it to Clarence, who is blissfully ignorant of all this work that was done on his behalf.

There is a variant of this whole process used for invoking methods through the IDispatch Invoke method. Remember, this is the method that allows systems like ASP to choose, as late as possible, what methods it wants invoked. Basically, the IDispatch Invoke method works like any other method invocation. The "parameters" to IDispatch contain method identification and parameters that need to be sent over the wire. It is the Invoke entry point in the component process DLL that is responsible for interpreting the method ID and parameters and re-invoking the correct method. But this is not COM+'s concern. So although it seems that IDispatch is a very different type of method invocation, from the perspective of COM+, it is just another method, no different than CGetInfo.

Simple, isn't it? No? Actually, it gets even more complicated when we add in the COM+ runtime environment. But we'll wait for that until Chapter 7.

Instance Creation

Before Clarence can actually invoke a method on a component, somebody needs to create the middle-tier instance. This is the responsibility of a special component called the *class factory*. In theory, the implementor of the class is also responsible for implementing the class factory, but most COM+ friendly languages (such as Visual Basic) will do this automatically. It is probably useful to be aware of, in case you have some special needs that are not taken care of by the default class factory, but we are not going to spend time on it here. The class factory is whom you ask to create an instance, but most languages support some simple create object API to shield you from the class factory. In this book I will assume you are using the default class library and the create object API.

Transaction Organization and Rollback

In commerce systems, the transaction is king. The idea that a bunch of work can be packaged together into a bundle that either all of which will execute (*in toto*) or none of which will execute (*in nihilo*) is the single most important concept in commerce systems. I discussed the importance of transactions back in Chapter 3, "Transaction Processing Monitors," so I won't reiterate that here.

I discussed the general algorithm of transaction boundary management in COMWare systems in Chapter 4. COM+ follows this algorithm (in fact, its predecessor, MTS, invented this algorithm). Let me briefly review this algorithm. As I discussed in Chapter 5, COM+'s close friend MS-DTC is responsible for coordinating the so-called two-phase commit protocol that I described in Chapter 3. The two-phase commit protocol is essential if transactional units of work are to span database connections, or even nondatabase connections, such as to MSMQ message queues (as I discussed in Chapter 5). But MS-DTC can do the right thing only if somebody lets MS-DTC know when the transaction has officially begun and when it has officially ended. In a pre-COMWare environment, this is the responsibility of the business logic implementor. In a COMWare environment, this is the responsibility of the runtime environment.

I also pointed out in Chapter 4 how important it is to have methods designed as transactional units of work. This, too, holds true for COM+. In the next chapter, I discuss exactly how the COM+ runtime manages the transactional boundaries.

You can see that a good part of the transactional management ideas in COM+ are similar to other COMWare platforms. Nevertheless, there are several twists that are unique to COM+. These twists have important implications for your component design, and yet are not often discussed in the traditional COM+ literature. It is, therefore, worth spending some time on them.

Let's start with some illustrative components. Say we are tasked with creating a banking application. The bank has checking accounts and savings accounts, which we implement as checkingAccount and savingsAccount components. Both of these components support deposit and withdraw methods. The bank wants to allow people to transfer money from one account to another, so we create a transfer component that coordinates this activity. One of the methods on transfer is fromSavingsToChecking, and one is fromCheckingToSavings (this is rarely used in practice, but is included just for completeness). The pseudocode implementation of the fromSavingsToChecking method looks like this:

```
fromSavingsToChecking(savingsID, checkingID, amount, error)
{
  error = FALSE;
  savings = createObject("savingsAccount");
  checking = createObject ("checkingAccount");
  savings.withdraw(savingsID, amount);
  checking.deposit(checkingID, amount);
}
```

One thing you might notice is that this implementation has no error management code. Without error management code, how do we ensure that the transfer either completes both the withdrawal *and* the deposit, or that it does neither? What if there wasn't enough money in the savingsAccount to complete the withdrawal? What if the checkingAccount database declines to accept the deposit because of some lock conflict? Shouldn't we put the money back in the savingsAccount?

In fact, the basic transactional framework will take care of all of this. The COM+ transactional framework makes the following assumptions:

- Any data whose integrity we care about is stored in a database, or at least some transactional storage medium.

- Any data that is in the instance is about to be lost anyway, so we need not worry about its integrity.

- A given method need only worry about whether or not its internal business logic was successful.

So how does this whole thing work? From a programmer's perspective, there is very little to it. The savingsAccount implementor, say Sarah, is responsible for letting the system know whether her business logic was happy. There are several ways she can do this. The most common is to configure the component so that it assumes everything went fine unless she "raises an error condition." Exactly how she "raises an error condition" is language dependent. For example, she might have pseudocode that looks like this:

```
withdraw(savingsID, amount)
{
  dbc = getDatabaseConnection(myUserID, myPassword);
  balance = readBalance(dbc, savingsID);
  if (amount exceeds balance)
  {
    releaseDatabaseConnection(dbc);
    return error "Inadequate balance to cover withdrawal";
  }
  updateBalance(dbc, savingsID, balance + amount);
  releaseDatabaseConnection(dbc);
}
```

The checkingAccount deposit logic could have similar error checking logic. For example Charlie, the checkingAccount implementor, might not accept more than two deposits in any one account in one day, for fear of money laundering.

The important point is that Sarah and Charlie can limit their worrying to business logic errors; they need not worry about errors in the database. In fact, database errors are difficult to worry about, because they may not occur until much later, when the transaction end point has been reached. Neither Sarah nor Charlie knows when that will occur. And in general neither knows, once that point has been reached, whether a commit request or a rollback request will be issued. The one exception to this last statement is when either Sarah herself or Charlie himself has raised an error condition because of a business logic error. If Sarah has raised an error condition, she still doesn't know when the end of the transaction will occur, but she does know what will happen when we get there. We will roll back. Sarah knows that because she is the one that raised the error condition.

Charlie, on the other hand, has no clue that a rollback is the ultimate destiny of this transaction. The general rule is that if you have raised an error, you know that a rollback is inevitable. If you didn't, then you have no idea what will happen. If somebody else raises an error, then a rollback will occur. If nobody raises an error, then a commit will occur. In any case, it's out of your hands.

Looking again at the transfer code, you can see that the checking-Account is being asked to do a deposit, even though it may have been predetermined that the transaction will eventually roll back. We could optimize for the error condition by having the transfer's from-SavingsToChecking not bother to invoke the checkingAccount's deposit if an error occurred in the savingsAccount's withdrawal. If we do this, it is strictly an optimization—it is by no means necessary. The transactional framework itself will ensure that, from a database perspective, the deposit will never occur. And one of the assumptions of this framework is that the database is all we care about.

In the next chapter, I cover how the COM+ runtime environment makes all this happen. For now, I am concerned only with explaining the implications for the component implementor. These implications are simple: let us know if anything bad happened, and leave the rest of the driving to us.

Now let's take a closer look at the commit point. This follows the basic transactional boundary management I discussed in Chapter 4, but let's review here. When we configure a component for COM+, we tell COM+ what the transactional needs of that component are. For the three components here—transfer, savingsAccount, and checkingAccount—all should be configured as "Requires a Transaction," which is pretty much the standard transaction configuration for most middle-tier components.

When a client makes a request on a transfer instance (indirectly, of course, through a proxy) the COM+ runtime notices that the transfer component was configured as requiring a transaction. It will therefore start off a new transaction on behalf of that client. As I discussed in Chapters 4 and 5, this lets MS-DTC know that it is time to start the contemplative phase of the two-phase commit.

When the transfer instance makes a request of the savingsAccount instance, it too has been configured as "Requires a Transaction." But in this case, COM+ notices that there is already a transaction in progress, so it just lets the savingsAccount instance piggyback off of the transfer instance's transaction.

The transaction will end upon returning from the method that started the transaction, in this case, the fromSavingsToChecking method invocation. At the transaction end point, COM+ will issue either a commit or a rollback request to MS-DTC, depending whether or not both Sarah and Charlie were happy with the way their business logic went. If both were happy, then COM+ issues a commit. If either was unhappy, then COM+ issues a rollback.

Once the commit is issued (assuming Sarah and Charlie were both happy) we find out if the databases are willing to accept the changes. Just because Sarah and Charlie were happy doesn't mean their databases are going to be happy. So now MS-DTC goes into the consensus phase of the two-phase commit, asking each database if it is willing to accept the transaction. When MS-DTC has heard from every database, it goes into the final phase, telling the databases whether or not they should all go ahead and commit or rollback. If all the databases said they were willing to accept the commit in the consensus phase (as described in Chapter 3), MS-DTC tells all the databases to commit. If any of the databases were in a bad mood in the consensus phase, then MS-DTC tells them all to roll back.

If Sarah's instance raises an error, Charlie's instance can still do its deposit, for all the good it will do him. When the transaction end point is reached, a rollback will be issued and his changes will be undone faster than you can say "COMWare."

Notice how critical it is to this algorithm that all data whose integrity we care about is stored, not in the instance, but in a database. In the COM+ transactional model, any instance data is not going to be rolled back if the transaction as a whole rolls back. This is true of most COMWare platforms. So the simple answer is, don't put any data in the instance. There is, by the way, a word we use to describe instances that don't have any data associated with them: *stateless*. Have you heard this word before? I can promise you, you are going to hear it again many times before the end of this book. The transaction framework is just one of the places COM+ has dependencies on a *stateless* component implementation.

The COM+ Stateless Model

Since we are on the subject of state, now is a good time to discuss the COM+ model for statelessness. First of all, the term stateless is a bit misleading. Nobody believes that components should not work on state. What we really mean is that the state should not be stored in the component; it should be stored someplace else. So it is really not so much a model for statelessness as it is a model for state management.

Although all COMWare platforms agree that state management is a must if the system as a whole is to work as it should (high scalability, transactional integrity, etc.), they differ radically over how state should be managed. In one sense, the COM+ state management model is the ultimate in simplicity and flexibility. It really does nothing for you, so you can do anything you want. Enterprise JavaBeans (EJB) takes the opposite approach, doing a great deal for you. However much of what it does, it does at a considerable performance cost. I discuss the various EJB models for state management in Chapter 10, "Enterprise JavaBeans."

All of the different COMWare models for state management have identical goals:

- To move state from the transactional data source (usually, but not necessarily a database) to the instance at the beginning of a transaction.
- To move the state back to the transactional data source at the end of a transaction.

Since all COMWare platforms also agree that a transaction is equivalent to a method, we can simplify this from the programmer's perspective. Read in state at the beginning of the method. Write it back out at the end of the method. For such a simple idea, you wouldn't think there would be so much room for disagreement.

Although COM+ does not enforce any model for state management, there is one programming pattern that will be so common that we might as well think of this as the COM+ state management model. It goes like this:

- Every method takes a special parameter that identifies the state location in the data source.

- Every method begins with code that reads in the state from the data source.

- Every method that has modified that state ends with code that writes the state back to the data source at the end of the method. If the method needs no state, then don't worry about any of this.

That's really about it. Just do those three things (parameter, read, and write), and you can take full advantage of the most important features of COM+.

Let's go back to the banking application I discussed in the previous section, and see how these rules are applied. The transfer component's fromSavingsToChecking method really doesn't have any state. Its purpose in life is just to coordinate two other component instances, the savingsAccount and the checkingAccount. So it doesn't do any state management. Here it is again:

```
fromSavingsToChecking(savingsID, checkingID, amount, error)
{
   error = FALSE;
   savings = createObject("savingsAccount");
   checking = createObject ("checkingAccount");
   savings.withdraw(savingsID, amount);
   checking.deposit(checkingID, amount);
}
```

The savingsAccount does need to work with state, namely that state that represents the savings account. So its code does follow the COM+ state management algorithm:

```
01. withdraw(savingsID, amount)
02. {
03.    dbc = getDatabaseConnection(myUserID, myPassword);
04.    balance = readBalance(dbc, savingsID);
05.    if (amount exceeds balance)
06.    {
07.       releaseDatabaseConnection(dbc);
08.       return error "Inadequate balance to cover withdrawal";
09.    }
10.    updateBalance(dbc, savingsID, balance + amount);
11.    releaseDatabaseConnection(dbc);
12. }
```

In line 1, we see the database ID passed in as a parameter (savingsID). In line 4, we read the necessary state. In line 10 we write it back out. And we are done. In Chapter 4, I discussed the importance of statelessness for instance management, and the relationship between instance management and scalability. In the next chapter, I'll show you how all this works within the context of COM+.

I should repeat here a point I made in Chapter 4. There is nothing about COM+ (or any other COMWare platforms) that requires that you move the state out of the instances. It's just that if you don't do so, you won't be able to take advantage of much of what COM+ has to offer.

Security

There is one final area to discuss that really does span both this and the next chapter. This is security. The reason it spans both chapters is that there are really two aspects to security. One is horizontal, the other is vertical. I'll explain both of these in a moment, but both build on the general idea that security in a COMWare environment must move from the database into the middle tier, an idea I first introduced in Chapter 3 and then expanded on in Chapter 4.

From the discussion of state management, you know that any important data is not in an instance, but in a transactional data source. Most likely, this data source is a traditional database. Since there is no important data in the instance itself, it follows that protecting this data is not a major issue. However the data in the data source is another issue. This data we care a lot about.

Most traditional data sources, especially in the commerce world, can be thought of as collections of similar things. In a relational database, we have collections of rows, each of which has the same columns. In a company personnel system, for example, we may have thousands of rows of employee information. Each employee row, or record, has, say, a unique employee ID, a salary, and a manager ID. It probably has a lot more information, but we will keep it simple. We may have similar collections of departments, employee evaluations, employee benefits, health records, and so on.

When I talk about *vertical security*, I mean the ability to restrict access to certain collections or information within collections. So, for example, I might consider an employee's health information extremely confidential, and limit the ability to look at it to only certain people in the human resources organization. I call this vertical security because it is based on a vertical subset of information in the database, namely columns if we are dealing with a relational database. Only human resource folks can look at those columns that make up health information.

When I talk about *horizontal security*, I mean the ability to restrict access to certain records within the system. For a relational database, records would equate to rows. So, for example, I might allow a manager, say Mary, to look at only employee information for employees that report to her. I call this horizontal security because it is based on a horizontal subset of information in the database, namely records. Mary can look at only those rows that show her employee ID as the manager ID.

If we only care about data in the data tier, why do we want to do security in the component tier? This was the discussion of Chapters 3 and 4, which I will briefly review here. In any kind of a three-tier environment, scalability depends largely on the ability to multiplex database connections. The reason we need to multiplex these connections is that they are in limited supply.

Traditionally, security is considered a problem for the database to manage. Databases have tons of code that is involved with saying exactly who is allowed to access what data under what circumstances, and then enforcing those constraints. Though this works well in a two-tier environment, it doesn't work well in a three-tier environment. The database can manage security only if it knows who is trying to access what information. It determines who the user is at the time the database connection is created. Putting security in the database, therefore, requires that the database connection contain information on the individual user who owns that connection.

In order to scale, we must multiplex our scarce database connections one way or the other. In order to multiplex, we must make the connections uniform. But if they are uniform, they can't contain user-specific information. And if they don't contain user-specific information, we can't put security in the database. So we get to choose: scalability or security in the database. Scalability wins, so we need another way to deal with security.

Even though we don't really care about the data in the component instances, we still do our security at the component level. By protecting our middle tier, we indirectly protect our data tier. In a Web-based commerce system, users have no way to get to the database except through the component tier, so if we restrict what they can do with middle-tier components, we effectively restrict what they can do with the database.

COM+ gives us the ability to administratively restrict which users are allowed to use which components. This restriction can be either at the method, interface, or component level. These types of restrictions are best thought of as vertical security. By restricting a particular user to a particular method, you restrict the columns that that user can access to the columns used by that method. If only human resource employees can access the showMedicalHistory method, and that method is the only one that provides access to medical information, then effectively you have allowed only human resource employees to access the underlying columns with employee health information. This security is similar to what was provided by MTS, except that MTS did not provide method level granularity. Since vertical security is really more of a runtime issue, I will discuss it in more depth in the next chapter.

COM+ also gives us the ability to restrict which rows a given user can see; in other words, horizontal security. Unlike vertical security, horizontal security cannot be defined administratively. It must be defined programmatically. Therefore the component programmer must write lines of code that, for example, check Mary's employee ID against the manager ID of the employee record. Only if they match will Mary be allowed to look at that record. This is not unlike how databases provide horizontal security, except that in the database world, this code is placed in the database, not in the business logic.

To write the code that does horizontal security, you need to know the user ID that invoked this particular method. And if this method was invoked by another component instance, you need to know the user ID that invoked the method on that instance that invoked this particular method. In other words, you need to be able to follow the calling chain back to the original client.

COM+ makes all of this information available to you. How it keeps this information is more of a runtime issue, so I will discuss it in the next chapter. But it is important to understand the difference between horizontal and vertical security, and that if you want horizontal security, you need to program it yourself at the component level. Fortunately, COM+ gives you all the tools you need to make this work.

Microsoft Terminology

Microsoft often uses confusing terminology to describe its component systems. I thought I better give you a quick look at some of the terms you are likely to run across, and how they relate to terms I use.

Microsoft often uses the term *component* as a synonym for the DLL that implements the component. That DLL contains not only the component implementation, but the type library, information on how that component should be configured, and class factories all packaged together. When you see the term *component* in Microsoft literature, it often refers to the binary package that contains all of these things.

Microsoft often uses the term *COM+ class*, or sometimes *COM class*, or sometimes *coclass*, to describe what I call a component. I find this term easily confused with object-oriented classes, and in fact, historically Microsoft, like most of the industry, tended to confuse object technology with component technology. Just to add to this confusion, what I call a *component instance*, Microsoft often calls an *object*.

Microsoft uses the term *COM+ application* to describe a collection of COM+ components (i.e., DLLs, in the Microsoft jargon) that are bundled together. This replaces the *package* concept that was used in MTS. Microsoft often describes three types of COM+ applications. A *server* application is a DLL that will be loaded into a middle-tier component process. This is the type of application on which I focus in this book. A library application is a COM+ DLL that will run in the client process. This type of application is most often used on the client tier, and I won't be discussing library applications. An application *proxy* is a DLL that is also intended to run in a client process, but this is the proxy information needed to marshal information over to the server application. In essence, an *application proxy* is the client view of the *server application*.

As I have already pointed out, the generic idea of *surrogates* is called by Microsoft *proxies* (on the client side) and *stubs* (on the component side). Just to confuse things, Microsoft also uses the term *surrogate*, but to mean something quite different, as I will discuss in the next chapter.

Finally, Microsoft distinguishes between *configured* and *nonconfigured* components. The easiest way to think of a nonconfigured component is that it is an old COM/DCOM/MTS component that hasn't yet been configured to take advantage of all the neat new features of COM+.

Once it gets configured with that new information, it becomes a brand spanking new COM+ *configured* component.

This is the Microsoft terminology as of press time. I wouldn't get too attached to any of it, though, since it has a tendency to evolve.

Guidelines

There may seem to be a lot of information in this chapter, but actually, developing COM+ components is quite easy if you just follow six simple guidelines. Here are my general rules for developing COM+ high transactional throughput commerce components:

Use a COM+ friendly language. Don't worry about performance of the language itself. Any difference in language performance is going to be lost in the general cost of distributed method invocation, COM+ runtime management (which I discuss in the next chapter), and database updates.

Get a reading familiarity with IDL. You may never need to write it yourself, but it helps to understand it.

Use one interface, derived from IDispatch. I don't see any reason for complicating your system with multiple interfaces in a single component.

Make your components stateless. This is required for transactional integrity and instance management (which I discuss in the next chapter).

Make your methods self-contained transactions. This will allow your components to work well with the transactional boundary management provided by COM+.

Do not pass back references to instances. If you need to pass something back, pass back database IDS. This will greatly simplify locking, life cycle, and general component management.

In the next chapter I discuss the other half of the component story, the component runtime environment.

CHAPTER 7

The COM+ Runtime Environment

I'm not sure I would like it. Imagine being buffeted about like so much flotsam. Having no control over your destiny. Never knowing when you will be dragged out of your sleep to fulfill somebody's spur of the moment request. Completely at the beck and call of whatever riffraff gets a hankering to withdraw a few dollars, purchase a few shares of stock, or charge his latest midlife fantasy.

A component's life is the pits. But the absolute worst part of the whole deal, the one thing that would drive me over the edge, is the utter and complete lack of privacy. Anybody who wants to know anything about you—every last detail about childhood, your birthmarks, your needs, your dreams for the future—just has to fire up that dreaded *Microsoft Management Console* (MMC), and everything about you is laid bare for the world to gawk at!

Human beings have quite a different perspective on MMC. For us, it is the Gates to Oz. It is our first look into this land of happy components, where everybody does what they are told, walks in straight lines, and has these utterly charming beatific smiles on their faces as they quickly hop from one task to another.

MMC is our window into the dreamy land of the COM+ runtime environment. It is how we introduce components into COM+, define our components' characteristics, create homes for these components, tell them who their friends will be, tell them who their friends will not be, watch them run their busy lives, help them adjust to the demands of their environment, and tell them how to coordinate their activity with their neighbors.

The COM+ runtime environment is the heart of COM+. It is the foundation of the COM+ Component-Oriented MiddleWare (COMWare) architecture. It is the intermediary between COM+ clients and component instances. For COM+, it is the world of the middle tier.

COM+

As you know by now, COM+ is a COMWare technology. It supports high transactional throughput component development that can be scaled to Web proportions. It supports a distributed architecture in which a client lives in one process (called the *client process*) and a component instance lives in another process (called the *component process*). Usually these two processes are on entirely different machines.

As I discussed in several chapters, clients and instances do not talk directly to each other. They talk through surrogates. The client process has a surrogate for the actual instance, called a *proxy* in the COM+ world. The component process has a surrogate for the client, called a *stub* in the COM+ world. These surrogates know how to communicate and send information back and forth, as I described in Chapter 6, "COM+ Components."

I am somewhat at odds with the Microsoft terminology. Microsoft uses the word *surrogate* to describe an entirely different concept. In the context of COM+, Microsoft usually uses the word *surrogate* to describe what I call the *component process*, the executable in which the instance lives. Using the word *surrogate* to describe the component process is misleading. *Surrogate* is defined as "one that takes the place of another." We can often recognize surrogates by a characteristic one-to-one relationship between a specific surrogate and that which it replaces.

The component process in no way takes the place of the client, the client process, or anything else that I can imagine. It is an entirely different process with an entirely different purpose. It is the milieu in which the component instance runs. It is the environment that defines how the instance interacts. It is an instance's home, a home shared with many other instances being used by a great many other clients. There is nothing even remotely close to a one-to-one relationship between anything on the client tier and the component process. If there were, we would be in serious trouble, because such an architecture would never scale.

Using the term *surrogate* to describe proxies and stubs, on the other hand, is entirely logical. In the client process, the proxy is obviously a surrogate for the component instance. There is, at least conceptually, one proxy for every component instance (we will see soon that this is an illusion, but an important illusion). The client talks to the proxy thinking it is talking to the instance. In the component process, the stub is obviously a surrogate for the client. Here, too, there is a one-to-one relationship; one stub for every client. The instance takes requests from the stub entirely convinced that it is taking requests from a client.

Microsoft Management Console (MMC)

Since MMC is your view into the COM+ runtime, it is probably a good place to start your tour. Once you have created your components (as described in Chapter 6) you are ready to introduce them into the COM+ runtime. And MMC is how you do this.

What is MMC? MMC is Microsoft's integrated administrative tool that lets you administer many of the services of your computer. Each service that is to be administered through MMC has an associated "snap-in" that allows it to share the look and feel and overall organization with the rest of the services that are administered with MMC. Overall, MMC has an explorer-like interface in which each of the managed services can be expanded to make its administrative facilities available. One of these services is the *COM+ runtime environment* that is administered with a snap-in called the *Component Services*. In Figure 7.1, you can see the MMC running with the Component Services expanded, ready for COM+ administration tasks.

From the perspective of COM+, there are four categories of administrative functions we carry out through MMC:

- Introduce COM+ components into the COM+ runtime environment.
- Define component runtime characteristics.
- Create component packages that can be installed in other client or COM+ environments on other machines, a topic I will discuss in the next chapter.
- Monitor those components as they go through their paces.

Let me take you through these.

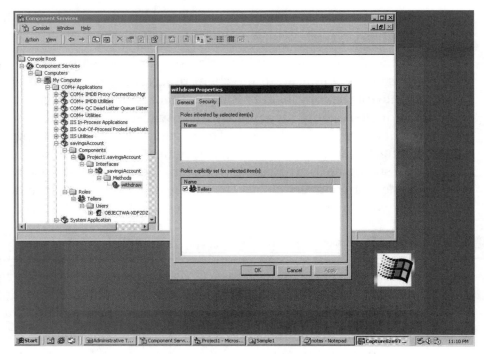

Figure 7.1 Microsoft Management Console with Component Services administration.

Introducing Components to the COM+ Environment

The introduction of a COM+ component to the COM+ environment is done through the creation of what Microsoft now calls an *application,* and what MTS called a *package.* An application is a funny name to describe what is really nothing more than a collection of components that will run together inside a single component process, but it is no worse than calling it a package.

When we use MMC to create a new COM+ application, we are really defining a new collection of components that will run together. You create a new COM+ application, or collection of components that will run in a single component process, by expanding the MMC COM+ Applications tab and right-clicking, which gives you the option to create a new COM+ application. About the only major intellectual exercise you need to undergo is deciding on the name of your new application, or collection, and the process identity under which it will run.

Once we define the application, we can introduce COM+ components into it. We are, in effect, telling the COM+ environment, "You know that collection that includes customers and savingsAccount components? Well, I have one more component that I would like you to run in the same process as those do. Here it is, it is the checkingAccount over here."

As I discussed in the last chapter, components typically are created and saved in the form of DLLs that includes type library information. It is these DLLs that are added to a given COM+ application. As each DLL is introduced to one of the COM+ applications, the administrative database is updated to include that component's class information and DLL location, and the application to which it has been added.

Administering Component Runtime Characteristics

The second administrative function of MMC is to allow application administrators to define component runtime characteristics. It is these runtime characteristics that intellectually distinguish Microsoft's COM+ from its pre-COMWare (i.e., pre-MTS) technology. The goal of COMWare is to simplify programmers' lives by allowing them to focus on business problems rather than environmental problems. It eliminates the need to use baroque APIs to design serious multitier applications. You administratively let the component runtime environment know what needs to be done, and it does it. No API. No nothing. So the administration of component runtime characteristics is critical, and we can learn a lot about what the environment will do for us by seeing what characteristics MMC allows us to define.

MMC allows us to define runtime characteristics at levels of granularity ranging from the coarsest (component collection, or "application") to the finest (the method). The most important runtime characteristics you can administer are these:

- Security
- Transactions
- Threads (administered indirectly) and Concurrency
- Instance Management

I will discuss each of these in the next sections. There are a few other areas you administer in MMC not on this list, such as queued components and events that are generally considered to be services. I discuss these in Chapter 8, "The COM+ Services."

Security Administration

At the COM+ application (component process) level, the main thing we worry about is security. In most operating systems, a process is a basic unit of trust. We trust the other things running in this process, within reasonable constraints. Since all components in a given application will be running, by definition, inside a single process, the COM+ runtime worries about protecting components inside the process from the nasty world outside the process, and trusts other components running inside that same process.

The first administrative security decision is to enable security. This tells the COM+ runtime environment to include security information, along with the rest of the environmental issues it tracks. I'll discuss how this works later in this chapter when I explain how the environment context works.

After the security is enabled, we can set the authentication level. Authentication uses the underlying security of the operating system to make sure that method requests are really coming from whom you think they are coming. MMC allows you to define how paranoid your process will be about requests coming in from the outside world. Keep in mind that there is a tradeoff between paranoia and performance. Configuring your process to be more paranoid than necessary will cost you performance. Configuring it to be not paranoid enough will open up security holes. So the rule of thumb is to be as paranoid as you must be, but no more.

Your possible authentication levels range from *None* to *Packet Privacy*. At the lowest level, you can probably figure out what *None* means. It is the COM+ equivalent to "Don't worry. Be happy." The next level is *Connect*, which means the COM+ environment will verify that the client is authorized to make requests into this process only when the connection is first established. Next is *Call*, which upgrades the client authorization check to every single method request. Next is *Packet*, which is the default for COM+ middle-tier applications, and means that COM+ will authenticate the client and verify that all parameters were passed for each method request. Next up the paranoid scale is *Packet Integrity*, which not only authenticates the client credentials with each method request, but makes sure no dastardly person has modified the parameters (or anything else) since the request left the client. And finally, for those that are 100 percent fully and certifiably paranoid, there is *Packet Privacy*. At this level, COM+ not only authenticates the client with every method invocation, but encrypts the method, parameters, and client identity so that even if somebody does intercept the information, they will have no idea what it says. That's a lot of security you can build into your system without using a single API.

Now, turning the component process into a raging paranoid isn't much good if you can't tell the runtime environment exactly who is allowed to access a given component. We could configure every single user of the system and tell COM+ exactly what Darlene, Carla, Charlie, Corinne, Carl, Cathy, Caitlin, and Christine are each allowed to do in meticulous detail, but this would be painful to administer. So MMC allows us to create *roles*, such as CustomerServiceRepresentatives, and assign individuals to one or more roles. When we specify who is allowed to do what with our component, we do so with roles, not individuals. When Carla gets promoted from CustomerServiceRepresentative to Manager, we don't have to try to figure out every new component to which she now needs access. We just change her role from CustomerServiceRepresentative to Manager, and the system takes care of the rest.

To simplify the administration further, we can assign system groups to roles. This unifies the security of the operating system to the security of the component runtime. This is optional, but for many systems, this will be the way roles will be administered.

Unlike authentication, access rights can be assigned at a much finer level that the component process. We can decide that CustomerServiceRepresentatives can access specific components in the process or specific interfaces in the components, or even specific methods on the interfaces. Method level access is new with COM+; the rest have been available since MTS.

The relationship between levels of paranoia (authentication level), access granularity, and roles is often confusing, so let me try to clarify this.

We classify users by *roles*. A particular role is used to describe all of the users with a common security need. When we assign a role, we are saying, "Here is a new user Michael. Michael is a SystemAdministrator, so anything that SystemAdministrators can do, Michael can do. And by the way, if we ever change what SystemAdministrators can do, automatically make that change for Michael."

We decide how cautious the COM+ runtime environment will be in allowing roles to access components in a particular application through the application's *authentication level*. The higher the authentication level, the more cautious the runtime environment will be. At the lowest level, it says, "Oh, you say you are Michael? Fine. I believe you. Michael is allowed to invoke this method. Go ahead." At the highest level, it says, "Oh, you say you are Michael? You don't look like Michael. Excuse me while I check out your encryption keys."

Access rights are used to define what a user can and can't do. At the coarsest level of granularity, we can tell COM+ to allow particular roles to use anything (or nothing) in the entire COM+ application, including all methods of all interfaces of all components. At the finest level of granularity, we can specify on a method-by-method basis exactly what methods people in a given role are allowed to invoke. We can say, for example, that SystemAdministrators can use only methods in the administration component in the COM+ Bank application.

Authentication level and access rights are related, but independent issues. We can be very paranoid (high authentication level) but still define access rights at a very coarse grain (say, the process) level. This is like saying, "One of Michael's roles is SystemAdministrator. SystemAdministrators can do anything they want in this particular application. I don't believe you really are Michael, but if you can prove you are, I will let you do anything you want in this application." Or we can be very trusting (low authentication level), but define access rights at a fine grain (say, the method) level. This is like saying, "Michael's only role is AdministrativeAide. AdministrativeAide's can only use one method, the generateDailyReports method of the Reporting interface of the Admin component of the Bank application. You say you are Michael and I trust you. So go ahead and invoke generateDailyReports method."

There are two other security-related characteristics we set at the component process level with MMC. One is the principal (combination of user name and password) of the process that will run this particular collection of components. The second characteristic is to administer *impersonation*.

Impersonation is the component process's ability to take on the identity of the client. Let's say you have configured the component process of the

Bank application to run as "Sam." Using client impersonation you can arrange to have the process temporarily take on the principal of its client, say "Natalie," while processing her method requests. The only reason you might want to do this is to allow a paranoid database to check the access rights of a client (Natalie) that is accessing that database indirectly through the middle-tier component process (Sam), as shown in Figure 7.2. The ability of a component process to impersonate a client is a negotiated right between the component process and the client.

Impersonation is necessary if you are going to design a system in which the database manages the security of the data rather than the COM+ runtime environment. Having the database manage security is not a good idea. As I discussed in Chapter 3, "Transaction Processing Monitors," and Chapter 4, "COMWare," a system in which security is managed by the database is not scalable; it can't share scarce database connections among clients. Security *must* move from the database to the middle tier runtime environment in any system that expects to have a large number of clients.

Once we move security from the database to the middle tier component runtime environment, there is no longer any reason to do client impersonation. Security will then be done either with a combination of role-based security and authentication levels, as I described earlier in this chapter, or with programmatic security, as I will discuss later in this chapter. There is no room for impersonation security in the middle tier. Therefore I will not discuss impersonation further, beyond my recommendation that you not use it.

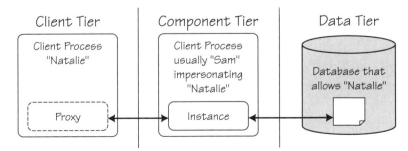

Figure 7.2 Security by impersonation.

Transactions

If your world is commerce, *transactions* are your bread and butter. They are probably your dessert as well. They may well be the air you breathe. I discussed transactions in detail in Chapter 3, transactional boundary management in Chapter 4, the role of the Microsoft Distributed Transaction Coordinator (MS-DTC) in Chapter 5, "COM+ and Friends," and the implications of COM+ transactional boundary management on component implementation in Chapter 6. I'll give just a brief review here.

When we design business systems, we typically have a bunch of business logic that we want treated as a single unit of work. We need to be sure that the entire bunch of logic is done or that none of it is done. This is the basic notion of a transaction that has been provided by database vendors since time immemorial. The transaction as provided by the database vendors has one serious limitation. It works only if all updates within the transaction are going through one single connection to one single database.

Transaction Processing Monitors (TPMs) extended this notion of transaction with the two-phase commit algorithm. This algorithm is oddly named because it is really three phases: a contemplative phase, a consensus phase, and a final phase. The purpose of the two-phase algorithm is to allow updates to multiple databases to be treated as one single unit of work. They all succeed or they all fail. Nobody is left out or everybody is left out.

The two-phase commit algorithm is actually even more flexible than this. It will coordinate not only updates to multiple databases, but updates to multiple database connections in the same database. It even will coordinate updates to nondatabase resources. The only requirement is that the underlying resource must be able to participate in the two-phase commit algorithm as implemented by MS-DTC. Among other things, this means that the resource must know how to carry out a commit and how to carry out a rollback request.

Although MS-DTC can coordinate multiple resources within a single logical transaction, it needs some background information. Specifically, it needs to know when the transaction begins, when the transaction ends, and what should happen when the end point is reached. The beginning and the ending of the transaction are called the *transaction boundaries*. The transaction boundaries define the collection of logic that, taken as a whole, makes up the transaction.

The transaction boundaries trigger MS-DTC phases. The beginning transaction boundary triggers MS-DTC's contemplative phase. The ending transaction boundary triggers MS-DTC's consensus phase and, indirectly, the final phase. In traditional business systems, the demarcation of transaction boundaries is the responsibility of the business logic. The beginning of the transaction is demarcated with a beginTransaction request. The end of the transaction is demarcated with a commit or a rollback request.

The code used for demarcating transactional boundaries has two problems in the component world:

- It breaks encapsulation; it requires intimate knowledge on the part of the client about the implementation of the component.
- It is very fragile; the replacement of one component implementation by another can easily break existing client code.

In NT 4.0, Microsoft's MTS product introduced an innovate solution to the problem of demarcating transactional boundaries in distributed systems. "Don't bother," MTS said. "Just tell me what the transactional needs of the components are, and I will manage the transaction boundaries for you. I will let my good friend MS-DTC know when the transaction starts and ends." The world was very impressed by this idea, and soon every COMWare platform followed MTS's lead.

COM+ uses the same transactional characteristics as did its predecessor, MTS. Transaction characteristics can be set only at the component level. I can configure my component to have any of five transaction characteristics:

- Disabled
- Not Supported
- Supported
- Required
- Requires New

"Disabled" means the component's ability to participate with the COM+ runtime in managing transactional boundaries has been disabled. This is for compatibility with older-than-dirt COM (pre-MTS) components. "Not Supported" means that the component will never participate in transactions. "Supported" means that I don't really care; if a transaction is going, fine, if not, don't bother starting one on my behalf. This will be the most common setting for components that do not themselves use transactional resources such as databases. "Required" means that I am using a transactional resource, and I must have a transaction in place before I can execute my code. This will be the most common setting for components that use transactional resources. "Requires New" means that I want to start a brand new independent transaction, even if my caller already had a transaction in place. This will not often be used.

Although MTS was able to take on the responsibility for starting and ending the transaction, it did not know what should happen when the end of the transaction was reached. MTS has no way of knowing whether a commit or a rollback should be issued. In NT 4.0, the component implementor was responsible for letting MTS know if the transaction should commit or roll back, when the end transaction was finally reached. So if Sally was implementing a checkingAccount component running within MTS, she would use a method called setComplete to let MTS know that, as far as she is concerned, at transaction completion a commit should be issued. If she finds some business error, such as inadequate funds, she uses a different method called setAbort to let MTS know that she wants the transaction to abort upon completion.

In COM+, Sally no longer has to tell the runtime environment that she is happy with the transaction. With COM+, we can configure the component to assume the implementation is happy with the transaction unless it says otherwise by raising an exception. Although this is hardly a revolutionary idea, it does make for slightly simpler code for Sally, and I recommend that you use this feature. To do so, use the MMC to "enable" the auto-done property for each method of a given component. As of press time, this is not available at either the interface or the component level.

Threads and Concurrency

In Chapter 6 I discussed the IUnknown interface supported by all components, and its methods AddRef and Release. Those methods manage the life cycle of component instances. I said these methods were needed mainly because of the problems caused when people pass around references to instances as if they are so many business cards. "Oh, you went to school with my son's best friend? Here, let me give you a proxy to my instance. Sure, make copies and pass them on to your whole family, no problem."

I said people do this as a side effect of the fact that they store state in their component instances. And by now, you know that I think this is a bad idea in large commerce systems because of the heavy toll it takes on scalability. In this section, I'm going to discuss another situation in COM+ that has been made much more complicated than necessary by stateful components. This is *thread management*.

To be fair, I should point out that this is in no way specific to COM+. Thread management, like life cycle, is a general issue for all COMWare platforms, and, in all of these platforms, it is stateful components that ultimately cause the problems. And, of course, it isn't really the components' fault. Instances don't put state in instances. Programmers do. And it certainly isn't COM+'s fault—COM+ is just trying to make the best of a bad situation.

But I'm ahead of myself. Let's start with a simple question. What is a thread? Actually, maybe we should start with something even simpler. What is a process?

A *process* has traditionally been the unit of execution in a computer, at least until threads came on the scene. The process includes a huge glob of virtual memory, some of which is dedicated to holding data and some of which is dedicated to holding instructions. Any instruction inside that glob potentially can refer to any of the memory inside the glob. By default, the instructions process sequentially, at least until they hit branch points.

Computer operating systems take processes very seriously. They do not get the sequence of instructions in one process mixed up with those of another. They protect the virtual memory in one process from the actions of another process. They make sure that processes are associated with principals that can be assigned access rights to specific system resources.

Operating systems can allow multiple processes to run in parallel. When one process has made a request that will take a long time to process, the operating system allows some other process to run for a while. This allows the system resources to be used effectively.

But sometimes this compulsive over-protectiveness of the operating system can get in the way of accomplishing work. For example, if two processes *want* to share information, they must go through a relatively expensive interprocesses communications system to do so. If two processes both want to access a database, the operating system will require them both to obtain their own expensive database connections.

We often find that we would like to get the benefits of multiple processes (parallelism) without its high cost (separation of work into processes). A *thread* is a compromise between these two. A thread is a sequence of instructions that can execute in parallel with other sequences of instructions in the same process. All of the process resources are potentially available to all threads in that process. If, for example, a process has a database connection, any thread in the process potentially can use that database connection. Any thread in the process can update any of the process's virtual memory. Any thread in the process can use system resources under the general security constraints of the process of a whole.

A component process is an excellent example of a process that needs threads. Imagine a component process that does not use threads. By definition, that process can run only one sequence of instructions at a time, even if those instructions are dribbling in at a very slow rate. If two clients both have proxies to a Customer instance, those two instances have to live in two different processes. Otherwise one of the clients will be blocked until the other client has finished using its instance. This means every client needs a dedicated process for every proxy. This is unbelievably expensive, and will greatly limit the number of clients a given machine can support.

We can make this work much more efficiently if we use threads. With threads, instead of blocking one client until the other is completely finished, we simply kick off a new thread for each new method request. You can see this in Figure 7.3.

Generally, the only thing that makes thread programming complicated is the possibility of thread conflicts; for example, if one thread is trying to read a location in virtual memory while another thread is updating that same location. Or two threads are both trying to update a database using the same database connection at the same time.

The beauty of our component process is that it is protected automatically against thread conflicts, assuming that each instance is well behaved, meaning that it modifies only its own state. On the client side, a proxy can be hooked up only to one instance and, because method invocations are synchronous, cannot possibly invoke a second method request until the first has completed.

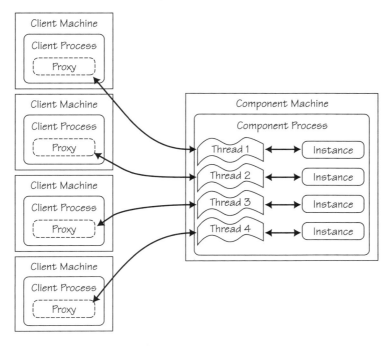

Figure 7.3   Threads and instances.

Threads are kicked off in response to method invocations. Looking again at Figure 7.3, it is possible that thread one will be modifying the first instance's state at the same time thread two is modifying the second instance's state. But that doesn't create a thread conflict. A thread conflict arises only when two threads try to work with the same instance at the same time. And, since we have only one proxy per instance, we don't need to worry about that. Or do we?

We wouldn't have to worry about this, except for one thing. We *can't* assume that proxies and instances are in a nice, healthy, monogamous one-to-one relationship. Remember, our instances have state. And what's the point of *having* state, if you can't share it with all your friends? And how else do you share state, but to hand out proxies to everybody in your family, and all their friends, and all their friends' friends? Who knows how many proxies exist to a given instance? Nobody knows! So the reality is that the nice simple Figure 7.3 may not be true at all. Reality might be much closer to Figure 7.4. And from the perspective of thread conflict management, Figure 7.4 is a very ugly picture indeed.

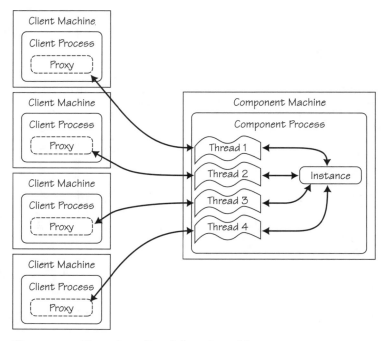

Figure 7.4 The ugly reality of threads and instances.

The reason it is so ugly is that we have no idea how many clients might make requests of a single instance at one time. Let's consider some of the bad things that can happen when two clients make a request of the same stateful instance at the same time.

Let's look at a restaurant reservation system in which one day in the life of a restaurant is represented by a component instance, and people make reservations at the restaurant on that day do so through the use of methods on the component. Our restaurant component supports the following methods:

- *getReservations*, which takes a time and returns an XML string that contains the names of all of the parties and the number in each party with reservations at that time.

- *makeReservation*, which takes a party name and a time, and returns an error if there are no reservations available at that time. To simplify the implementation, I am going to assume the restaurant allows only one party to make a reservation in a given hour.

Assuming we had decided to implement this as a stateful component, we will, by definition, store the information about the reservations in the instance state. We could do this in a 24-element array called *times*, where each element contains an empty flag (if true, it means that a reservation is available at that time) and a party name. This is obviously an overly simplistic reservation system, but I am trying to explore thread, not reservation issues. Our makeReservation code (in pseudocode) is shown in Figure 7.5, with lines numbered for reference.

What happens if we have two clients wanting to make reservations for the same time? They each will get a proxy to the restaurant instance. They each will make a method request at the same time. In the middle tier, the component process will kick off a thread for each method request. But now we have the potential for thread conflict. It is quite possible that both threads will execute lines 3 and 4 at the same time, and that both will therefore conclude that they have made the reservation. In this case, whoever executes line 6 last will win, overwriting the first. Both clients will think they have a reservation, but from the system's perspective, only the last one to execute line 6 will really have a reservation.

You might mistakenly believe that making the component stateless will also make it thread safe. It doesn't. Consider, for example, the stateless implementation of the reservation component shown in Figure 7.6.

If we have two proxies pointing to the same stateless instance, we still can still thread conflicts. For example, if one thread is working on line 6 and 7, and another thread is working on line 4, we are going to have the

```
Reservation::makeReservation(hour, newName, ok)
{
    look at the hour element of the times array in myState;
    if (the empty flag is TRUE) {
        set empty flag to FALSE;
        set the name to newName;
        ok = TRUE;
    }
    else {
      ok = FALSE
    }
    return;
}
```

Figure 7.5 Stateful implementation of makeReservation.

```
Reservation::makeReservation(day, hour, newName, ok)\
{
  dbc = getDatabaseConnection(myUserName, myPassword);
  readFromDatabase(dbc, day, hour, empty);
  if (empty = TRUE) {
    set empty to "FALSE";
    set the name to newName;
    updateDatabase(dbc, day, hour, empty, newName);
    ok = TRUE;
  }
  else {
    ok = FALSE;
  }
  releaseDatabaseConnection(dbc);
  return;
}
```

Figure 7.6   Stateless implementation of makeReservation.

two threads trashing each other's work. In fact, this code is probably even more thread fragile than the stateful implementation, because of the delicate database connections.

In fact, the stateless implementation *is* more thread safe than the stateful implementation—not because the code itself is more thread safe—but because we are highly unlikely to end up with two threads working on the same state in the first place. If there is no state in the instance, we have no reason to have multiple proxies referring to the same instance. And without multiple proxies referring to the same instance, we will not have multiple threads working on the same state. At least, not working on the same state in the instance. We are likely to have multiple instances sharing state in the database, but this sharing can be managed using standard database locking.

I should point out that even a stateless component that scrupulously avoids instance sharing is not necessarily thread safe. There are other issues that can arise. For example, one or more of the underlying language libraries used in the component implementation may not be thread safe. Or the component implementation itself can shoot off some threads (a practice that is strongly discouraged). But there is little COM+, or anybody else, can do to protect in these situations.

Despite my recommendation against sharing instances, COM+ does support this practice. There will be, however, major costs associated with this, so you still shouldn't do it. But let's see how COM+ prevents thread conflicts, when the instances are shared (or when there is a thread conflict for some other reason).

The first thing you must do is request (through MMC) thread protection for your component. To do this, you configure your component as "requiring synchronization." In theory, synchronization should be required only for components that support instance sharing. "Instance sharing" is not a configuration option. In practice, you must configure *all* components as requiring synchronization, since, at least in the current release, COM+ requires synchronization of any component that supports transactions. As I discussed earlier in this chapter, transactional support should be the default assumption for all middle-tier components.

The best way to think of the synchronization system is to imagine that there are a series of locks controlling access to instances. Every instance is controlled by only one lock at a time, but one lock can control multiple instances, as shown in Figure 7.7. When a client, say Carla, makes a request of a proxy, the proxy, always eager to please, attempts to make that same request of the actual middle tier instance on Carla's behalf. Unbeknownst to Carla or her proxy, that request must go through a stub. Remember, the stub is the client surrogate in the component process. Before COM+ will allow that request to be made, it forces Carla's stub to acquire the instance's lock. If the lock is in use by some other client's stub, say Darlene's, then Carla's stub (and Carla) must wait until Darlene's stub (and indirectly, Darlene's instance) has completed its request. When Darlene's request has been completed, COM+ will release her lock and Carla's stub will be allowed to make its

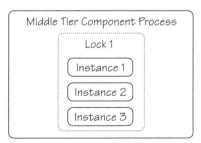

Figure 7.7. Relationship between locks and instances.

request. I am simplifying this discussion by assuming you have followed my advice in Chapter 4, and designed your methods to be self-contained transactions.

If Carla's component instance itself has proxies to other instances, all instances will be controlled by the same lock. Let's say Carla is using the banking transfer component I discussed earlier in this chapter. That component supports a FromSavingsToChecking method. This method was implemented by creating a savingsAccount instance called fromAccount and a checkingAccount instance called toAccount. The program logic then requested a withdrawal from the fromAccount and a deposit into the toAccount. Assuming the transfer, the savingsAccount, and the checkingAccount components were configured as "requiring synchronization," all instances will be placed under control of the same lock. This means that nobody else will be able to use Carla's fromAccount or Carla's toAccount instance until Carla's transfer has completed. Even when Carla's fromAccount has completed the withdrawal method and that instance is no longer needed by Carla, it can't be used by anybody other than Carla. It is controlled by the same lock as the transaction instance, and Carla has not released that lock yet.

In the world of stateless components, client blocking by lower level instances (such as fromAccount) by a lock that is controlled by a higher level instance (such as the transaction instance) is not likely to be a problem. Nobody else will be using those same instances. People other than Carla, say Darlene, may be (and probably will be) using other instances of the transfer, savingsAccount, and checkingAccount components. But as long as Darlene is using her own instances, she doesn't have to worry about Carla's locks. Locks are on an instance basis, not a component basis. As long as Darlene doesn't have a reference to Carla's *particular* instances of transfer, savingsAccount and checkingAccount (and there is no reason for her to do so in a stateless world), Darlene can forget about Carla.

If, for some reason, the implementor of the banking system ignored my advice and created an implementation that shared references to the account instances, as shown in Figure 7.8, then Darlene could have a problem. In this scenario, if she needs to share Carla's transfer instance, she can't get it until Carla is finished. Even if she doesn't share a transfer instance, but shares a lower level checkingAccount instance (per-

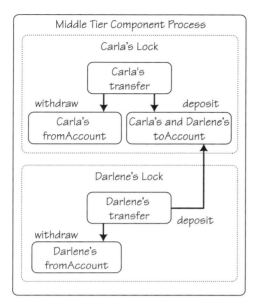

Figure 7.8   Lock blocking by shared instances.

haps because both Carla and Darlene have a joint account), Carla will be blocked until Darlene is finished.

It is possible to allow Carla and Darlene to share a lower level checkingAccount instance and still not block each other unnecessarily. If the account component is configured as "requiring new synchronization" rather than merely "requiring synchronization," then the locking of the checkingAccount will be independent of the locking of the transfer instance, as shown in Figure 7.9. *If* you are sharing lower level instances (which I recommend against), then this is a useful trick to minimize blocking. However, as you can see from Figure 7.9, the locking itself becomes more complicated. Basically you are trading less lock blocking for more complex lock management.

The more locks you have, the more difficult you make COM+'s life. You may be saying to yourself that COM+'s difficulties are its problem, not yours, and to some extent that is true. But if performance suffers because COM+ is spending too much time trying to deal with all the locks you have created, then COM+'s problems can rapidly *become* your problems.

COM+ has a special name for the collection of instances that share a single lock: *activity*. Personally, I find the idea of multiple instances sharing

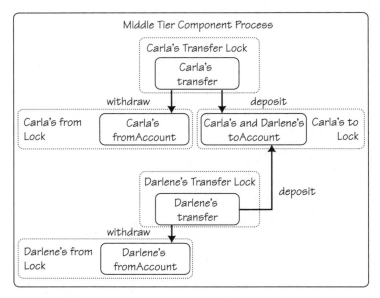

Figure 7.9 Using "Requires New Synchronization."

a lock more intuitive than the idea of multiple instances living together in an activity. But to each his own.

My recommendation is that you use stateless instances, that you do not share instances among proxies, and that you use "Requires Synchronization" rather than "Requires New Synchronization." Keep it simple. Give COM+ a break. But if for some reason you feel compelled to design a component that uses shared instances, then you should probably configure that component to "Requires New Synchronization."

Instance Management

Thread management is the beginning of a scalable middle-tier infrastructure, but it is not enough. It increases by an order of 100 the number of clients supportable with a given middle-tier environment, because it allows multiple clients to share a single component process. If we were required to dedicate a single process to each client, we would be looking at supporting a few dozen clients with a given middle-tier machine. With threads, we can increase this to a few hundred, or to as many threads and other system resources as we have available. But a few hundred is just a drop in the bucket when that bucket is the Web.

To increase this by another order of 100, we need another technique: *instance management*. Instance management algorithms allow us to share threads and system resources among many clients. With instance management algorithms on top of thread management algorithms, we can increase our client support to the tens of thousands.

Instance management won't be the end of our scalability. In the next chapter I talk about load balancing, a COM+ technology that supports clients into the millions. Load balancing is usually classified as a COM+ service, which is why it is discussed in Chapter 8.

Thread management, instance management, and load balancing all can be considered *scalability algorithms*. These are algorithms that allow support for large numbers of clients, one of the key concerns of COMWare. Each of these algorithms builds on the other. Thread management is the foundation for scalability; it allows multiple clients to share a single process. Instance management is dependent on threading; it allows multiple instances (and therefore clients) to share a single thread. Load balancing is dependent on instance management. It allows instance management to be spread out over a large collection of machines. Mathematically, we get a theoretical prediction of the total number of clients we can support with a given system from this equation:

```
C = M x I x T x P
where C = Clients, P = Processes (hosting components) per machine
T = Threads per process, I = Instances per thread,
M = Machines (used for load balancing)
```

If P ranges from 10 to 100, T from 50 to 200, I from 50 to 200, and M from 1 to 16 (all reasonable ranges), you can see that the total number of concurrent clients running on a COM+ application can range from 25,000 ($10 \times 50 \times 50 \times 1$) to 80,000,000 ($100 \times 200 \times 200 \times 20$) depending mainly on work requirements of each client, the machine power, and the number of machines used for load balancing.

I have already discussed instance management algorithms in Chapter 4, "COMWare," so I will just briefly review them here. Instance management algorithms are used to solve the lazy client problem. The lazy client problem states that clients are typically very inefficient in their use of middle-tier instances. Clients often instantiate instances early on and hold onto their instances for long periods of time. During most of that time they are not actually using their instances. Instance management algorithms allow the system to effectively multiplex instances among many clients, so that while an instance is not working for one client, it (or the resources it represents) can work for some other client.

There are two common instance management algorithms:

- Just-In-Time Instantiation (JITI) algorithm
- Instance Pooling (IP) algorithm

The JITI algorithm instantiates middle-tier instances only when a work request is received, and deinstantiates them as soon as the work request is completed. The IP algorithm keeps unused instances in a common process-wide instance pool. When client requests are received, instances are grabbed to service the request. When work is complete, those instances are returned to the pool.

COM+ supports both algorithms, although as of press time, support for IP is limited and untested in actual production. Support for JITI has been available in MTS for years. There are several problems with IP that hopefully will be fixed soon.

One problem with IP is limited language support. Because of underlying threading restrictions, only C and C++ can be used for writing components that support IP, and these languages are by far the most difficult languages to use for COM+ component implementation. I consider C and C++ unsuitable for most commerce developers except for the truly diehard byte brained bug hunters. For business programmers used to working with simple languages like Visual Basic, having to learn C++ in order to work with COM+ will be even more complicated than having to learn Java to use Enterprise JavaBeans (the topic of Chapter 10).

Another problem with IP is the complexity of managing transactions in an IP component. Assume that you have acquired your resources (say, database connections) at the initial instantiation of your instance, the main reason you would use IP in the first place. You must then manually "enlist" the resource into your transaction. This is an unnecessary pain in the neck, and many people will avoid it by waiting until the last possible minute to get the resource. Getting the resource *after* the transaction has already started allows it to be enlisted automatically in the transaction, without having to use any API. However, this defeats the main advantage of the IP algorithm over JITI. Given this and the language restrictions, I recommend that for the near future you stick with JITI. Fortunately, JITI works just fine, is supported by all languages, and has withstood the test of time (having been in use in MTS since 1996).

Regardless of whether you use JITI or IP, you will need to define and implement your component with the needs of instance management algorithms in mind. This means you must make your components stateless, a topic I discussed in Chapter 6. As I pointed out in Chapter 4, stateless programming is a requirement for any COMWare technology, whether you use instance management or not. The COM+ model for statelessness is no better or worse than that of Enterprise Java-Beans, CORBA, or any other COMWare platform.

Microsoft has a funny way of categorizing instance management algorithms. It uses the term *Just-In-Time Activation* (JITA) to describe the last minute association of an instance with a client side proxy/stub, an idea that is common to both JITI and IP. It then uses the term *Object Pooling* to describe the specific algorithm that I call *Instance Pooling* (IP). For hopefully obvious reasons (by now) I think *instance pooling* is a much better term than *object pooling*. As of press time, Microsoft has no term to describe JITI. If you configure your component to use JITA and Instance Pooling (or, as Microsoft calls it, Object Pooling), you get IP. If you configure your component to use JITA but not Instance Pooling, you get JITI. But COM+ does not have a term to describe JITI. Perhaps I should use the term *Just-In-Time Activated But Not Instance Pooled* and the acronym JITABNIP. To me, JITABNIP sounds more like a *Star Wars* creature than a software algorithm.

Of course, you *can* configure your component to use neither JITA nor Instance Pooling. Then you get your basic, unscalable component. But you wouldn't do that, would you?

Managing the Runtime Environment

With all these different configuration options at granularities ranging from the process to the method, you may be getting the idea that the COM+ runtime environment is preparing to do some serious work for you. You would be right. I sometimes find the terminology Microsoft uses to describe its COMWare rather random. But this should not be taken as a lack of respect for the COMWare itself. A good motto for COM+ might be, "With terminology like this, the technology has *got* to be good!"

Before we look at the component runtime, let's briefly review some basic COM+ component concepts. In most of my pictures of components I show client-side proxies hooked up directly to middle-tier instances. But this is a simplification in that it ignores the component process stub. The stub serves as the client surrogate in the component process. A more realistic view of the component architecture is shown in Figure 7.10.

If you are using Just-In-Time Instantiation (JITI), which I assume you are, then Figure 7.10 gets a little more complicated. It now has two versions: one after the client has instantiated its "instance," but in between method invocations. Assuming that the method is a self-contained transaction boundary, it is only during the method request that the actual instance exists. This, of course, is the whole point of JITI. The difference between an instance that is waiting for a method invocation and one that is processing a method invocation is shown in Figure 7.11.

A client, say Darlene, may think that she is instantiating a middle-tier instance. But what she really is instantiating is a proxy (in her process space) and a stub (in the component process space). Only when she actually makes a method invocation does an instance actually get associated with that stub. Microsoft calls the association of an instance and a stub *activation*. There are two ways of activating an instance. If you are using the JITI algorithm, you first create the instance and then associate it with the stub. If you are using the IP algorithm, you first grab an instance from the pool and then associate it with the stub. Either way,

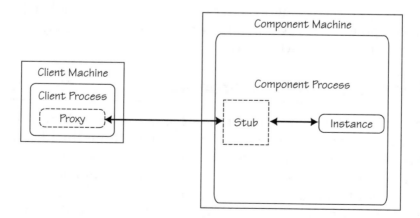

Figure 7.10   COM+ components with stubs.

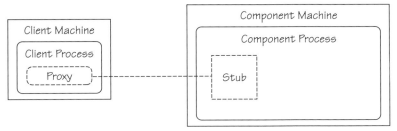

After instantiation, in between method invocation

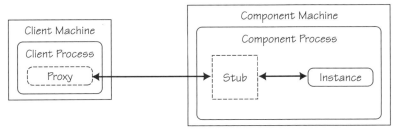

During method invocation

Figure 7.11 COM+ JITI with stubs.

when activation is complete, you have an instance hanging off the stub in the component process.

This stub architecture is used even when one instance instantiates another instance. Take, for example, the banking transfer operation I described earlier. In this scenario, we have an instance of a transfer component instantiating a savingsAccount instance for the withdrawal and a checkingAccount instance for the deposit. If Carla instantiated the original transfer instance, and all three components are configured to live in the same component process (or, in COM+ lingo, live in the same COM+ application) then the whole blown-out stub architecture will look as shown in Figure 7.12. Notice that this figure is shown with instances waiting for the next method invocation.

Let me walk you through Figure 7.12. In this discussion I'm going to assume that all of the components are stateless, that we are using the JITI instance management algorithm, and that transfer was configured as requiring a transaction.

To start, Carla has invoked FromSavingsToChecking on her transfer instance. The implementation of this method instantiates a savings-

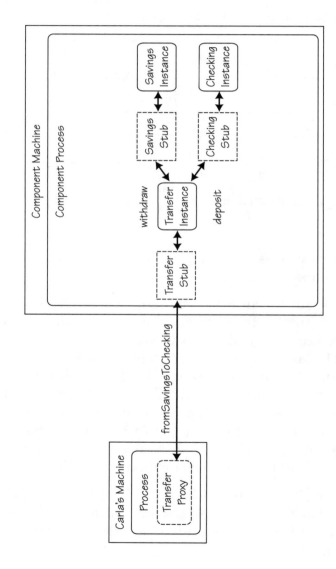

Figure 7.12 Stub architecture of a transfer component.

Account and a checkingAccount instance. They are returned to the transfer instance. But what is returned is not literally a pointer to the instance; it is a pointer to the proxy (in the client process) that is referencing a stub (in the component process). In COM+, we never return pointers to instances. Whenever you want to get to an instance you must first go through the stub and to get to the stub you must first go through the proxy. The *only* thing that can invoke a method on an instance is the stub for that instance. Everything else must make requests through the proxy/stub.

Keep in mind that stubs may or may not be connected to actual instances. If we are using JITI, the stub is connected to the instance only when a method is invoked, and only for as long as the transaction containing that method is active. If the component has been well designed, the transaction will end when the method ends.

There are cases where the proxy may or may not be necessary. The proxy, remember, is the component instance surrogate living in the client process. If the client and instance are in the same process (as may be the case when one instance is a client of another instance), the proxy may not be necessary. How do we know if a savingsAccount proxy will be returned or a direct pointer to the stub? COM+ will do whatever is most efficient. If it can return a direct pointer to the stub, it will do so. If it can't, it won't.

So how does COM+ know if it can return a direct pointer to the stub or if it needs to return a proxy? A proxy is needed if there is any significant difference in the runtime environment defined for the transfer component and the savingsAccount component. If there *is* any significant difference between the two environments, a proxy will be required to make sure that the proper mediation occurs between the two environments.

Let me give you an example of significantly different component environments. Suppose the savingsAccount was configured to require a new transaction. In this case we know that the savingsAccount instance is going to do its work in a different transaction than the transfer instance. That is the meaning of requiring a new transaction. Working in one transaction is significantly different than working in another transaction. Somebody is going to need to start up the new transaction as we move from one instance to the other. So if the savingsAccount requires a new transaction, we know that some type of proxy will be returned to the transfer instance, a proxy that will somehow ensure that the new transaction is started before entering the savingsAccount instance.

Here is another example. Suppose the savingsAccount was configured to require synchronization, and the transfer instance was not so configured. Now, the savingsAccount would have been happy to use the synchronization lock of the transfer, if the transfer instance had a synchronization lock. But it didn't, because it wasn't configured to require synchronization. When we move from the transfer instance to the savingsAccount instance, somebody is going to need to acquire a new lock. So, some type of proxy is going to be returned to the transfer instance, a proxy that will somehow ensure that a new lock is acquired before entering the savingsAccount instance.

Let's look at one more example. Suppose that the transfer component was configured to require a transaction and the savingsAccount was configured to merely support transactions. This seems different, but it really isn't. The savingsAccount is willing to live with a transaction, transfer has a transaction, so as long as savingsAccount is happy with that, we don't need an environment adjustment and therefore we don't need a proxy returned. At least, we don't need a proxy returned for the sake of transactions; there may be some other environmental incompatibility between the two.

And finally, the most obvious example: Suppose that the transfer component and the savingsAccount component are transaction compatible and synchronization compatible, and everything else compatible, but they just happen to run in two different component processes (i.e., were configured to live in different COM+ applications). Running in different processes is a major difference in environments, so a proxy is returned. This is the reason why a client in one process instantiating a component instance in another process *always* gets a pointer to a proxy, and *never* gets a direct reference to a stub, regardless of how similar their environments might otherwise be. Crossing a process boundary always needs major environmental readjustment.

Not all proxies are equal. If we are starting up a new transaction, COM+ might be able to get by with a lightweight proxy. If we are crossing a thread boundary, COM+ might need a heavier weight proxy. If we are crossing a process boundary, then we need an even heavier weight proxy. And the most extreme proxy is needed when we are going from one machine to another.

How does COM+ figure out if the environments are different? I believe that we are now getting into more detail than we need for the purposes of this book, but let me give a quick explanation for those that may be interested. Feel free to skip past this next section.

The information about a given proxy's environmental requirements (and therefore the environmental requirements of the JITI instance, once it gets activated) are stored in a special object (and I think *object* really is the appropriate term here) called a *context*. Each context object represents a particular environment configuration. Every stub is associated with one and only one context, the specific context that represents its particular environmental requirements. There are no duplicate context objects. If two stubs have exactly the same environmental requirements, then they are both associated with exactly the same context object. This is shown in Figure 7.13.

The association between a stub and a context occurs at the time the stub is instantiated and does not change until the stub is deinstantiated. When the stub is instantiated, the COM+ runtime figures out the environmental requirements from the configuration database. If the runtime can find an existing context object that represents those environmental requirements, it associates this stub with that context. If the runtime can't find an appropriate existing context object, it creates a new one, and then associates this stub with the new context.

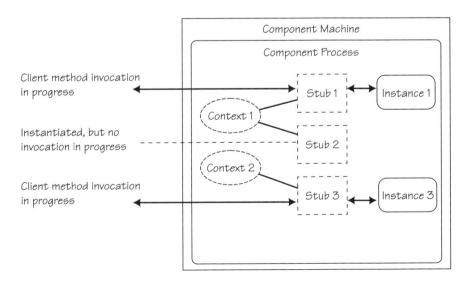

Figure 7.13   Stubs with the same environmental requirements.

If one component invokes a method on another, it may or may not be going through a proxy, as I described earlier. If it is going through a proxy, then we must be invoking from one instance associated with one context to another instance associated with another context. If the two instances were associated with the same context, then the environments would be identical, and we wouldn't need a proxy in the first place. If the invocation is going through a proxy, then the proxy can use the information in the invoker's context and the invokee's context to determine how the environment should be adjusted. The process by which the environment is adjusted is called *interception*.

Object Context

The environmental context objects discussed in the last section are expensive, but they are shared among a large number of clients (and therefore stubs) and are only created at the time of instantiation. There is another type of context that is associated with a particular method invocation rather than a number of stubs, called the *object context*.

The object context contains information related to this specific instance, and the method invocation to which it responds. In particular, these three pieces of important information are likely stored here:

- The specific ID of the transaction associated with this method invocation

- The specific ID of the synchronization associated with this method invocation

- The specific information about the caller of this method (if security has been configured to allow this)

The first two of these will be stored in the form of a GUID. GUIDs are discussed in Chapter 6.

Useful APIs

I don't think it is helpful here to give a long list of COM+ APIs. Most will never be used and should you need them, you can easily read the COM+ API documentation. However I will at least make you aware of the most important APIs available.

If you are implementing a component, and you need to access your instance's context, you can do so with a COM+ provided function GetObjectContext. Once you have the object context, you can use the IObjectContext methods, probably the most useful one of which is is-InTransaction, which can tell you whether or not you are currently in a transaction.

For programmatic security, you will want to use GetSecurityCallContext to get an instance of the SecurityCallContextObject, which can help you find out the process ID that invoked this method, and every other method right back to the original client.

If you use Instance Pooling (IP) as your instance management algorithm, you will need to work with an interface called IObjectControl (not to be confused with IObjectContext). One of the requirements of a transactional component that supports instance pooling, at least as of press time, is that the component support the IObjectControl interface. Since there is no logical reason why this should be so, I wouldn't be surprised if this requirement goes away, but let me briefly take you through them, just in case this requirement sticks around.

IObjectControl supports three methods:

- Activate
- Deactivate
- CanBePooled

None of them take any parameters, and only CanBePooled is expected to return a value (a Boolean). Activate and Deactivate are completely unarchitected. You can do anything you want with these methods. The COM+ runtime guarantees to call them on your instance at specific times, in case you want to get involved in the activation/deactivation cycle of your instance.

The COM+ runtime invokes Activate on an instance immediately after the instance is associated with a stub and a context, as I discussed in the instance management section. For an IP component, this would be after the COM+ runtime finds an instance not doing anything in the pool and attaches it to a stub/context. For a JITI component, this would be after the COM+ runtime instantiates a new instance and attaches it to a stub/context. If you have an opinion on what should happen next, Activate is where you get to express that opinion.

Deactivate is the mirror image of Activate. The COM+ runtime invokes Deactivate on an instance just before it pries it loose from the grip of the stub/context. Deactivate is the signal to the IP instance that it is about to be returned to the pool from whence it came. For the JITI instance, Deactivate is when it gets to state its last words before being sent on to the great bit bucket in the sky.

You might think that Activate would be a good time to read in state from the database, and that Deactivate would be a good time to write it back out. And you would be right, except for one thing. There is no way to pass in a database ID to Activate, which takes no parameters. So there is no way you can read instance-specific state from the database in that method.

There was a time when I advocated for a change in the component architecture to allow a database ID to be associated with the client side proxy and then automatically passed into the Activate method through a parameter. This would allow the read code that now must live in the business logic to move to the Activate method and would give COM+ a persistence model very similar to the entity bean model of EJB, a topic I will discuss in Chapter 10.

I have since come to believe that the EJB entity bean model is flawed. Associating a database ID with a proxy is a bad idea for two reasons:

- It makes the cost of proxy creation too expensive because of the transactional database access needed to ensure the validity of the database ID.

- It makes the client code dependent on maintaining that proxy.

In the long term, I see client side proxies going away in favor of an XML-based method invocation system. In these future systems, clients will invoke methods by creating XML strings that contain the component name, method name, and parameters, and then just passing them through to a generic invoke procedure. This will be very efficient on the client side and will make the client code independent of the actual COMWare technology in the middle tier. None of this will be possible if the client must depend on the proxy to maintain a database ID.

Not to get too far off track, but this is not an argument against EJB, only against entity beans. The session beans, which are very close to the COM+ component model are still a good idea. Given this discussion, I see little value in the Activate and Deactivate methods, but perhaps you will find something to do with them. In any case, you must support them, even if you do the obvious implementations of these two methods, which is to do nothing.

The third method in the IObjectControl interface is the strangest of all. It is CanBePooled. This method is invoked on the instance just before it is returned to the pool, to see if being returned to the pool is acceptable to the instance. If the instance returns TRUE, back to the pool it goes. Not that it has much of an alternative. If the instance returns FALSE, it will be sent to the bit bucket. Why an instance would prefer the bit bucket to the instance pool is beyond me. Maybe this is one of those "Give me liberty or give me death" things.

You will find other APIs scattered throughout the COM+ documentation. But keep in mind an important point. With COMWare products, we don't measure success by the size of the API. We measure success by how infrequently we must use that API. For COMWare APIs, size does matter. In this case, the smaller, the better.

Monitoring

The MMC monitor function allows us to pry into the private lives of component instances. Figure 7.14 shows MMC ready to monitor client usage of a savingsAccount component. As new clients come up and instantiate proxies/stub combinations, we can monitor the system usage through each of the columns shown on the right-hand side of the monitor. This information is very useful for understanding where we may have throughput problems. These columns are as follows:

Prog ID. The official human interpretable name of this component. If there are multiple components in this application, one will be shown per line.

Objects. The number of clients with active proxies to instances of this component.

Activated. The number of instances currently attached to client stubs.

Pooled. The number of instances available in the pool.

In Call. The number of instances currently processing method invocations. This will be some number equal to or less than the number that are activated, since only activated instances can process a call.

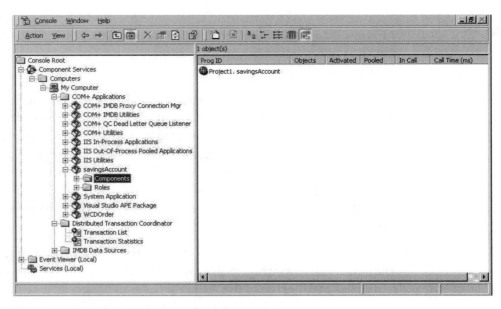

Figure 7.14 Using MMC to monitor components.

Call Time. The average time needed by an instance to process a method invocation.

There are a few things you might look out for here.

You should have as many "objects" as possible. This shows how many clients you have right now pumping money into your corporate coffers. On the other hand, you don't want your "call time" to be very high, or many of your clients may spend most of their time waiting for something to happen (and getting annoyed in the process).

The number "activated" should be about equal to the number "in call." Only "in call" instances are doing work. If the number "activated" is much larger than the number "in call," then you have a lot of middle-tier instances tied up by clients that are not actually doing any work. This is an early indication of a poorly designed system that will not scale well as more and more clients come online.

MMC has other monitoring screens as well, but I have found this particular screen to be one of the most useful.

The COM+ runtime environment is where you live your life, if you are a component instance. The environment determines when you live, when you die, and for whom you will be working in between. It provides your protection from the elements. It defines your transactions. And MMC is how you are administered.

In the last chapter I discussed the COM+ component model. In this chapter I discussed the COM+ runtime environment, the most important part of the COMWare architecture. In the next chapter we are ready to start looking at some of the COM+ services.

The COM+ Services

We already have spent a great deal of time looking at COM+. In Chapter 5, "COM+ and Friends," I discussed some of the helper technologies to COM+, primarily MS-DTC and MSMQ. In Chapter 6, "COM+ Components," I explored the basic COM+ component model, and in Chapter 7, "The COM+ Runtime Environment," I talked about the COM+ component runtime environment.

Very little of the material discussed up until this point is new for Windows 2000 COM+. Most of this material is similar to what was provided in NT 4.0 with COM, DCOM, and MTS. A few additions were made to the API, a lot of functionality was repackaged, and much of the underlying runtime environment was re-implemented to better align the component model and the component runtime environment. But none of these changes had a significant impact on component implementors or even system administrators.

In this chapter, we enter newer territory. COM+ has several new capabilities added over and above what was available in the collection of COM, DCOM, and MTS. Microsoft lumps these new capabilities together under the general category of *COM+ services*. The COM+ services address some important issues faced by implementors of large distributed commerce systems.

Although Microsoft is not entirely consistent about what is considered the COM+ runtime environment and what is considered the COM+ services, it usually describes the following four capabilities as COM+ services:

Queued components. Queued components is a funny name for what I call *asynchronous components*. Asynchronous components allow method invocations to be stored and processed at future times. For example, an online store might configure its Shipping component to be asynchronous so Shipping instances can process orders at night, when system load is much lower.

Events. Events allow component instances to respond to events initiated by other instances. For example, an online store might have its Ordering component trigger a security alert if the cost of any one order exceeds some specified amount. Special security components can be waiting for that event to check for possible fraud.

Component load balancing. Component load balancing allows component workload to be distributed among a large number of machines. For example, an online store could have its Ordering component configured to be dynamically load balanced over three machines, so that the system can take orders at rates beyond what any one machine could process. Component load balancing was part of COM+ until shortly before the scheduled release, but has now been removed from the standard COM+ version. Microsoft plans to incorporate this into a new product tentatively being referred to as Application Server. However, since I expect that COM+ Component load balancing will be available in one form or another, I will discuss the general concept in this chapter.

In-Memory Database. The In-Memory Database (IMDB) provides a shared per-machine memory region that can be used to share information among component instances running on that machine. For example, an online store's retail application could store a catalog of the items and prices it sells in the IMDB. The IMDB was part of COM+, but was removed at the same time as component load balancing. Like component load balancing, I expect some of its functionality to reappear in some future product so I will give a general discussion here and speculate about where we could see its functionality in the future.

Let's go through each of these, starting with the two services that, as of press time, are still scheduled to make up the COM+ services.

Asynchronous/Queued Components

Queued components are one of the bright stars in the COM+ constellation. Queued components represent probably the best attempt of any of the COMWare technologies to bring together message queuing and methods. Queued components will almost certainly become the standard against which future asynchronous technologies will be measured, much like MTS was the standard for its generation of COMWare.

In Chapter 5, I discussed the Microsoft Message Queue Server (MSMQ). Back in NT 4.0, MSMQ was the only technology available for asynchronous communications between component instances. If a banking component wanted to make an asynchronous request to an auditing component, MSMQ was the technology to use.

In Chapter 5, I described several capabilities of MSMQ. MSMQ allows the requestor and the requestee to be working at different times. MSMQ allows work to be done on disconnected machines, like Baby, who can happily process away at Starbucks and save up requests until we next return home and get around to plugging into the network. And MSMQ, because it works within the two-phase commit framework of MS-DTC, allows the sending and receiving of messages to be coordinated within a larger transactional business logic.

The only real problem with MSMQ is that it uses a whole different communications API than does COM+. With Microsoft's COMWare products as they existed in NT 4.0, synchronous component communication and asynchronous component communication looked entirely different. Synchronous communication is based on the idea of method invocations. Asynchronous communication is based on the idea of message queues. Although neither idea is complicated, they are quite different. Many programmers familiar with methods from their days as object-oriented programmers have never seen a message queue. And they have no interest in learning a whole new API when all they want to do is invoke a method, but not wait around for the result. In other words, they want a component to operate asynchronously.

COM+ solves this problem by providing a veneer on top of MSMQ. Microsoft calls this veneer *queued components*. I don't like this terminology, because the fact that these asynchronous components are built on top of a message queue is an implementation detail. What is important about these components is that they are asynchronous, so I will describe these as *asynchronous components*. Besides, it wouldn't do for Microsoft to get the idea that I agree with them on any terminology issue.

The idea behind asynchronous components is to make it as easy as possible for programmers familiar with synchronous components to be able to implement and make use of asynchronous components. To a larger extent than in any other COMWare product, this has been realized. Consider the following pseudocode fragment:

```
fromAccount.withdraw(fromAccountID, amount);
toAccount.deposit(toAccountID, amount);
```

You can't tell from this particular code fragment if the withdraw and deposit methods are invoked synchronously or asynchronously. However, not all code can be either synchronous or asynchronous. This slight modification on the code eliminates the possibility of asynchronous invocation:

```
error = fromAccount.withdraw(fromAccountID, amount);
if (no error) toAccount.deposit(toAccountID, amount);
```

The second code segment *must* be synchronous because the invoking code uses the return value from the withdraw method to decide whether or not to process the deposit. If the withdraw method is asynchronous rather than synchronous, then we have no way of knowing when, if ever, the business logic behind withdraw will be executed.

At some level, the requirements for asynchronous components are a subset of the requirements for synchronous components. Any asynchronous component potentially can become a synchronous component. The inverse is not true. Synchronous components have more latitude in their design than do asynchronous components. For example, synchronous components can return information through parameters; asynchronous components cannot. After all, what would it mean to return information through a parameter when the method may not execute until days later? So if a component returns information through a parameter, it is going to be a synchronous component. If it doesn't, it may be either synchronous or asynchronous.

The decision as to whether a component is synchronous or asynchronous is made at configuration time, as the component is introduced into the COM+ runtime through the Microsoft Management Console I described in Chapter 7, "The COM+ Runtime Environment." This, at least, is the COM+ story as presented by Microsoft. We will see later that this is a bit simplistic. However it is true that, in general, there is a *no special code* rule in effect for asynchronous components, as there is for most of the COM+ features.

The one exception to the no special code rule is at the client-side instantiation of the asynchronous component. Instantiation is slightly different for asynchronous components than it is for synchronous components. I have heard two explanations of why we have difference instantiation code. The first is that this allows initialization parameters to be passed in while not requiring compiler extensions. Personally, I think the value of initialization parameters is questionable. The second explanation of this difference is that it allows some clients to instantiate the component as asynchronous and allows others to instantiate the component as synchronous. However, as I will point out, there are too many differences between synchronous and asynchronous components for me to imagine that a given component will be used in both modes. In any case, the difference in instantiation between asynchronous and synchronous components is at most a minor irritation.

The asynchronous components architecture, as shown in Figure 8.1, is just a glue layer between COM+ and MSMQ, the venerable Microsoft message queuing product. The glue layer is provided by three pieces: a *recorder*, a *listener*, and a *player*.

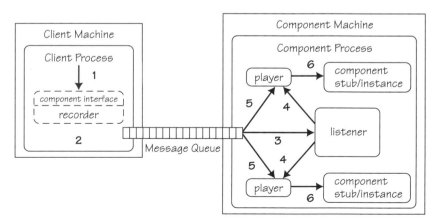

Figure 8.1 Architecture of asynchronous (queued) components.

A recorder is analogous to a proxy. It is specific to a specific asynchronous component, and supports the same interface as does the asynchronous component. It lives in the client's process, and, from the client's perspective, it *is* the component instance. Referring to Figure 8.1, it is what receives the method request from the client (1). Like a proxy, the recorder does not actually contain any business logic, but contains the logic necessary to transport that method request (2) over to a component process. Unlike a proxy, however, the transport is not based on the COM+ transportation mechanisms, but instead is based on message queues.

The listener typically lives in the component process. It monitors the message queue, waiting to see when there is an available message. Since there can be thousands of message queues in the system, it must agree with the recorder on which message queue exactly is being used to transport method requests. Once the listener notices that there is a method request in the message queue (3), it asks a player, via a method (4), to deal with that message. The player receives the message from the message queue (5), translates the message into a method invocation, and invokes that method directly on the stub to the asynchronous component (6). Because the player and the instance stub live in the same process and share all of the COM+ runtime characteristics, the use of a proxy can be eliminated, allowing direct communication between the player and the stub.

The player plays an important role in managing the overall transaction. It is configured as requiring a transaction. So when the listener asks it, via a method invocation, to process the next asynchronous request, it will kick off a new transaction, as will any self-respecting component instance that requires a transaction. When the listener then invokes the method on the actual asynchronous component instance, that method executes within the player's transaction. So if the instance updates a database, that database update will also be within the player's transaction. If the database update then fails, the entire transaction will fail, including all updates within the transaction.

What were the updates within the transaction? There were two updates within the player's transaction. The first was the removal of the message from the message queue that started this whole mess in the first place. The second was the update by the instance of the database. So if the database update fails, the message is returned to the message queue. This is how COM+ guarantees that if the message is delivered, it will be executed. If, for any reason, it cannot be executed successfully, it will be undelivered. This is critical to the overall transactional semantics of asynchronous components, which guarantee that asynchronous methods will *eventually* be executed—it just doesn't guarantee *when* they will be executed.

There is an exception to this guaranteed execution: if the method is somehow "poisoned," so that its invocation always fails. In this case, the message gets moved to a "dead" queue. This is all built on top of the standard MSMQ error management capabilities.

This overall architecture is quite efficient at processing asynchronous method requests. The listener has access to many different players, each running on its own thread. By delegating the actual removal and processing of the method request to a player, the listener can orchestrate asynchronous method requests as fast as they can come off the queue, or until its process runs out of power.

So there are three distinct pieces of the asynchronous component architecture. There is the listener/receiver/player, which translates from method requests to message queues and then back again. There is the MSMQ system, which actually provides the asynchronous transport services. And there is COM+, which processes the method request using its normal synchronous processing once that message has been received asynchronously by the player from MSMQ.

Difference between Synchronous and Asynchronous Components

As I said earlier, the decision as to whether a component is synchronous or asynchronous is made at configuration time. Because there is no special code that goes into an asynchronous component, this statement is literally true. But the likelihood that a given component will sometimes run synchronously and sometimes run asynchronously is unlikely for a variety of reasons, all of which are related to the use of MSMQ as the underlying interprocess transport mechanism for asynchronous components rather than COM+, as is used for synchronous transport. Let's look at the differences inherent in these two transport mechanisms.

To begin, what is being transported, and between which processes? In both cases a stream version of a method invocation is being transported. At a minimum, that stream will include information that identifies the method, the specific stub that is the target for the method, and all of the parameters that are passed into that method. The stream is created in the client process; that is, the process that actually invoked the method originally. The stream must then be transported to the component process; that is, the process in which the stub lives and in which an instance will eventually be assigned to process the method using the instance management algorithms I described in Chapter 7.

Once the stream has been created, we need some mechanism to move it from the client process to the component process. For a synchronous component, we use the COM+ transport mechanism. This mechanism is often described as DCOM, because, in fact, it is exactly the same transport mechanism that has been used since DCOM was originally introduced. This transport mechanism is a *synchronous* transport mechanism, in that the transport is done as quickly as possible and the client process is blocked until the transport has been completed. For an asynchronous component, we use an entirely different transport mechanism: an MSMQ message queue. MSMQ message queues are an *asynchronous* transport mechanism, in that the transport is done when it is convenient, and the client process is not blocked until the transport has been completed.

When I discussed MSMQ in Chapter 5, I talked about how MSMQ works within the overall transactional framework of MS-DTC, the distributed transaction coordinator of the COM+ world. I'll review this again, since the relationship between MSMQ and MS-DTC determines the relationship between asynchronous components and transactions. To simplify this discussion, I will treat stubs as synonymous with instances, although by now I'm sure you are aware of the ephemeral relationship between these two.

In a COMWare environment, methods are typically configured as being transaction boundaries. When a method is received by such an instance, a start transaction notification is sent over to MS-DTC. When the method is returning from that instance, an end transaction notification is sent to MS-DTC. MS-DTC is responsible for coordinating all the transactional resources so that they either all make their changes or none do. One of these transactional resources is the MSMQ message queue.

When a method is invoked on an instance, that invocation typically triggers the start of a new transaction. Let's say that method updates two databases and places a message in a message queue. Later, when that invocation has completed, it will trigger an end transaction and a commit. At that point MS-DTC wakes up and asks the two databases and the message queue if each is okay with the commit. If everybody says yes, MS-DTC will tell everybody to commit. If anybody is not okay with the commit, then MS-DTC tells everybody to rollback.

From the message queue's perspective, a commit means placing the message in the message queue, where it can at some point be transported to whomever is waiting for the message. The commit does not mean that the message has actually been delivered; delivery may not occur until days later. And, in fact, since the message queue must be prepared to expel the message if it gets told to do a rollback, it *can't* deliver the message until sometime after the commit is issued (if it is issued).

It is also possible that a method implementation includes the retrieval of a message from the message queue. This, too, is governed by the MS-DTC commit protocol. If a commit is eventually issued, the instance is allowed to keep the message. If a rollback is eventually issued, the message queue will act as if the message was never removed. The next request to read from the queue will get that same message again.

None of the underlying transaction semantics change just because we have introduced a recorder and a listener as intermediaries between the client placing messages in the queue and the instance taking messages out. The only changes are at the next level up, the method level. So, where we had been talking of the transactional semantics of placing a message into and getting a message out of the message queue, now we need to layer this same transactional semantics on the method invocation (which results in the recorder placing a message in the message queue) and on the receipt of the method invocation (which is a result of a listener receiving a message from the message queue).

Let's look at these higher level transactional asynchronous method semantics based on the lower level transactional message queue semantics. For purposes of discussion, I'll use the following scenario. We have a bank component that supports a transfer method. That transfer method invokes a withdraw method on a savings component, a deposit method on a checking component, and a log method on an audit component. All three of these methods update databases. The audit component is asynchronous, and the bank, savings, and checking components are all synchronous. The savings, checking, and log components all update their respective databases as shown in Figure 8.2. All of the components are configured as "requiring a transaction;" that is, if their caller has a

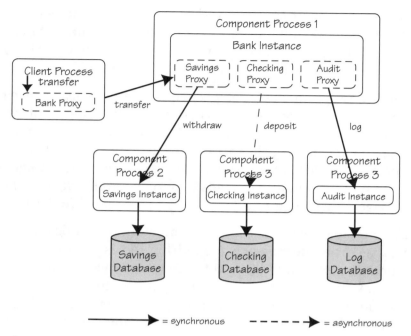

Figure 8.2 Sample application.

transaction, they will piggy-back; if not, they want a new transaction started.

If all of these components were synchronous, then the transactional semantics of this application would be straightforward. The client invokes transfer on the bank instance, triggering a new transaction. The bank instance invokes withdraw, deposit, and log in sequence on the savings, checking, and audit instances, respectively. All want transactions, but we already have a transaction in progress, since we are still within the transfer method that started the transaction. The savings, checking, and audit instances update the savings database, checking database, and audit database, respectively. All of these updates are contained in the transactions started by the transfer invocation. When the sequence of withdraw, deposit, and log have all completed, the transfer is complete, the transfer method returns, the transaction completes with a commit, and MS-DTC coordinates the commit with all three databases. If any one of the databases can't commit, MS-DTC will tell all three databases to rollback, and the world is returned to the state it was in before the transfer began. If all the components are synchronous, this whole scenario should be, by now, fairly obvious.

But, of course, all of the components are not synchronous. The audit component is asynchronous, and therefore dependent on the underlying transactional semantics of MSMQ. Let's see what happens with this one little itsy bitsy change: reconfiguring the audit component to be asynchronous (or *queued*).

The new scenario starts as the last one did. The client invokes transfer on the bank instance, which triggers the start of the transaction. The bank instance invokes withdraw, deposit, and log on the savings, checking, and audit instances, respectively. All still want a transaction, so, as before, they piggy-back off the transaction in progress. The withdraw and deposit method invocations both result in updates to the savings and checking databases, respectively. However, the log invocation does not. The log invocation, in fact, does not even go to the audit instance. Instead, it goes to the recorder. The recorder translates the method invocation into a message that gets placed in the message queue.

When we return from the transfer invocation, MS-DTC goes through the commit protocol. But now the commit protocol includes not the three databases, but the savings database, the checking database, and the message queue. The audit database is not included in the commit protocol. It would make no sense to include it in the commit protocol, because it hasn't been updated yet. And I don't mean that it *may* not have been updated yet. I mean it *can't* have been updated yet—it can't be updated until the message is committed to the message queue, and that can't happen until the transfer commit has been completed.

During the coordination of the commit protocol, MS-DTC asks each of the updated databases and the message queues if they are willing to commit. If any say no, then the database changes are rolled back and the message is taken back out of the message queue.

Once the transfer commit has completed, then and only then is the log method available in the message queue for delivery to the audit listener, and ultimately to the audit instance. But this, too, must go through transaction semantics. Keep in mind that the audit component was also configured as "requires a transaction." And, like the savings and checking instances, it also piggy-backs off of its client's transaction. But unlike the savings and checking instance, its client is not the bank instance, but the listener. The listener starts a transaction, removes a method invocation from the message queue, reconstructs an actual method invocation, and invokes that method (the "log" method) on the audit instance. The audit instance piggy-backs off of the listener's transaction. And the audit instance, as part of its business logic, updates its database.

The transaction governing the audit is entirely independent of the transaction governing the withdraw and deposit. The withdraw/deposit transaction is the one that starts when the transfer method is intercepted and ends when the transfer method is completed. The log transaction is the one that starts when the recorder asks a listener to pick a method out of the message queue, construct a log method, and invoke that log method on the audit instance.

What happens if the database update within the log method of the audit instance does not survive the MS-DTC commit protocol? In this case, all updates that are part of this transaction will be rolled back. There are two such updates: the database update and the removal of the method information from the message queue by the listener. Both of these will be rolled back. But, and this is a critical point, the withdrawal and deposit will *not* be rolled back. They are not part of this transaction. They are part of the withdraw/deposit transaction.

So it is entirely possible that the withdraw and deposit will commit without ever having done the audit log. Although this seems like a major problem, it really isn't. Sooner or later, the audit log will get done. If the log database fails, the method just goes back into the message queue, where it waits for another opportunity.

You can see that the seemingly simple change of configuring a component to be asynchronous rather than synchronous has some major implications as to the transaction semantics. And transactional semantics is not the only thing impacted by this seemingly innocuous configuration change.

The other major change, which occurs with the transition from synchronous to asynchronous, is to workflow. The easiest way to see this is to imagine changing the savings and checking components to be asynchronous as well as changing the audit component. If we make this change, our entire system changes. We now have three methods being invoked (withdraw, deposit, and log) in a random order and all at some indeterminate time in the future. And, of course, all in their own transactions.

All kinds of odd scenarios are now possible. For example, we could end updating our checking account today with a deposit, and not find out until tomorrow that we never had enough money in the savings account to cover the transfer. Or we could make the transfer, and then make another transfer before the updates resulting from the first transfer had been made. Or we could log the transfer and then have a failure of the transfer itself. None of these are good things. We need some very specific workflow semantics. We want the withdraw and deposit effectively to happen simultaneously, and the log to occur sometime (we don't really care when) later.

It is possible to modify our component implementations so that the methods are at least guaranteed to execute in a specific order. But this cannot be done administratively; this requires new programming code. Figure 8.3 shows the new implementation that would guarantee an order of withdraw, deposit, and then log. Basically, we need to have each component instance invoke the next method in the workflow line.

The discussion on workflow is very reminiscent of the discussion of MSMQ workflow in Chapter 5. The changes we must make to guarantee correct work flow are analogous to the changes we would need to

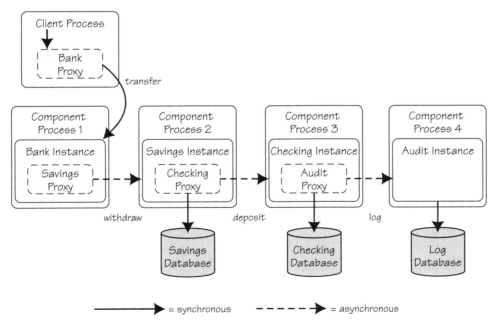

Figure 8.3   Sample application, version 2.

make if the work requests were going through MSMQ without the benefit of asynchronous components. This, of course, is no coincidence. It is the use of MSMQ as an underlying transport layer that governs the workflow.

It is important to realize that although we can change our code to guarantee a correct ordering of method invocations, there is no change we can make that will give our asynchronous components the desired transactional semantics—namely, a unified withdraw/deposit transaction followed by a log transaction. No matter how we torture our code, we are still going to end up with a separate withdraw and deposit transaction. The *only* way around this is to have the savings and checking components configured as synchronous. Or to write our own transaction management code.

I hope it is clear from this discussion that moving from synchronous to asynchronous processing (or vice versa) is much more complicated than just reconfiguring a component. The change has major implications both to transactional semantics and workflow. We cannot randomly change either the transactional semantics or the workflow of a component and still expect the business logic to work correctly. Microsoft sometimes presents an idyllic world in which synchronous components can be magically transformed into asynchronous components as easily as flicking a switch. In fact, the synchronous or asynchronous nature of the component is burnt into the component implementation, and even the component design, and is not likely ever to change without major redesign and re-implementation effort. This is certainly not Microsoft's fault. This is inherent in the nature of synchronous and asynchronous work. This will be true of any asynchronous component technology.

So if asynchronous components are so different, why use them? The benefits of asynchronous components are potentially enormous. And, in fact, I have already discussed them in Chapter 5, in which I discussed the great value of MSMQ message queues. To recap, the three most important benefits I discussed were these:

Work load averaging. The ability to postpone some of the work arriving at peak times to times of lower system usage. Let's say that a system that peaks, at its absolute busiest time, at P transactions per minute, but that its average throughout the day is only A transactions per minute. We don't know what P and A will be, but A can never exceed P, and for most systems, A will be much lower than P. Without workflow averaging, you must purchase a system that can handle P transactions per minute. With workflow averaging, you only need to purchase a system that can handle A transactions per minute. You can look at this as saying that either your cost will be A/P^{th} as much, or that for a given cost, you can handle P/A times as many transactions per minute. If N is 3 and A is 1, meaning average transaction load is one-third the peak transaction load, then your system cost with work load averaging is one-third as much as it would be without work load averaging. Or you could say that for a given cost, your system can handle three times more transactions with work load averaging as it could without.

Shortened client wait time. If a method is going to take a long time to execute, making it asynchronous can mean the client doesn't need to sit around waiting for the work to be completed before going on its next task.

Disconnected workflow processing. If the client is running on a machine, such as a laptop, that is not currently hooked up to the network, the client can just pile up work locally and then process it when it is convenient to hook up to the network.

All of these benefits of MSMQ message queues apply equally to asynchronous components. And asynchronous components have a major benefit MSMQ message queues do not have: they are much easier to use. For a programmer already familiar with COM+ components, they introduce no new API. If a programmer can invoke a COM+ method, that same programmer can make an asynchronous request of a component appropriately implemented and configured.

There is one important caveat. As of press time, Microsoft requires that COM+ run not only on the component machine hosting the asynchronous component, but on the client machine using the asynchronous component. This is a serious problem for disconnected workflow, which will often run on laptops. COM+ is strictly a Windows 2000 technology. Using asynchronous components, therefore, limits clients who expect to get disconnected workflow to the Windows 2000 platform. Although I have been running my laptop with Windows 2000 for some time now, many laptops will not run Windows 2000 in the near future. These laptops will be unable to run applications built as disconnected workflow applications, if that disconnected workflow is based on COM+ asynchronous components. This is a serious limitation that we do not see, for example, with pooled components, a topic I discussed in Chapter 7, "The COM+ Runtime Environment." Pooled components are usable by any client that has DCOM. Technically, there is no reason Microsoft couldn't similarly support asynchronous clients on any platform that supports MSMQ, which is every Microsoft platform. But for unknown reasons, Microsoft so far has chosen not to do so.

The net result of this decision not to support non-COM+ asynchronous clients is that if you want to have portable clients involved in disconnected workflow, you can't use asynchronous components. Instead, you must use MSMQ, the technology that provides the underpinnings to asynchronous components. This situation is so clearly ridiculous that we can only assume that Microsoft will soon rectify this problem. As of press time, however, Microsoft has announced no plans to do so. In any case, this problem is limited to the disconnected workflow scenario. There are simple workarounds to allow portable clients to get the other benefits of asynchronous components.

Enough, already, on asynchronous (queued) components. Let's move on to loosely coupled events (LCE).

Loosely Coupled Events (LCE)

It's hard to think about events before getting a morning Doppio. Getting a Doppio Macchiato at Starbucks requires two interactions: First, I order, then, I get. Ordering is the annoying part. My local Starbucks often has a line of 10 people waiting to order their own coffee concoctions, all seemingly oblivious to the obviously higher priority my own order should get. So I wait. Once I tell Mark what I want (as if he doesn't know) I go into the next phase, the get phase. The get phase is much easier for me. I go and find a comfortable chair. Take out Baby. Start thinking Very Important Thoughts. At some point, I hear Mark's distant voice calling out, "One Doppio Macchiato, one sugar, extra foam!" Then, and only then, do I mosey over and pick up my drink.

The annoying thing about ordering is that I am trapped in a constant cycle of having to check to see if the line has moved up and if it is finally my turn to order. It's almost impossible to do any work while I'm in line. I can try to do something very simple, perhaps read a newspaper, but even this is difficult. As soon as I make any headway in an interesting article, I need to put the paper down to see if the line has moved again. Then I reopen the newspaper, and by the time I find where I left off, it's time to check the line again. If I check too often, I get absolutely nothing done. If I don't check often enough, I end up with a big gap in front of me and a rapidly growing, increasingly annoyed, severely caffeine-depleted mob scene behind me. Either way, I lose. The actual work involved in moving up, in those rare situations where the line has actually moved, is minimal. It's the constant checking that drives me crazy.

Getting often takes longer than ordering, but I don't care. I don't care because I can do other things while I am waiting for the get to be completed. What if it does take five minutes? That's five minutes longer I have to think Very Important Thoughts, like what am I going to tell Kathryn, my developmental editor, when she asks why my next chapter is three weeks late. Of course, in some parallel Starbucks in New York City, Kathryn has also survived the ordering process and is now comfortably waiting for her tall decaf skinny cappuccino, while thinking what new threats she can use to convince me to get back to work. You might think that these two Starbucks would cancel each other out, like matter and anti-matter, but instead they seem to hold everything together in some kind of precarious universal balance.

What is the essential difference between how Kathryn and I *order* and how we *get* our morning addictions? *Ordering* is what we call a *polling* system. In a polling system, I am responsible for constantly checking back (polling) and seeing if something I care about (the line has moved forward another two inches) has occurred. *Getting* is what we call an *event* system. In an event system, I don't need to check constantly to see if that special thing I care about has occurred; when my Doppio Macchiato is ready, I trust Mark to raise the *Doppio Macchiato, one sugar, extra foam* (DM1SXF) event. Kathryn, even if she were in my Starbucks, would ignore this event. She is waiting for the Tall Decaf Skinny Cappuccino (TDSC) event.

There are a couple of interesting observations I would like to make about the relationship between Mark, myself, and the DM1SXF event. First, Mark, at least in theory, has no idea who is going to respond to the DM1SXF event. Scott takes the order and hands it off to Mark. Scott tells Mark to make a DM1SXF. He doesn't tell Mark whom it is for. Mark doesn't really care. When Mark has finished his artistry, he raises the event. Not just any event, but specifically the DM1SXF event. Anybody who cares about that event is free to rush forward. So far, I seem to be the only one who ever cares about that specific event at that time of the morning. Which is a good thing, because *nobody* gets between me and my Doppio.

Just as Mark has no idea who is going to respond to the DM1SXF event, I have no idea who raised the event. I know Scott took my money, but I don't know what happened after that. And frankly, at seven o'clock in the morning, before I have had my first shot of caffeine, I don't care. All I know is that when I hear the magic words I will know that the first of my morning dosages will be waiting for me on the counter.

Among event cognoscenti, Mark is called the *publisher* of the event. He is the one who actually announces to the world that some specific state of affairs (DM1SXF is ready!) has come to pass. The DM1SXF is called, of course, the *event*. The event is the occurrence that ties me to Mark, though neither of us knows about the other. I am called the *subscriber* to the event. The subscriber is the one waiting with baited breath for the blessed event to occur. When Mark yells out "Doppio Macchiato, 1 sugar, extra foam," he is said to be *raising* an event. When I tell Mark that I want a "Doppio Macchiato, 1 sugar, extra foam," I am said to be *subscribing* to the event.

There are also others working behind the scenes. These are the ones who have defined what events are allowed to occur. They are the event gods, living in their palaces in Mount Olympus, who have decided that DM1SXF is a valid event at Starbucks, while L16SMSW ("Lagavulin, 16 year old Single Malt Scotch Whiskey") is not. They live in a land that Mark and I will never know. We are merely pawns in their larger game.

Component-oriented software systems often have requirements very similar to mine in waiting for my DM1SXF. Take, for example, a supermarket with 20 cashiers. As each cashier scans in an item, that item is deducted from the inventory. When the inventory reaches a predefined low point, we want to send off a general complaint to the world that somebody needs to deal with the inventory. If that complaint arrives between 7:00 A.M. and 9:00 P.M., we want our stocking department to immediately jump into action. If that complaint arrives between 9:00 P.M. and 11:00 P.M., we don't want to do anything, because we know at 11:00 P.M. the stocking clerks go through the entire store restocking everything anyway. We might just want to log the low inventory, so a manager can double-check that the restocking really was done in the morning.

There are many other examples of event systems. A telephone call center can monitor response time, and use events to notify managers when more people are needed to staff the phones. A banking system could use events to notify branch offices of bad accounts. A law enforcement system could use events to issue all-points bulletins. A weather monitoring system could use events to issue storm warnings. A security system could use "intruder" events to trigger phone calls to the police, set off alarms, and hurl sharpened spears randomly through the walls. A credit card company could use an "unusual activity" event to let managers know about an unusual pattern of credit card usage, so that somebody can contact the credit card holder to verify that purchases really are authorized, and that the unusual activity is not due to the theft of the credit card.

One way to think of events is as a loose coupling between a particular state of affairs and those that will respond to that particular state of affairs. It allows me to write code to let the world know that something has occurred, without having to know who is going to deal with the situation, how they will deal with the situation, or even *if* they will deal with the situation. With a hard-coded method invocation, I as a programmer know exactly what component is going to receive a work request.

An event is like an information announcement. I am announcing to the world, "World, something has happened." Who cares that something has happened is something that, for events, gets configured, not hard-coded. One day, I can have five different components that all jump into action when that something happens; the next day, it could only be two, the next day, none. My code is the same in all cases; only the configuration of the event changes. For this reason, Microsoft calls this system *Loosely Coupled Events* (LCE). They are loosely coupled because neither the event publisher(s) nor the event responder(s) need know about the other, and, in fact, either may change without notice to the other.

Three categories of components work together to process an event. The *publisher* is the component that actually fires off the event. The publisher does not necessarily need to be a component—it could be client code. The *event* component (called an *event class*, in the unfortunate Microsoft terminology) is really a trigger component. Each of the methods supported by the event component is a trigger for one event. The event component will support some event interface, and the methods defined on that interface are effectively the event triggers that that event component supports. The subscriber component is the consumer of events. The subscriber component supports the same interface as the event component, namely, the event interface. The subscriber may support more than that basic interface, but it must support at least the event interface. The event component becomes an intermediary between the publisher and the subscriber(s).

Let's look at an example to clarify how these components work together. Let's say I am a cell phone company and I am designing a billing system. Once a month I must go through each of my customer's accounts and calculate each customer's bill.

Calculating the monthly bill for a given customer is complicated by the fact that I have a variety of rate plans. Some customers are not charged for calls until they have exceeded some number of minutes per month, are calling long distance, or are calling outside of their home city. Others are not charged unless they are calling outside of their state. Others are charged for neither roaming nor long distance, unless they exceed some number of minutes per month, a number that can vary from 150 to 2000 minutes per month.

As I go through a typical customer's records for the month, I would like to do three things. First, I want to figure out what the customer actually owes, not an insignificant task in itself. Second, I would like to see if that customer would have saved more if they had purchased an upgraded rate plan. Finally, if that customer is a good candidate for an upgraded rate plan, I want to let my customer service department know this so that this customer can be called with a suggested a rate plan change.

Although the event system has nothing obvious to offer the first two tasks, it is ideal for the third (the notification of the customer service department). This is just a suggestion we are passing off. If anybody responds, fine. If nobody responds, it's not the end of the world. The customer will still be there next month.

So let's go through the process of creating, registering, subscribing to, publishing of, and responding to this particular event.

The first step is to create the event. This means defining the interface and event trigger methods. We don't need to implement any of the methods; this will be done by COM+ itself. In fact, the only thing we really need to do is create a type library, as described back in Chapter 6. A type library, remember, is a machine-readable description of a component and/or interface description.

We can create a type library one of two ways. We can write an IDL file and then use COM+ utilities to create a type library. However, writing IDL is not for the weak of heart. Most of us are better off going the second route: using one of the language development tools to develop the type library for us. Visual Basic, for example, has a good component development wizard that will take you through the steps of designing a component. It will leave you with empty implementations, but this is fine, since we only need the type library anyway. The actual implementation of the event component will be provided by COM+. Using Visual Basic, we create a DLL containing the type library. Let's say we define a ServiceDept interface that looks like this:

```
interface ServiceDept {
  suggest(CustomerID, RatePlanCode);
}
```

Next we can register the event, using the same Component Services Snap-in (CSS) that we have been using for all our administration tasks. We register the DLL we created in Visual Basic (or whatever) as an event. At this point, we are ready to publish our event. Unfortunately, publishing won't be very interesting, because we don't have any subscribers yet. This is in the, "If a tree falls in a forest and there is nobody there to listen" category.

To create a subscriber, we must first implement a component that can respond to the event. This means implementing a component that supports the ServiceDept interface, the interface we defined in the last step. Let's say we call this component a ServDeptEvProc, for Service Department Event Processor. The names aren't important; you can call these interfaces and components anything you like, as long as you are consistent. We tell Visual Basic that the ServDeptEvProc supports the ServiceDept interface. We implement the suggest method, so that, let's say, it looks up the Customer ID, and creates a text file with the last bill, the suggestions rate plan description, and the contact information for the customer. That file is then e-mailed to a service representative who can then make the customer contact.

Now that we have a potential subscriber, we go back to the CSS tool, and add our ServDeptEvProc as a subscriber to the event that is triggered when somebody invokes the suggest method on the ServiceDept.

Notice that the subscriber needs to implement the same event interface as is supported by the event component. This is a bit confusing because we have two different components both implementing the same interface (ServiceDept). The *event* component is the component that is implemented by COM+ to provide the intermediary between the publisher and the subscriber. The event designer defines the interface, and COM+ provides the implementation. Then there is the *subscriber* component. The subscriber's interface is defined by the event designer, but it is implemented by the subscriber implementer.

Let me go through the event flow of control, referring to Figure 8.4. First, we need a publisher. That is our billing instance. Our billing instance wants to publish the suggest event. To do so, it creates an instance of the ServiceDept component (the one defined by the event designer and implemented by COM+) and invokes the suggest method (1). Once the billing instance has instantiated a ServiceDept instance and invoked the suggest method, the COM+ Event Service's implementation of suggest checks the configuration database to see who is subscribing to this particular event (2). It discovers that the ServDeptEvProc component is subscribed (3). By definition, the ServDeptEvProc must also support the ServiceDept interface; anything else would be an error. So the COM+ event component instantiates a ServDeptEvProc and invokes suggest on the newly created instance (4), passing through any of the original parameters the publisher used in its invocation.

All three of the components involved in the event processing (publisher, event, and subscriber) are normal, run-of-the-mill COM+ components.

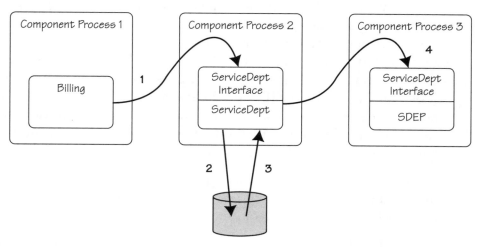

Figure 8.4   Event processing.

They can be configured like any COM+ components; that means they can require transactions, have security placed on their usage, and be asynchronous. The combination of these attributes is predictable.

Configuring an event component as synchronous and requiring a transaction will guarantee that any work done by the event instance is included in the transaction of the publisher. Having an event component configured as requiring a new transaction will guarantee that the work will be an independent transaction.

Configuring a component to be asynchronous (queued) means that the event will be invoked at some later time, using the transactional and workflow semantics I discussed for asynchronous components earlier in this chapter. I suspect that most events will be asynchronous. Asynchronicity seems a natural fit with the laissez-faire approach to disconnected processing inherent to the event model.

Security can be used to ensure that only those clients in specific roles will be allowed to publish the event.

Unlike many other features in COM+, this is really the first release of the event system. Although there was an earlier event system in COM/DCOM, this was very rudimentary, and the current system is a complete redesign of events. So it should not be surprising that there are still some limitations in the system.

To me, the biggest limitation seems to be the lack of distribution in the subscription administration. The subscriptions are stored on one machine, and only one machine: the machine on which the event component is installed. This introduces a significant bottleneck in the event system. But I assume this is going to be fixed in a coming release.

Component Load Balancing

COM+ Component Load Balancing Service (CLBS) is the architecture for allowing the component workload to be distributed over a collection of machines. Up until shortly before product release, CLBS had been planned for part of the base COM+ product. Microsoft recently announced that CLBS would be removed from the basic COM+ and made part of another technology tentatively called Application Server. Very little is known about Application Server as of press time, but I expect that the ability to distribute the component work load in the

Application Server product will look similar to beta versions of CLBS. Therefore I will describe the CLBS architecture here.

NT 4.0 was often criticized for being unscalable. I always thought this was interesting, given that Microsoft database technologies supported database connection pooling, a key scalability requirement, and MTS pioneered the field of instance management, introducing ideas that have since become widely adopted throughout the COMWare industry. I discussed instance management in Chapter 4, "COMWare," and Chapter 7.

Despite the importance placed on scalability by MTS and Microsoft in general, there was a grain of truth in the criticisms of NT 4.0. In fact, I often told people that NT 4.0 was both very scalable and not scalable. It was scalable because of the focus on getting as many clients as possible around a single machine. At some point, though, you saturated the capability of the machine. And once that happened, there was no way to enlist other machines to help out with the workload.

In Chapter 7, I introduced the following equation to predict the number of clients supportable on a given middle-tier configuration:

```
C = M x I x T x P
```

where C = Clients, P = Processes (hosting components) per machine, T = Threads per process, I = Instances per thread, and M = Machines (used for load balancing).

The name of this game is to get C (the number of supportable clients) as high as possible. In theory, this can be done by increasing any of M (the number of machines available for load balancing), I (the number of instances per thread), T (the number of threads per process), or P (the number of processes per machine). In practice, I, T, and P were already close to fully optimized in NT 4.0. The one variable that was neglected by NT 4.0/MTS was M. COM+ load balancing focuses on M.

COM+ load balancing is a fairly straightforward extension of the COM+ (and MTS, for that matter) instantiation architecture, which is itself an extension of the COM+ distributed component architecture. So let's start by reviewing briefly the distributed component architecture and the nonclustered instantiation architecture.

Distributed Component Architecture

Keep in mind that COM+, like all COMWare technologies, has two conflicting goals. The first is to provide a very rich middle tier infrastructure that can make use of as many tricks as possible to provide scalability, security, transactional integrity, and all of the other qualities of life that make life in the middle tier possible. The second is to hide as much of this infrastructure as possible from both the client and the business logic programmers.

To accomplish both of these goals, COM+ maintains a careful relationship among a proxy, a stub, and an instance. Though Carla, a client, may think she has a component instance in her process, she actually has a proxy. The proxy is best thought of as a client-side surrogate for the instance, but in fact, it is a client-side surrogate for the stub. It is the stub, living in the component process, that is actually hooked up to the instance, and this hooking up occurs at the whim of the instance management algorithms I described in Chapter 7. The relationship among Carla's proxy, stub, and instance is shown in Figure 8.5.

The proxy, stub, and instance all have different purposes in life. The client-side proxy is there to shield Carla from the complicated details surrounding the middle tier infrastructure. The component-side stub is there to coordinate the point of interception algorithms that I have described throughout this book. The instance is there to perform the business logic. Carla is there to reap the windfall of all this technology.

If we want to be 100 percent technically correct, Carla really doesn't have a proxy, she has a pointer to a proxy. And what I call a proxy is really a blob of memory containing a pointer to a VTable and state, as I described back in Chapter 6. But this is more detail than we need for the

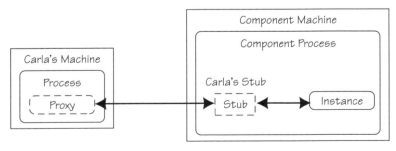

Figure 8.5 Proxy/Stub/Instance architecture.

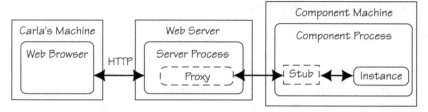

Figure 8.6 Proxy/Stub/Instance architecture on the Web.

purpose of this discussion. We can just simplify this to Carla, the proxy, the stub, and the instance.

As a further reminder, if Carla is working on a Web browser, the situation is a little different. In this case, her machine is hooked up by HTTP to the Web server. And it is the Web server that actually contains the proxy. This is shown in Figure 8.6.

Non–Load-Balanced Instantiation

It is ironic that we think of instantiation as creating an instance of a component. In fact, this is about the only thing that instantiation *doesn't* do. The two real goals of instantiation are to create the proxy in the client process (realizing that the "client" can be the Web server) and creating the stub in the component process. Once the proxy and stub are in place, we have everything we need to acquire the actual instance when the time is ripe. Let's go through the process of creating a proxy and stub in the non-clustered architecture, as shown in Figure 8.7.

For normal (non–load-balanced) instantiation, a client (1) starts with an instantiation request (2). If COM+ is being used on the client side, then the client COM+ runtime will ask (3) the local component catalog (4) which machine is hosting that particular component. Placing this information in a machine wide catalog makes it easy to update all applications running on that machine by updating a single location. There is, however, no requirement that COM+ be running on the client. This can just go through normal COM/DCOM processing.

Once COM+ knows the target machine, it sends the instantiation request over to that machine (5), where it is picked up by a COM+ server process, sometimes called the *activator* (6). That server process then looks up (7) the component in its local component catalog (8) to figure out the

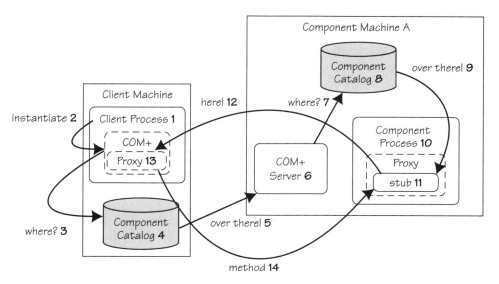

Figure 8.7 Instantiation architecture of COM+.

local process in which the instance should be created. It then passes the request (9) over to that process (10), which creates a local stub (11) to represent that particular client proxy. The COM+ runtime then returns (12) the proxy (13) to the client. Although this may seem complicated, it happens only at instantiation time. Further method requests (14) travel directly from the proxy to the instance stub after passing through the appropriate point of interception algorithms.

All of this happens as a result of a client side instantiation request, which in Visual Basic looks like

```
Set Customer = CreateObject("Bank.Customer")
```

Although the client thinks of the instantiation request as returning an instance, we know that it really returns a proxy representing that instance. And, in fact, the proxy does not really represent that instance, it really represents a *stub* that represents that instance. The actual instance will be assigned through the normal instance management algorithms described in Chapter 7, and may not appear until much later. The stub, however, will stay around until the client proxy is destroyed, which, in Visual Basic, looks like:

```
Set Customer = Nothing
```

Load-Balanced Instantiation

The COM+ load-balancing algorithms add a level of indirection to this instantiation process. The client makes the instantiation request exactly as in the non–load-balanced scenario. But instead of the instantiation request going to the machine that will create the stub, it goes to a machine that is responsible for choosing a machine that will create the stub. This intermediary machine is called the Component Load Balancing (CLB) Router. And since the machine that the CLB Server chooses to create the stub will eventually create the instance, indirectly the CLB Server is choosing the machine on which the instance will eventually run.

The CLB Router can assign the instantiation request only to machines that have been appropriately configured. If it is going to assign the instantiation to one of Dopey, Sleepy, or Grumpy, then Dopey, Sleepy, and Grumpy all need to have the Bank COM+ application installed, the Bank DLLs available, and access to any other system resources those DLLs might require (such as databases) available. The set of machines that are identically configured for load-balancing purposes is called an *application cluster*. The router itself can participate as part of the application cluster.

Let's look at this load-balancing instantiation in more detail, as shown in Figure 8.8 (which can be compared to Figure 8.7, for the non–load-balanced instantiation). Load-balanced instantiation starts out just like non–load-balanced instantiation. A client (1) makes an instantiation request (2). The local COM+ or COM/DCOM system checks (3) with the local component catalog (4) to find out where the component lives. The catalog believes that the component lives on the COM+ router machine hosting the CLB Server (5). The COM+ runtime environment (6) looks up (7) the component in its catalog (8) and discovers the component is load balanced (9). The runtime environment passes the instantiation request over to the CLB Server (10), which can then forward the instantiation request to any machine in the application cluster; in other words, to any of Dopey, Sleepy, or Grumpy. Assuming that it decides Grumpy is the most available, it sends the instantiation request (11) over to Grumpy (12). Grumpy reluctantly creates a local stub (13) and, through the COM+ runtime, returns a proxy to that stub back to the original client (14). Subsequent method invocations via that proxy then go directly to the stub (15).

COM+ can only load balance if everything has been configured correctly. This means making sure the CLB Server knows that the compo-

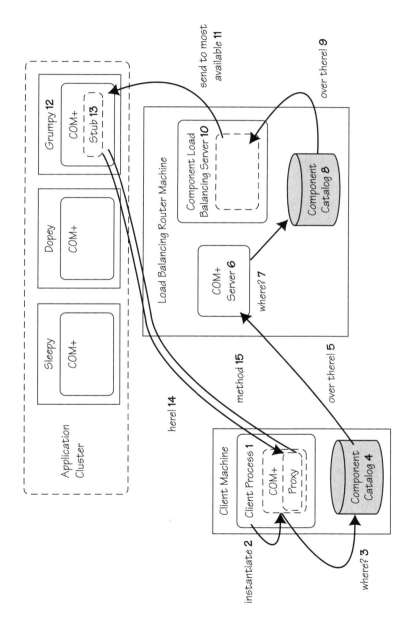

Figure 8.8 Load-balancing architecture of COM+.

nent is load balanced, making sure that all the cluster machines have the application installed, and making sure all the client machines have the necessary client-side application pieces installed. If we are talking about commerce applications on the Web, most likely the "client" will actually be a Web server.

Most of the configuration tasks were done (in the COM+ beta) with the Component Services snap-in (CSS) of the Microsoft Management Console I described in Chapter 7, or with the COM+ administration API, or with scripts. When component load balancing is moved to the Application Server, I assume this administration will become part of the Application Server snap-in. But this will probably have a similar look and feel to the beta CSS. In CSS, when Sally, the system administrator, configures the COM+ Bank application to run clustered (load balanced), she completes the following steps:

1. She configures a particular machine to act as the CLB Server. This is the machine that will assign machines to specific instantiation requests.

2. She configures a set of machines to act as the application cluster. These are the machines that will serve as host machines for the Bank application.

3. She defines a new COM+ application called Bank.

4. She adds the component DLLs to the Bank application. She might, for example, add DLLs containing components for SavingsAccounts, CheckingAccounts, BankTransfers, Customers, and Branches.

5. She configures each of the Bank components, including options for security, transaction, instance management, and any other particular component requirements, as I discussed in Chapter 7. Among whatever options are appropriate, she configures the component as supporting dynamic load balancing.

6. She exports the Bank application for cluster installation. This creates an installation file that, when installed on a cluster machine, will install the Bank COM+ application.

7. She exports a proxy Bank application for easy installation on client machines. This creates an installation file that, when installed on a client machine, will automatically install the Bank proxy DLL and type libraries.

8. She imports the Bank application on each machine on the Bank cluster.

9. She installs the proxy application on each client machine.

In Chapter 4, I talked about load balancing algorithms as a subset of blob algorithms. Blob algorithms are those algorithms that allow a bunch of computers to act together as a single blob. The blob figures out how to share the workload and the blob figures out how to manage things when a member of the blob dies.

In Chapter 4, I described the common notion of blob management as a subcategory of point of interception algorithms. I said that most COMWare platforms intercept methods and decide at invocation time which blob member should receive the request based on both overall system throughput and availability.

This idea of blob management as a point of interception algorithm is also true of COM+, but in an odd way. Although COM+ could theoretically do blob management at point of interception, today blob management is limited to the interception of the instantiation request. When the client, say Carla, creates an instance, she gets a proxy in her process connected to a stub in some component process, as I described earlier. Once that stub has been created, it doesn't move. Relegating blob management to point of instantiation rather than the more general point of interception has some positive and negative effects.

On the positive side, doing blob management at the point of instantiation significantly reduces the cost of blob management. As you can guess from discussion on instantiation with load balancing, blob management can be a significant bottleneck in a system. If blob management is done with every invocation of every method on every instance by every client, you can imagine the workload on the blob manager. By limiting blob management to point of instantiation we potentially can reduce the workload on the blob manager.

On the negative side, limiting blob management to point of instantiation has two potential problems. First, the ability to redistribute system load is limited. Let's say we somehow end up with 500 clients on Dopey and 50 clients on Sleepy. We have no way to redistribute any of the Dopey clients to Sleepy, unless the clients cooperate by releasing and re-instantiating their proxies. If there is a fair amount of dynamism in acquisition and release of proxies, then blob management at point of instantiation is probably fine. But applications in which proxies are attached like glue to clients for very long times can find their workload nonoptimally distributed.

The other problem with blob management at point of instantiation has to do with failover support. Failover means that if one machine fails, another machine takes over its workload automatically. In an ideal world, we would like the client to be totally oblivious to failures of machines in the blob. If Sleepy goes to sleep and Grumpy gets too grumpy, we should be able to reroute their workload over to Dopey without Carla having to bat an eyelid. The ability to reroute work from an unhappy machine to a happy machine is what we call *failover*.

Failover is a straightforward extension of load balancing. In load balancing, the CLB Server checks to see which system is most available for new work assignment. If we just extend this also to check to see which systems are still alive, then load balancing *becomes* failover.

Actually, no system can guarantee to Carla that she will not to lose *any* work during a failover. But the work Carla loses should be limited to the current transaction in process. And since Carla followed my advice in Chapter 4 and other places, and made her transactional boundaries equal to her method boundaries, the loss of the transaction in process translates to the loss of her current method. But who cares? As I discussed in Chapter 3, "Transaction Processing Monitors," uncommitted transactions can always be lost, and by definition, a transaction in process is an uncommitted transaction. No system in the world can guarantee not to lose a transaction in process. The only guarantee is that the transaction is either lost or committed *in toto*.

COM+ does not do as well with failover as some other systems. Because the blob management, including both load balancing and failover, is limited to point of instantiation, the only opportunity COM+ has to check system availability is at instantiation time. If the CLB Server assigns Carla's stub to Sleepy and then Sleepy goes down, Carla will have a stub on a dead system. The next time she invokes a method on that stub via her proxy, she will get an error. Systems that do load balancing and failover checking at point of interception, rather than point of instantiation, can automatically reroute the method to another system without the client's proxy being any the wiser.

Actually, all it would take for COM+ to solve this problem and give Carla true failover would be to add a few more smarts on the part of the proxy. Specifically, the proxy needs to check the return status of the method from the stub. If the return status is an error because the stub machine is down, then the proxy should re-instantiate itself. At re-instantiation, the

CLB Server would once again get involved, realize that Sleepy is down, and create the new stub on some other machine in the cluster. Once the re-instantiation is complete, the proxy can once again re-invoke the method without Carla ever knowing what happened. A proxy that does this automatically can be considered a *failsafe proxy*.

Unfortunately, COM+ proxies today aren't failsafe. Perhaps they will be some day, and I wouldn't be at all surprised if this becomes part of the Application Server project. But even if Microsoft doesn't create failsafe COM+ proxies, you can create your own. But this is more detailed programming than I am going to cover in this book.

If Carla is using a system that does not provide failsafe proxies, then she can still take steps herself to make her system failsafe. She needs to check on each method return for a dead machine error. If she finds such an error, she needs to re-instantiate the proxy and re-invoke the method. This is exactly what the failsafe proxy would do, if it existed. So one way or the other, it is possible to get true failover support with COM+, even though blob management is limited to point of instantiation.

In any case, the delta between what COM+ provides and true failover is fairly small. COM+ is doing all of the hard work today, namely, figuring out which machines are running. The extra work, re-instantiating, when necessary, is relatively small, regardless of whether this work gets done automatically, inside a programmer created failsafe proxy, or directly, by Carla's code.

The jury is still out on whether blob management is best done at point of instantiation (as done today by COM+) or at point of interception (as done by some other COMWare technologies). Which is best depends on exactly how proxies are being used. The overall theory describing proxy usage is, however, poorly understood, and is likely to evolve rapidly over the next few years. So conditions that favor blob management at instantiation time today may well not favor such blob management in another two years, and vice versa. One advantage of the COM+ approach is that it is cautious. It is doing the least it needs to do today, while leaving the door open for more invasive approaches in the future.

In a true failsafe system, any one computer should be able to go down without impacting clients. Assuming Carla is using either failsafe proxies or has used failsafe method invocation, she will be very close to having a failsafe system. But there are still two possible points of failure.

One is the database; the other is the machine hosting the CLB Server. Let's consider why each of these is a point of failure.

The database machine is used to store the state of the instance. This, of course, assumes you are following my advice about creating stateless instances. This topic was discussed is Chapter 6. All instances of the component, regardless of which machine in the application cluster they happen to run, are going to use the same database for their state storage. If the database is on a single machine, and that machine goes down, there isn't much the CLB Server can do to help you.

The CLB Server is the other point of failure. It is the one place everybody must go through in order to find out which machines are running. If the CLB Server machine itself is not running, then neither the load balancing nor the failover mechanisms can work.

The solution to both the database and the CLB Server points of failure is the same: the Microsoft Cluster Server (MSCS). MSCS is the Microsoft product that allows two machines to work in such a way that if one machine stops working, the other can automatically take over its workload (or failover). There is a MSCS API that applications must use in order to take advantage of this failover capability, but both the CLB Server and the Microsoft Database products do support this failover capability, so both can be clustered in the MSCS sense of the word.

I think it is also quite possible that MSCS will get folded into the Application Server project. It would be a much tighter integration between failover and load balancing, so I wouldn't get too attached to the concept of an entirely independent MSCS product.

Just to further confuse this issue, there is yet one more Microsoft technology that is involved with failover and load balancing: the Windows Load Balancing Server (WLBS). WLBS allows multiple machines to act as a single IP port address. Effectively, this becomes a way of load balancing HTTP requests coming in from clients. Figure 8.9 shows the relationship between MSCS, WLBS, and CLBS, as it exists today. But again, the general packaging of load balancing and failover seems likely to be rethought with the Application Server, so consider this diagram as more conceptual.

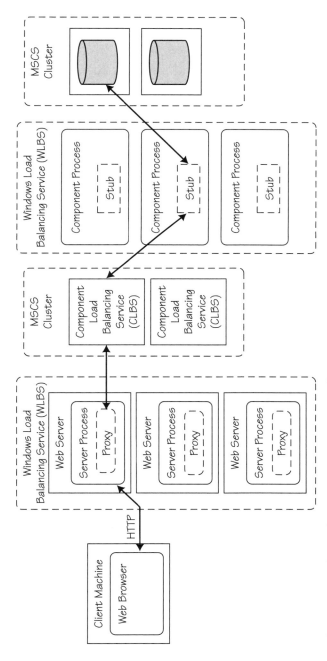

Figure 8.9   Relationship among WLBS, CLBS, and MSCS.

In-Memory Database (IMDB)

The last of the COM+ Services is the *In-Memory Database* (IMDB). The IMDB was designed to solve one very simple problem. Reading data from a database is expensive, especially if that database is on some other machine. If we can find a way to turn a read from a remote database into a read from local shared memory, we potentially can save a great deal of time. IMDB did this by creating a local memory cache of the remote database.

IMDB is no longer with us. As of press time, Microsoft has made no announcement about repackaging its technology into some other product. However, the following points are fairly clear to me:

- IMDB, if it worked, would solve an important problem: the high cost of moving data between the data tier and the middle tier.
- IMDB didn't work, because its cache was not integrated into the database cache scheme.
- If the IMDB cache were tightly integrated into the database cache, then it would be a very useful technology.
- There is one database cache that Microsoft owns, and could potentially integrate into a middle tier cache: the cache of SQL Server.

I'm going to go out on a limb here, and predict that the functionality of IMDB will be integrated into some future release of SQL Server or some SQL Server add-on technology. However, I should point out that this is all speculation based on what would obviously make sense. Microsoft has as of press time made no such announcement to do this work, or even dropped any hints of such a possibility. So if you are just interested in current functionality of COM+, rather than future speculation, feel free to skip this section.

I'm briefly going to describe IMDB as it existed before its recent demise for several reasons. One, as I said, I believe its functionality will be revived in the future without the problems of the recent implementation. Two, the same problems that made IMDB unreliable also plague another middle tier technology: the Entity Beans model of Enterprise JavaBeans. I will discuss Entity Beans in Chapter 10, "Enterprise JavaBeans," but I think a general discussion of the problems involved in multiple but disconnected caches will be useful here. So let's take a tour of IMDB, as it exists today, but will not for long.

A component theoretically can use an IMDB in the same way it could use a database, only the I/O will be much faster, since it is going directly to local shared memory. In fact, the API typically used for the IMDB is a subset of the API used in the Microsoft world to access databases (ADO), so, at least in theory, there is very little difference in using an IMDB and a back-end relational database, except for speed.

An IMDB is probably most often used as a cache for an actual database. In this mode, a table and its associated indexes are loaded from the back-end database into the IMDB. This loading can occur either at system startup or on demand. Once information has been loaded from the database into the IMDB, component instances can access information directly from the IMDB, which is in fast local memory from a database, which is on slow remote disk. The use of an IMDB as a cache for a remote database is shown in Figure 8.10.

Notice that in Figure 8.10 I show the flow of information between the IMDB and the back-end database as being two-way. It is, in fact, possible for updates to the IMDB to be propagated to the back-end database. It is also possible for the updates to stay in the IMDB, and not to be propagated. It is even possible for the IMDB to be entirely in memory and local, and have no relationship at all with a back-end database.

Although Microsoft had described the IMDB as being a database cache, in fact, it has very little true caching capability, and you will probably get yourself in quite a bit of trouble should you actually try to use it as a database cache. Let me take you through some of the missing functionality you would expect from a true database cache.

There is no cross-machine coherency. Let's say you have an online store with purchasing components living in a machine dedicated to processing your business logic. With every purchase, you want to update the total sales for the day. Instead of storing that information

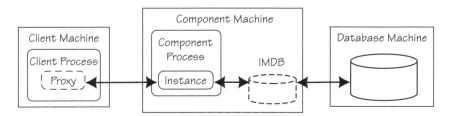

Figure 8.10   IMDB as a database cache.

in the slow-as-molasses database, you decide to put it in the supersonic IMDB. You design a component that updates the back-end database on an hourly basis, just in case the component machine goes down. Everything works great, until one day when your store is featured as the site of the week in a major newspaper. You realize you must scale up, and scale up quickly. No problem. You have read *COM+ and the Battle for the Middle Tier* by Roger Sessions, and have followed his very sage and highly enlightened advice. Your components, therefore, are ready to take advantage of every scalability option COM+ offers. Since you are maxed out on your component machine, you decide to buy two more machines and set them up as an application cluster (as described earlier in this chapter).

Then you notice something odd. Although you are now processing three times as many purchases every day, your total store sales haven't increased a dime. What could possibly account for this? Your problem is that your IMDBs have no cross-machine coherency. So when a purchase is made on Dopey, the total sales are updated in the IMDB on Dopey, but this doesn't make any changes in the IMDB on Sleepy. When a purchase is made on Sleepy, it updates the total sales stored in the IMDB on Sleepy but not on Dopey. So as the total sales are flushed back to the database, each IMDB overwrites the changes reflected in each other IMDB.

There is no true database coherency. Let's say you have loaded a table from the database to the IMDB, and some other application updates the underlying database tables. Let's further imagine that this update application has the audacity to update those database tables *without* going through the IMDB. Your IMDB tables are now no longer up to date with the database. But you'll never find that out! And what if you should then flush your IMDB updates back to the database? Guess what's going to happen to those updates made by that now long-gone update application? You've got it! Roadkill!

Caching is at too coarse a granularity. A true database cache typically works on a page level, where one page of information is brought into memory at a time, and only when the page is accessed. The IMDB works on a table level, where an entire table is brought into memory, whether it is all needed or not. This means that for large tables, most of the data in the IMDB will never be used. Unfortunately, even though it won't be used, you still get to pay the price for bringing it into memory. All of the pain, none of the glory.

All of these problems would be solved by tightly integrating the IMDB cache into the database (e.g., SQL Server) cache. This would guarantee that all middle tier machine caches were kept synchronized. It would mean that non-IMDB database applications would still update the IMDB cache. And it would make the IMDB cache granularity matched to the database cache granularity. Will we see a middle tier/database cache integration? We will just have to wait and see.

Summary

In this chapter, I have introduced the interesting COM+ Services. One of them, the Component Load Balancing Service, will be repackaged into another product. Another of them, In-Memory Database, didn't make it, but probably will be resurrected in a better form. But the other two services will be important to COM+ developers. Asynchronous, or queued components, allow the invocation and the execution of a method to be decoupled in time. In an analagous way, events allow the invocation and the execution of a method to be logically decoupled; the publisher and the subscriber have no knowledge of each other whatsoever.

This is the end of my general introduction to Microsoft's COMWare technology. I have discussed the many technologies Microsoft provides for COM+ components to interact with each other. In the next chapter, I look at some of the technologies Microsoft supports to allow COM+ components to interact with the non-Microsoft world.

COM+ Interoperability

Microsoft often gets beaten up in the press for not supporting standards. I find this surprising, given the impressive body of standards in which Microsoft has participated; in particular, those standards involving the Web. But there is some truth to this notion of Microsoft ignoring standards. The world of standards can be split into two categories: those that have to do with portability and those that have to do with interoperability.

Portability standards try to define common veneers that can be layered on a wide variety of hardware and/or software strata. The goal of any portability standard is to agree on a single API that can be implemented anywhere, in theory, making it possible to write code that can move very easily from one platform to another. Examples of portability standards are SQL (in the database world), UNIX (in the operating system world), CORBA (in the component world), and Enterprise JavaBeans (in the COMWare world). All of these portability standards suffer from an unresolvable clash between two ideals.

On the one hand, a portability standard must be highly generic, defined in such a way that it gives no preference to any one underlying system. In the case of the Java platform (as distinguished from the Java language), we often hear that it can run on a toaster, a mainframe, or anything in between. But the flip side of this is that the standard can support only features that can be *implemented* on both toasters and mainframes. The standard cannot take advantage of any of the good features of either toasters *or* mainframes, both of which have features that make them uniquely qualified for certain tasks.

On the other hand, implementors of standards must find ways to distinguish their product. If a product is truly nothing but a generic implementation of some standard, then there is no reason why a customer would choose one over the other. So vendors try to add value. They add new APIs that work only on their systems. They encourage customers to buy their systems because of how much better their value-added API is than those of their competitors.

So there is this constant clash between vendors touting their products as faithful implementations of some standard which allows customers to readily port code from one vendor to another and vendors trying to convince customers to use their special vendor-specific value added API thereby locking customers into their particular product.

To a large extent, this conflict is unavoidable. A portability standard must, by its nature, be limited. And rarely, if ever, is the limited standard allowed by the rules of portability sufficient for doing production work. Even if it were, the vendors would still be driven by the highly competitive nature of the industry to enhance, enhance, and enhance.

Given this conflict, you might wonder why we even have portability standards. Who cares about them? Probably not the customers, since the vendor-specific enhancements eliminate any real hope of portability. These standards are of interest only to the vendors, and only to a specific group of vendors.

The vendors that care about portability standards are the little guys. When a vendor is not big enough to interest the world in an API specific to that vendor, the standard course of action is to team up with a bunch of other little guys. Their goal is to convince the world that the API is *not* specific to one and only one vendor, but is supported by an entire industry. In fact, this is rarely true. The API as implemented by any one vendor is largely specific to that vendor, with only some generic subset of that API available throughout the industry.

The vendors that do *not* care about portability standards are the trendsetters. Some vendors become important enough so that their APIs are of interest to the whole world, even if they are the only vendors supporting that API. These vendors are in the enviable position of not having to box themselves in to some arbitrary industry designed-by-committee standard. These vendors have the freedom to define whole new industries. MTS, for example, followed no industry standard. Instead, it defined a brand new industry.

So portability standards are problematic, at best. They represent the most generic of capabilities, and become rapidly eroded by the very vendors that are pledged to support them.

Microsoft follows portability standards only when trying to move into an already established technology area, such as it did with SQL Server. SQL Server is their relational database, and was introduced after relational databases were already well established. So Microsoft supported the "industry standard" and then immediately did what every other relational database vendor did, embellished the standard with vendor-specific ornaments that seduce customers, lure them in, and make it as difficult as possible for them to leave. Can customers move from one relational database to another? Of course! Like lobsters can move from one lobster trap to another! Microsoft often gets accused of "embrace and dominate." It does, but this is not unique to Microsoft. This is exactly what every vendor in the world tries to do with every portability standard it supports. Some succeed, some don't. But they all try.

In those emerging industries that Microsoft is defining, such as COMWare, portability standards are of no interest. Nor should they be. These are the new frontiers—these are technologies that need creativity, not committees.

But there is another type of standard that is of interest, even in the new frontiers: interoperability. Interoperability standards have an entirely different goal than portability standards. Interoperability standards are there to recognize that one size doesn't fit all in the software industry. Let toasters toast and mainframes mainframe. Let's just make sure that when the toast is done, there is a way to let the mainframe know so that it can process the information.

Microsoft has designed Windows 2000 and COM+ to solve specific problems very well. Microsoft recognizes that other systems will solve other problems very well. Its attitude is that customers should choose systems that are best suited to specific problems, and then focus on finding ways for those systems to work together. Working together is an interoperability issue, not a portability issue.

Most large corporations would prefer to buy rather than build anyway. When they buy an application, they *run* it, they don't *port* it. They run that application on whatever platform the provider has chosen for whatever reason the provider has chosen it. The nightmare these large corporations face is not porting the application, but getting it to work in concert with the hundreds of other applications they have purchased. This is an interoperability issue. *Interoperability is the key issue facing corporate information technology departments today.* Interoperability, not portability.

Microsoft does recognize this, and fully supports those standards that have to do with interoperability. It is actively working on standards with:

ANSI (American National Standards Institute)

ECMA (European Computer Manufacturing Association)

ETSI (European Telecommunications Standards Institute)

IEEE (Institute for Electrical and Electronics Engineering)

IETF (Internet Engineering Task Force)

ISO (International Organization for Standardization)

ITU (International Telecommunications Union)

NCITS (National Committee for Information Technology Standards)

W3C (World Wide Web Consortixum)

This does not even include standards organizations of which Microsoft is a member, but does not actively participate, such as the OMG (Object Management Group).

Microsoft is now participating in more than 100 different standards activities. Some of the most important, from the perspective of commerce applications, are:

- *SQL.* An ANSI standard for relational database access.
- *GIF.* A graphical interface standard from Compuserve.
- *JPEG.* Joint Photographic Experts Group standard from ISO and IEC.
- *MPEG.* Motion Picture Experts Group from ISO and IEC.
- *PostScript.* Graphics Programming Language from Adobe.
- *TIFF.* Tagged Image File Format from Adobe.
- *IMAP.* Internet Message Access Protocol from IETF.
- *IRC.* Internet Relay Chat protocol from IETF.

- *LDAP.* Lightweight Directory Access Protocol from IETF.
- *MIME.* Multipurpose Internet Mail Extensions from IETF.
- *DNS.* Domain Name System from IETF.
- *FTP.* File Transfer Protocol from IETF.
- *HTTP 1.1.* Hypertext Transport Protocol from IETF.
- *IP.* Internet Protocol from IETF.
- *IPX/SPX.* Internetwork Packet Exchange/Sequenced Packet Exchange protocol Novell.
- *ISND.* Integrated Services Digital Network (ANSI).
- *Kerberos.* Security management infrastructure from IETF.
- *PKI.* Public Key Infrastructure from IETF.
- *DOM.* Document Object Model from W3C.
- *XML.* Extensible Markup Language from W3C.
- *XSL.* Extensible StyleSheet language from W3C.
- *XML Schemas.* From W3C.
- *XML Namespaces.* From W3C.

If your favorite standard is not here, do not despair; there are more than 100 others that I did not list.

As a result, Microsoft operating systems and applications can interoperate with virtually any machine in existence—a UNIX, an Apple, or an IBM AS/400 system—and most of them in one of several ways.

There is no way to cover the entire area of Microsoft interoperability in one chapter. I will limit myself to a few key areas that are most likely to impact you in your efforts to get your COM+ commerce applications to interact with the non-Microsoft world. I will look at three different areas of middle tier interoperability: with non-Microsoft clients, with non-Microsoft middle tier applications, and with non-Microsoft databases.

Client Tier Interoperability

When we think about interoperating with non-Microsoft clients, we are generally talking about the world of Web browsers. This makes it a little more complicated to discuss the relationship between the component tier and the browser, because we have another tier in between, namely, the Web tier. In the Microsoft world, the Web tier is Internet Information Service (IIS). Our assumed configuration is a Microsoft COM+ component tier interoperating with the Microsoft IIS Web tier, and IIS interoperating with non-Microsoft browsers. This is shown in Figure 9.1.

Interoperating with non-Microsoft browsers is complicated by the rapid evolution of standards in the browser area and the relative slow evolution of up-to-date browsers that implement those standards. Even though we have standards for XML and its related technologies for describing data, and DHTML for describing dynamic user interfaces, if we want to write systems that will interoperate with the widest possible variety of browsers, today we can assume only support for HTML. This should be changing over the next year, so in planning for the next generation of systems, it is probably not too soon to start thinking of systems that make good use of all the *ML technologies. Microsoft has been among the first of the companies to jump on the DHTML/XML bandwagon, and support for these technologies is strong in the Microsoft Web tier.

Let me briefly describe the various standards for which we can assume support in the next generation of client side browsers. The *ML standards can be subdivided into two categories: those that describe the general appearance of a Web page, and those that describe data. The "appearance" technologies are the venerable HTML (HyperText Markup Language) and the up-and-coming DHTML (Dynamic HyperText Markup Language). The data technologies are XML (eXtensible Markup Language), which describes data itself, and XSL (eXtensible Style Language), which can describe either how that data is to be presented, or how that data is to be transformed. XML can be used to describe any data, including data describing the data itself, or what we usually call metadata.

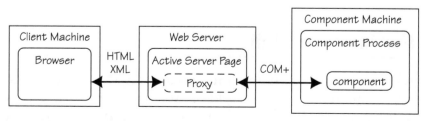

Figure 9.1 Client side interoperability.

When we use XML in this way, we call the XML a *schema*, and some of the standards being developed have to do with standards for describing schemas.

Most people are familiar with HTML. This is the standard string of text that describes a Web page. The biggest problem with HTML is that it is static. The text is created on the Web tier and sent over to the browser where it is displayed. But requests for new Web pages need to go back to the Web tier, which generates new HTML descriptions and sends them back to the browser. This results in a slow user interface experience; most updates to the display need to wait for a new HTML description from the Web tier.

DHTML is designed to eliminate, as much as possible, the trips back to the Web tier for updates to the client machine display. Most of the new display decisions now can be made on the browser machine. Between HTML and DHTML, we have very good ways to describe the layout of Web pages.

XML is to data what HTML/DHTML is to layout. XML gives us a standard way of describing data. In one sense, XML is nothing new—it is really just a text string containing data. We have had text strings for a long time. Most of us have written programs that have returned data as a string. For example, you could write a method called lookupBook that takes a string containing an ISBN number and returns a string containing information about the book. The returned string could contain information about the title of the book and the author. You could then send that text string over to some client side technology that could parse and display the string. Here are several possible strings that could be returned by lookupBook:

- "Romeo and Juliet: William Shakespeare." We interpret this as two substrings separated by a ":". The first substring is the title of the book and the second is the author.

- "title: Romeo and Juliet author: William Shakespeare". We interpret this as four substrings: a field name ("title"), a data value for that field ("Romeo and Juliet"), another field name ("author"), and the data value for that field ("Shakespeare").

Both of these string formats have advantages. The first is shorter, because we don't need to send over data field names; they are assumed. The second is more flexible, because we can send over any arbitrary data about a book. You can imagine the same parser that understands the second string format easily being extended to understand this string: "title: Romeo and Juliet author: William Shakespeare publisher: Classic Tales."

The flexibility of the second string comes from the fact that it is *self-describing*. The string contains information not only about the data ("Romeo and Juliet"), but information on how the data is to be interpreted ("title"). So if I get a string that looks like "title: Romeo and Juliet publisher: Classic Tales" I can still interpret this string. I can assume that this string describes a book whose title is *Romeo and Juliet*, whose publisher is Classic Tales, and whose author is unknown.

There is no limit to the number of ways you could have a string self-describe itself. All of the following are valid self-describing strings:

- "title: Romeo and Juliet author: William Shakespeare"
- "<title> Romeo and Juliet <author> William Shakespeare"
- "title <Romeo and Juliet> author <William Shakespeare>"

Although all of these are valid self-describing strings, they are useful only if both the creator of the string and the consumer of the string agree on how the string is to be interpreted. If a string creator creates a string of the first format and a string consumer assumes it is receiving a string of the second format, we are going to have a problem.

XML is nothing more than an industry-wide agreement on how strings will self-describe themselves. This guarantees there will be no disagreements between the string producer and the string consumer even when the string producer is Microsoft and the string consumer is Sun.

The XML standard says that the data string contains a series of field names and data. Field names are identified by the substring <field-name>. Everything following the field name is assumed to be the data for that field, up to the substring </field-name>. This is assumed to terminate the data for that field name. The following XML substring describes the title of a book:

```
"<title>Romeo and Juliet</title>"
```

and the following XML substring describes the author:

```
"<author>William Shakespeare</author>"
```

We also need to show how these two substrings are related. If we just have the string "<title>Romeo and Juliet</title><author>William Shakespeare</author>", then we don't know how, or even if, these two data items are related. So we would enclose both data items within a larger data item that shows they are both part of the larger concept of book:

```
"<book>
<title>Romeo and Juliet</title>
<author>William Shakespeare</author>
</book>"
```

There is also a standard for the XML schema that explains how to describe what the string can contain. This is more detail that I am going to get into here, but keep it in mind.

How does this impact the middle tier? In a sense, not at all. It is the responsibility of the Web tier to create the XML strings and return them to the browsers. But in another sense, XML is going to have an increasingly large impact on the components themselves.

The most obvious way XML will impact components is on the expectations of how components will return information. Many people are already designing components to return information as XML strings. Programmers making the transition from object-oriented programming to component programming often have difficulty designing their interfaces. They are used to designing interfaces with individual methods to return specific data items. So we could have a book component, for example, that looked like this:

```
interface book
{
  setTitle(ISBN, titleName);
  setAuthor(ISBN, authorName);
  setPublisher (ISBN, pubName);
  string getTitle(ISBN);
  string getAuthor(ISBN);
  string getPublisher(ISBN);
}
```

Why are they passing in an ISBN number? Because they are doing stateless programming, and the ISBN number is the database key. But we still see another rule being violated, the "method = transaction" rule. We could adhere to this rule with this interface rewrite:

```
interface book
{
    setBookInfo(ISBN, titleName, authorName, pubName);
    getBookInfo(ISBN, titleName, authorName, pubName);
}
```

but this code seems a bit fragile. After all, what if we decide to add information on the price? We will have broken our interfaces.

One solution is to pass information in and out of the method via XML strings, in which case we rewrite our interfaces as such:

```
interface book
{
    setBookInfo(ISBN, info);
    string getBookInfo(ISBN);
}
```

In this interface, both the info parameter passed into setBookInfo and the string returned by getBookInfo is assumed to be an XML string. This makes the data coming into and going out of the methods similar to the data that is passed directly back to the client.

I have seen a problem that occasionally occurs when this technique is applied. Some people use XML strings as a lazy way of defining interfaces. So rather than spend the time to design a good interface, some just avoid the issue and have one method that accepts and returns an XML string. You could, in fact, have an entire business system defined with just this one interface:

```
interface myStuff
{
    string doSomething(XML);
}
```

Presumably you use such a system by passing in an XML string that contains information of what to do, whom to do it to, and what information is needed to do it. Here is such a string:

```
"<action>
<verb>update book</verb>
<ISBN>111-12345</ISBN>
<field>author</field>
<data>William Shakespeare</data>
</action>
```

This is legal but it is not good design. Most of the COMWare design, including security, load balancing, instance management, and most of the other issues I have discussed in this book, assume components with well-designed interfaces. I encourage you to use XML strings where appropriate and not as a way to avoid spending the time on good interface design.

This does, however, bring up another usage for XML strings that I expect to become widespread in the next few years. This is as a generic way to invoke a method on a component without having to know anything about the component technology used to implement the component or the COMWare technology used to support the component. The client just makes requests through XML strings that contain the name of the component, the name of the method, and the parameters. The general architecture for such a system is shown in Figure 9.2.

A client using XML as a proxyless technology could use an XML string like this:

```
"<method>
<component>book</component>
<methodName>update</methodName>
<ISBN>111-12345</ISBN>
<price>$50.00</price>
</method>"
```

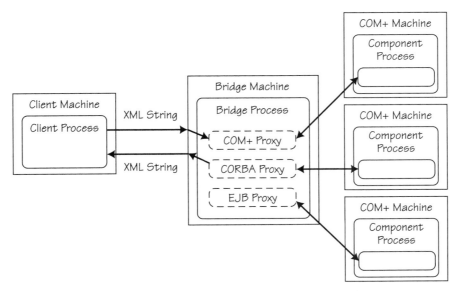

Figure 9.2   XML-based proxyless architecture.

Notice this proxyless XML string looks a lot like the string I just told you not to use, but there is a subtle difference between the two. The first string was used to avoid designing an interface. This second string is used to avoid using a proxy. In this last XML string, I still assume the interface is there, and that this XML string is just another way to invoke a method on that interface.

The nice thing about this architecture is that the client no longer has proxies. Proxies are technology dependent. Get rid of the proxies, and you get rid of the client's dependency on the underlying component technology.

Not only do you eliminate the component technology dependency when you eliminate client side proxies, you also eliminate one of the major performance costs. Creating client side proxies is expensive; perhaps not as expensive as database transactions, but expensive nevertheless. Eliminate client side proxies, fold your bridge machine into your component machine, and you have a component system that runs faster than greased lightening.

Notice that this proxyless architecture works well if you have been designing your components along the rules proposed in this book, around stateless programming, and following the "method = transaction" rule. It does not work if you assume that there is instance state associated with the proxy.

Most well designed component models, such as those of COM+, will work well within a proxyless architecture. Unfortunately, there is one component model that will not. This is the entity bean model of Enterprise JavaBeans (EJB). Sun has been pushing the entity bean model strongly, since it is the main new idea Sun introduced in EJB 1.1 in 1999 over and above what has been in MTS since 1996. I will discuss the EJB architecture and the general problems with entity beans in Chapter 10, "Enterprise JavaBeans." For now, I'll just say that entity beans effectively associate database IDs with client side proxies, and this makes the proxy something that needs to have a long life. Long proxy life is incompatible with proxyless architectures. In proxyless architectures, the proxy has the shortest possible life, no life at all (at least on the client side). The poor ability to play within a proxyless architecture, such as this one based on XML, is just one of the many problems with entity beans and one more reason programmers should avoid them.

In the case study in Chapter 12, "Silknet: Treating Customers as People," I will discuss a customer that has built a whole system around an XML-based proxyless architecture very similar to what I have described here.

Middle Tier Interoperability

No place is interoperability more complex than in the middle tier. And in no place are there more choices, and probably, more confusion about what is needed to achieve interoperability, and even the basic issues of interoperability.

XML in the Middle Tier

The use of an XML-based proxyless architecture, such as I have just discussed in the context of client tier interoperability, can be an effective way to tie together the middle tier. When a middle tier component invokes a method on another component, the invoking component becomes a client, just like any other client. Figure 9.3 shows a similar architecture to the XML proxyless architecture being used to provide a bridge between a COM+ and an EJB component.

COM/CORBA Bridges

There is another bridge technology that is specifically available to tie COM+ components to CORBA components. I will discuss CORBA in

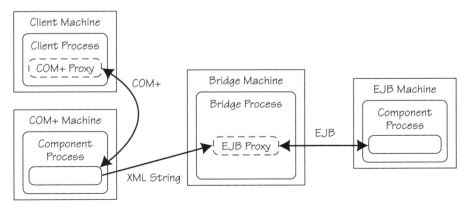

Figure 9.3   XML-based middle tier bridge architecture.

more detail in Chapter 11, "CORBA." The bridge technology that ties together COM and CORBA components is the *COM/CORBA bridge*.

The COM/CORBA bridge is the official OMG (Object Management Group) approach to interoperability between COM+ and CORBA. The OMG standardized a series of mappings between COM and CORBA in September 1997. I am not aware of any company that has used these mappings between COM+ (as opposed to COM) and CORBA; however, there is no obvious reason they should not work for COM+ as well. These mappings can therefore presumably be used to build intermediary components that know how to speak both COM+ and CORBA, and how to translate between the two languages. The OMG defined these mappings mainly to solve the problem of allowing pre-COM+ COM on the client to invoke methods on CORBA in the middle tier, but bridges based on these mappings still could be used to tie together components of the two technologies. Bridge architecture based on the COM/CORBA mappings is shown in Figure 9.4.

Although Microsoft doesn't push this bridge technology, it does cooperate in COM/CORBA bridges. It has licensed the COM source code to companies like IONA, which have built COM/CORBA bridges based on the OMG mappings.

But there are problems with these bridges. First, since COM/CORBA bridges are based on component interfaces, we can use such a bridge only if we can find appropriate component interfaces for linking the two systems together. There is no reason to assume that such interfaces exist. Sec-

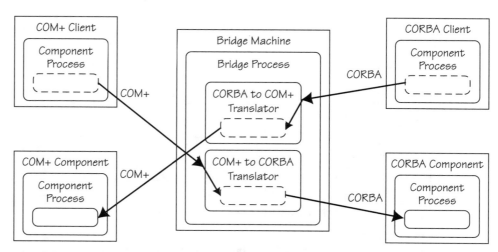

Figure 9.4 COM/CORBA bridges based on OMG mappings.

ond, these bridges are typically synchronous. A CORBA method is received, it is translated to a COM+ method, and it is invoked immediately. These bridges generally do not have the capability to store the methods for later processing. These bridges, therefore, are limited to working between applications that are both up and running at the same time.

Given these two problems, I don't see COM/CORBA bridges as being well suited for middle tier bridging. In fact, I don't even see the problem such bridges solve (component-to-component interoperability) as being the major issue facing the middle tier. From what I have seen, middle tier interoperability is more often a problem of getting *applications* to cooperate, not *components*. In other words, the interaction needs to occur at a higher level than components.

Message Queues as Bridges

If we think about middle tier interoperability as being an application-to-application issue rather than a component-to-component issue, then we have a ready-made solution in the form of message queues. I discussed Microsoft's message queue product, MSMQ, in Chapter 5, "COM+ and Friends." Message queues have a long history in use for interconnecting applications. They will work equally well when those applications happen to be based on component and COMWare technologies. The nice thing about asynchronous message queues is that you get to control the sending, the timing, the format, and the receipt of the message. This is a lot more control than you will ever get from a synchronous component/component bridge.

There is, however, one problem with using MSMQ as an interapplication bridge technology. MSMQ is strictly a Microsoft product that runs only on Microsoft operating systems. By itself, it can't provide an interoperability solution. The most popular message queue product for non-Microsoft platforms is another message queue product, IBM's MQ Series. MQ Series runs on Windows 2000, but does not integrate as well into the COM+ technologies (for example, with asynchronous components) as does MSMQ. So for many people, the best solution will be to use MSMQ on the COM+ platform, MQ Series on the non-Microsoft platform, and an MSMQ/MQ Series bridge to move from one to the other. Although Microsoft does not directly support MQ Series, it does support an MSMQ/MQ Series bridge. The MSMQ/MQ Series bridge was developed by a company named Level 8 and is now licensed and sold by Microsoft. Figure 9.5 shows a

Figure 9.5 Interoperability based on message queues.

typical application/application bridge based on MSMQ, MQSeries, and the Microsoft MSMQ/MQ Series bridge.

Transaction Cooperation

Sometimes interoperability is less about transparent flow of data from one system to another and more about cooperation within a common transaction. Imagine, for example, wanting to make both hotel and flight reservations. You want to book the trip only if both the flight and the hotel are available. But suppose the business logic for the flight is on one vendor's technology and the business logic for the hotel is on another. We don't need to get any data between the two systems. We do, however, want them to act as a unified transaction.

I discussed transactions, distribution transactions, and the so-called two-phase commit protocol in Chapter 3, "Transaction Processing Monitors." Standard distributed transaction coordinators (DTCs) work well when they are responsible for coordinating the work. But suppose the work goes across DTCs. For example, the hotel reservation system is an EJB application and the airline reservation is a COM+ system. And just to make matters more interesting, both are on the Web. How will you get the CORBA DTC to cooperate with the COM+ DTC?

Microsoft has been working with other companies that are experienced in complex transaction processing, such as Tandem (now Compaq), to develop a vendor-neutral protocol that can be used to coordinate transactions across the Web. This protocol is called Transaction Internet Protocol (TIP), and has been submitted to the W3 Consortium as a standard, where it appears to be heading for approval.

COM/DCOM on Other Platforms

Although COM+ in its entirely runs only on Windows 2000, Microsoft has made the basic COM+ component and distribution technology (the original COM and DCOM technology) available on other platforms. This makes it possible to wrap legacy applications running in, say, UNIX, and have them appear as COM+ components. Unlike the component and distribution technology, the COM+ runtime has *not* been made available on these platforms. This makes these other platforms a fairly undesirable platform for the development of new applications (which is probably exactly the reason Microsoft *didn't* port the runtime), but at least we can make use of these existing applications while using a general COM+ component approach. Much of this early COM/DCOM porting effort was pioneered by Software AG, which still sells some of the non-Microsoft COM/DCOM products.

COMTI/Babylon

One final product warrants mention: SNA Server, the new version of which has been going by the name of Babylon. This is Microsoft connectivity technology for mainframes, the most important of which is probably the COMTI technology that allows back-end CICS and IMS IBM mainframe applications to work within the overall framework of COM+. From the CICS or IMS perspective, COMTI is just another client. If you are looking to integrate your IBM systems into the COM+ framework, this will be important technology.

Database Interoperability

Microsoft would love to convince the world to abandon their legacy database base products and turn over everything to SQL Server. This is not going to happen, at least anytime soon. Regardless of how inexpensive SQL Server is and how good it is, legacy systems are here to stay. There is no more inertia anyplace than on the data tier. There is one simple reason for this: it is too hard to move existing data. So Microsoft realizes that if it is to have a serious shot at the middle tier, it must interoperate with a variety of back-end data tier products.

Figure 9.6 gives an overview of Microsoft's database interoperability. The business logic uses a set of data access components called *ActiveX Data Objects* (ADO). ActiveX is a historical term that is no longer relevant, but still rears its head in various product names.

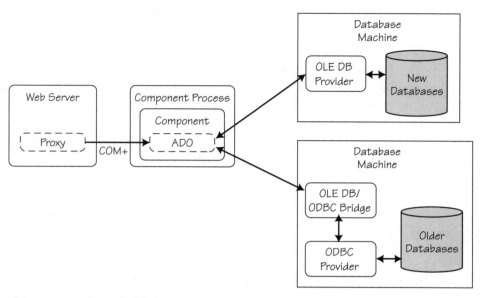

Figure 9.6 Microsoft database interoperability.

ADO is designed to be a general component-based interface for data access, and to work well for a variety of database products. ADO is the client-level interface. Data products can plug into ADO through two different Service Provider Interfaces (SPI): ODBC and the OLE DB.

ODBC is the original Microsoft API and SPI for data access, intended mostly for relational database access. ODBC has since been turned over to standards body, and is now considered something of an industry standard.

OLE DB is the new SPI, intended to be supportable by all data storage products, relational or not. It is closely aligned with the client level API, ADO. Microsoft is trying to encourage data storage providers to write to the new OLE DB SPI, but because of the number of existing technologies based on ODBC, Microsoft provides an OLE DB/ODBC bridge. This bridge allows any database product written for the older ODBC SPI to work as an OLE DB technology, and therefore to be accessible through ADO.

The Microsoft data access strategy is confusing because of the various APIs that have been favored at different times. For the last several years, ADO (on the client side) and OLE DB (on the SPI side) seem to have emerged as viable long-term strategies. According to the Microsoft Web site (www.microsoft.com/data/partners/products.htm), OLE DB providers exist for DB2/400, Oracle, Sybase, Informix, SQL Server, RDB, Ingres, Non-Stop SQL/MP, Non-Stop SQL/MX, RMS, DBMS, MUMPS, Adabas, IBM RS/6000, and ObjectStore, and other database products.

Summary

I think it is clear that Microsoft has put a great deal of thought into interoperability at almost every level. Although I can't cover the entire field of Microsoft's efforts in this area, I hope I gave you a taste of the depth and breadth of the offerings. Interoperability is clearly a strength of the Microsoft technology. Interoperability, not portability. Microsoft believes every platform should do the job for which it was designed, as well as it can do it. But interoperability is critical. Once you have these great platforms, you need to get them to work together.

PART THREE

Competition

The rest of the world isn't standing still while COM+ marches ahead. This part discusses the two primary technologies that are competing with COM+ for control over the middle tier. The Java world, led by Sun, is championed by Enterprise JavaBeans. I'll discuss how EJB works, how it compares to COM+, and the pros and cons to using EJB on the middle tier. The OMG is releasing its COMWare technology, CORBA Component Specification (CCS). I discuss the characteristics of CCS and how it compares to COM+. It is COM+ versus EJB versus CORBA in the software battle of the new millennium: the battle for the middle tier. We have seen what COM+ has to offer. In this section, I look at the other two main factions.

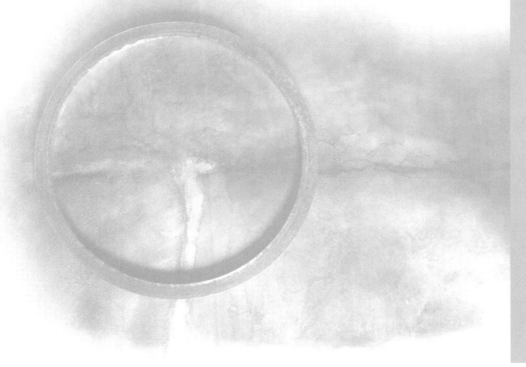

CHAPTER 10

Enterprise JavaBeans

If COM+ will have any serious competition in the next two years, that competition will come from *Enterprise JavaBeans* (EJB). EJB tries to do for Java what COM+ does for COM. Java, of course, is the most recent programming language to hit the airwaves. If you are in the software industry and you haven't heard of Java, then you must have been living in a very dark pit for the last two years.

Considering how many people are enamored of Java, it's interesting how little agreement there is on exactly what Java is. Here are four interpretations of what we mean by the word *Java*.

Java is an object-oriented programming language, much like C++ but better. C++ programmers will appreciate the automatic array checking, automatic garbage collection, and stronger support for interfaces. As a programming language, it has a well-defined syntax and rules for its usage. If you are writing code that follows this syntax and rules, then you are using Java.

Java is a virtual machine, like Visual Basic, but more extensive. The virtual machine is designed to run code that is in a format called byte codes. If you are running something that can be turned into byte code format, then you are using Java.

Java is a portable operating system, like Windows 2000, but supported by more vendors. Since the Java operating system can be layered on top of any real operating system, it provides a layer of operating system independence that allows you to write code that can run anywhere.

Java is an API, like Windows Foundation Class, but cooler. There are pieces of the Java API for virtually any functionality you can think of. Swinging user interfaces? Database access? Online commerce? Whatever your heart desires, somewhere there is a Java API to meet your needs.

EJB is in the spirit of Java as a portable operating system. EJB tries to be the operating system for the middle tier. It defines a runtime environment for components, and the interactions they need to be successful in a multi-tier environment.

Oddly enough, this is not the first attempt to make a portable operating system for Java. The first attempt to define a portable operating system was for the client tier. Much of the early years of Java were spent in an attempt to define a portable operating system that could be layered on any real operating system, which would allow programmers to develop applications that could run anywhere. This would have been a great boom for the software industry, which was then (and now) faced with developing different versions of products for Windows 95/98/2000, OS/2, and Unix, to mention a few. There was great enthusiasm in the industry for a portable operating system that would allow a large application to run anywhere, on any platform, as long as there was a standard version of the Java operating system for that platform.

Unfortunately, that goal was not met. The products that attempted to use the portable Java client operating system were unable to compete, either in functionality or performance, with applications that were developed for the native operating systems. The most visible effort to attempt a large application written 100 percent for the Java operating system was by Netscape. Netscape announced its intention to rewrite its browser for the Java OS. Just a year later Netscape announced that the 100 percent portable Java operating system on the client was inadequate for doing competitive user interfaces, and that it was abandoning the Java OS browser.

Companies faced many obstacles in using Java on the client. Long downloads, restricted security, slow client-server communications, and generally slow and restricted user interfaces were some of the biggest problems faced by designers. To be fair, Java has made recent strides on the client side. Many new improvements were made with Java2 and Swing (an API for creating user interfaces). None of these existed when Netscape was doing their rewrite. But these technologies remain unproven in the world of commerce, and most large companies have lost interest in rich (or so-called "fat") clients anyway, and are now looking to thin client technologies such as HTML, XML, and DHTML. Of the many companies with which I have spoken, few are still considering using Java on the client.

Although the Java OS remains unproven on the client tier, many people hope for a better result on the component tier. They believe there would be two benefits of a component tier Java OS:

The ability to develop middle-tier components that were not tied to one particular operating system. Components could be developed for Windows 2000, and then if Windows 2000 turned out to be unreliable or unscalable, in theory these components could just be moved over to a large Unix system.

The ability to buy components from any source and use them as building blocks for your new application. Components would not have to be developed for just the Windows 2000 platform; they could be marketed at anybody using the Java component tier OS, regardless of the host OS.

The Java component tier OS is *Enterprise JavaBeans (EJB)*. EJB is a specification, not a product, but in order to be successful, that specification must support products that have great middle-tier functionality, performance, and portability.

Keep in mind that performance means something different on the component tier than it does on the client tier. Client tier performance is measured in client response time. On the component tier, performance is measured in transactional throughput. It is beyond the scope of this chapter to discuss the performance of various renditions of EJB. This market is evolving quickly, and only time will tell if and which of the EJB vendors can match the performance throughput of COM+; a product that, unlike an EJB product, is tightly integrated into the underlying operating system, and has a pedigree going back to 1996.

In this chapter, I will focus on the functionality of EJB. And even on this, I am going to have to limit myself. The latest preliminary version of the 1.1 EJB specification is more than 300 pages, not including interface and class descriptions. EJB, like COM+, is just one part (although the most important part) of a middle-tier solution. A full discussion of Java's middle-tier architecture requires a book of its own, and several good ones have been written. I've listed a few suggestions in the bibliography. Here, I will focus on selected aspects of EJB, namely, those design features that distinguish EJB from Component-Oriented Middleware (COMWare) in general and from COM+ in particular, and on some of the implications of these features that seemed to have been missed in the general EJB press.

I have tried to keep this book relatively non-technical, focusing on concepts rather than programming details. For EJB, I will have to go into slightly more depth than I have up until now. EJB has added several highly visible features over and above those offered by COM+. In order to evaluate whether these features are good ideas, fluff, or perhaps even bad ideas, I will need to examine the EJB architecture in some depth.

EJB Component Types

One of the first things we notice about Enterprise JavaBeans is the proliferation of component types. We start with the two main types, *session beans* and *entity beans*, and by the time we add variants on each of these, we have five different possible bean types. (By the way, what I call a component, EJB calls a bean, or strictly speaking, an Enterprise JavaBean.)

The difference between the two basic types, session bean and entity beans, is probably the single most confusing thing about EJB.

Here are some of the qualities that define a session bean, according to the EJB specification.* A session bean "executes on behalf of a single client." It "does not represent directly shared data in the database, although it may access and update such data." It is "relatively short-lived." And session beans are those that are "removed when the EJB Container crashes. The client has to re-establish a new session object to continue computation."

---

*All quotes are taken from the Enterprise JavaBeans™ Preliminary Specification v1.1, ©1999 by Sun Microsystems, Inc., August 10, 1999.

Here are some of the qualities the EJB specification says define an entity bean. An entity bean "provides an object view of data in the database." It also "allows shared access from multiple users." And finally, an entity bean "can be long-lived (lives as long as the data in the database)."

In my mind, the real difference between a session bean and an entity bean has little to do with shared or unshared access; long-lived or short-lived objects; or crashed or uncrashed containers. The single most important difference between a session bean and an entity bean has to do with database IDs, and how they are passed around.

I should point out that my perspective is not shared by many EJB proponents. Most would say that an entity bean is a persistent object, meaning an object that stores its state in a database. They would consider a *customer* an entity bean. They would say that a session bean is more like a business process, one that does not have state in the database. They would consider an *interest calculator* a session bean.

However, I disagree with this differentiation of session and entity beans. Any so-called persistent object can be implemented as *either* bean type. In fact, as I will discuss in this chapter, most persistent objects would be better off implemented as a session bean. The real difference between these bean types is how you will manage the database ID for that persistent object. For entity beans, the system will manage the database ID for you. For session beans, you are responsible for managing the database ID yourself.

To get a better idea of why I consider the database ID management such a linchpin differentiator, let me take you through an example of a bean implementation. Let's go through the process a programmer, say Bernice, goes through to create a Customer bean. Bernice's Customer bean will have two things it can do:

- Retrieve a customer's name, address, and social security number.
- Update a customer's name, address, and/or social security number.

Retrieving and updating data is a fairly simple front for some tables in a database.

Should Bernice make Customer a session bean or an entity bean? Based on its update and retrieval functionality, and the specification's admonition that an entity bean is "an object view of data in the database," the entity choice would be logical. Customer is also "long-lived;" we don't expect to lose the customer when the client program goes away. However, to give some insight into the crucial differences between session beans and entity beans, we are going to have Bernice implement Customer both ways.

An Entity CustomerBean

Bernice starts implementing Customer as an entity bean. The first thing she does is create the Enterprise Bean's home interface. A home is a special type of component, a kind of finder/creator component, that knows how to create and/or find an instance of the bean we care about, a Customer in Bernice's case. Every class of bean has an associated home object that implements Bernice's home interface.

Notice that I am using slightly different language from what I have used in previous chapters. I'm trying to use more of the terminology of EJB, so it won't be too confusing for those of you in the home audience trying to follow along with your own EJB specification.

Back to our home bean story. Each bean type has one and only one home in each component process. Component processes are referred to as *containers* in EJB lingo. Strictly speaking, a container could be something other than a component process, but this will be the most common implementation. So in EJB lingo, each container has a Customer home object, along with homes for any other components it happens to be hosting.

The eventual client, whom we'll call Curly, will use that home object to create a customer. Actually, this will just be an illusion, we'll discuss the reality later. But from Curly's perspective, when he wants a Customer bean, the first thing he must do is find an appropriate CustomerHome object. Once he has this object, he can ask it nicely to create a Customer, and assuming the CustomerHome is happy with the way Curly made the request, out will pop a fully formed Customer bean, ready and willing to do Curly's biding. Under the covers, the CustomerHome object must also insert a record into the database, to reserve the appropriate Customer ID. Once created, this bean will be returned to Curly as a surrogate, as I described things back in Chapter 2, "Components," or, as it is called in the EJB literature, a *reference* to a Customer remote object. The underlying mechanism of the surrogate, or reference, is determined by the implementation of the Java Remote Method Invocation (RMI). The process of Curly creating a Customer bean, from Curly's perspective, is shown in Figure 10.1.

So what must Bernice do to implement the CustomerHome object? It actually turns out to be simple. All she has to do is define an interface for CustomerHome, and the EJB system she is using will automatically generate the code for the CustomerHome object. Let's assume for the purpose of this discussion that Bernice is using the ABC company's EJB system, and therefore ABC's toolset. ABC, by the way, stands for *A Better Container*.

The fact that ABC can automatically generate the code for Bernice's CustomerHome object may seem remarkable, considering that she has wide latitude in defining the interface. How in the world can an automated code generator create code for algorithms that would tax the abilities of most real programmers? I will describe how this works in a moment. But first, let's look at Bernice's CustomerHome interface.

The rules for creating a CustomerHome interface say that it must be derived from the EJBHome interface, which is provided as part of the Java2 extensions to the Java platform. Keep in mind that CustomerHome is an interface, not an object, so it contains no implementation. The implementation will come from the ABC code generator, which will generate a class that we will call ABCCustomerHome. The ABC-CustomerHome will contain generated implementations of the methods Bernice defined in the CustomerHome interface, and those methods inherited from the EJBHome interface. The overall inheritance relationship between the different interfaces (and methods they define) and classes (and methods they implement) related to the Customer-Home is shown in Figure 10.2.

There are at least two methods Bernice will probably define in the CustomerHome interface, assuming, as I said, that Bernice is implementing Customer as an entity bean. She will typically define one or more *create* methods and one or more *find* methods. The create methods are used for creating a Customer bean and the find methods are used for finding an existing Customer bean. There may be none, one, or more than one of each of these, but there must be at least one find method.

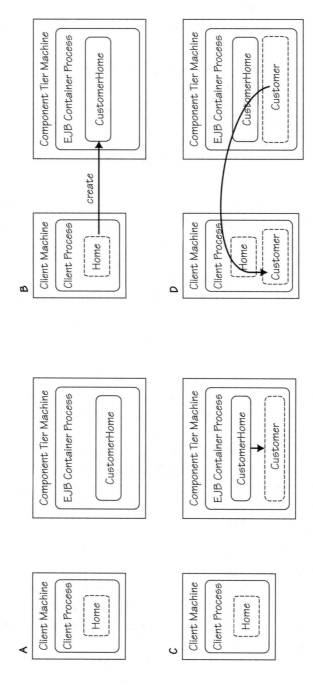

Figure 10.1 Client view of creating a customer bean.

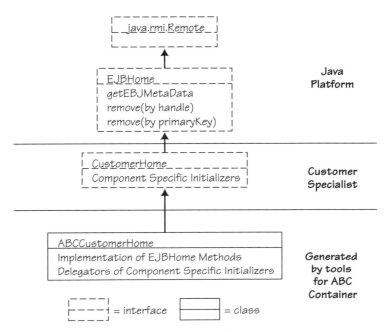

Figure 10.2 The CustomerHome family tree.

The create methods are actually misnamed. They are not used for creating the Customer bean, rather they are used for *initializing* an already created bean. The bean will be *created* using a default constructor on the CustomerBean class. The find methods are used for finding existing beans. Remember, entity beans are beans that the EJB specification says have a lifetime beyond that of a given process. So in theory, we would rarely create entity beans and instead would usually find existing entity beans. In practice, there is no such thing as a bean whose life extends beyond that of a given process. The container is designed to give that illusion. A much better way to think about this is that an *existing* bean is one whose data already exists in some database. If the data already exists, use *find* to get the bean. If it doesn't, use *create*.

Once Bernice has created the CustomerHome interface and generated the ABCCustomerHome class using the ABC code generator, she is ready for the next step: defining the Customer interface. In our case, Bernice will define three methods in this interface:

■ The retrieve method, which returns the information related to a customer.

- The update method, which is used to change information related to a customer.

- The constructor, which is used to actually instantiate a Customer.

The rules for creating a Customer Interface tell Bernice she must derive it from the EJBObject Interface, which is itself derived from java.rmi .Remote. It is this last derivation that defines for Java RMI an interface that can be treated as a remote component. She doesn't actually implement these methods; implementation comes later. Once Bernice has defined the Customer Interface, she uses the ABC code generator to implement the code for the actual Customer object to whom Curly's reference will eventually be speaking. The overall inheritance relationship between the different Customer related interfaces (and the methods they define) and classes (and the methods they implement) are shown in Figure 10.3.

Now it is implementation time. Remember Customer implementation code generated by the ABC tools? Well, it turns out that this code only takes care of the COMWare responsibilities of transactional boundary

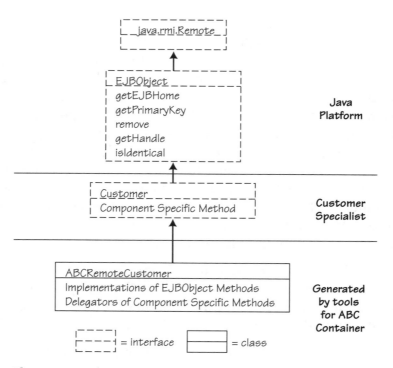

Figure 10.3 The Customer interface family tree.

management, instance management, and all the other niceties that make life worth living in a COMWare world. The real business logic is delegated to another object. Now Bernice has to implement the class to whom all that delegated work will be sent: the actual, factual, honest-to-goodness Customer Bean!

The business of implementing a Customer Bean takes the form of implementing the CustomerBean Java class. For an entity bean, the Customer-Bean class implements a Java-platform-provided interface called EntityBean. Had the bean been a session bean, it would have implemented, guess what? SessionBean interface! EntityBean is an interface derived from another Java-platform-provided interface called EnterpriseBean, which is derived from java.io.Serializable.

Had Bernice been implementing a session bean, she would have had to make another decision: whether or not to implement the Session-Synchronization interface also. Since she is not implementing a session bean (but will later in this chapter), I will postpone my discussion of this interface until then.

Once Bernice has completed the implementation of the CustomerBean class, she again runs her fingers over the magic ABC code generator and produces another class called ABCCustomerBean. The implementation of this class is not specified in the EJB specification, but could be derived from her CustomerBean class and therefore include (via inheritance) all the code she created for CustomerBean plus the newly generated code for ABCCustomerBean. Whatever code is in ABCCustomerBean is specific to ABC's containers, and includes whatever ABC feels is necessary to get the bean to act like a mench in the ABC environment.

The overall inheritance relationship between the different Customer-Bean related interfaces (and the methods they define) and classes (and the methods they implement) is shown in Figure 10.4.

One of the methods Bernice had to implement in her CustomerBean is setEntityContext, a method defined in the EntityBean interface. This method takes a single parameter, which is a Java object that supports the EntityContext interface. When Bernice implements the setEntity-Context method, she should store a reference to the EntityContext object. It will come in handy later on.

The last step is optional. Bernice implements a Primary Key class. This class will serve as a primary key for customers, and will be used in the

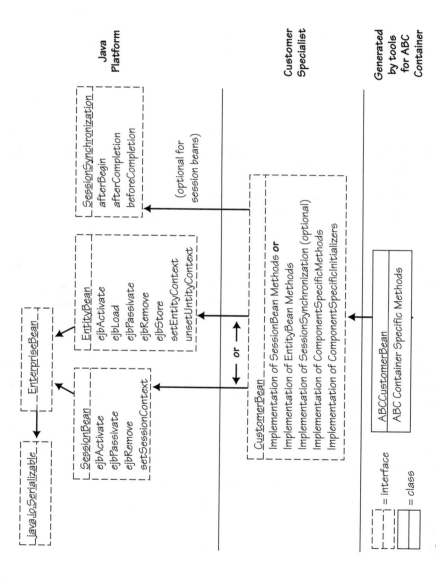

Figure 10.4 The CustomerBean family tree.

implementation of at least one of the find methods defined in her Customer interface. How will it be used in the find methods? Ask Bernice. She is the one who not only gets to define and implement the primary key, but also gets to implement those methods that will use the key, at least for what I believe will be the most usage patterns for entity bean. Should she choose not to implement this class, she can either use a Java string class, or defer this development until deployment.

Just to make sure Bernice didn't forget anything, let's go through what Bernice had to do for her entity CustomerBean:

1. Define the Customer interface.
2. Define the CustomerHome interface.
3. Include in this interface at least one create method and at least one find method (typically).
4. Have the container generate the ABCCustomerHome class.
5. Implement the CustomerBean class (this is where all the real work comes in).
6. Generate the ABCCustomerBean class.
7. Implement the CustomerKey class (typically).

Plugging in the Database

If Bernice is implementing a commerce system (and if she wasn't, she wouldn't be in this book) then we know that someplace out there lurking in the shadows is a database. Commerce systems and databases are inseparable. That tells us that Bernice is going to need to figure out how to get the data from the database into the Customer Bean and back out again.

There are two ways Bernice can manage data flow with an entity bean. The first is through something called *container-managed persistence*. With container-managed persistence, the container itself takes responsibility for moving data from the database to the Customer Bean and back again. To use container-managed persistence, Bernice need do no more than specify which fields in the Customer Bean should be treated as persistent data, use some tool to map those fields to database fields, and the container takes care of the rest. This works great if Bernice isn't too fussy about how or where her Customer's data is being stored. In most real-life situations, Bernice will care a lot, and will probably have data storage requirements that exceed the ability of these tools to cope. She will have specific databases she must use and specific, and often complex data formats she must follow to maintain compatibility with non-JB applications. So the usefulness of container-managed persistence is limited to a few rare situations, at least until these tools improve.

In the real world, Bernice will need to do something a little more complicated than container-managed persistence, something the EJB specification calls *bean-managed persistence*. With bean-managed persistence, Bernice depends on the container only to tell her when she needs to interact with the database, but the interaction itself is Bernice's responsibility.

The container lets Bernice know when it's time to interact with the underlying database by invoking methods on the Customer Bean. When the container invokes ejbCreate, it is time to create new data in the database for this Customer. When the container invokes ejbRemove, it is time to delete this Customer's data from the database. For ejbFind, it is time to find existing data in the database. For ejbLoad, it is time to reload the Customer's data, and for ejbStore, it is time to store the Customer's data. Note that all of these methods (except ejbCreate and ejbFind) are defined in the EntityBean interface, one of the interfaces CustomerBean implements. The methods ejbCreate and ejbFind are just two of the required conventions of entity bean creators.

If Bernice is going to write code to store information to the database, she needs to know some unique IDs to tell her where in the database she should be adding, reading, writing, deleting, and/or finding. Where does Bernice get that information? She gets that information from the associated EntityContext object, the inheritance relationship illustrated in Figure 10.5. From where does she get an EntityContext object? From the setEntityContext method that I discussed earlier. This method is guaranteed to be invoked before any of the database notification methods. Bernice presumably followed my advice and set a local variable to the EntityContext object that was passed in during the setEntityContext method. Now it's time to use that local variable to access the EntityContext object. That is important because the EntityContext interface supports a getPrimaryKey method that returns the primary key for this particular customer. If Bernice is smart, the primary key for the Customer will be closely related to the database ID for the Customer's data in the database. If Bernice is not so smart, then all this coordination by the container will be to no avail.

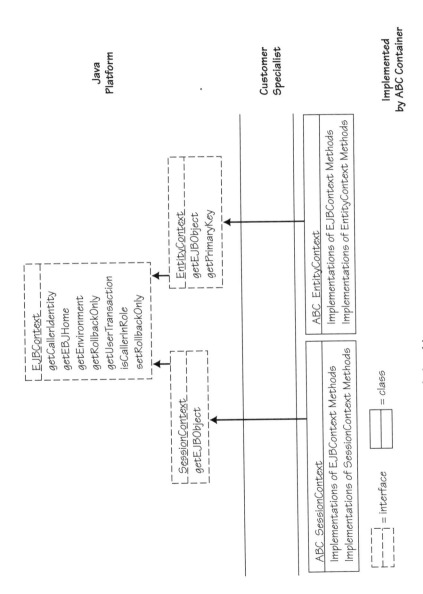

Figure 10.5 Context inheritance relationships.

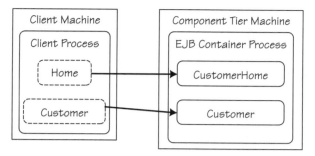

Figure 10.6 Curly's naive view of the world.

By the way, how does the EntityContext find out about the primary key? This is up to the container to figure out, but one way or the other, it must do so at one of the two places EJB can create client references. Client references can be the result of either client-side create or client-side find method requests on the CustomerHome object.

How does Curly the client know a primary key to pass into the find request? That is really Curly's problem. If Curly used a CustomerHome object to create the Customer bean, then he could have asked the newly created object for its primary key through the getPrimaryKey method of EJBObject. A primary key is expected to be serializable, which essentially means it can be turned into a string. Curly can do anything he wants with that string, including write it into a file, and, at a later time, turn it back into a primary key. It is that primary key that is now passed into the find request. If the bean's data found its way into the database through some other application (probably the more common case), then it is up to Curly to figure out what the primary key is.

If we put all this together, we find the world looks a lot more complicated than Curly the client thinks. Curly, dolt that he is, thinks the world looks as shown in Figure 10.6. Hah! Like the world is flat! The real world, the world Bernice knows only too well, looks as shown in Figure 10.7. If Curly only knew. But of course, this is the whole point of EJB; the value of any COMWare product is in how well it shields clients from the complexities of the real world.

There's No Place Like Home

Before Curly can do anything with an entity Customer component, either creating or finding, he must first get a reference to the CustomerHome

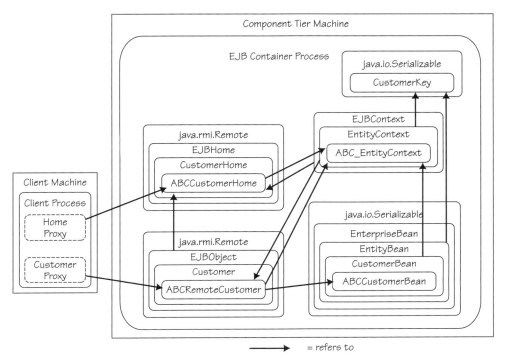

Figure 10.7 Bernice's world for entity beans.

object. The key to the container is through that home object. Curly finds the home object using another part of the Java API, the *Java Naming and Directory Interface* (JNDI). This API allows us to find distributed objects by preassigned names. The process of installing a home object into a Java container includes the process of installing its name into the JNDI system. So as long as Curly knows the name of the home object, he can use the JNDI to find it. And once he has found the home object, he can use it either to create or to find entity instances, such as a Customer.

EJB as COMWare

None of this bean stuff is very interesting unless EJB can provide some serious Component-Oriented Middleware (COMWare) functionality, à la Chapter 4, "COMWare." Just in case you have forgotten, some of the expectations we have of a COMWare environment are scalability, automatic transaction boundary management, and configurable security. All of these require a *point of interception*, a spot at which the component runtime environment (the container, in the EJB case) can intercept methods as they travel from the client to the component instance and then back again. The most important of these point-of-interception algorithms are the instance management algorithms I discussed in Chapter 4. These are the algorithms that form the basis for scalability.

Where is the point of interception in EJB? It is in the ABCRemote-Customer class, the one to which Curly's reference naively points. This is the object that receives all of Curly's reference's requests, and that will eventually pass these request on to the business logic contained in CustomerBean. But what happens between the time when the ABC-RemoteCustomer gets the request from Curly and when it passes it on to the CustomerBean is entirely up to the container, as long as it follows the general rules laid down by the specification. And what exactly it will do will be based on the configuration of the CustomerBean, such as the security constraints, the transaction boundary configuration, and how the component has been configured for instance management. As you can see, the point-of-interception architecture of EJB is almost identical to that of COM+, as I described in Chapter 7, "The COM+ Runtime Environment." And the COM+ point of interception architecture is almost identical to that of Microsoft Transaction Server (MTS), introduced three years earlier than EBJ.

Entity Beans versus COM+ Components

Because the point of interception model for entity beans is very similar to COM+ components, there is no essential difference between the COMWare capabilities of the two models. However there are two advantages to the entity beans model that are not related to COMWare capabilities. These advantages have to do with the *client usage model* and the *component implementation model*.

The client usage model of entity beans is more attractive than that of COM+ components because clients do not need to pass the database ID in as a parameter to every single method. As I showed in Chapter 7, this *is* a requirement for COM+ components. The reason clients of entity beans do not need to pass in the database ID is because the component code can figure out for itself the database ID from its EntityContextObject's getPrimaryKey method.

The implementation model of entity beans is also more attractive than the implementation model of COM+ because of where the database access code is located. In an entity bean with bean-managed persistence, this code is located in a few well-partitioned methods that do not clutter up the main business logic. In an entity bean with container-managed persistence, the database access code is within the container, where you never see it.

In COM+, the database restore and store code must start and end each method respectively, as I discussed in Chapter 7. This is because in COM+ there is no well-orchestrated scheme for the runtime environment to let the component code know when it is time to restore and store, and no concept of persistence built into the container itself. We might assume that the restore and store code could go in the activate and deactivate methods (also discussed in Chapter 7), but these methods have no way to let the component know about the database ID, without which it's pretty hard to do much with the database. So the only place left to place that code is in the business methods proper where the database ID can be made available as a parameter. Not having database access code anyplace is not an option; it must be there and it must be there in such a way that its usage is coordinated with the overall transaction boundaries (as discussed in Chapter 4). Otherwise the instance management algorithms cannot work. If the instance management algorithms cannot work, then scalability is out the window, and the main point of COMWare is lost.

So the entity bean model is better that the COM+ model on two counts:

- Not forcing the client to pass in the database ID on every single method invocation is clearly a preferable client-programming model.
- Not having to clutter up the business logic with database access code is a nicer implementation model.

Both of these advantages come to entity beans because of one essential design feature: the database ID is effectively associated with the reference (indirectly, through the EntityContext), and is therefore available to every method (or at least the methods about which we are concerned) at any time.

The strength of the entity bean model is also its greatest weakness. The fact that the database ID is associated with the reference means that once the association between a database ID and a reference has been made, it can't be changed. There is no way in the entity bean model for a client to tell a reference that its database ID has changed.

It *is* possible for the container to tell an EJB EntityBean that its database ID has changed. You can do that by changing its EntityContext. And in fact, this happens quite regularly in EJB as a natural side effect of the instance management algorithms. But only the *container* is allowed to reset an EntityContext; this is not an option available to clients. The client doesn't even have access to the EntityContext. The *client* model is that once a database ID has been associated with a bean, it can't be changed.

The potential problem with all this is that the creation of a reference to an entity bean is a very time-consuming operation in EJB. It requires the following:

1. A call to find a remote name context to the Java Naming and Directory Interface (JNDI).

2. A remote method call to that name context to find the Home object and get a reference to it.

3. A remote method call to the Home object to get a reference to the bean.

4. A search in the database to find the appropriate object data and possibly load the data (depending on the EJB implementation), requiring a transaction.

Step 4 is by far the most expensive of all of these, because it requires a database search and a transaction. Even if we have efficient search indexes set up, this is going to be costly. Because neither COM+ nor session bean references require this step, these are both much faster at reference creation. In some situations, this cost is not going to matter, in others, it will. It mainly depends on how long you are going to use that reference once you have it. If you are going to make many requests to that same remote object, then the cost of the reference creation as it becomes amortized over those many requests will eventually drop to negligible. But in situations where you are going to use that reference only briefly, you may find that the cost of using a remote entity bean is almost entirely dominated by the cost of acquiring the reference.

So although the EJB entity bean model is attractive from both a client and a programmer perspective, it is also a very expensive model. Whether or not it is a better model overall than the COM+ model depends on whether or not that expense can be justified by long-term reference usage. Nobody is going to put up with a model that has a 100 to 200 percent performance penalty, which is what the cost is likely to be for short-term entity bean reference usage, just because the model is more aesthetically pleasing. But for long-term entity bean reference usage that penalty could drop to less than 10 percent, a reasonable cost for aesthetics. So which is more likely? Short-term or long-term usage?

In some programming situations, you can reduce some of the reference acquisition costs. If you are going to create a large number of bean references and you can figure out a way to hold onto the reference for the home object, then you might be able to create the home object reference once and use it over and over. This eliminates the need to create the home reference for all but the first bean creation, steps 1 and 2 For example, you might imagine a Bank bean that supports a method to get information about a customer. It might create a home object when the Bank bean is first initialized, store it in a local variable, and then use the same home object for every customer query. But the remaining costs are fixed. There is nothing you can do to eliminate them. And especially for step 4, the database search, this is a real potential problem.

The question of how long a typical client will use an entity bean reference is a question to which we will return. But first, let's look at the EJB alternative to the entity bean model: the session bean.

A Session CustomerBean

Bernice has finished creating her Customer as an entity bean, and is now ready to tackle the session bean implementation. The general ideas are very similar. She defines the CustomerHome interface derived from the EJBHome interface and uses the ABC code generator to create the ABC-CustomerHome. She creates the Customer interface derived from EJBObject and uses the ABC code generator to create ABCRemoteCustomer.

When she gets to the CustomerBean, she must define her class as implementing the SessionBean interface, rather than the EntityBean interface as she did to make the Customer an entity bean. The SessionBean interface has fewer methods than did the EntityBean interface, and one method changes. The changed method is setSessionContext, which takes as a single parameter a SessionContext object. When Bernice was implementing Customer as an EntityBean, the method analogous to setSessionContext was setEntityContext, which took an EntityContext as its parameter. You might refer back to Figure 10.4, which shows the inheritance relationship of session beans.

Like before, Bernice must implement the setSessionContext, which should be implemented by setting a local variable to the SessionContext object that was passed in. For session beans, Bernice will have less use for this object, but still, it could come in handy.

The major difference between a session and an entity bean is in the associated context object. If you refer back to Figure 10.5, you can see the difference between SessionContexts and EntityContexts. The most important difference is that whereas the EntityContext supports the getPrimaryKey method, the SessionContext doesn't. This one difference has a huge implication to what you can do to a session bean.

Without the getPrimaryKey method, there is no way for anybody to get a primary key for a session bean Customer. Since you can't get the primary key, there is no real point to having one, and in fact, the EJB model for session beans is that they don't have a primary key. So they have no find methods, which, among other possibilities, would be expected to take a primary key. Bernice's world for session beans is shown in Figure 10.8, which should be contrasted with Bernice's world for entity beans shown back in Figure 10.7.

Oddly enough, even though the EJBSessionEntity does not support getPrimaryKey, the ABCRemoteCustomer object, the object to which Curly

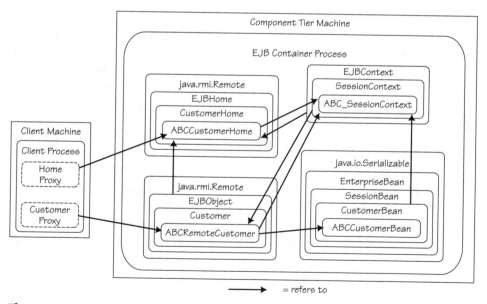

Figure 10.8 Bernice's world for session beans.

the client's reference points, does support getPrimaryKey. How can this be? If Curly invokes getPrimaryKey on a session bean, it returns an exception.

There is no reason why the ABCRemoteCustomer's derivation pattern (as shown in Figure 10.3) shouldn't parallel the derivation pattern of the CustomerBean (as shown in Figure 10.4), which would have solved this problem. EJB proponents claim this was done to "simplify" the interface inheritance. If this were true, we would expect a similar "simplification" in the derivation of the CustomerBean and the entity interfaces.

More likely, this odd inheritance was an oversight, an oversight whose correction would now require breaking existing code, and perhaps an admission that even Sun can make mistakes. In any case, I am told that Sun is not planning on any changes in this area, and the longer they wait to fix this, the more code they would break by doing so. It looks like future generations of programmers will be stuck with trying to understand this rather bizarre use of inheritance. I am sure they will be quite happy to hear how this has "simplified" their lives.

The bottom line then is that session beans don't have primary keys. The reason for this is that in the EJB design philosophy, session beans exist only for this session. Primary keys imply a bean that existed before this session began and will end sometime in the distant future.

Let's review what Bernice wants her Customer component to do. She has two goals for her component. First, it must retrieve a customer's name, address, and social security number in some type of a get-CustomerInformation method. Second, it must be able to update a customer's name, address, and/or social security number in some type of an updateCustomerInformation method.

The getCustomerInformation method needs to read the customer's information from the database, and to do so, it must have a primary key for that customer. How will it get it? Since it isn't available any other way, Bernice must design the method so that it accepts another parameter, which is the database ID.

The updateCustomerInformation method needs to update the customer's information in the database, and to do so, it also must have a primary key for that customer. How will it get it? The same way the getCustomerInformation method got it, through a parameter.

Since each of the methods is getting its database key through a method parameter, where will any necessary read/write code go? The answer is that the read code will be in the beginning of each method and the write code will be at the end. This will also be required to get the code working properly for instance management and boundary management, as discussed in Chapter 4.

Notice that something very odd is happening here. The programming techniques we need to use for EJB session beans are starting to look a lot like the programming techniques we need to use for stateless COM+ components, as I discussed in Chapter 6, "COM+ Components." And in fact, they are alike, at least from a bean implementor's perspective. Of course, there are a myriad of minor differences in the details, but at a high level, these two component models are very compatible. In both cases, the database ID is passed in as a method parameter. In both cases, the method starts with a restore from the database and ends with a store to the database.

At a client level, the difference between session beans and entity beans are a little less apparent. Session beans, like entity beans, still are instantiated through their home object. There are two major differences from Curly's perspective. One is that he must now pass in a database key to each method invocation. The other, that I have already discussed, is that he will get a little electrical shock should he ask the unsuspecting session bean to get its primary key.

The Stateful Variant

There is a variant on the session bean that is called a *stateful session bean*. This is a misnomer, since the Customer session bean I have just been discussing is also stateful; it's just that its state is stored in a database, as you would expect from any self-respecting commerce component. What the EJB folks mean by a stateful session bean is one that acquires state over the course of several method invocations. Such a bean violates the design rule of "method=transaction" that I have discussed throughout this book, but EJB advocates would probably counter, saying that they don't buy into that design rule in the first place. Whether or not you use the stateful variant will therefore depend on how you feel about the relationship between methods and transactions.

The SessionSynchronization Variant

There is another variant on the stateful session bean. This is a stateful session bean that supports the SessionSynchronization interface, shown in Figure 10.4. The purpose of this interface is to let the bean know when transactions are starting and ending. Since stateful session beans are not supposed to (according to Sun) readily map to a traditional database, it's not clear to me how this information is useful. If we had access to a primary key, we could potentially do some database synchronization, but because this is a variant of a session bean, we don't have this access. In any case, if you are designing your bean around the recommendations of this book, your method boundaries will be the same as your transactional boundaries, so an additional interface to let you know when transactional boundaries have occurred seems unnecessary.

Comparing the Entity and Session Beans

Bernice has now implemented the Customer bean two ways: as an entity bean and a session bean. Which is a better implementation? The standard Sun answer would be that the entity bean implementation is not only the *better* implementation, but the *only correct* implementation. Your bean represents persistent data, they would say, therefore it *must* be an entity bean. But, rebels that we are, would like to evaluate this for ourselves, so let's look at both implementations, with three different bean usage patterns.

Pattern one will be the simplest. In this pattern, Curly is concerned with creating one customer and getting its credit limit, period. Here is Curly's code for Bernice's entity bean in pseudocode:

```
nameService = getNameService;
CustomerHome = lookup (home for Customer Bean);
customer = CustomerHome.find("1234");
display (customer.name());
```

Here is Curly's code for pattern one using Bernice's session bean:

```
nameService = getNameService;
CustomerHome = lookup (home for Customer Bean);
customer = CustomerHome.create();
display (customer.name("1234"));
```

Which of these is better? Most EJB folks would recommend the former, as the customer seems to fit the general notion of a bean that will outlast the client's process. But the entity implementation has a problem. It is much less efficient than the session implementation. This is because the cost of the reference creation is much higher for the entity bean than for the session bean. The reason it is higher is because it, unlike the session reference creation, requires a database lookup. It requires a database lookup to make sure the "find" has actually "found" an existing customer. There is no way to tell this without going to the database.

We might assume that the database lookup in the find method will be paid back by not having to do a database lookup in the invocation of customer.name(). But this is not true. The customer.name() invocation will also require a database lookup. If we try to avoid the second lookup, we risk the transactional integrity of the bean; someone else might have come in and changed the bean's data since we did the find. As I discussed back in Chapter 4, all COMWare, including EJB, requires that transactional boundaries be the same as method boundaries. This means the bean's data has no protection between the find and the display. The display *must* therefore reread the data from the database.

Pattern two is a little more complicated. In this pattern, Curly wants to show the credit limit for three different customers. Here is Curly's code for Bernice's entity bean:

```
nameService = getNameService;
CustomerHome = lookup (home for Customer Bean);
...
customer1 = CustomerHome.find("1234");
display (customer1.name());
...
customer2 = CustomerHome.find("1212");
display (customer2.name());
...
customer3 = CustomerHome.find("1111");
display (customer3.name());
```

Here is Curly's code for pattern two using Bernice's session bean:

```
nameService = getNameService;
CustomerHome = lookup (home for Customer Bean);
customer = CustomerHome.create();
display (customer.name("1234"));
...
```

```
display (customer.name("1212"));
...
display (customer.name("1111"));
```

In some scenarios, we can have the CustomerHome find a collection of beans. But this only works when we know all of the beans that we want to find before we have found any. Often we are in a much more interactive and dynamic environment, in which future finds are based on past finds, and present interactions with the client. In those scenarios, which I believe will be more common, we need to find the beans individually. Here the cost for the entity reference is now much more expensive than the session reference. Not only is the cost of the first reference higher (as it was in the pattern one usage), but we must create three times as many references to do the same job.

The final pattern is a variant on pattern two. In this pattern, Curly is not using the Customer directly, but is interacting indirectly through some other blob of software. That blob has the following characteristics: it is initialized the first time it starts, then the body of the blob executes over and over with each request from Curly, Carla, or any other client. The code written by Curly (or Carla) that uses this blob looks the same for either the entity or the session bean:

```
request blob to displayCustomer ("1234");
```

The blob code using Bernice's entity Customer looks like this:

```
initializer (executed once):
  nameService = getNameService;
  CustomerHome = lookup (home for Customer Bean);
main body (executed many times):
  customer = CustomerHome.find("1234");
  display (customer.name());
```

The blob code using Bernice's session Customer looks like this:

```
initializer (executed once):
  nameService = getNameService;
  CustomerHome = lookup (home for Customer Bean);
  customer = create();
main body (executed many times):
  display (customer.name(ID));
```

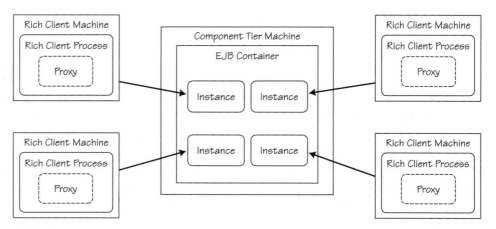

Figure 10.9   Rich client scenario.

For this pattern, the initialization costs for the session bean is actually higher than for the entity bean since it includes the customer reference creation as well as the Customer home reference creation. But initialization costs are usually not important in this type of scenario, because it occurs very infrequently. The much more important cost is the cost of executing the main body, which happens over and over, perhaps thousands of times for every one initialization. The main body using the session bean will execute much faster than the main body using the entity bean. The session code completely eliminates the cost of the reference creation.

So let's summarize the state of affairs. If we use an entity bean instead of a session bean, we get a questionable improvement in aesthetics and no improvement in functionality. In return for that, we pay moderate performance cost in a pattern one scenario, a significant performance cost in a pattern two scenario, and a considerable performance cost in a pattern three scenario.

The next question is which of these patterns will be the most common? It turns out that pattern one, the pattern for which entity beans do the best, is by far the least common. A typical rich client scenario, as shown in Figure 10.9, is probably as close as we will ever come to a pattern one, even though it will often look more like pattern two than pattern one.

The most common usage of the bean is a thin client scenario, where the bean client proper is actually a Web server. In the pure Java environment, the actual bean client will be a Java servlet, as shown in Figure 10.10. We

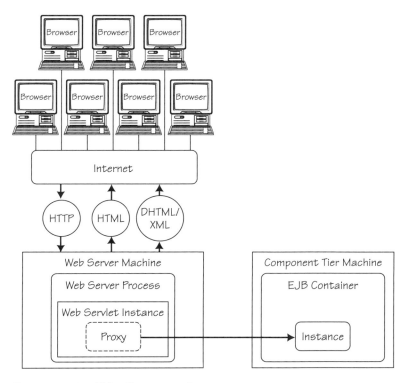

Figure 10.10 Thin client scenario.

aren't going to spend time discussing servlets in any detail here, but there is one point that is important to understand. A Java servlet is a blob of software that follows pattern three.

We see then that the most common scenario for running beans is exactly the scenario for which entity beans have the worst possible performance. Thus if Bernice wants her bean to give the best performance in the most common usage scenario, she should create it to be a stateless session bean. In fact, if she wants it to perform well in any usage scenario, she should make it a stateless session bean.

Now if Bernice is absolutely positive her clients are always going to be pattern one clients, then she might decide to implement her Customer as an entity bean, even knowing her bean will be somewhat less efficient. But this is a huge risk. What if she wants to sell her bean to somebody using pattern three? There is no way Bernice's entity Customer, with its constant need for expensive reference creation, can compete with somebody else's session Customer, with its infrequent need for inexpensive reference creation.

Even worse, once Bernice realizes the error of her ways and decides to reimplement her entity Customer as a session Customer, she can't! She is trapped! Once she has clients using her entity Customer, she has a contractual obligation to continue as an entity Customer. This is because the client side contracts are *different* for session Customers than for entity Customers. Bernice's existing client base is dependent on the *entity* contract. Bernice has painted herself into a corner.

Given this analysis, I make the following claim. Although entity beans may seem to offer a more attractive programming model in some scenarios, that aesthetic advantage is more than outweighed by performance considerations. Given the increasing importance of thin (pattern three) clients, for whom entity beans do the absolute worst, it is difficult to imagine that anybody will want to implement any business logic using this inefficient model.

Rehabilitating Entity Beans

There is one issue concerning entity beans that makes them difficult to avoid in real life. Sun has mandated that entity beans are the official way to implement persistent objects. This in itself wouldn't bother me. After all, what do I care what Sun mandates? But unfortunately, the tool vendors do care, and have designed their tools around the assumption that persistence means entity beans. So, if you want to use most vendors' tools to implement persistence, you must find some way to use entity beans without paying too high a performance penalty for the extra database access. There are two ways to do this.

One way you can use entity beans without taking the performance hit is to assume that you are using a high end EJB product that does some type of instance caching. In this scenario, the container only goes to the database if it can't find the instance in an in-memory cache. In the worst case, the container would go to the database to accomplish the find, and would then store the object in the in-memory cache. This eliminates the need to go back to the database to get the data, since that object would now be in the cache. Although the entity bean still performs no faster than a session bean, at least it now performs no slower. Unfortunately, there are several problems with this approach.

The first problem is that this approach is highly dependent on the container implementation. It will only work on containers that implement an in-memory cache, and such a cache is not part of the EJB specification. If you depend on an in-memory cache to make up for deficiencies in the entity bean model, you are going to find your portability limited, and portability is presumably one of the main reasons you are using EJB in the first place.

The second problem with depending on a cache is that it makes your implementation very fragile. EJB container caches work only when *all* updates to the database go through a single EJB container. In most common scenarios, updates occur through a variety of legacy and third party applications, none of which could care less about your container's cache and its problems. And even if today all updates are going through your EJB container, how do you know some new non-EJB application won't turn up tomorrow with a need to update your database and threaten your cache?

The only way to guarantee that all database updates are reflected in the instance cache is to use a highly specialized container, most likely developed by the database vendor. But this code is highly nonportable.

So we can eliminate the container cache as a solution to the performance problems of entity beans. Notice that the problems I described here are very similar to the problems I described in Chapter 8, "COM+ Services," for the COM+ In Memory database. Any cache that is not directly tied to the underlying database is a cache that cannot be guaranteed to be in synch with the underlying database. And a potentially out-of-synch cache is a time bomb waiting to explode. It may not explode tomorrow or even next month. But sooner or later, probably when you least expect it...BOOM! The need to make the cache part of the underlying database to ensure cache coherency is a basic law of computer science. Microsoft can't change it. Sun can't change it.

But there is another solution to the performance problem of entity beans, and this solution has more promise. To see how this solution works, let's re-examine the underlying problem with entity beans. The performance problem occurs because the creation of the entity bean proxy requires a separate transaction from the transaction required for the data access.

But what if we didn't need a separate transaction? What if we could accomplish both method invocations in the same transaction? This would eliminate the need to go back to the database, because we wouldn't release the locks acquired by the first method invocation (the find) until we have completed the second method invocation (the data access). But this seems to violate the basic COMWare principal that says that a method equals a transaction.

How do we reconcile, on the one hand, forcing multiple method invocations into one transaction, and on the other hand, having a rule that says a method equals a transaction? We can do this by guaranteeing that an entity bean will never be visible to the client; that it will always be buried under a session bean. We are then saying, in effect, that entity beans are not part of the component model of EJB *per se*, but simply an implementation tool that you may or may not use to implement the real components, which are session beans.

When we bury an entity bean under a session bean, we can make sure that both method invocations occur within the same transaction. An entity bean does not require a *new* transaction, just *some* transaction. If the enveloping session bean is configured as requiring a transaction, and all the entity bean invocations occur from within a single session bean method, then all of the entity bean method invocations will be contained within the transaction started and ended by the session bean method.

There is nothing special about EJB here. This is the standard transaction model for all COMWare platforms, as I described in Chapter 4. Once we have wrapped the entity bean method invocations inside a session bean method invocation (and therefore a session bean transaction), the entity bean performance is acceptable again. But don't forget: this works *if and only if* the entity bean is always hidden by the session bean. As soon as you make the entity bean visible to the client, each of its methods becomes a separate transaction again and performance drops off precipitously.

Perhaps someday you won't have to worry about all of this. Perhaps the tools vendors will realize the limitations that result from Sun's mandate that persistence is only an entity bean issue. Or even better, perhaps Sun will see the problem of the entity bean model and un-mandate its usage. But I wouldn't count on either of these occurring in the near future.

Overview of EJB Beans Types

EJB offers five main options in creating beans, all of which I have already discussed, but I will summarize them here.

Entity beans with bean-managed persistence. This is a bean where the container manages the database ID (the *entity* part), but not the format or location of the stored data (the *bean-managed persistence* part), which is controlled by the bean. This is generally an undesirable bean because of the performance overhead of the reference creation, unless it is buried as an implementation detail of a session bean. This type is not supported by COM+.

Entity beans with container managed persistence. This is a bean where the container manages both the database ID and the format and location of the stored data. This is generally an undesirable bean both because it allows too little flexibility when working with standard databases and suffers from the same performance overhead in the reference creation as does the Entity bean with bean-managed persistence. This type is not supported by COM+.

Stateful session beans. This is a bean that holds state across method invocations. This type is supported by COM+, although I don't recommend its use (either in COM+ or EJB) because it violates the "method=transaction" rule

Stateful session beans with SessionSynchronization. This is a stateful session bean that has transactional boundary notification turned on. This additional information doesn't help solve the problem of synchronization with traditional databases, and therefore offers no significant advantages over stateless session beans. This type is not supported by COM+

Stateless session beans. This is a bean that has great flexibility in working with databases and has very efficient reference creation. And, like all good components living in a COMWare environment, can take full advantage of instance management algorithms (and is therefore highly scalable). Now that is a bean! (And it *is* supported by COM+.)

Notice something strange about all this? EJB offers five bean types. Four of them have limited, if any, value. One of them is very useful and also happens to be the one that is favored today by COM+ and by MTS since 1996. Spooky, isn't it?

COM+ versus EJB

You may think, after all this, that I hate Enterprise JavaBeans. Not so. My point here is not that EJB is bad, but that only that it offers no important functionality (for distributed commerce applications) over and above what has been offered by MTS since 1996 and what COM+ offers today. Its bean model is no better than the COM+ stateless component model. Its overall functionality is no better than COM+. In fact, COM+ has several things going for it that EJB doesn't have:

COM+ is mature. It is the second generation of COM/DCOM/MTS, technology that has been with us since 1996 and has proven itself in mission-critical commerce applications, two of which I have given case studies for in this book. EJB is immature and unproven technology.

COM+ offers capabilities not matched in EJB. COM+ has asynchronous components, a better event model, load balancing, failover support, and excellent interoperability. None of these are in the current EJB specification. Any products that do include these features today do so in proprietary manner.

COM+ does not tie you to one language. You can write a COM+ component in any language: Visual Basic, C, C++, Java, COBOL, and others. EJB beans can be written in one and only one language: Java.

Most of COM+ is free, or at least, it comes with Windows 2000. If you buy Windows 2000, you have COM+. If you don't use it, Microsoft is not going to give you any of your money back. EJB must be purchased as an add-on to Windows 2000. And though some versions of it will be available inexpensively, these are not the versions you are going to trust for your mission-critical application. Mission-critical applications will require very sophisticated high-end EJB implementation, the kind you will get from companies that have strong backgrounds in Transaction Processing Monitors. Those versions are *not* going to be available inexpensively.

The major thing EJB has going for it is that it is supported by many vendors on many operating systems. Unfortunately, it is *not* supported by Microsoft, the one vendor whose operating system, according to most industry analysts, is likely to dominate the component tier. But other vendors can create versions of EJB for Windows 2000. The problem is that these versions will be layered on top of Windows 2000, not integrated tightly into the operating system, as is COM+. Therefore Windows 2000 EJB projects are unlikely to run as well as COM+. And, of course, these versions will not be free.

But still, EJB does offer a promise of portability. That promise is overstated in the specification, which says, "Enterprise JavaBeans applications will follow the Write Once, Run Anywhere philosophy of the Java programming language. An enterprise Bean can be developed once, and then deployed on multiple platforms without recompilation or source code modification."

Although it is potentially true that the home interface definition, the business logic interface, and the bean implementation may not require modification, it is highly unlikely that any of the code generated from one vendor's tools will be compatible with the expectations of any other vendor's container. This generated code includes the ABCCustomerHome, shown in Figure 10.2, the ABCRemoteCustomer, shown in Figure 10.3, and the ABCCustomerBean, shown in Figure 10.4. If you are using bean-managed persistence, the generated code will also include database mapping logic.

Code generation, especially the database mapping code for container managed entity beans, is likely to be a significant task, requiring expertise with the tools from a particular vendor. The newly generated code, once it has finally been generated, is going to have to be compiled before it can be used. So to imply that beans can be downloaded from anyplace and used without requiring recompilation, as described by the EJB specification, is inaccurate.

But there is no question that some degree of portability will be achieved. EJB-based products will be available that run on many operating systems. As long as you are willing to stick with one vendor, you can run on any operating system that vendor supports. You can even achieve some degree of vendor independence, as long as you are willing to write only to the standard EJB API.

The idea of a standard EJB API will probably exist more in theory than in reality. All vendors will try to differentiate their EJB products by offering special, cool, extremely attractive add-on services. We have already discussed one important differentiation, the in-memory object cache. The specification allows this, saying, "Specialized containers can provide additional services beyond those defined by the EJB specification." But you use these services at the expense of portability. As the specification continues, "An enterprise Bean that depends on such a [value added] service can be deployed only in a container that supports the service." In fact, the specification is slightly inaccurate on this last point. Since these value-added services will not be standardized, beans using them will not even be portable to other vendors that have equivalent services. The specification should say, "An enterprise Bean that depends on such a [value added] service can only be deployed in *the* container for which it was developed."

Language Neutrality

Probably the biggest problem with EJB is the lack of language flexibility. The specification says that "The Enterprise JavaBeans architecture will provide interoperability between enterprise Beans and non-Java programming language applications." Non-Java clients will make use of Java beans through interoperability with the CORBA specifications. I will discuss the CORBA middle-tier architecture in the next chapter. From Java's perspective, a CORBA client makes use of a still-to-be-proven technology called *Remote Method Invocation* (RMI) on *Internet InterOrb Protocol* (IIOP).

IIOP is the wire protocol for the distributed CORBA architecture. Historically, Java has ignored IIOP and developed its own wire protocol for RMI. Over the last two years, great pressure had been exerted on both the CORBA community and the Java community to come up with some interoperability story. For a long time it looked like that portion of Sun that was focused on Java would simply ignore the rapidly dwindling portion of Sun that still cared about CORBA. Finally, a compromise was reached—that RMI would be rewritten to use the IIOP wire format by default.

Rewriting RMI to use IIOP would mean that the same IIOP that, at least in theory, allows one CORBA vendor to talk to another, would also allow one EJB vendor to talk to another, an EJB client to talk to a CORBA component, or a CORBA client to talk to an EJB component. This is shown in Figure 10.11.

While IIOP helps address interoperability, in reality, it addresses only the lowest level wire protocol issues. The EJB specification also defines

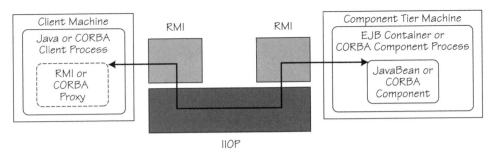

Figure 10.11 IIOP as an interoperability standard.

a fuller mechanism for a non-Java client to make use of EJB components, including such important details as how transactional and security contexts will flow from a non-Java client.

But this technology is still in the future. As the specification says, "The use of the EJB to CORBA mapping by the EJB Server [that would allow non-Java clients to access EJB components via CORBA] is not a requirement for EJB 1.1 compliance." So at this point, if you are a seller of EJB components, you had better plan on limiting your sales to EJB customers. Apparently integration to non-Java languages, even at this minimal level, is pretty low on the Sun priorities. One might assume from this that Sun has little interest in encouraging (or even supporting) the use of non-Java programming languages for anything, even on the client tier.

Even when a mapping between CORBA and EJB is mandated (if ever), it still will not solve the biggest of the language problems: Java is the *only* language that can be used for developing business logic and creating components. This is a serious problem for the business community, where Java programmers are rare and even training in object-oriented programming is more the exception than the rule. These businesses face a huge retraining effort before they will be able to use this technology. This retraining effort is not needed in the COM+ world, which allows the development of components in traditional programming languages already familiar to most business programmers.

Corporations that choose EJB are tied not only to Java now, but to Java for the foreseeable future. And for all of the great press Java has received (and I myself am a great fan of Java), it is still a language that can hardly be said to have withstood the test of time. The software industry is notoriously poor at predicting future language popularity. It was only a few short years ago that Smalltalk was going to take over the world, and before that, Eiffel, Pascal, APL, and probably several others I have forgotten. Is Java going to be the language you will want to be using five years hence? If so, it would be a first for our industry.

In Short

Enterprise Java Beans (EJB) is the standard COMWare platform for Java. Whereas COM+ provides a component runtime environment for the Windows 2000 platform, EJB offers that same capability for the Java middle-tier virtual operating system. The overall component model of EJB is richer than COM+, offering four component types that are not matched by COM+. However those additional four component types offer limited, if any, value. COM+, on the other hand, offers several useful capabilities that are not matched by generic EJB, although one or more of those capabilities may be matched by specific vendors.

On the other hand, EJB does offer the essentials for a good COMWare platform. There is enough flexibility in the standard to allow companies to add serious value by providing additional functionality like very high availability, generally at the expense of portability. EJB is, in many respects, very similar to COM+, and was obviously strongly influenced by MTS. The EJB security model, transactional model, and point of interception algorithms, as just a few examples, all come directly from MTS.

Both the strongest and weakest point about EJB is that it is a Java technology. If you like 100 percent pure Java 100 percent of the time, you will love EJB. But if you only like 95 percent pure Java 95 percent of the time, you feel probably feel quite differently. EJB requires a thorough, complete, and long-term commitment to both Java as a platform and Java as a language. Although it appears Java shows promise as a language in the short term, its ability to provide a robust programming platform for the middle tier is far from clear, based on its previous history.

If you are ready and willing to make this an all-Java gamble and want operating system independence, EJB is definitely the way to go. It offers the best possible platform for middle-tier, operating-system-independent Java components. Vendor independence is still a myth and probably always will be, so you should choose very carefully which vendor you are going use. Of the 25+ EJB vendors around today, probably fewer than 4 will survive more than another 3 years, similar to the historical consolidation in both the relational database world and the TPM world.

If you want to use Java but are willing to write your components for Windows 2000, COM+ still offers an attractive alternative. As of press time, there is still confusion over the future of Java within Microsoft, because of Sun's attempt to prevent Microsoft from adapting Java to the COM+ environment. My guess is that Microsoft will soon be allowed to continue its innovation of Java, although it may be forced to call the language something else.

If you are not ready to lock yourself into either a language (and thus EJB is not an option) or an operating system (and thus COM+ is not an option), then you have yet another choice: CORBA. I will discuss CORBA in the next chapter.

CHAPTER 11

CORBA

I f any group ushered in the era of distributed components, it was the Object Management Group (OMG). The OMG began in 1989 with eleven companies that banded together to define some common standards for what were referred to back then as distributed objects. Over the years the OMG has created some historical and technically advanced standards for distributed component development. Some of the most important standards that the OMG passed were:

- An architecture that allows clients in one process to invoke methods on instances of components/objects in remote processes. This architecture is called *CORBA* (Common Object Request Broker Architecture).

- Language bindings that allow clients written in any language to use components written in any language.

- Common wire formats that allow different CORBA implementations to pass method requests between them.

- Common APIs that allow component instances to interact with their host process. This is called the *Portable Object Adapter* (POA).

In this chapter, I give an overview of the CORBA architecture, discuss how this architecture is evolving with the adoption of the CORBA Component Specification, and compare this architecture to COM+ and EJB.

I present a high-level view here since the new Component Specification is too immature to attempt a programming example. We will have to wait to see how providers of this technology interpret this specification in actual products.

Basic CORBA Architecture

From a high-level architectural perspective, the basic CORBA architecture is shown in Figure 11.1. Calling this a CORBA *architecture* is actually redundant, since CORBA stands for Common Object Request Broker *Architecture*, but most people still refer to this as the CORBA architecture. The architecture consists of several important pieces. In the client process, we have IDL stubs, which are generated from *Interface Definition Language* (IDL) files—files that define the interfaces to what the OMG calls *objects* and what I call *components*. A stub is specific for a given component interface. Referring to the figure, when a client makes a method request (which CORBA calls an operation request), it goes through the IDL stub (a).

The stub is responsible for turning the request into some kind of vendor-specific format and transferring the request to that vendor's Object Request Broker (ORB) (b). The term ORB usually refers to some vendor implementation of the CORBA architecture. Once the request is in the ORB, it transfers over to the destination process. One of the nice features of CORBA is that the ORB used by the client need not be the same ORB used by the destination process. The OMG defines a common protocol, called Internet InterOrb Protocol (IIOP), which all ORBs must support, either directly or through a bridge. If the client ORB and the destination

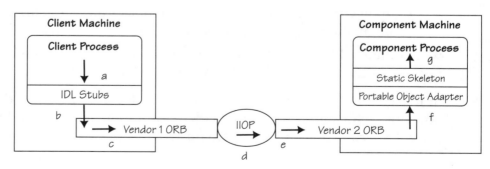

Figure 11.1   Architectural view of CORBA.

ORB do not use the same transfer protocol, they will use a common IIOP bridge to move requests between the two (d).

Once the request has been transferred to the destination ORB, it moves toward the destination process, passing through a Portable Object Adapter (POA) (f), which provides a standard interface for objects/components to interact with the underlying ORB. The POA was introduced fairly recently to the CORBA architecture to standardize the interactions between the component and the hosting process. From the POA, the request passes to the skeletons, which like their analogous client-side stubs, are generated by the IDL compiler, and matched to specific IDL files. And finally, the request is delivered to the hosting process ((g) and a running instance.

The client-side stubs and the component-side skeletons provide one of the most important features of the CORBA architecture: language neutrality. The CORBA standard defines how these stubs and skeletons are generated for a variety of languages in a series of standards collectively referred to as language bindings. Since the stubs and skeletons are independent of each other, a C++ client using C++ stubs can make method invocations through COBOL skeletons to a COBOL component implementation. In fact, there is no need for the CORBA client to have any idea what language was used to implement the back-end component. This idea of language neutrality was perhaps the single most important contribution by the OMG to the component industry.

There are other parts of the architecture not shown here. For example, there is an ORB API that can be used for various purposes. Perhaps the most important function of this API is that which supports dynamic method invocation. A dynamic method invocation is used to construct method requests at runtime, and includes a database that contains information about the components and their interfaces, and an interface used for constructing method requests. Although the dynamic method architecture is important, it is mainly useful to tools vendors, such as interpreters and code designers. I will not discuss this part of the architecture, since it is not relevant for most commerce application designers for whom this book is intended.

Most of the ORB API is hidden from the client. The client sees a simple programming model, very much like the simple COM/DCOM (sans MTS) model that was presented to programmers in the Microsoft world pre-COM+, and shown in Figure 11.2. The client has a local

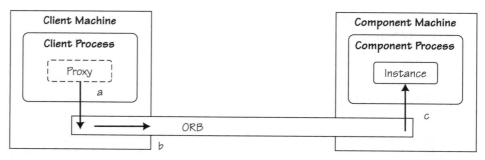

Figure 11.2   Client view of CORBA.

object reference (which I call a proxy) on which methods are invoked. Referring to the figure, this proxy passes the methods over the ORB (b) and to the target instance (c). If there is any bridging necessary between different vendor ORBs, that is hidden from the client.

The CORBA architecture has a unique take on the object reference that makes it more than just a local proxy. The object reference is considered to have a life beyond that of a given process. The object reference can be transformed into a string that can be saved and rehydrated at a later time to get back an equivalent object reference—in other words, a reference to an object that is the "same" object as the one to which the original reference referred. Exactly what is meant by the "same" object is not specified, and is left up to the particular ORB implementation to decide.

In addition to this basic distributed component architecture, there are a number of so-called object services. These are OMG standardized APIs for solving many common programming problems with components. Object services range from object persistence (which I worked on), object transactions, security, queries, collections, and many others.

This is where the CORBA architecture starts to get ugly. Most of these object services are recent additions (relative to the basic ORB architecture) to the CORBA design. Many represent difficult compromises between companies with hugely different opinions on how something should be done. All were effectively designed by committees. Because the committees that designed each service were largely independent of the committees designing the other services, there is relatively little coordination with the overall architecture.

The CORBA Component Model (CCM)

In June of 1997, the OMG began a project to define a CORBA Component Specification. The project started out as an effort to define a client-side model for fitting together components intended to replace the failed OMG OpenDoc specification. But people soon realized that problems on the middle tier were much more serious than problems on the client tier, and the project evolved into an attempt to accomplish two important goals:

1. Bring the ungainly CORBA Object Services API under control. As the specification says, "CORBA's flexibility gives the developer a myriad of choices, and requires a vast number of details to be specified. The complexity is simply too high to be able to do so efficiently and quickly."

2. Define a common middle-tier infrastructure along the lines of Microsoft's (then) MTS and Sun's EJB—in other words, an attempt to define COMWare for CORBA.

In August of 1999, after more than two years of negotiation, the Component Specification passed the most important hurtle to becoming an official OMG standard: a vote by the ORB Object Services task force (ORBOS) charged with responsibility for the object services. Although this specification could still face some hurdles, it now looks like (barring unforeseen problems) this standard will become part of the official OMG repertoire by midyear 2000.

This specification is officially called the CORBA Component Model (CCM). Keep in mind that this is a brand spanking new specification, with very little opportunity for industry scrutiny and no actual implementations. Much of this chapter is speculative, based on my own (hopefully informed) interpretation of the specification, and my years of experience with the other CORBA standards.

The CCM gets rid of the CORBA API using the same trick as does EJB and COM+. It introduces an environmental infrastructure to manage the lives of components. It trades a complex API for a flexible and configurable component runtime environment.

Like both EJB and COM+, the CCM runtime environment is unobtrusive. Programmers make requests on proxies (CORBA's *object references*).

Component instances (CORBA's *objects*) receive these requests and respond by executing business logic. Behind the scenes, like a giant, invisible, puppet master, the CCM runtime environment (CORBA's *container*) pulls all the strings. The object services APIs are still there, but you let the CCM runtime environment worry about making sense out of them. All that the component sees of the runtime environment is a handful of methods that must be implemented to fulfill the expectations of the environment. These methods are sometimes referred to as the CCM *container contract* since they define those methods through which the environment interacts with the component instance.

Figure 11.3 shows the general CCM architecture. The client interacts with the proxy, which, as always, supports the same business interface as does the back-end instance. Requests are sent over the ORB to the instance using the same business interface. The instance also accepts requests from the runtime environment through the contract interface. The runtime environment interacts as necessary with the object services to get the client's work done efficiently.

CORBA has not taken as strong a stand as COM+ or even EJB on the issue of API versus runtime environment. Perhaps because of the strong historical CORBA attachment to API, the CCM still defines an API to the object services. But the API is much simpler than the original object

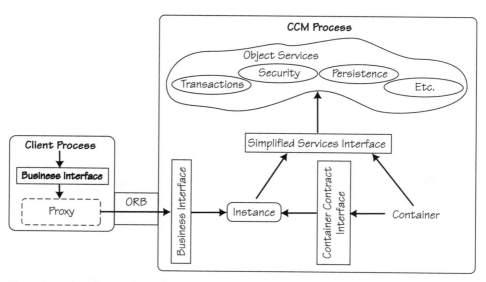

Figure 11.3 CCM architecture.

services API, is much better organized, and politely ignores the large collection of object services that have failed to withstand the test of time. In any case, the best approach in the middle tier is not to use the API at all, but to use the runtime environment.

Like all COMWare technologies, CORBA is dependent on point of interception algorithms. I described the point of interception algorithms in detail in Chapter 4, "COMWare." These are the algorithms that manage transactional boundaries, security, and instance allocation. I won't repeat these algorithms here, since CCM is a standard COMWare technology in this regard.

The CCM implementation of point-of-interception is much closer to COM+ than EJB. I described the EJB implementation of point-of-interception in Chapter 10, "Enterprise JavaBeans." EJB makes the point-of-interception visible to the component implementor, through the remote object. CCM takes more of a COM+ approach, where the point-of-interception is not made visible to the component implementor. Although CCM defines a point-of-interception architecture, the component implementor need not be aware of it; therefore, I will not discuss it here.

Component Implementation Definition Language (CIDL)

Programmers can define characteristics of components using a newly introduced language called *Component Implementation Definition Language (CIDL)*, or, more likely, through tools that will generate CIDL. CIDL is used to define implementation characteristics of components that the CCM container will want to help manage, such as the state contained by the component, the database ID, and which of the supported component models this particular component will use. The purpose of CIDL is to drive automatic code generation and/or runtime environment management.

CIDL is based on the OMG defined Interface Definition Language (IDL), which is used to define interfaces for components. IDL is language neutral, and concerns itself with interface only and not with the implementation. You can use IDL to define which methods are supported in a particular interface, which parameters each method takes, and which exceptions the method returns. This is all information that can be thought of as part of the contract between the component implementor and the component client.

There is a third OMG-defined language also related to CIDL and IDL, the Persistent State Definition Language (PSDL). PSDL is a relatively new addition used to define the persistent state of a component.

So we now have three OMG languages:

1. IDL, for defining the components interfaces.
2. CIDL, for defining the runtime characteristics of components.
3. PSDL, for defining the persistent characteristics.

Welcome to the land of IDL, CIDL, and PSDL.

The CCM Basic Architecture

The CCM defines two architectures: a basic and an *extended* architecture. A component developed for the basic model is said to be a *basic CORBA component*, and one developed for the extended model, an *extended CORBA component*. I'll start by discussing the basic architecture, since it is a subset of the extended architecture.

The basic CCM architecture is one that is designed to be functionally equivalent to the EJB 1.1 COMWare model that I described in Chapter 10. EJB has had a major influence on CCM, and this is particularly clear in the basic architecture. CCM uses similar terminology to that found in much of the EJB specification, calling, for example, the component runtime environment a container. It also uses a similar concept to the EJB home to find and create instances. It is essentially EJB 1.1 ported to CORBA. However it introduces slightly different terms to describe the component models.

Like EJB 1.1, the basic architecture supports three different models for state management. Recall from Chapter 4, "COMWare," that all COMWare technologies must find techniques for moving state out of the middle-tier instances. The different platforms differ only in how they accomplish this. The three models for basic components are:

1. Service components, which have behavior but no state and no database ID. These are equivalent to EJB stateless session beans. The component implementor is responsible for managing any and all state used by the component.

2. Session components, which have behavior, state (but not state that will be stored to a database), and no database ID. These are equiva-

lent to EJB stateful session beans. If the container chooses to manage the state of these components (it is not required to do so), then it does so as it sees fit.

3. Entity components, which have behavior, persistent state, and a database key. These are equivalent to EJB entity beans. Their state can be either stored/restored by the container as defined by component/ database mapping tools (equivalent to entity bean container managed persistence), or stored/restored by the component itself under direction of callback methods invoked by the container (equivalent to entity bean managed persistence).

These three models match exactly the notions of stateless session beans, stateful session beans, and entity beans that I described in Chapter 10. In that chapter, I gave the arguments against using entity beans and, to a lesser extent, to the stateful session beans, but let me review those arguments briefly.

The session component (equivalent to the stateful session bean) does not allow the component implementor to define how or even if the instance state will be managed. As I have discussed in many places throughout this book, instance management requires stateless programming. Session components have no provision for allowing the programmer to manage the state.

To support session components, the vendors will either have do the state management in some proprietary way, or disable instance management (and scalability) altogether. The different choices that the different vendors select will make it impossible to predict in general how session components will work or if they will scale. An application that works well in one vendor's implementation could work poorly or not all in some other vendor's implementation. Since session components provide no functionality that can't be programmed with a service component (equivalent to a stateless session bean), and the use of session components greatly limits the portability of the resulting application, I see no compelling reason for using them.

The entity component (equivalent to an entity bean) is also highly dependent on the vendor's implementation. The basic problem they present is that they require an additional transaction for the proxy creation, because the database ID is associated with the instance at proxy creation time. Associating a database ID with a proxy requires consultation with the database to see if the database ID is already in use (when creating a new instance), or to make sure that it is in use (when finding an existing instance).

Since most vendors will find the additional database access for the database ID lookup too expensive, they will be compelled to find some way to reduce this cost. Some vendors will only support entity components if they are used within a service component, so that the proxy "transaction" is subsumed within the higher level transaction. This is similar to the argument some make that entity beans should be used only by session beans. Some vendors will cache the entity instance so that it doesn't require the expensive database access, thus eliminating the worst of the proxy creation cost. Some of these cache providers will be tightly coupled to the database caches, so that they can guarantee database consistency. Most won't be tightly coupled to the database caches, and these can work only when all applications use the CCM for database access, a highly unlikely scenario.

Like the session components, how you use an entity component effectively will be highly dependent on your own vendor's interpretation of the specification. Implementations that work well for one vendor will work poorly for another. Also like the session components, anything you can do with an entity component you can do with a service component, and without any of the resulting portability problems. So, like the CCM session components, I recommend against using entity components.

The service component (equivalent to the EJB stateless session bean and the COM+ component model) on the other hand, is a fine model. It can be used in a wide range of component applications. It is very clear how you go about creating a component that is highly portable and maps well to all of the COMWare technologies. I have no problem with the use of service components.

The CCM Extended Architecture

The extended CCM architecture is one that is designed to offer a series of interesting enhancements, going well beyond the EJB model. It introduces several new ideas to the CORBA world.

The extended CCM architecture supports four different models for components. The first three models are the same as those of the basic architecture: service, session, and entity components that match their

EJB stateless session bean, stateful session bean, and entity bean counterparts. In addition, the extended architecture supports a process component. Like an entity component, a process component also has behavior and state, but the state is not visible to the client. Only the instance's identity is visible to the client. The specification says this type is useful for "representing business processes, rather than entities. Examples include applying for a loan, creating an order, etc." The differences between a process component and a session component are not obvious, so we will have to wait for further clarification from the vendors on this issue.

Some of the other advanced capabilities of the extended CCM model include the ability of components to support multiple interfaces, the ability to navigate between these interfaces, a new event model, and segmented components.

Segmented components are a particularly interesting idea. They are component instances for which data is read in as segments, where each segment corresponds to one of the interfaces the component now can support. Up until the CCM, CORBA components could only have one interface, but support for multiple interfaces is one of the new features of this specification. In the EJB entity beans model (the only EJB model that officially recognizes persistence of state), data must be read in all at once and in toto for an instance.

In the COM+ model, segmentation is not specified, but is easily supported by just reading in the state necessary to process a single method. We might even argue that the COM+ model is naturally segmented. However, the debate is academic as far as this book is concerned. Segmented objects have little use in the world of electronic commerce, where an instance's state typically maps to a relatively small number of records, all of which can fit into memory with plenty of room to spare. But in other specialized realms I can imagine segmented components as being extremely useful.

CCM/EJB Bridges

The CCM permits "two way interoperability between components and allows the construction of applications made up of both enterprise beans and CORBA components." The interoperability is limited to only basic components. Extended components are not part of this scheme.

The CCM technology that supports interoperability is CCM/EJB bridges. The CCM/EJB bridge architecture is shown in Figure 11.4. A bridge is a component that knows how to accept either EJB or basic CCM requests, and how to pass those requests through to an internal proxy to an actual back-end instance of the opposite type. If the request comes from a basic CCM client, it will be directed to a CORBA component that has an EJB proxy. If the request comes from an EJB client, it will be directed to an EJB bean that has a CORBA proxy.

CCM defines the bridges and the internal mappings between the CORBA features and attributes and their functional equivalents in EJB. Since the basic CCM model, by design, supports no functionality beyond that of EJB, it is a fairly simplistic mapping.

This bridge architecture allows an EJB client to use a basic CORBA component, and a CORBA client to use an EJB bean transparently. However, it falls short of true interoperability. A true interoperability solution needs to go further than defining how clients of one system use components of another. It needs to define how the components themselves work together. And in particular, it needs to define how transactions are coordinated. The CCM does not define how CCM component instances are used to coordinate their transactional activity with EJB beans. For example, if an EJB bean makes a request of a CORBA component, how does the transaction started by the EJB bean's method invocation pass through to the CORBA component? This problem is supposed to be solved by the CORBA transaction service, not the CCM. Unfortunately,

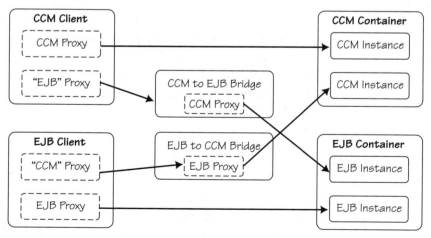

Figure 11.4 CCM/EJB interoperability.

at this point none of the major commercial implementations of the transaction service support this level of interoperability. Without this support from the transaction services, the CCM/EJB bridges will be of limited value.

The Two Models

I see the support for both a basic and an extended architecture as a fairly typical OMG compromise. In this case, the compromise was between those that wanted a CCM that would merely stamp the EJB architecture with an official OMG stamp of approval and those that wanted to boldly define a new architecture and advance the state of the art in interesting new areas. The CCM tries, a bit schizophrenically, to fulfill both of these goals.

Component designers will have to choose whether to design for the basic or the extended architecture. The extended architecture offers a number of innovative features that will be quite attractive, such as the segmented components I discussed earlier. However, only the basic architecture is compatible with EJB, so if the designer wants the component to appear as an EJB bean to EJB clients (and sell those components to EJB buyers), the basic architecture must be used exclusively.

The choice between the basic and extended architecture is likely to be greatly simplified by the reality of availability. I think it is highly unlikely that any major vendor is going to support the extended architecture anytime in the near future. As I write this, nearly three months after the OMG vote ratifying the CCM, not a single major vendor (in which I include BEA, Sun, IBM, Oracle, and IONA) has publicly committed to supporting the CCM. In contrast, all have issued numerous and vociferous public statements pledging undying loyalty to EJB. So it seems likely that if they support the CCM at all, they will support only the basic architecture.

However, even support for the basic CCM architecture is a major improvement over EJB. First of all, even the basic CCM architecture offers language neutrality. The single biggest flaw with EJB is the total commitment required to one and only one programming language. Second, the model is simpler, since it hides the details of point of interception from the component implementor.

One of the reasons the CCM basic model can be simpler than EJB is that is does not get sidetracked on the issue of portability. Sun is almost obsessed with portability and adds considerable architectural complexity to EJB in an ultimately doomed attempt to provide it. CCM never claims that CORBA components, either basic or extended, will be portable. Instead, it merely claims to add nothing to make components less portable than they otherwise would be.

In fact, I think the OMG is being overly modest in its accomplishments in the portability realm. The CCM simplification and consolidation of the object services is a major advance in portability. It goes a long way toward enabling the development of components that can move from one CCM implementation to another with much less effort than if they were being moved from one pre-CCM CORBA implementation to another. We still do not have a download and run mentality, but, unlike Sun's claims for Java, this is not part of the CCM vision.

COM+ versus CCM

The basic distributed architecture of COM+ and CCM is very similar. Both use client-side surrogates to communicate with the back-end component instance, and component-side surrogates to represent the front-end client. Both use language bindings to allow clients using one language to invoke methods on components of another language.

The COMWare architecture of COM+ and CCM is also similar, in that both use point-of-interception algorithms to provide transaction boundary management, security, and instance management. Both assume that the COMWare provider is implementing the executable in which the components will run. For both, this is a new idea; COM/DCOM and CORBA pre-CCM assumed that the component implementor provided the runtime executable.

Both architectures use an IDL to define the component interfaces. The CORBA IDL, in my view, is better designed. However it seems that most CORBA vendors and Microsoft are deemphasizing the use of IDL, providing IDL generation tools that are more dialog-based.

CCM supports four different component models: service, session, entity, and process. Only the first three of these are likely to have any widespread support, since they are defined in the basic architecture. Only the service component is supported by COM+. However, the two that are not supported (session and entity) are poorly understood and will be highly dependent on vendor-specific technology, as I discussed earlier. The component model that I recommend (the COM+ component model, stateless sessions bean, or service components, depending on which system we're discussing) is supported by both COM+ and CORBA.

The CORBA specification has one major goal that is not part of COM+: compatibility with EJB. At least half of the architecture is designed to provide a CORBA façade on EJB. In addition, it provides for synchronous bridges between CCM components and EJB beans. Although these bridges are not perfect, in that they provide as yet unproven support for transaction flow, at least they are moving in the direction of interoperability between these two component models. There is nothing in COM+ that recognizes EJB as brethren in the component industry.

Of course, the biggest difference between COM+ and the CCM is maturity. From a basic component perspective, CORBA has a three-year lead on COM+. The first CORBA component technologies were available in 1992. But from a COMWare perspective, COM+ has at least a five-year lead on CORBA. COM+ is the next release of technology that has been around since MTS 1.0, available in 1995. Given that the CCM specification hasn't finished clearing OMG hurdles yet and that it runs well over 400 pages, the first beta implementations of CCM are not likely to appear before 2001, and stable products until 2002, if they appear at all.

At this point, the OMG CCM specification is nothing but paper, without even promises of support by the major vendors. The OMG will rebut this argument, saying that the OMG rules require that companies that cosubmit specifications submit letters of intent (LOI) from corporate executives promising to implement the specifications if and when they are adopted. IBM, Oracle, IONA, and BEA, among others, must therefore have submitted LOIs promising to implement the CCM, since they have all contributed to the CCM. However these LOIs were submitted almost three years ago, before these companies had shifted their attention from CORBA to EJB. Even without a three-year delay in technology adoption, there are numerous examples of LOIs being ignored by companies once specifications were accepted. The persistence, relationship, and licensing object services are just three among many examples. The OMG has no policing policy to ensure that LOIs are adhered to; most never are, and there is no reason to assume that the CCM LOIs will be taken any more seriously.

Conclusions

The CCM has many good architectural ideas. However until we see serious plans for such implementations, any company betting on the CCM becoming a reality is taking a risk. I hope CCM does get support, because it is clearly a useful technology, one that deserves exploration, and one that is critically important to CORBA's long-term viability. Without CCM, CORBA has no architecture to support the middle tier.

Although it is unlikely that anything other than the basic CCM architecture will ever see the light of day, even that would be an important step forward for the CORBA vendors. It would give us a standard component model that is language neutral and operating-system independent. We will just have to wait to see if any of the major middle-tier companies support even this much of the CCM architecture.

We need CORBA and we need the CCM. The CCM specification is the only COMWare technology other than Microsoft's that understands the value of multiple-language support. If the CCM goes by the wayside, CORBA will not be far behind. Then it will come down to just Sun's Java-centric EJB and Microsoft's Windows 2000-centric COM+. Those simply aren't enough choices for the middle tier.

PART FOUR

Case Studies

O kay, so COM+ has some good ideas. But can you really use it to build serious systems? Will it scale? Will it handle the transactional load of real Web commerce systems? In this part, the rubber meets the road. I discuss how three companies—Silknet, Dell, and Acentris—use Microsoft technologies to create the next generation of commerce on the Web.

Nobody wants to use a technology that has not proven itself in the market, yet COM+ is still in Beta. How do I write a case study about a technology that, as of press time, has not yet been released? Fortunately, while we don't have COM+ yet released, we do have its immediate precursor technology, MTS, and have had it for several years. So I have chosen for two of my case studies mission critical applications based on MTS. These applications use most of the COM+ algorithms, COM+ design patterns, and COM+ supported languages. In fact, these applications should port to COM+ with few, if any, changes, except those changes needed to take advantage of the newer features of COM+. You can be sure that if these applications run today on MTS, they will run better on COM+.

But still, I know you want to see at least something written in the latest and greatest COM+. So I have chosen for my third case study an application that is 100% COM+ to the core. It isn't released yet, but it is close, and it has completed an impressive array of benchmarks.

CHAPTER 12

Silknet: Treating Customers as People

Company Profile

Silknet Software Inc.
50 Phillippe Cote St.
Manchester, NH 03101
Phone: 603.625.0070
Fax: 603.625.0428
www.silknet.com

Products/Tools Used

- Microsoft Transaction Server (MTS)
- Microsoft Cluster Server (MSCS)
- Microsoft Message Queue Server (MSMQ)
- Internet Information Server (IIS)

Application

Silknet provides tools to companies for building sophisticated electronic Customer Relationship Management (eCRM) systems. These tools help keep track of what customers have purchased and what products can be marketed to them in the future, how to better deliver customer service, and in general, make sure that your customers are 100 percent happy with their interactions with you. Silknet recently was a recipient of the Mass eComm 10 Award by the Massachusetts Electronic Commerce Association. Silknet customers include Altus Mortgage, Southwestern Bell, Geac, PCConnection, Sprint, and BankAmerica. For a young company, they have made a real impression on the industry. Let me take you through an example of how a good eCRM system can become part of your corporate strategy, especially if your business is centered around the Web.

Shopping on the Web doesn't have to be a miserable experience, leaving you feeling depersonalized and uncared for. A well-designed Web site can make you feel like a valued customer, or even better, like a real person! It may be one of the great ironies of the next millennium that some Web sites may turn out to be more personable than some of the people we know. How do you create a personable Web site, one that is interested in more than just selling you a service, and one that creates an ongoing relationship with you? What would such a site even look like?

Let's contrast two hypothetical companies that sell computers on the Web. The first company I will call *Bytes for Less*. The Bytes for Less Web site treats the customer as a source of income, pure and simple. It offers cheap prices, period. Customers come to the site, look up the desired configuration, figure out the cost, and place the order. Then the good times are over.

The second company I will call *Holistic Computers*. Holistic Computers focuses on the long-term customer relationship. Like Bytes for Less, the site is easy to find and order from, and the prices are in line with the competition. But the Holistic Computers site focuses on creating a long-term relationship with the customer. It wants customers that return again and again because of the services the site provides and the trust it instills.

Here is my hypothetical interaction with the Holistic Computers Web site. The first time I access the site, I register some basic information, including my name, address, and expected uses for my new computer.

The site then asks me some questions about my needs. These questions are asked in a friendly dialog, not an impersonal radio button display. Is the system for home or work? If for work, what kind of work do I do? If for home, do I have children? If so, how old? Do I want a laptop or desktop? What applications will I run?

Once the site has my basic statistics, it can start to make recommendations. Because I want the computer for work and I travel a lot, the site suggests I consider a FastTrack Z12, a new mid-end laptop. The site asks what operating system I want to run. I choose Windows 2000. The site tells me that the FastTrack Z12 hasn't been tested with Windows 2000, but that the FastTrack Z30 has received rave reviews running Windows 2000, and they are currently offering a special when that machine is purchased with Windows 2000 preinstalled.

"Great," I say, "I'll buy it." Since I am buying the system for work, the site asks if I would like to purchase Office 2000 preinstalled. "Sure," I say. Since this is a laptop, the site suggests an online backup service through their Web site for only $15.00 per month. Online backup costs only $15.00 per month? Cool, I think.

I buy my system and it arrives a week later. But our relationship has just started. In two weeks I get some e-mail from Holistic Computers. I haven't done an online backup yet, do I need any help? They have a customer service representative who would be glad to walk me through my first backup, or I can click on the enclosed hyperlink for online directions. I feel a little foolish and do my first online backup.

In two months I get some more e-mail from Holistic Computers. My standard warranty is about to expire, would I like to purchase an extended warranty? It's easy to buy, I just click on the link in the e-mail, and I am brought to a Web page that has all of my information already filled in. All I need to do is decide whether I want an on-site or drop-off warranty, click on the appropriate button, and the warranty is mine. A screen pops up telling me exactly what I need to do in the unlikely event I need service. If I chose on-site, I am given the appropriate phone number to call. If I chose drop-off, I am given the names and addresses of all service centers within 100 miles of my zip code.

Two months later I receive another piece of e-mail from Holistic Computers. A new BIOS version has just been released for my particular system. This fixes several problems that have been reported with the

FastTrack Z30 running Windows 2000 in low-battery situations. A link is included in the e-mail. All I need do is click on the link, my browser fires up and I am brought directly to the page with the download for the new BIOS. I click once to download. At the end of the download, instructions come up telling me exactly how to install the new BIOS on a FastTrack Z30 complete with screen shots that walk me through which options to choose and how to select them. I print out the Web page and complete the installation.

When a new device driver is released for my system, I get e-mail from Holistic Computers that includes a direct link to the Web page with the new driver. Holistic Computers sends me e-mail only about drivers that are designed for FastTrack Z80s running Windows 2000, since others are not relevant to me. If I call customer service with a problem, the representative can tell exactly which drivers I have downloaded, and suggest ones I might have overlooked.

Usually when I have a system problem I don't bother to call customer service. I just go back to the Holistic Computers Web site and look though their extensive and easy to use knowledge base. Since I see only information relevant to FastTrack Z30s running Windows 2000, it is easy to locate the specific information I need. The site presents information in a variety of ways. It uses text files, videos, still photos, and online manuals, choosing the medium that will best communicate the necessary information.

If I need personal help, I go to the Holistic Computers Web site and click on the *chat* button. I immediately go into a chat conversation with a service representative—no waiting 20 minutes for somebody to pick up a phone. No annoying, "This call is very important to us" message, which, of course, really means "this call would be very important to us if our pizza wasn't getting cold right now."

If the online chat representative can't solve my problem, the representative can arrange for a specialist to call me for a person-to-person conversation. The specialist calls me while looking at a pop-up screen that shows my entire history with the company. When my problem has been diagnosed and solved, the specialist enters the new information into the site's knowledge base, so that future customers with this same problem can more easily find the solution.

I tend to go back to the site periodically, just to make sure I am fully up to date on software and that there is no new information that is specific to my system. Since the site remembers me, it doesn't annoy me with having to wade through generic Web pages and agonizingly slow search engines. From the beginning, I see only information that is relevant to me and only to me. When new hardware and software becomes available for my system, I learn about it immediately. When I want to make purchases, I do so easily by pushing a single Web button. I start to believe the site actually cares about me. It's an illusion, I know, but it's a pleasant illusion nevertheless. Since the site seems to know so much about me, I trust the recommendations it makes.

Now it is time to buy my next computer. Sure, I could save a few hundred dollars if I purchase through Bytes for Less. But who is going to look after me once the money has transferred hands? I have saved hundreds of hours of my valuable time over the last two years because of the ready availability of information at the Holistic Computers Web site and the superb attention of its dedicated support staff. Frankly, my time is worth more than money. I'm spoiled! I admit it! Holistic Computers has made it easy for me to be productive, and, incidentally, has made quite a decent income selling me useful software, hardware, services, and extended warranties in the process. Holistic Computers is profitable. I am productive. All relationships should be like this. There is no way I am going to give up all this to save a few hundred bucks at Bytes for Less.

Enterprise Relationship Management

The systems that manage relationships between companies and customers are called *electronic Customer Relationship Management* (eCRM) systems. You can see that they can offer a huge competitive advantage to a Web site engaged in commerce. The demands on such systems are enormous. They must be easy to update. They must be robust. They must scale to huge numbers of users. They must manage complex transactions that consist of large amounts of information. There is probably no more demanding Web-based application than an eCRM system.

Web-based eCRM is the business of Silknet. It provides an open framework and tools for the development of eCRM systems. Silknet calls its product Silknet eBusiness, which we will just call eBusiness for short. The eBusiness architecture is used by corporations to set up eCRM systems. It allows business analysts to define customer relationship rules that are specific to that company. It allows the technical staff to create extensive knowledge bases that can be made accessible to customers. It allows support systems to be set up that offer intensive online help to customer-service representatives. Silknet's eBusiness is exactly what Holistic Computers needs to manage its long-term customer relationships.

All indications are that eBusiness is going to be very successful. One of Silknet's customers, a large telephone company, built its entire customer relation system using eBusiness. It processed over 16,000 customer interactions in the first two weeks of operations, resulting in a reduction of more than 15,000 calls to their customer service representatives. Less work for their representatives and more satisfied customers. Not bad for the first two weeks.

eBusiness Requirements

The eBusiness architecture offers many lessons on how to build large scalable systems, and Silknet has been generous in sharing these lessons. eBusiness is built with the Microsoft COMWare technologies. It uses the algorithms and strategies that I covered throughout this book. It has built a three-tier plus architecture based on components in the middle tier, made its components stateless, relied heavily on MS-DTC to coordinate transactions, and used the instance management algorithms provided by MTS (and now COM+) to allow very efficient use of the component instances.

Early in the eBusiness design process, Silknet laid out certain requirements as essential to the success of this project. It turns out that many of these requirements are typical of most commerce systems.

Varied clients. First of all, Silknet envisioned three different types of clients for the eCRM systems developed with eBusiness: internal clients, trusted partners, and customers.

Internal clients are those that work directly for the company building the eCRM, say Holistic Computers in our hypothetical example. Internal clients include customer service representatives that work directly with end customers through phone-in support lines, information managers that keep the eCRM system well fed with new information, and systems implementors that tailor the eBusiness system to meet specifically the needs of Silknet's customers. Internal clients typically come into the eCRM system through Wide Area

Networks (WANs) through computers that have known configurations that support DHTML, client-side components, client-side scripts, or whatever technology you like.

Trusted partners are clients in companies that work closely with Silknet's customers. For Holistic Computers, trusted partners might include chip manufacturers, software vendors, and documentation specialists. Like internal clients, trusted partners also need to access and update information in the eCRM. Unlike internal clients, trusted partners usually come in over the Internet on computers that have a variety of software configurations. Holistic Computers can make only minimal demands of its trusted partners, such as the use of a certificate-based authentication scheme.

Customers are clients whose relationships are the focus of the eCRM. Customers are the most fickle of all clients. You can assume virtually nothing about your customers other than that they are running some Web browser that recognizes HTML.

Each of these clients uses potentially different technologies to access the eCRM system, so the business logic has to be entirely independent of the presentation logic.

Unlimited scalability. Ultimately, it is the relationship with customers that makes an eCRM system successful and the more customers, the better. So it must be possible to add support for as many customers as necessary by simply adding more hardware onto the system. Silknet knew it would be working with companies whose customers would number in the hundreds of thousands.

Robustness. It had to be possible to guarantee the eCRM systems built around eBusiness will run 24 hours a day, 7 days a week, 52 weeks a year. Silknet knows that the Web never sleeps. Nothing frustrates a customer more than needing information, needing it now, and not being able to get it. A customer in Finland doesn't care that it is 4:00 A.M. in Austin where Holistic Computers is located. It is the middle of the business day in Finland.

Ease of Deployment. It must be possible to take an eBusiness system and tailor it for the needs of a specific customer very easily. Since that customer's needs will change in time, it must be possible to update the system equally easily. The Web is no place for a static system. *Dynamic* is the Web's middle name.

Vendor neutrality. Although Silknet was betting heavily on the Microsoft COMWare technologies, it wanted to be able to move eBusiness to other platforms should business needs dictate.

Asynchronous Messaging. Another requirement was a rich collection of communication options. Synchronous methods were adequate for many of the business interactions, but others required asynchronous methods and yet others required publish and subscribe capabilities.

Security. Much of the customer-specific information is sensitive, and customers have the ability to make purchases using pre-established credit card information. The fact, therefore, that customers are coming through the public side of the system in no way decreases the need for excellent security.

Legacy Wrapping. Many, if not most, of Silknet's customers have others systems that need to be tied into this overall architecture, such as information management packages from SAP and/or PeopleSoft. The eBusiness system needs access to information from these legacy applications.

eBusiness Architectural Overview

The various requirements for eBusiness quickly drove Silknet into the direction of COMWare. The need for presentation independence dictated a dedicated business logic tier. The need for ease of deployment dictated a component technology. The need for scalability dictated the need for a TPM-like technology. Put these things together and they spell COMWare.

The basic eBusiness architecture is shown in Figure 12.1. You can see that the architecture follows a standard *N*-tier pattern with a Web tier hooked up to human beings, a presentation tier that houses the Web servers, a component tier that houses the business logic, and a data tier that houses the data. Perhaps not so standard is the depiction of a legacy tier that interoperates with outside systems.

The component tier can be split into two subtiers, one that reads the configurable business rules and uses them to control the overall eCRM process and one that contains the nuts and bolts code that accomplishes specific business tasks such as credit card validation. The component tier is the main guts of the system. Silknet has over 60 components that represent more than 15 different business processes. All of these run in the MTS component runtime environment.

The data tier can also be split into two logical tiers, one that holds the business knowledge (such as how to check a computer for a low battery condition) and one that holds the business rules (such as "Does this customer have a corporate discount? If so, look up their negotiated discount rate."").

As I go through this architecture, you can see how many of the eBusiness requirements were met. The discussion that follows uses numbers that refer back to Figure 12.1.

Varied Client

The *varied client requirement* is met by having two different presentation layers, one for internal users (1) and one for external users (2). It may seem odd that internal users get a richer presentation experience, but this is dictated by two facts. First, only internal users can be assumed to have computers that support client-side technologies like DHTML and ActiveX components, technologies that allow the richest possible client experience. Second, internal users have more demanding needs of the system. They can do anything an external user can do, but they also need access to customer information, to be able to monitor work flow, and to be alerted to defined events in the system (such as customers that have excessively overdue accounts).

External clients can be counted on only to support standard HTML, which is more limited than the technologies available to internal clients. Still, a very rich presentation experience is possible using standard HTML, including video, audio, photos, and documentation delivery, and eBusiness has taken every advantage of HTML's capabilities.

Ease of Deployment

The *ease of deployment requirement* is met two ways. First, eBusiness uses late binding of business rules through special components that can read business rules at runtime and can adjust process flow accordingly. Second, eBusiness makes extensive use of components in the middle tier (3). Most of these components are developed by Silknet specifically for eBusiness, but Silknet also purchases outside components wherever possible. Most of these outside components come from Microsoft's

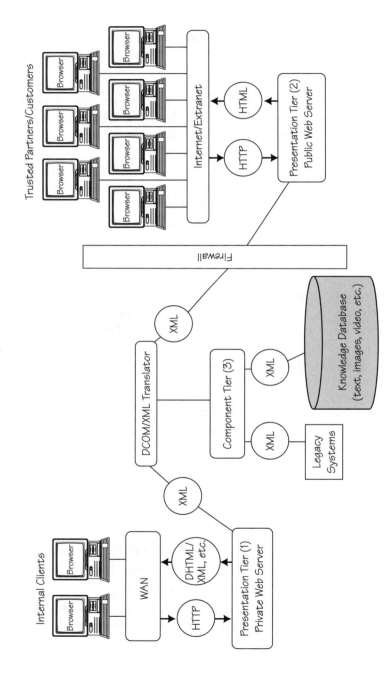

Figure 12.1 Overview of the eBusiness architecture.

eCommerce collection, which includes components for managing many standard electronic commerce needs such as shopping carts, credit card authorization, and catalogs. The use of eCommerce components has allowed Silknet to focus on what it knows best: the management of customer relationships.

Scalability

The *scalability requirement* was met using three techniques. First, the use of the HTTP protocol as the entry into the system is believed by Silknet to be very scalable, since it is a series of stateless calls into the eBusiness system. I am not sure I agree with Silknet on this assessment, since HTTP requires a constant recreation of middle-tier proxies in the presentation tier, but I agree with the choice of HTTP in any case to allow support for the external eBuisness clients.

The second technique for scalability was running the component tier under control of MTS. MTS was the precursor to the COM+ runtime environment and uses one of the two instance management algorithms supported by COM+. Instance management provides very efficient use of middle-tier resources for those components that are designed appropriately, and Silknet's components are all designed to use instance management.

The final technique used to establish scalability was *load balancing*. Had COM+ load balancing been available when Silknet was developing eBusiness, it could have been used, but only MTS was available back in 1996–1997 when eBusiness was developed. Silknet therefore chose to implement its own load-balancing algorithm. Because it was in close communication with the development teams at Microsoft, Silknet was able to implement a load-balancing algorithm that is very close to what will be implemented for COM+. Once Silknet upgrades their system to COM+ and has convinced themselves of the effectiveness of the COM+ load-balancing algorithm, the Silknet load-balancing algorithm can be eliminated in favor of the COM+ algorithm. Because of the closeness of the two algorithms, this will have minimal impact on the eBusiness system.

The load balancing/robustness architecture designed by Silknet is shown in Figure 12.2.

Let's go through the information flow in Figure 12.2 to see how both load balancing and robustness are both achieved by the same basic eBusiness

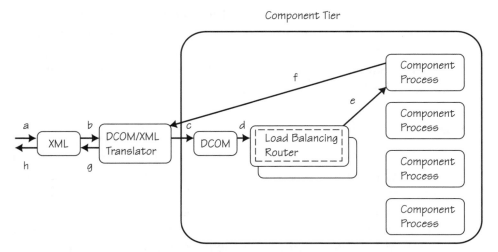

Figure 12.2 The eBusiness load balancing/robustness architecture.

architecture. The first thing to realize is that Figure 12.2 is an enlargement of the component tier (3) in Figure 12.1. Requests come in from the presentation tier as XML requests (a). These are sent into the DCOM/XML translator (b) that turns these into standard DCOM requests (c).

The DCOM requests are sent to the Load Balancing Router (d). The router chooses one of several identical component processes running on different machines to process that request based on overall system load. Since these component processes are identical, they are interchangeable, from the router's perspective, and it can choose one based only on current system load. The router keeps track of various statistics about the component processes, including CPU idle thread utilization, disk I/O, thread load, and overall response time, and uses this information in a sophisticated heuristic to decide on method assignments. Silknet calculates that the overhead associated with the router is significant, but manageable. Should the overhead associated with the COM+ router prove to be less, I suspect they will switch over.

The system is highly scalable because new machines can be added at any time to accommodate increased client load. You just buy a new machine, configure it, and add it to the router.

The system is also robust. If a component process hosting machine goes down, there is no particular problem. The router will quickly notice this and discontinue any further method requests to that machine. In the worst case, the transaction in progress will be lost (always a possibility anyway), and the XML request from the client will have to be reissued. Since all client requests are coming in as XML requests from the presentation tier, we don't have to worry about invalidation of the proxy on the presentation tier, which is a potential problem in a rich client scenario.

The machine hosting the routing function is protected by normal Windows Clustering (the old Microsoft Cluster Server (MSCS) technology in NT 4.0). So if it goes down, the router function can be dynamically taken over by a backup machine. This is also true of the machine hosting the knowledge base (not shown in this figure). This technique is also used to protect the COM+ router.

There is one further point worth exploring with regard to system robustness: system upgrades. The use of the router means that the system doesn't have to be taken off-line to do software upgrades. This is an essential requirement for $24 \times 7 \times 52$ availability. The router allows component hosting machines to be brought down as needed for updates. As long as those machines are down, the router will not route requests their way. When the update has been completed, the machine is brought online again, and once again, it becomes fair game for routing.

Once the request leaves the router it is sent on to the chosen process (e), which returns information to the DCOM/XML translator (f). The translator turns the information back into XML format where it is returned to the presentation tier either to be sent on as XML (for an internal client), or turned into a more generic HTML format (for an outside customer).

Asynchronous Messaging

Asynchronous messaging is one of Silknet's requirements. There are at least three situations in which asynchronous messaging is important to the eBuisness system.

One need for asynchronous messages is to eliminate unnecessary blocking of the caller during a method invocation. Synchronous messaging means that the caller must sit and wait for the callee to finish work, even when the caller doesn't need any immediate results from that work. A good example of this is when a customer places an order. That order may require the participation of many subsystems. We might decide to block the caller until all of these subsystems have completed (synchronous order processing), but we also might assume the order will be accepted and arrange to have the customer called later if something went wrong (asynchronous order processing).

A second need for asynchronous messages is when you want to buffer the system work load. A system that is capable of handling peak work loads of, say, 200 transactions per second can find itself in a situation where over the day it is averaging only 25 transactions per second, but at peak times (say, at lunch hour) it is averaging 400 transactions per second. With synchronous messaging, users will experience a significant slowdown during peak periods as they are forced to wait for component resources to become available. With asynchronous messages, users simply queue up requests to be processed when the work load has quieted down a bit. At peak periods, it may take five or ten minutes for the system to get around to processing some clients' requests, but those clients won't care because they won't be left hanging.

A third need for asynchronous messages is to allow for system outages. In the Microsoft COMWare platform, asynchronous messages have always been persistent and able to survive system failures. This is because asynchronous messages are stored in a transactional database until processed. If a system goes down, the normal transactional integrity of the database protects the outstanding message until all systems are back online.

When eBusiness was created, Microsoft's COMWare did not support asynchronous components. This did not become available until COM+. The earlier COMWare supported an asynchronous message queue technology called Microsoft Message Queue (MSMQ), and in fact, the asynchronous messaging of COM+ is based on MSMQ. The eBusiness asynchronous messaging is therefore based on MSMQ. When eBusiness ports over to COM+, I expect Silknet to make use of the simpler facilities of COM+ asynchronous components.

Publish and Subscribe

Publish and subscribe is another business requirement. It allows a component or a client to register interest in the occurrence of a particular event, and to be notified when that event occurs. A typical *event* in an eCRM deployment can occur when customers are waiting, on average, more than two minutes for a customer support representative to answer the phone. When this happens, a particular eCRM system can be configured to alert automatically all of the managers of the unacceptable wait times so that they can bring in more customer service representatives.

In a system without support for publish and subscribe, every managers' computer systems must constantly poll the eCRM system to monitor phone response time. In a system with publish and subscribe, the managers' computer systems register interest ("subscribes") to the excessive-phone-hold event. The component that is generally monitoring phones can, as part of its overall functionality, keep track of the hold times. It can then publish the excessive-phone-hold event when and if it occurs. If that event does become published, the subscribed managers will be notified that the excessive-phone-hold event has occurred, and specialized components on their systems can pop up menus, set off alarms, or take any other appropriate action.

System resources are used much more efficiently in a publish and subscribe system than in a polling system. In a polling system, every manager needs to constantly poll, and every poll is a drain on the system resources. With a publish and subscribe system, managers just passively wait for the event to occur. Resources are required only at registration time, which happens infrequently, and at publish time, which may not happen at all.

Silknet has created an adaptable event service that supports this publish and subscribe capability and can integrate a variety of events into the overall eCRM system. Both the publishing and subscribing are done through Silknet's asynchronous messaging system, which, as I discussed, is based on Microsoft's MSMQ. The fact that the publish and subscribe is layered on top of the Silknet asynchronous messaging facility ensures that neither publishers nor subscribers are blocked while waiting for events to be published or while waiting for subscribers to respond. This layering also guarantees that a subscriber will not lose an event if the subscriber's machine happens to be down at the exact moment the event was published.

Microsoft has promised to deliver a publish and subscribe system as part of COM+. When it does become available, Silknet may be able to remove their own publish and subscribe system in favor of the one provided by COM+.

Silknet describes its interactions with existing systems such as SAP, as *legacy wrapping*. I would probably use the term *interoperability*. In any case, the problem is to get information to and from systems over which Silknet had no control. Silknet takes advantage of its generic XML routing technology. Basically, eBusiness includes components that look a lot like the DCOM/XML translator shown in Figure 12.2, but instead of translating between XML and DCOM, they translate between XML and native requests to some foreign technology. These components are called SilkDataObjects, and are best thought of as data layer that can map to either a relational database or a legacy system. This is shown in Figure 12.3.

Vendor Neutrality

Another of the business requirements was *vendor neutrality*. Silknet is primarily leveraging XML as a vendor neutral mechanism for passing around data. Should Silknet ever need to abandon Microsoft, it will probably have to replace its business logic (not a trivial task) and its XML/DCOM Translators, but the presentation part of the system could remain intact. The presentation layer itself is actually already vendor neutral. Silknet has versions available for both Microsoft and Netscape Web server systems. Since both versions generate the same XML, the component tier doesn't care which is used.

Security

The final business requirement is *security*. The COM+ administative security model has not proven itself adequate for Silknet's needs. This is not

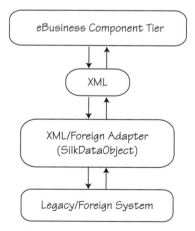

Figure 12.3   Legacy wrapping in eBusiness.

so much a COM+ issue as it is a COMWare issue, since all COMWare platforms deal with security in a similar way. Although Silknet relies heavily on the underlying Windows 2000 security capability, it rolls its own security at the component level using a horizontal security model, similar to what I discussed in Chapter 6, "COM+ Components."

Horizontal security requires a programmatic approach. Silknet's security layer uses Web server authentication to get a token identifying a user. When possible, this uses Secure Socket Layer (SSL). The authentication user token is encrypted using standard MTS runtime encryption and is a well-known parameter to all component level methods. The token is trusted (and therefore no longer encrypted) once inside the middle tier.

System Benchmarks

Work is underway to determine the limits of eBusiness. At this time, even the largest Silknet customers have not been able to overstress the system. Silknet calculates that a single application server can support at least 6500 of what it calls *cases* per hour. A *case* is a single customer interaction with the system, such as me checking the Web to see if any new device drivers have been issued for my computer. A case is far more complex than your run of the mill business transaction. It typically includes the running of several presentation tier scripts, an average of 20 separate SLQ updates, many component interactions, several translations back and forth between XML and DCOM, and sometimes translations between XML and foreign systems. Silknet calculates that each new component server can increase the workload potential by an additional 3200 cases per hour.

Lessons Learned

Silknet is a pioneer in the use of COMWare technology and has learned many lessons. It has made good design decisions up front, decisions from which many other companies can benefit. Here are some of the most important lessons I see coming out of the Silknet eBusiness project.

1. Put your biggest effort into up-front design. Focus on such concepts as how the system will work, how the components will interact with each other, and how users will maintain business logic. Worry later about the details, such as whether you use a linked list or a hash table to store order items.

2. Systems must be designed with rapid change in mind. Use late binding of business rules in the form of scripts to allow nonprogrammer staff to make system modifications.

3. Plan for scalability early and often. Use instance management, but don't limit your imagination to instance management. Leverage load balancing, asynchronous messaging, publish and subscribe, and every other technology you can find.

4. Plan for fault tolerance at the earliest stage of design.

5. Leverage COMWare technologies to the greatest extent possible. If you must build pieces of the infrastructure, do so with the goal of replacing them.

6. Make sure your tiers are carefully separated. Keep each tier independent of the others.

Silknet and Microsoft

Silknet chose Microsoft's COMWare platform because at the time of the initial development of eBusiness (around 1996), Microsoft technology was the only COMWare available. EJB had not yet come out, and of course, CORBA COMWare was a distant dream. Back then, Silknet was on the cutting edge. Even Microsoft was still figuring out how to make sense of its own COMWare platform. Nobody had built any large applications with this newfangled technology.

Silknet uses many of the Microsoft COMWare capabilities extensively, including MTS's instance management, MSMQ's asynchronous messages, and MSCS's cluster technology. Silknet can leverage many of the new COM+ capabilities, such as queued components, application clusters, and the publish-and-subscribe event system. There are a few COM+ capabilities that Silknet will probably never use, the most obvious being the COM+ administrative (vertical) security system.

Silknet found that teaching programmers to use the Microsoft COMWare technologies was very easy. Programmers were able to focus on the business problem at hand, using the language of their choice. The core of the system was built with C++, and most of the higher-level business logic was developed in Visual Basic. In my experience, this is typical of many large commerce applications.

It is clear that Microsoft's COMWare capabilities have been a very solid foundation for eBusiness. It is also clear that Silknet has added considerable value to that foundation. Silknet has made some excellent decisions in the build versus buy tradeoff. It has wisely decided not to reinvent the wheel. Instead, it has purchased existing wheels and used them to create some fantastic cars.

Some Drawbacks

The biggest problem Silknet has had with the Microsoft technologies is in selling eBusiness to shops that are not willing to consider Microsoft technology except on the desktop. Microsoft is relatively new in the corporate market and is just coming up to speed with the support structure (such as consulting services and telephone support) needed by large companies. Windows NT 4.0 also lacked many of the tools necessary for large-scale system administration and was generally considered to be less robust than the top of the line Unix systems. As a result of this, many companies still consider Windows 2000 unproven for mission critical applications.

Silknet has laid in a strategy to address this issue. Of course, their preferred strategy would be to use Microsoft-provided ports of COM+ to Unix systems, which would allow eBusiness to run on more than just Windows 2000. Since Microsoft has announced no plans to do this, Silknet is starting to develop a parallel system on Enterprise JavaBeans (EJB).

It will be very interesting to watch Silknet's EJB effort unfold over the next 16 months. My own prediction is that over the next 16 months Windows 2000 will prove itself to be an incredibly reliable and inexpensive option for corporate computing, and the resistance to purchasing mission critical systems built on Windows 2000 will evaporate. If I am right, Silknet's EJB effort will soon dwindle in importance. If I am wrong, the EJB effort will become critical to Silknet's future.

One thing is clear about Windows 2000: it is going to make or break Microsoft in the corporate market. If Windows 2000 does as I expect, then Unix is largely finished as a viable middle-tier platform, and the major incentive for EJB goes away with it. On the other hand, if Windows 2000 screws up, then Microsoft is finished in the corporate market. The corporate market is not a forgiving one and it will be a long time before Microsoft is given another chance.

All of this uncertainty makes for a lot of stress on companies like Silknet. I can well understand their reasons for hedging their bets on an EJB version of eBusiness. I will be watching with great interest to see if this particular bet pays off. As will much of the software world.

I asked Eric Carlson how he felt about building systems with Microsoft's COMWare technology. Eric Carlson is the chief technical officer of Silknet, and has been the guiding light behind the Silknet project. He thought for a moment, trying to imagine building a comparable system without such a supportive COMWare architecture. He finally summed in one sentence the value of this technology. "It allows," Eric said, "mere mortals to build these systems in the Internet time frames." As a fellow mere mortal, I know how he feels.

CHAPTER 13

Dell: Commerce on the Cheap

Company Profile

Dell Computer Corp.
One Dell Way
Round Rock, Texas 78682
Phone: (512) 728-8315
www.dell.com

Products/Tools Used

- COM
- DCOM
- MTS (beta testing COM+)
- Site Server Commerce Edition
- NT 4.0
- MSMQ
- SQL Server 6.5 (beta testing SQL Server 7.0)

- ADO
- ASP/IIS 4.0, Front Page

Application

In late 1995, Dell Computer decided to take on the big boys. At that time, the rules of computer retailing dictated that PCs were sold in stores, stores that had cozy relationships with established companies like Apple, IBM, and Compaq. Dell had met with limited success in the retail channels, where they had to play second fiddle to the better-known brands. If Dell was to compete seriously with the big boys, it couldn't do so on turf owned by the big boys.

So Dell decided to rewrite the rules for computer marketing. It would no longer leave its future in the hands of indifferent retailers. It would market its computers directly to the end users.

Soon after, Dell made another fateful decision. It would use, for one of its primary marketing tools, an untested commerce technology: the Internet. Dell bet on the Internet, and bet big. It would bypass the middleman and market directly to the consumers. And its storefront would be the Web.

Today, if you want to purchase a Dell system, the chances are you will do so through the Web. You start your purchasing experience at www.dell.com/store. You can browse through all of the different Dell offerings and configure a system exactly as you want it. You choose the processor, the amount of memory, the size of disk drives, the speed of modem, and the type of service options. The Dell system automatically calculates your price and even offers you a business lease option. When you have your dream system configured, you add it to your shopping cart. Add a printer, a monitor, and some business critical software packages (like 3D Ultra Pinball) and place your order. Dell will take your contact and credit card information, and before you know it, your system will be on the shop floor, being built to your exact specifications. You can go back to the Dell Web site to check on the status of your little darling at any time. Within a few days, your system arrives at your home without you having had a single interaction with a human being, other than the driver who delivers the system to your home.

This is a great way to purchase computers. You get to purchase the system when and where it is convenient for you. You get good prices, because you are buying directly from the manufacturer. The Dell store is always open, so it is as convenient to purchase systems at 2:00 A.M. as it is at 3:00 P.M. From Dell's perspective, once they have you in their "store," you are a captive audience. No IBM, Apples, or Compaqs to distract you from the systems Dell wants you to buy. And no sales commissions.

Once you have completed your purchase, Dell is there with its extensive Web-based support. Go to the Dell support page, tell the system your computer's serial number and you can download device drivers, diagnostic utilities, desktop management utilities, flashBIOS updates, and network drivers that are specific to your particular system. The system can even answer your questions. How do you make backup copies of the Windows95 registry and system files? Check out the Dell knowledge base. Why did your system just turn itself off? Ask Dudley, the Dell automated support specialist (once, of course, you get your system turned back on).

You can get a sense from all of this on how seriously Dell takes its Web site. The Dell Web site is more than a portal to Dell. For many of Dell's customers, the Dell Web site *is* Dell. It is how they purchase their systems, support their systems, even resell their systems once they have outgrown them.

Dell's Internet Strategy

We can think of the Dell strategy as having three components:

1. Dell sells directly to customers, avoiding the markup associated with retail channels. This allows it to significantly undercut the price of its large competitors.

2. Dell sells and supports through the Internet. This allows as much workflow as possible to be done without the intervention of human beings. Human beings are the single most expensive resource at a corporation like Dell.

3. Dell has built its Web site using the absolute lowest cost technology it can find: Microsoft COMWare running on commodity hardware. This allows it to process Web-based transactions at a fraction of the cost had these systems been based on large mainframe systems.

The biggest risk of this whole strategy came not so much from the Internet as from the idea of direct sales. Back when Dell first set this project in motion, there was no precedent for direct sales of computers. The common wisdom was that consumers wanted to play with computers before purchasing them. Who would think that consumers would buy systems sight unseen? Dell dealt with this problem by offering a liberal return policy. If you weren't happy with your system, you could return it for a full refund within 30 days, no questions asked.

Soon it was clear that consumers were willing to buy without having to touch the computer first. Once this was established, moving to the Internet was a natural next step.

Requirements

Dell will probably sell more than 12 billion dollars worth of hardware and software through its Web site in the year 2000. If their system is down for even four minutes, it costs Dell more than $100,000. So as you can imagine, they have rather stringent requirements for robustness and reliability. Dell expects to continue its enviable growth, so their systems must be scalable. Dell is very focused on the bottom line, so they want to deliver commerce at the absolute lowest cost possible. To do this Dell wants to base its entire commerce system on a simple, easy-to-write-for software platform that runs on the Windows platform, and can therefore run on Dell computers.

There are three guiding rules to the Dell Internet strategy:

1. Use the most cost-efficient systems available.
2. Provide redundancy at every critical point.
3. Gather extensive metrics on every aspect of system usage and use those metrics to proactively plan for future system load.

The Dell Internet Architecture Overview

Dell has chosen to base its entire Web sales and support system on Microsoft technologies, with some value-added layers that Dell has provided. Architecturally, the system is laid out in four tiers. The ratio of machines in each tier is approximately as follows:

- 10 percent dedicated to serving static pages (the Web tier)
- 35 percent running business logic using Microsoft Site Server components—COM, DCOM, MTS, and MSMQ (the component tier)
- 10 percent processing data using SQL Server (data tier)
- 45 percent running miscellaneous back-end functions, such as mirroring, staging of information, prototyping, testing and development, and general infrastructure (such as load balancing)

The entire system is designed to be fully functional 24 hours a day, 7 days a week, 52 weeks a year.

The standard machine was, as of early this year, a PowerEdge Server with about 1GB of memory and six 9 GB hard drives. I calculate the retail cost (what you and I would pay) of this machine at around $9,000. Dell at that time had about 131 of these machines split over four tiers. It is probably up to 180 of these machines as of press time, for a total retail cost in hardware of around $1.6 million. The total retail value of the hardware running the Dell Web site is about equal to the revenue stream that the hardware produces for Dell in a single hour and a half of operation. Not a bad return on investment.

On the Web tier, Dell is committed to Microsoft Internet Information Server (IIS) 3.0 with plans to move to IIS 4.0. These machines also run MTS, which allows Web scripts to be coordinated in the overall transaction along with the middle-tier business components. Secure sockets are used for commerce transactions.

On the middle tier, Dell uses Commerce Site Server 2.0, COM, DCOM, and MTS. Commerce Site Server is a Microsoft product that provides commerce-related business components for companies to use as building blocks in creating commerce applications. Commerce Site Server is built on COM, DCOM, and MTS. MTS is used to provide instance management. Dell plans to move to Site Server 3.0 with COM+ and Windows 2000 to be in synchronization with the next generation of Microsoft technology. MSMQ is also used for asynchronous processing.

On the database tier, Dell uses ADO as an access technology and SQL Server 6.5 for data storage. Dell is testing SQL Server 7.0 for the next generation of its data tier. The operating system for all of this is NT 4.0. Dell is beta testing Windows 2000 for future generations of the data tier.

Throughout, Dell uses Microsoft Cluster Server (MSCS) for failover, a technology I described in Chapter 8, "The COM+ Services."

Dell designs its systems to be fully load balanced across multiple data centers and application servers. If any one machine goes down or becomes overloaded, its workload can be redistributed to a redundant sibling machine. It uses its own proprietary software layers to do this. The main Dell site in the United States is mirrored both in Europe and Japan, to ensure a proper Web experience to its entire worldwide customer base.

Dell ensures that its systems are running smoothly through a continuous process of reporting and measuring. Externally, Dell measures the average of both download performance and the percentage of none or slow response time. On the network, Dell measures usage and path characteristics and constantly checks the site for maximum optimization. Dell monitors CPU, memory utilization, I/O bottlenecks, disk space usage, changed URLs, and the general health of HTTP, FTP, and core IIS services. All in all, Dell takes more than 7 million measurements each and every day of the usage patterns of its site. These measurements allow Dell personnel to take immediate corrective action when necessary to ensure a quality customer experience.

Dell looks for trouble before it begins. It has a series of online stress tests that can simulate multiple browsers running concurrently. This allows most performance problems to be located long before applications are ever deployed.

Cost per Transaction

Dell is making a healthy profit. For quarter two of 1999, Dell had a net income of $507 million on a revenue base of $6.14 billion. Part of the reason Dell is profitable is that they are running their company on such cost-effective hardware and software systems.

We can get an idea of exactly how cost effective the Dell systems are by looking at results submitted to the Transaction Processing Council (TPC). The TPC is an organization that compares different hardware/software configurations in terms of their transaction processing capability. To compare these different systems, the TPC has defined a standard benchmark called the TPC-C benchmark.

The TPC-C benchmark is designed to mimic a typical commerce application. The benchmark defines a "company" that has a number of warehouses. Each warehouse stocks all of the 10,000 items the company sells.

Each warehouse services 10 districts, and each district services 3,000 customers. Customers place orders with the company. Each order consists of an average of ten items. The benchmark includes a variety of different types of business transactions, primarily new orders, but also payments, order lookups, deliveries, and stock inventory lookups. Full details on the TPC-C benchmark are available at the TPC Web site (www.tpc.org).

TPC measures the performance of various hardware/software combinations in transactions per minute, referred to as tpmC, for transactions per minute of the C benchmark. A system rated at 100,000 tpmC is one that was able to process 100,000 of these transactions per minute.

The tpmC metric is only part of the equation. We also need to consider how much it costs to process a given transaction. The TPC-C benchmark includes information on the cost of processing transactions. The cost of processing transactions is calculated by dividing the entire system cost (over five years of ownership) by the number of transactions per minute the system is capable of processing. This number is referred to as $/tpmC. A system that is rated at 20 $/tpmC is a system that costs $20 for each transaction per minute it can process.

Once we know the $/tpmC, we can calculate the cost to design a system that can process M transactions per minute, which is M × $/tpmC. This assumes that the cost of building the system is linear with transactional throughput capability, but this is a reasonable first-guess approximation.

Unfortunately, the Dell system as configured was not one of the systems for which the TPC reported either tpmC or $/tpmC as of press time. But there are a variety of systems included that are extremely similar to the Dell configuration. And in fact, of all the systems running COM+, there was remarkably little difference in either the measured tpmC or the $/tpmC.

As of press time, TPC includes measurements on seven systems running COM+, mostly Compaq systems, which are very similar to Dell systems. The $/tpmC they measured were 14.62, 18.26, 16.62, 18.7, 18.46, 17.88, and 17.96. The average of these numbers is 17.5, so this is a good guess as to the $/tpmC we would have seen for Dell. Based on this, we can assume that the cost to build a Dell system that can process 1000 orders per minute would be 1000 × 17.5, or $17,500, give or take $1000. To build a Dell system that can process 10,000 orders per minute would be 10,000 × 17.5, or $175,000. Keep in mind that your transactions may or may not be similar to the TPC-C benchmark. The point is not to predict what your throughput will be as much as to give you a tool for comparing systems.

How does the $175,000 cost of a Dell system processing 10,000 orders per minute compare to some other systems? As of press time, the fastest system for which we have TPC-C measurements is the Sun Enterprise 10000 Starfire Servers with the Solaris operating system and Oracle 8 Data Server. The tpmC for the Sun system exceeded 115,000. This is fast. However it is also expensive. The $/tpmC measured for the Sun system is 105.63, meaning it costs over $100 for every order per minute the system can process. To build a system based on the Sun Enterprise 10000 Starfire Server that can process 10,000 tpmC is, therefore, $105.63 × 10,000, or $1,056,300, or more than five times the cost of the Dell/COM+ system doing the same work. And this assumes you can scale down the Sun system so that you don't have to pay the $12 million price tag the standard system would cost.

Although the $/tpmC value of the Sun Enterprise is high, it is typical of mainframe-based systems. The Sequent NUMACenter 2000 running Oracle8 Enterprise Edition and TUXEDO, which can process more than 93,000 tpmC, costs 131 $/tpmC, or $1,310,000 for the equivalent processing to the $175,000 Dell/COM+ system. An IBM AS/400e Server Model S40 running DB2 and CICS can process more than 43,000 tpmC and costs 128 $/tpmC, or $1,280,000 for the Dell/COM+ equivalent.

However, the cost of machines isn't everything. It is well worth spending more money on large mainframe systems if those machines can handle huge traffic loads, never go down, and/or have geographic redundancy. But these are exactly the requirements that Dell had for their commerce systems. And what Dell has shown us is that we can have commerce systems that are both highly reliable and very cheap.

System Benchmarks

The Dell strategy was hugely successful. In 1999, Dell became the number two supplier of NT workstations and went from being a virtually unknown company to number 78 among the Fortune 500 companies. In its latest quarter, it made over $6 billion. Barring some catastrophe, over the next year Dell's revenues will exceed $30 billion. According to Michael Dell, as of August 17, 1999, "We are now the largest direct company within the worldwide home and small-business market, and are significantly more profitable in that space than our nearest direct competitor." We can assume that part of the reason Dell's profit margin is so strong is because the commerce systems they are using to sell their systems are so inexpensive to build.

Almost 40 percent of Dell's revenues are from its sales over the Internet. Over the next year, its Internet sales will most likely exceed 12 billion dollars. That is more than 32 million dollars a day. Or more than 1.3 million dollars per hour, 24 hours per day, 365 days per year. If the Dell system goes down for four minutes, it costs Dell the equivalent of a full-time person's salary for a year. When Dell says it wants its systems up and running 24/7/52, it isn't kidding.

Lessons Learned

By early 1999, the Dell site was hosting over 2.5 million visitors per week. Dell has proven that commerce over the Web can be a huge success, and it has forced every major computer maker to start its own Web sales/support system. Dell has fundamentally altered the rules for selling computers, and has had a huge impact on the entire retailing industry. It is safe to say that Dell takes the Internet seriously.

Dell believes that its embrace of the Internet has been the key to its success. Building on its success in sales and service, Dell is looking to expand the use of the Internet throughout every part of its business. Dell no longer sees the Internet as a tool to be used in doing business, but sees the Internet as what now *defines* its business. As Michael Dell said at DirectConnect, Dell's global customer conference, held August 25, 1999, "The Internet must become your business. The use of the Internet throughout the business will be what ultimately distinguishes successful firms in all industries."[1] Dell now uses the Internet as its primary means of communicating with customers, suppliers, and employees. It distinguishes itself by making as much information as possible available to as wide an audience as possible. Again, Michael Dell:[2]

> Information can no longer be guarded like the crown jewels of your business. It must be shared with customers and suppliers, over the Internet, as a powerful source of differentiation. Businesses that don't provide better information, faster to customers, in a way that makes it easy to use, will quickly lose their advantage.

[1] August 25, 1999, Michael Dell at the DirectConnect, Dell's global customer conference.

[2] Ibid.

Today, Dell has started to make this prediction a reality. The Dell Web site is your entrance into the world of Dell, offering much more than sales and support. Through the Dell site you can take lessons in how to network your home, create a home theater, or protect your system from viruses. You can view the Dell annual reports, learn about the Dell executives, and learn much more than you ever wanted to know about Michael Dell (Did you know that Michael Dell prefers to work standing up at his desk?).

At the Dell site you can apply for a job at Dell. Are you an expert in Microsoft Word? Go to the Careers at Dell page, do a search by keyword for "Microsoft Word" and you will find 19 current job openings at Dell for which proficiency with Microsoft Word is a requirement. Are you interested in Customer Service? You are in luck. Search for job openings in the Customer Service Department, and you can take your pick from among 65 open positions. If you don't have a resume to send in, no problem, go to Dell's Resume builder, answer the interactive questions, and create an impressive resume on the fly.

You say you don't want to work at Dell because it means moving to Austin, Texas? Silly you, you don't know Austin. But fortunately, on the Dell site you can learn all about Austin's 14,000 acres of parkland and greenbelts, Austin's 100 live music venues, even Austin's beloved 1.5 million Mexican free-tailed bats (no mosquitoes, here!).

Dell is even getting into the general portal business. Click on dell.net from the Dell home page, and you can check out the latest news, weather, stock reports, and sports scores; send e-mail; chat; set up a personal Web page; and even read your horoscope (Today, I am told to spend a lovely evening with my mate. Unfortunately, my mate is told to seek new romantic interests. . .).

If Dell has learned one lesson from its use of the Internet, it is that one should never underestimate how tightly integrated the Internet can become into one's business. In the future, the Internet will become only more pervasive at Dell. As Michael Dell says, Dell will seek ". . . to move all core capabilities online, creating a super-efficient organization that leverages the Internet in every part of its business."[3]

Using the Internet effectively is only part of what Dell has learned. The other part is how to build Web based systems economically. This is

[3] *Scalable Enterprise Computing (SEC) White Paper*, July 12, 1999. Dell Computers

where the Microsoft technologies have played a key role. These technologies allow Dell to build Web-based commerce systems at a fraction of the cost of building such systems on large mainframe systems. The economy comes from the low cost of the Microsoft systems themselves, but even more important, from the fact that these systems run on low cost, commonly available hardware platforms.

Dell and Microsoft

Dell has been happy with its use of Microsoft technology to run its Web-based systems. Based on its success with Web commerce, Dell believes it is ready to take the next step: to run the entire Dell operation using nothing but Dell technology based on Microsoft systems. Dell believes that the Microsoft technology is ready for corporate prime time. The mainframe is not yet completely dead at Dell, but it is dying fast.

Dell sees the Microsoft technologies as the enabling technology for the next great change in the server market. According to Dell's Scalable Enterprise Computing White Paper, July 12, 1999, this is the evolution from boutique systems and specialized, high-end hardware to what Dell calls the "commoditization of the server market."[4] By this Dell means corporate class business servers running Web systems and business logic on inexpensive and widely available hardware and software. In other words, the evolution from a highly specialized hardware market to a commodity hardware market.

The ability to run corporations on commodity machines running inexpensive software plays to Dell's strength. This new generation of relatively inexpensive server machines just happens to be exactly the machines that Dell manufactures. And this new generation of machines is a fraction of the cost of the traditional big iron machines that, up until now, has dominated the corporate IT departments.

Dell sees the success of Microsoft middle tier technologies as being intimately tied to its own success. It believes that as the whole world starts to move to the Dell model for corporate IT management, Dell will be in an excellent position to grow. So Dell is not only building its own IT technology using Microsoft/Dell technology, it is proudly showing off its accomplishments to an increasingly interested world.

[4] Ibid.

Drawbacks

When Dell first chose to make the Microsoft/Dell technologies the cornerstone of its commerce and IT strategy, it was taking quite a risk. To the best of my knowledge, Dell was the first Fortune 500 company to make such a major commitment to this kind of technology. Most of its IT programmers came from traditional IT programming backgrounds, and had to learn new systems and new ways of doing things. Much of the early work was done with early versions of MTS, and Dell was at the bleeding edge of large COMWare projects.

There is still skepticism among some of the IT staff as to whether Microsoft technology is up to the task. Much of the skepticism revolves around SQL Server 6.5, which some believe was not ready for mission critical work. The initial experience with SQL Server 7.0 is much more positive.

I have had many Dell employees in my public classes, and I have personally seen a shift in attitude. A year ago, I encountered a lot of hostility towards Microsoft systems among Dell students. But in recent months, most Dell employees seem excited about what they have been able to build using Microsoft products. They feel the current projects have been successful and are willing to give Microsoft a chance in ever more mission critical areas.

At the high level, I have seen no evidence that the confidence in this technology has wavered at all. Today, Dell seems more committed than ever to making its "Dell on Dell" vision a reality.

Wrap Up

Dell has proven that the days of relying on large expensive mainframes for reliable corporate computing are over. We are entering a new age: the age of the commodity server. We now know how to put together farms of these commodity servers into a large super-server. This allows us to choose systems based not on throughput, but on the cost of processing transactions. In this area, COM+ based systems offer a huge cost advantage over their mainframe ancestors.

Commerce over the Internet is largely governed by cost. Companies that offer better values will be those that succeed. To succeed, companies *must* be able to process transactions as cheaply as possible. There is no room for cost inefficiency. It is the cost of processing transactions that, in most cases, will be the primary determinant to corporate profitability.

COM+, running on inexpensive server hardware, offers companies a huge advantage over companies using expensive mainframes for transaction processing. It is hard to imagine how companies using mainframes are going to survive over the next five years. The dinosaur's time has run out. The race is now to the swift and nimble. Dell has set the pace for the next generation of commerce.

Acentris: Transactional Gusto

Company Profile

Acentris Wireless Communications
127 SW 156th Street, Suite 100
Seattle, Washington 98166
www.acentris.com

Products/Tools Used

- Microsoft ADO 2.5
- Microsoft Message Queuing Services
- Microsoft SQL Server 7.0, Service Pack 1
  - Microsoft Data Transformation Services (DTS)
  - Microsoft Free Text Search
- Microsoft Visual Studio 6.0, Enterprise Edition

- Microsoft Windows 2000 Advanced Server
  - Microsoft COM+ 1.0
  - Microsoft Internet Information Services 5.0
- Dell PowerEdge Servers: Series 2000, 4000, and 6000

Application

In the last chapter I discussed Dell Computer. Dell is interesting, because it is a good example of a company taking advantage of one of the important features of Microsoft's middle tier technologies: the extremely low cost of processing a transaction. Dell is a showcase for how to design a corporate Internet commerce system around Microsoft COMWare and commodity hardware. There are no existing systems that can deliver a lower cost of transactional processing than can the Microsoft technologies.

In this chapter, I describe another company's use of Microsoft's middle tier COMWare: Acentris Wireless Communications. Acentris is an interesting case study because it focuses on the other important feature of Microsoft's middle tier technologies: the speed of processing transactions. Unlike the cost of transactional processing (for which Microsoft is unsurpassed), when measuring the speed of processing transactions, or how many transactions can be processed in a given time period, Microsoft is not up there with the big boys.

In the last chapter, I discussed the TPC-C benchmark. As I pointed out, there are two important measurements in the TPC-C benchmark. One is what the TPC calls tpmC, which is the number of transactions processed per minute, and the other is the cost/tpmC, which is the cost of the total system divided by the tpmC. Since the TPC-C benchmark mimics a typical order in its definition of a transaction, I usually refer to orders per minute (abbreviated OPM) rather than tpmC, and cost per order per minute (C/OPM) rather than cost/tpmC, since these terms seem more intuitive to me.

So Microsoft does well in the C/OPM, and not so well in the OPM department. This may or may not be a problem, depending on what your OPM needs are. For example, the fastest measured OPM is that of a Sun Starfire Enterprise 10000, measured at a blinding 115,395 OPM. Not far behind is the IBM RS 6000 Enterprise Server, measured at 110,434 OPM.

In fact, none of the top nine OPM systems is running a single piece of software written by Microsoft. As of press time, the top nine systems, the average OPM is clocked at more than 86,000 OPM. The fastest machine running COM+ is able to process only 40,368 OPM, less than half of the big-boy average.

However 40,368 OPM is still more than 58 million orders per day, or more than 21 billion orders per year. This may not equal the 60 trillion orders per year you could process with the Sun Starfire, but 21 billion orders per year is nothing to sneeze at. And this published TPC-C number was measured on an early build of COM+ running on NT Enterprise Edition 4.0. The released version running on Windows 2000 should be significantly faster. Also, these measurements are of orders as defined by the TPC-C benchmark. Many commerce transactions will be less complex than the TPC-C, and can expect throughput at two or more times these measurements.

In this case study, I will look at one company requiring high transactional throughput: Acentris. Acentris requires high throughput by most standards. It was able to achieve this throughput using systems that cost a fraction of what a Sun Starfire would have cost. It did so by leveraging COM+ and the Microsoft middle tier technologies described in this book.

I wanted to include the Acentris case study even though they are not in full production yet. Since COM+ is still in beta as of press time, there are no production systems yet. This is even more true of systems based on EJB and CORBA 3.0. However, Acentris is one of those that are closest to production. The work they have done can give us some important insights into the future of high throughput transactional processing. So let's take a look at Acentris.

Acentris is in the business of reselling wireless telecommunications services, including cellular phone services and paging services. They buy airtime in big chunks from wireless providers and sell it in little chunks to individual consumers or small companies. Their wireless providers include most major national carriers. Customers using Acentris' services get a variety of value-added services, including:

- *Lower rates.* Acentris can offer large blocks of time at the lowest possible rate, and pass on these savings to its customers.

- *Single point-of-contact customer service.* Acentris handles all of the customers' needs regardless of which company provided which service.

- *Simplified billing.* Acentris consolidates all of the customers' telecommunication services on a single bill, including local services, long distance, wireless, paging, and other telecommunication services. This is described as rebilling.

Historically, Acentris has been a phone-based service company. If customers want to ask questions about their bills, they phone service representatives. Acentris would like to move to Web-based service, where customers can view bills, change service options, and purchase new services directly through the Internet. It will still have telephone support staff available, but it would like to put as much information as possible directly into the hands of its customers.

Acentris has been in business since 1988. There are very few line-of-business suites for companies that sell products on a metered/time-based basis, which is why Acentris needed to write their own system rather than purchase an existing package. It started with a C and Fox-Pro application in the late 1980s. In 1994, it decided to rewrite parts of its application in Visual Basic and Access. In 1996 they started to use Visual Basic 5.0 and Access 97 to move into the Win32 world. Now they are hitting the limitations of this simple database system, and want to rearchitect their entire system for high transactional throughput and direct customer access through the Web.

Business Requirements

Acentris is designing the next generation of their business system. They are calling it the Reseller Billing System (RBS) 2000. It is specifically designed for companies that are buying services in bulk and reselling them in smaller packages. Here are some of the business requirements Acentris identified for RBS 2000.

Very low transaction cost. Acentris is walking a very thin profit line. It buys its time from wireless service providers and then resells that time competing with those same vendors. As you can imagine, this leaves very little room for profit.

Acceptable transaction volume. Acentris's current customer base is 20,000. It wants RBS 2000 to support one million customers, and up to 100 transactions per month per customer. Based on this, its system must be capable of supporting at least 100 million transactions per month.

Support for batch and online transactions. Transactions come in two forms for Acentris. Batch transactions come in the form of billing tapes from the phone companies that show the time used by Acentris customers and become the basis for customer bills. Online transactions come from both the Web and from the Acentris phone support staff.

Scalability. With one million customers needing to access their records, Acentris needs RBS 2000 to support large numbers of concurrent users. If the typical customer accesses the system twice a month, concentrated during the 800 business hours of a typical month, Acentris can expect an average Web load of 2,500 concurrent clients, and peak loads of perhaps four times that, or 10,000 concurrent clients.

Rapid deployment. Acentris needs to have RBS 2000 up and running within one year of their decision to rearchitect. This includes support for both thin and rich clients, an entirely new database architecture, porting of database data, reimplementation of all its business logic, design of the Web interface, testing, debugging, and full system deployment. In addition, Acentris must be able to respond to rapidly changing market conditions quickly.

Rich and thin clients support. Acentris wants RBS 2000 to support rich client interfaces internally, while allowing external clients to use thin client Web browsers. It wants both clients to share the same business logic.

Robustness. Acentris is in the business of manipulating databases. Data is coming in and being changed at a very fast rate. The loss of even small amounts of data could result in considerable loss of profits, and an even greater loss of time as Acentris would have to methodically reconstruct lost orders. RBS 2000 needs to support full backups that are highly robust.

Security. Acentris customers can order new services over the Web. Customers can also look at their private accounting information, including phone calls they have made. Acentris is therefore very concerned that RBS 2000 properly validate users coming in over the Web and ensure the privacy of their information.

Extensibility. Acentris wants the system to be able to handle a wide range of rebilling applications, such as accounting and consulting, so that the RBS 2000 can be marketed as an independent product.

The profit margins for reselling wireless services is extremely thin, so Acentris is sensitive to the cost of processing each transaction. It chose to develop RBS 2000 on COM+ and the Microsoft technologies because it believes these technologies will give them both low-cost processing and a proven COMWare platform for which development is extremely easy.

RBS 2000 needs to process transactions—a lot of transactions. Acentris expects to hit the ground running with more than two million orders per month (24 million per year) and wants to architect the system to handle 100 million per month, or about 1.2 billion orders per year. That is a lot of orders, but not nearly enough to require the big iron Sun Starfire priced at more than 12 million dollars for the configuration used in the TPC-C benchmark. This is well within the capability of a high-end COM+ system, priced at less than 450 thousand dollars for the TPC-C configuration. My guess is that, like RBS 2000, more than 80 percent of today's commerce systems could fit in a similar COM+ system. In fact, as Acentris found out, it could fit in a smaller COM+ system.

Architectural Overview

Acentris knew RBS 2000 needed a COMWare solution; it needed both a TPM-like infrastructure and a component programming model. A TPM solution without components would have been too difficult to program, and would have required significant training of the Acentris staff. A component solution without the TPM-like infrastructure could never have achieved the scalability and security requirements. They needed a solution that combined both TPM-like infrastructure and component-based flexibility and simplicity.

Which COMWare solution would they choose? They considered both CORBA and Enterprise JavaBeans, but eliminated both as immature. Of the more than 30 CORBA and EJB vendors, it was unclear which would survive the shakeup, and which, of those that survived, would remain committed to their technology. None of the systems had withstood the test of time, and none had been used to build serious commerce systems. As Darin Lang, Vice President and COO of Acentris, put it, "We are leery of 1.0 software." COM+ was based on existing technology (MTS, COM, DCOM). As Lang says, "Microsoft's COM+ is a proven, stable technology." It also felt that Microsoft was not likely to go out of business, and that Microsoft was deeply committed to its technology.

Enterprise JavaBeans (EJB) had other problems as well as its immaturity. Acentris had existing systems built in Visual Basic. It wanted to leverage these systems, not throw them out and rewrite them all in Java just so that they could run in EJB.

Acentris had to work with languages with which its programmers were familiar. Acentris, like many companies, had a valued programming staff that was intimate with Acentris' specialized business. Few were fluent in Java. It was not about to allow its next-generation system to be used as a training ground for teaching Java. As Lang puts it, "We don't want people developing mission critical applications while learning Java."

It's not that Acentris will not use Java. RBS 2000 will be rewritten in many languages. Most of the RBS 2000 business logic will be written in Visual Basic, because it is such an easy language to work with. Lang believes their system will follow the 80/20 rule: that 80 percent of the CPU cycles will be spent in 20 percent of the components. As they identify those critical components they will rewrite those in C++ or Java. So it's not that they are against Java, it's just that they want to use Java where it makes sense, instead of across the board.

One of the ways Acentris expects to use Java is for those components that need support for instance pooling, an instance management algorithm I discussed in Chapter 4, "COMWare." The current version of Visual Basic does not support the instance pooling algorithm, only the just-in-time instantiation algorithm. Although C++ components also support instance pooling, the development of COM+ components is currently much easier in Java.

Acentris knew it needed three-plus tier architecture for the same three reasons most companies choose three-plus tier architectures: manageability of business logic, scalability of clients, and flexibility in the user interface. Placing the business logic in the middle tier makes the system much more manageable, as business logic is located on a few central machines where it can be rapidly updated and easily maintained. Using the middle tier allows the COMWare algorithms to work full force to provide the scalability Acentris needed to support the number of clients it expected. And because the use of a middle tier enforces a clean separation of user interface and business logic, RBS 2000 can support both thin clients for its external Web clients and rich clients for its internal telephone support staff.

The RBS 2000 architecture is shown in Figure 14.1. It consists of five main tiers: a rich client tier, a Web server tier, a thin client tier, a component tier, and a data tier.

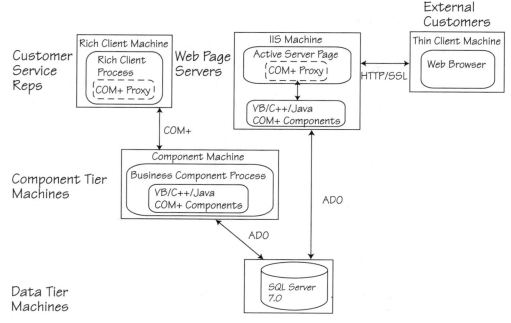

Figure 14.1 RBS 2000 architecture.

The thin client tier consists of Web browsers. This is the entry point into RBS 2000 for external customers. Because Acentris wants to minimize the expectations it makes on external customers, it accepts information from these customers through industry standard HTTP requests and returns information as industry standard HTML pages. Customers can use the operating system, Web browser, and Internet Service Provider of their choice. The Secure Socket Level provides the security over the Web.

HTTP requests are received by the Web server tier, which in turn generates the HTML pages that are delivered back to the thin, Web-based clients. The Web server tier is running Windows 2000, COM+, and Microsoft IIS. Two types of HTML pages are returned to the client: static pages, which never change, and dynamic pages, which are constructed on the fly as a result of processing business logic. Static pages can just be stored on the Web tier and delivered as requested. Dynamic pages must be generated by ASP scripts. These scripts make requests of the component tier business logic through standard COM+ proxies. Acentris has been using a Microsoft tool called the *Web Application Stress Testing Tool* to make sure that they have optimized the system for the best possible performance over the Internet.

Acentris staff typically does not go through the same access path as external clients do. Staff comes in through a rich client tier. Since staff can access the system through known machines with configurations that can be determined by Acentris, RBS 2000 can offer these users a much richer experience. These rich client interfaces use Visual Basic forms-based programs. Since these machines are running Microsoft operating systems, they can use COM+ proxies directly to access the business logic containing component tier. These Visual Basic interfaces are not only better, but much faster than what can be presented to a generic customer Web browser. These Visual Basic programs go directly to the component tier, eliminating the overhead associated with the generation of HTML pages, the running of scripts, and the repetitive regeneration of remote proxies.

The rich client tier sends its request to the component tier. The component tier is currently running only Visual Basic components, but some of these components will eventually be rewritten in C++ or Java if tests indicate that they would significantly improve overall system performance by doing so. There are about 25 business components running in this tier, with such functionality as customer management, invoicing, accounting, tax maintenance, application monitoring, and e-mail access. Since all of these components run on the central component tier, it is very fast and efficient to make modifications in business logic as the nature of the business evolves. To give the best possible performance to the Web tier, the business components run directly on the Web tier for the thin clients.

All of the middle tier components are designed around the requirements of the COM+ COMWare environment. They are stateless, so that instance management algorithms can be used to give high scalability. They have moved security into the middle tier, so that resource connections can be freely pooled. They have been designed so that each method represents a self-contained transaction, so that the COM+ transactional boundary management algorithms can automatically determine the correct place to start and stop each transaction. Acentris has sought opportunities to use asynchronous components for workload averaging, which allows some of the peak work load to be performed at times of lower system usage, a topic I discussed in Chapter 5, "COM+ and Friends."

The RBS 2000 contains information that is considered customer confidential. For example, customers are allowed to look at their billing information, but not billing information for other customers. This is an example of horizontal security. As I discussed in Chapter 6, "COM+ Components," COM+, like all COMWare platforms, does not administratively support horizontal security. Horizontal security must, therefore, be programmed using some sort of a security API. COM+ has such an API. Using this API, the component instance can determine exactly which user process is making requests, and can react appropriately. RBS 2000 uses this API to program its own horizontal security.

RBS 2000 components, like most well-designed commerce components, are designed to be stateless. This stateless programming allows the systems to scale up to large numbers of users. I discussed the need for stateless programming in many places, especially in Chapter 4. As I said there, stateless programming doesn't really mean that components have no state. It means that component instances must store their state in a place other than the instance. Most commerce components store their state in databases.

Components store their state in the SQL Server 7.0 database. The machine(s) with the database constitute the Data Tier. The existing customer information is stored in an Access database. To transition from the original Access databases to SQL Server 7.0, Acentris used Data Transformation Services (DTS). DTS is a tool that is used to move data from one data source to another. Lang believes that the use of this tool saved four weeks of development and testing time.

Acentris has been happy with SQL Server 7.0. One of the features that has made SQL Server 7.0 especially easy to use is the self-tuning ability. SQL Server can be set to monitor all queries, and automatically create indices where doing so would improve system performance. This makes the system easy to use and maintain by nondatabase administrators.

Once the basic system functionality has been tested, Acentris will start adding robustness and further scalability features. It will use the Windows Load Balancing Service, which does load balancing based on IP addresses, to provide robustness and scalability of the IIS server machines. It will use Microsoft's cluster technology (MSCS) to ensure robustness of the component router (as described in Chapter 8, "The COM+ Services") and the database machines.

System Benchmarks

As of press time, Acentris has completed all of the basic business components and has started doing some performance measurements to validate that it can obtain the scalability it needs. For the tests, it used two machines. One machine consolidated the Web tier and the component tier and the other machine served as a database server.

Both the Web/component machine and the database machine were inexpensive machines. The Web/component machine was a Dell Precision 410 (Single 450 MHz Pentium II) with 512MB RAM, 9.0GB drive, and running Win2000 RC2 Advanced Server, retailing for about $7000. The database machine was a Dell Precision 610 (Dual 550 MHz Pentium III Xeon) with 512MB RAM, 18.0GB drive, and also running Win2000 RC2 Advanced Server, SQL Server 7.0, and MS-DTC. This configuration retails for about $10,000.

The first series of benchmarks simulated a full running system. It used the worst possible case, with all transactions coming over the Web. Web-based transactions are particularly expensive, because the cost of creating the HTML pages is very high. It also requires frequent recreation of client side proxies.

The transactions Acentris measured covered all major aspects of the application including customer management, service item management, and accounting. Acentris believes the tested system load would be very typical of a high Internet client load with a batch billing cycle occurring simultaneously.

In this configuration, Acentris measured transactional throughput of 2887 transactions per minute. Dividing the cost of the system ($17,000) by the transactional throughput, we get a TPC-C like metric of $5.80 per transaction per minute, which would make this system one of the lowest cost transactional processing systems ever measured. We must be careful in comparing this number to the actual TPC-C numbers, since this benchmark is not the same benchmark as defined by the TPC-C. However unlike the TPC-C, this benchmark uses a significant proportion of Web-based clients. From a performance perspective, Web clients are the most difficult to manage, since there is considerable overhead associated with the processing of Web pages. Thus my expectation would be that this benchmark is much more demanding than TPC-C, not less. To be able to push 2887 transactions per minute out of low-end hardware that has not been optimized and is not yet using the IP load-balancing capabilities of the Windows Load Balancing Service is a remarkable achievement.

Acentris had defined 100 million transactions per month as its target goal. It has already surpassed this goal on its first benchmark. One can only imagine what the performance of this system will be once the workload is distributed over multiple middle-tier and Web-tier machines.

Lessons Learned

Acentris is happy with their choice of COM+ as its COMWare technology. They see COM+ as an essential element in their plan to shave every possible cent off of the cost of processing transactions in this highly competitive market.

Acentris is so excited about the potential of RBS 2000 that they are now making plans to market it as an independent application to be used for others that have a need for rebilling software in- or outside of the wireless telecommunications industry. In preparation for this, they have transferred the intellectual property rights of RBS 2000 to a separate company, Covault Corporation (www.covault.com).

Lang believes Microsoft's component technology has proven that it can make it easy to build robust business systems. The ability to use nonspecialized programming languages has allowed Acentris programmers to be immediately productive. COM+ has proven it can deliver the transactional throughput, and can deliver it at a cost that is without precedent in the industry.

Acentris and Microsoft

Acentris has a long history of working with Microsoft technologies. It has many programmers who have a good understanding of Visual Basic. It was slightly nervous about the transition from Access to SQL Server 7.0. They had expected the data transformations to be difficult and the maintenance required of a more serious database product to require major retraining. Neither of these fears came true. The data transformation was simple and SQL Server 7.0 has proven to be a very easy system to use and maintain. Acentris has a great relationship with

Microsoft, and is expecting to be building on Microsoft technologies for a long time to come.

Drawbacks

The decision to use COM+ as a COMWare technology means that Acentris is committed to Windows 2000 as a platform. It is hard to imagine a better platform for this type of an application. However, as Acentris decides to sell the RBS 2000 system to other companies, it will undoubtedly have to deal with some anti-Microsoft sentiment. NT 4.0 still has a reputation for being less stable than Unix among some companies. I believe this reputation is largely undeserved, and is due more to the common practice of adding random device drivers to the NT machines, whereas such a practice would never be tolerated in the Unix world. But undeserved or not, some companies still believe that Microsoft is unproven in the world of mission-critical computing.

The first six months of release will be critical to the long-term reputation of Windows 2000, and, indirectly, to RBS 2000. If Windows proves itself to be a highly robust platform, ready for mission-critical applications, then Acentris will have chosen a platform that will offer an unbeatable combination of price and quality. If Windows 2000 gets a reputation for unreliability, then Acentris will have to do a quick retreat from its current strategy.

Acentris has been beta testing Windows 2000, and believes Windows 2000 is the platform of the middle tier future. Windows 2000 has been subjected to more beta testing than perhaps any other product in software history. I think Acentris has made a good bet on Windows 2000. But we still must wait for the ultimate verdict from the industry.

Wrap Up

The Acentris case study is a useful adjunct to the Dell case study from Chapter 13, "Dell: Commerce on the Cheap." Dell showed how to develop commerce systems using Microsoft middle-tier technology and commodity hardware systems at a fraction of the cost of using traditional mainframe systems. But Dell was built on COM, DCOM, and MTS, not COM+. MTS is the previous generation of COM+. We could reasonably assume that the next generation will outperform the previous generation, but it would be nice to see some evidence of this. And there is another issue: The Dell case study focused more on cost of transaction rather than transactional throughput. Can COM+ handle the throughput necessary to support commerce?

Acentris answers these questions. Acentris proves that the high performance of COM, DCOM, and MTS was not a fluke. RBS 2000 is completely built on Windows 2000 technology and COM+, and achieves a cost per transaction per minute of $5.80 and a transaction rate of 2887 transactions per minute.

The mainframe vendors will respond to this by saying that 2887 transactions per minute may be good, but it is hardly fast compared to the 100,000 plus TPC-C transactions per minute achievable, say, on the Sun Starfire Enterprise 10000. We need to keep a few things in mind, however.

First, the TPC-C benchmark, which is what Sun used to achieve this 100,000 plus number, is based on a rich client scenario, not a Web-based scenario. So the Sun system achieved 100,000 plus transactions per minute only by eliminating the considerable overhead associated with Web management. The RBS 2000 COM+ system achieved 2887 transactions per minute *on top of* managing the Web system. In a typical Web-based commerce system, probably 90 percent of the overhead is associated, not with the business transactions, but with Web page management. Had the Sun system been required to manage Web pages as well as business transactions, as did RBS 2000, I suspect their transactional throughput would have been reduced by a factor of 10, bringing it down to 10,000 transactions per minute. In this case, we would be comparing a $12 million system processing 10,000 Web-based transactions per minute to a $17,000 system processing 2887 Web-based transactions per minute. Or, presented in cost per Web-based transaction per minute, a Sun system that costs $1200 per Web-based transaction per minute to a COM+ system that costs $5.80 per Web-based transaction per minute.

Second, RBS 2000 isn't even close to being fully optimized. Acentris uses only two machines, one of which runs both the Web and the business logic. It is not yet using the Windows Load Balancing Service, a technology I discussed in Chapter 8. It hasn't separated the Web tier from the component tier, as Dell has done. Without a lot of effort, Acentris should be able to scale RBS 2000 up from 2887 Web-based transactions per minute to 28,000 Web-based transactions per minute. At this point, I predict that RBS 2000 will far surpass the capabilities of the mainframe Sun hardware at a fraction of the cost.

Third, RBS 2000 is based on highly flexible COMWare technology using easy-to-write Visual Basic programs. The Sun system is based on highly inflexible Transaction Processing Monitor (TPM) technology using hard-to-write traditional programming languages and complex TPM APIs. Even Sun is telling people not to base future applications on TPM systems, but instead to migrate to COMWare technology. Sun has yet to prove that it can deliver acceptable performance using its COMWare technology, however, especially when that technology is used in conjunction with the Web. Acentris has proven that Microsoft COMWare technology can handle the highly demanding workload that is required to deliver commerce over the Web.

So the Dell and the Acentris case studies make a matched set. Dell shows how we can keep the cost of transactions to a level that is unprecedented in the history of the computer industry. Acentris proves that we do not have to sacrifice good transactional throughput in order to achieve this low cost. Between them we can sum up the Microsoft strategy for the middle tier: providing high volume, low cost transactions for the most demanding market in the world, the Web.

PART FIVE

Wrap Up

Many readers of this book will be in the process of trying to choose between COMWare technologies for their Web-based commerce applications. I have taken you through all of the technologies. Now I will summarize with a chapter giving you some guidance as to the most important issues you might want to consider when choosing between these technologies. I also leave you with a glossary that will give you a common language for discussing these technologies. Finally, I have included a list of resources you can use to continue delving into this topic, and, in many cases, gain an entirely different perspective on COMWare than mine. I hope that this material helps you make some intelligent decisions.

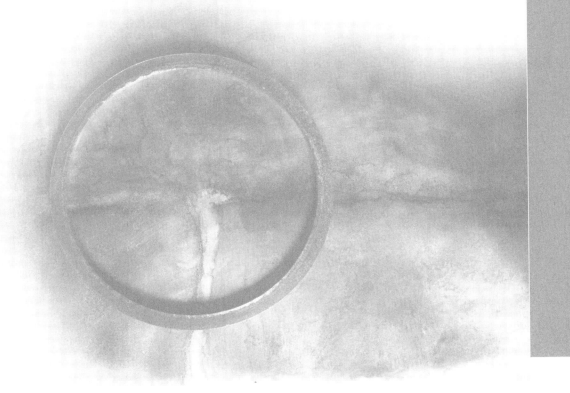

CHAPTER 15

Considering COMWare Technologies

If your company is struggling, trying to decide which COMWare technologies to adopt, take heart, you are not alone. The COM+ versus CORBA versus EJB debate is raging at most large corporations. I have visited hundreds of such corporations throughout the world, and have seen exactly the same issues being debated over and over again. In this closing chapter I will try to distill the main issues I think your company should consider when trying to choose a COMWare technology.

Portability versus Interoperability

I frequently give talks before audiences of 1000 or more. I often ask the question, "How many people think portability is important?" Usually, half the audience raises their hands. Then I ask the question, "How many of you are actively porting applications from one platform to another?" At this point, 95 percent of the hands go down.

At first, this confused me. Why do so many people think portability is important if so few are making use of it? I have finally come to the conclusion that people think they want portability. But what they really want is interoperability, and they don't understand the difference.

Portability is the ability to take an application and move it easily between different platforms. Interoperability is the ability to have your application interoperate with other applications on the same or different platforms.

In my experience, portability is a red herring. People do not port. They buy applications, and they buy the platforms on which those applications run. Then IT departments must figure out how to get those different applications to work together. This is an interoperability issue. In my experience, interoperability is the major issue facing corporate IT departments today—interoperability, not portability.

Think this issue through. Figure out which is really important to you: portability or interoperability. Then focus on the real issue in your COMWare evaluations.

Buy a Vendor, Not a Technology

When you buy into a vendor's technology, you are buying into a vendor. If that vendor goes out of business, you are going to be very sorry. There is simply no such thing as vendor-neutral technology in the middle tier. To build a successful middle tier application, you will have no choice but to use vendor-specific technology.

Do not buy into IBM's WebSphere technology because it is Enterprise JavaBeans compliant. If you buy it, do so because you like WebSphere. Evaluate it for the technology it is. If IBM discontinues support for WebSphere, the fact that it is EJB-based will be of little consolation to you. It will be almost as much work to port to another EJB vendor as it will be to port to COM+ or CORBA.

Vendor Longevity

Many companies have great technology. But great technology is not worth much if the company supplying it is out of business. I am frequently asked to evaluate some new COMWare product. I am told that some new approach is far superior to COM+, or EJB, or whatever.

From my perspective, technology is only as good as the business plan behind it. To convince me to take a technology seriously, you must not only convince me that the technology is good, but that you have a business strategy that can make it successful in this highly competitive market.

In my opinion, only these four vendors are likely to make a go of it in the middle tier:

- Microsoft, because they have seemingly limitless resources

- IBM and BEA, because they have excellent and well-established TPM products

- Sun, because they supply much of the hardware behind some of the largest transactional systems around and control the influential EJB specification

Beyond these four vendors, you're moving into high-risk territory. Perhaps Oracle will make it, because they have considerable momentum from their database product. Perhaps IONA will make it, because they were the most successful of the CORBA technologies. Who else? Who knows? Probably nobody.

Vendor Commitment

Make sure that your vendor is fully committed to your technology. Having your vendor be in business three years from now will be of no value if it has stopped supporting your technology. IBM, in particular, seems to have a history of walking away from distributed component technology. OS/2, SOM/DSOM, OpenDoc, Taligent, and CORBA are all technologies that IBM at one point "bet the company on," and then soon lost interest in.

If the COMWare technology you have purchased turns out not to make money for your vendor, what do you think its strategy will be? Will it abandon the technology and focus on other products where it is making money? Or will it have risked so much on this technology that it would be inconceivable that it could give up on this COMWare? How much of its own future development is based on its own COMWare technology?

Platform

What are your platform requirements? If you can live with running your application on Windows 2000, then COM+ is a very attractive COMWare technology. If you must run on some other system, however, COM+ is no longer an alternative. Can you choose a platform based only on the advantages and disadvantages of that platform? Or are their certain platforms you absolutely must support? Is it more important that you support one platform very well, or can you compromise the support for one platform in return for having other options? Both IBM and BEA support several platforms, although it seems that neither will support Windows 2000 as well as COM+. If you need to support multiple platforms, then you should choose a particular COMWare product that supports those platforms. Don't expect to support the other platforms by using another vendor's technology, even if it is based on the same "standards."

Skills

What are the skills needed to build for this particular COMWare technology? If you are a typical bank or insurance company, you probably have fewer than 10 percent of your programmers trained in object-oriented programming and probably fewer than 10 percent of those trained in Java. If this is your situation, then choosing a Java technology makes little sense. On the other hand, if most of your staff is highly trained in Unix, then shifting to Windows 2000 will probably be a painful exercise. As best as you can, leverage your existing skills. Retrain only as a last resort, and then determine which options will require the least in retraining.

Maturity

How long has the COMWare platform you are contemplating been available? What is the component model it is using, and how long has that been available? How much experience does the vendor have in building component technology? How long has the vendor been building COMWare? How much money are they making on their COMWare technology?

Throughput

When you are looking at performance, look at the important numbers. In general, response time is not important, as long as it is within acceptable levels. In general, the performance of the programming language is not important. The only important performance number to consider is for the middle-tier work throughput. How many transactions can you push through the system within a given time period? Will that number be able to handle your expected system workload?

Cost per Transaction

Once you have determined that a given COMWare product can meet your throughput needs, look at the cost of processing each transaction and compare this to your profit margin. If you are selling books and you stand to make only $1.00 per book sold, purchasing a system that will cost you $1.20 for every book sale is not exactly logical. When you consider the cost, try to consider not only the cost of the COMWare platform, but the cost of the supporting hardware, the ongoing maintenance costs, the cost and availability of hiring programmers to develop for that platform, and the cost and availability of programming tools for those programmers to use.

Religion

Try to keep religion out of the discussion. Many people hate Microsoft just because it is Microsoft. For these people, Microsoft can simply do no right. Anything but Microsoft is a familiar refrain in some companies.

You do not make money by hating Microsoft. You make money by developing systems that can process your particular business transactions as cheaply as possible. Keep focused on the issues that are important to you: making money for your company, not worrying about whether Microsoft is making money. If you are making money using a particular COMWare platform, then the better that COMWare platform does overall, the better this is for you. You don't want to use a COMWare platform that is not making money for its vendor.

Try Before You Buy

Finally, try before you buy. Once you buy into one of these technologies, it is very hard to change. Take a month to try out each of your top two choices. Have a few developers try to build some systems. Check out the resulting systems for ease of development, ease of maintenance, and scalability. You will learn more from a few months of building live systems than from listening to any number of presentations by sales representatives.

Wrap Up

If you are building Web-based commerce systems, then you cannot afford to ignore the field of Component-Oriented Middleware (COMWare). And if you are in the field of commerce, you cannot afford to ignore the Web.

Web-based commerce requires great agility. It also requires great technology, technology that can deliver exceptional scalability, low-cost transactions, and a total infrastructure package for supporting serious business logic. This is the commitment of COMWare. Every significant company in the world agrees that COMWare is the future of Web commerce. This is not a technology you can afford to ignore.

Microsoft has a particularly strong, mature, and cost-effective offering in this area. But COM+ will not be the only COMWare technology. We can count on at least several EJB-based products to prove their worth, and hopefully over the next two years, a few CORBA-based products.

These products will all be evolving rapidly over the next few years. This will be a highly competitive area. Keeping ahead of new developments in this field is going to be a challenge. But keeping ahead is critical. The alternative to keeping ahead is being left behind. And on the Web, being left behind is being left forever. The Web does not suffer stragglers. This race goes to the swift and the nimble and the bright, and to those that can see the vision of the future.

Glossary

abort (v).   A less desirable synonym for *rollback*.

activity (n).   A collection of COM+ instances that share a single lock.

application (n). What Microsoft calls the collection of components that will run together inside a single component process.

application cluster (n).   A collection of machines, any of which can run a particular COM+ application. This term is slightly archaic, since it refers to COM+ component load balancing, which has been moved out of the basic COM+ product.

ASP (Active Server Pages).   Microsoft scripting technology for Web pages.

asynchronous (adj.).   A work request for which the requester does not wait, and which will be processed at some indeterminate time. In contrast to *synchronous*.

asynchronous components (n).   A component that completes its work requests asynchronously with respect to the requester.

authorization security (n).   Security based on authorizing a user to make requests of the middle tier. In contrast to *impersonation security*.

bean managed persistence (n).   A subtype of *entity beans* in which the bean programmer is responsible for managing the bean's state within callback methods called by the EJB container. In contrast to *container managed persistence*.

blob (n).   A bunch of machines that work together so that if one fails, the others can take over its workload.

blob manager (n).   A process that coordinates a bunch of machines working together as a blob.

callee makes right (adj.).   A description of a technology that makes the component instance responsible for determining which code path a particular method invocation should follow. Example: Because components are a *callee makes right* technology, the client coding requires very few code branch statements.

caller makes right (adj.).   A description of a technology that makes the client responsible for determining which code path a particular method invocation should follow. Example: Because TPMs are a *caller makes right* technology, code modification is tedious and error prone.

CLBS (Component Load Balancing Service).   A name for a COM+ load balancing service that has since been removed from the basic COM+ and is expected to be repackaged as part of an application server.

client (n).   A process that is making requests of a component. Client is a term that is relative to the component accepting the request, so one component may act as a client relative to another.

client side component (n).   A component that is specialized for working inside a client process. An example would be a component that acts as a robust proxy, automatically reinstantiating itself if something happens to the instance with which it is associated.

client surrogate (n).   A stand-in for the client that lives in the component process and accepts method requests on behalf of a client process and passes those requests through to a local instance.

cluster (n).   A blob (see *blob*).

COM+ (n).   The main piece of Microsoft's Component-Oriented Middleware (COMWare), which provides the component runtime environment and related object services.

COM+ Runtime (n).   The part of COM+ that defines the runtime environment for COM+ components, including the coordination of *point of interception* algorithms.

COM+ Services (n).   The part of COM+ that defines services of which components can make use. The COM+ services include *asynchronous components* and *events*.

component (n).   An ambiguous term sometimes used to refer to a component instance, implementation, or type, depending on the context. Examples: empX is an instance of an employee *component* (here used to refer to a component implementation). empX is an employee *component* (here used to refer to a component instance).

component implementation (n).   A specific implementation of a component type.

component instance (n).   A particular blob of memory that can be called upon do work on behalf of a client. The term *component instance* is often shortened to just *instance*, although the term instance is sometimes also used to describe an object instance. A component instance is described by a component type and is associated with some specific component implementation. The association between a component instance and a component implementation is made at the point of instantiation. Strictly speaking, a method is invoked on a specific component instance. Example: empX is a component instance of an employee.

component process (n).   A process in which a component instance lives. Non-recommended alternative terms are *server* and *surrogate process*. Example: Unbeknownst to me, my purchase involved an instance of a creditCard-Verification component that lived in a *component process* in Australia.

component tier (n).   A collection of machines dedicated to running business logic packaged as components.

component type (n).   A collection of one or more interfaces that are supported by one or more component implementations. Example: Because empX is a component instance of an Employee *component type*, we know it supports the tellMeYourName method. Note: Often the term *component type* is left out, and merely implied, as in: Because empX is an instance of an Employee, we know it supports the tellMeYourName method.

commit (v).   A request to a database to terminate a transaction and attempt to perform all of the database updates that were part of the transaction. In contrast to *rollback*. Example: Since there is enough money in the savings account to cover the transfer, we allow the transaction to *commit*.

COMWare (Component-Oriented Middleware).   A collection of technologies designed to provide a middle tier infrastructure to support the runtime needs of middle tier components, especially those used to implement Web-based commerce systems.

container (n).   The word used by Enterprise JavaBeans to describe the middle tier runtime environment for components.

container managed persistence (n).   A subtype of *entity beans* in which the bean's state is managed automatically by the container, using component/database mappings defined by the component implementer. In contrast to *bean managed persistence*.

conversational mode (n).   A relationship between a proxy and an instance in which the instance remains associated with the proxy for some amount of time (the period of the conversation). Instances that are in a conversational mode are allowed to contain state, but may not participate in instance management algorithms. This is not generally scalable, and therefore generally not a recommended approach to programming middle tier components.

CORBA (Common Object Request Broker Architecture). This is the generic distributed component architecture defined by the OMG. Example: IONA sells an implementation of *CORBA*.

CTM (Component Transaction Monitor). A synonym for COMWare. Derived from the popular term OTM (see *OTM*).

Distributed Transaction Coordinator (n). A process that knows how to coordinate transactions across multiple databases and/or other transactional resources usually using the three-phase commit protocol.

DTC. See *Distributed Transaction Coordinator*.

DLL (Dynamically Loaded Library). A common way of packaging the compiled code that implements a component instance so that it can be loaded into a component process as needed. Example: We compile the Employee code and create a *DLL*.

DHTML (Dynamic HyperText Markup Language). An evolving standard for the next generation of HTML. One of the features of DHTML is a tight integration with XML.

DM1SXF. Doppio Macchiato, 1Sugar, Extra Foam (see *Doppio Macchiato*).

Doppio. See *Doppio Macchiato*.

Doppio Macchiato (n). Two shots of espresso with milk foam on top, like a cappuccino without the steamed milk. This stuff will grow hair on a ping pong ball. It is best enjoyed with one sugar in the raw, extra foam, and a light dusting of chocolate powder.

EJB (Enterprise JavaBeans). The COMWare technology championed by Sun that is closely associated with the Java programming language.

entity bean (n).   A type of component defined by EJB that has a database ID associated with each instance. (In contrast to a *session bean*.) Entity beans are typically subdivided into those that support *bean managed persistence* and those that support *container managed persistence*.

event system (n).   A system that coordinates events.

event (n).   An announcement of some occurrence by a client or a component (called a *publisher*), possibly being waited on by other components (called *subscribers*). Example: A variety of components were waiting for the Object-Watch stock split *event*.

failover (v).   The process of moving a collection of work from one machine to another in the event that the first machine has suffered a failure.

failsafe (adj.).   Something that will continue working even in the event of a system failure, such as a failsafe proxy.

failsafe proxy (n).   A proxy that will shield its client from a failure on the part of the associated instance.

fat client (n).   A less desirable synonym for a *rich client*.

GUID (Globally Unique ID).   Some type of an ID that is generated with an algorithm that guarantees that the ID will not be the same as any other GUID, even when that other GUID is generated on a completely different system.

HTML (Hyper Text Markup Language).   The standard language used to define pages for display by Web browsers.

HTTP (Hyper Text Transport Protocol).   The protocol used by a Web browser to make work requests, usually for the generation of Web pages.

home bean (n).   An EJB concept that refers to a bean whose special purpose is either to create new beans or (in the case of entity beans) to find existing beans.

IIS (Internet Information Services).   The main Microsoft technology used to control the Web tier.

IMDB (In Memory Database).   An archaic term used to describe a database cache-like COM+ service that has since been withdrawn from the product.

impersonation security (n).   Security based on a component process temporarily taking on the process credentials of a client process. Usually used in order to let the database handle security rather than letting the COMWare environment handle it. This type of security does not scale, so should be avoided in applications that expect to support a large number of clients. In contrast to *authorization security*.

instance (n).   In the context of components, this refers to a *component instance*. In the context of object-oriented programming, this refers to an instance of an object.

instance management algorithm (n).   An algorithm that manages the relationship between a client side proxy and a component instance, giving the illusion that the relationship is long lasting, whereas in fact, the instance resources are being shared among a large number of clients. Instance management algorithms are a subcategory of *point of interception* algorithms. The two instance management algorithms commonly used are *just-in-time-instantiation* and *instance pooling*.

instance manager (n).   Something that coordinates *instance management algorithms*.

instance pooling algorithm (n).   An instance management algorithm that returns an instance to a pool while it is not in use by one client, so that it can be used by other clients.

instance state (n).   Any information stored in an individual component instance that is specific to a particular client proxy.

instance surrogate (n).   A stand-in for the component instance that lives in the client process and forwards method requests over to the client surrogate living in the component process. A synonym is *proxy*. Example: The *instance surrogate* presents the illusion of a dedicated local instance to the client, even though the actual component may be on another machine entirely.

instantiate (v).   To create a blob of memory that will represent a component instance. Also used by object-oriented programmers to describe the creation of an object instance.

intercept (v).   To intercept a method invocation between a proxy and a stub.

interface (n).   A named collection of methods. Example: The employee *interface* includes the methods for changing an employee's name.

invoke (v).   To request that a component instance perform one of its behaviors. Example: Do not *invoke* the tellMeYourName method on the employee instance before *invoking* the yourNameIs method.

JITI.   See *just-in-time-instantiation algorithm.*

just-in-time-instantiation-algorithm (n).   One of the instance management algorithms that instantiates an instance only when it is needed and for as long as it is needed to perform work for a client.

lazy client problem (n).   The problem first tackled by transaction processing monitors in which clients spend most of their time *thinking* about using scarce system resources rather than actually *using* those system resources.

load balancing algorithms (n).   A general class of algorithms used to decide how to distribute work load across a blob of machines.

loosely coupled events (n).   A synonym for *events.*

MDCA (Microsoft Distributed Component Architecture).   A term I sometimes use to describe the collection of technologies that constitute Microsoft's middle tier architecture.

MIDL (Microsoft Interface Definition Language). The Microsoft language used to define interfaces and components.

mench (n). An entity that has earned the right to be proud of what it has accomplished, usually by carefully following the rules and regulations of its society.

method (n). A definition of one of the behaviors that a component supports. A method includes all of the information a client needs to know to invoke a specific behavior on a component instance. Example: If you want to get the name of the employee, invoke the tellMeYourName *method*.

middle tier (n). A collection of machines used to run business logic. When that business logic is packaged as components, this is usually referred to as the *component tier*.

MMC (The Microsoft Management Console). The graphical user interface tool used to administer the COM+ runtime environment and to define the needs of COM+ components.

object (n). In the object-oriented programming context, this usually refers to an instance of an object. In the component context, it sometimes refers to an instance of a component. In the latter context, the term *instance* is preferred.

object oriented programming language (n). A language that claims to support *callee makes right* (polymorphic) methods, inheritance, and encapsulation. Example: Java is the *object oriented programming language* du jour.

OMG (Object Management Group). A software consortium of companies that define standards for distributed components, especially CORBA. Example: The *OMG* has recently defined a new standard for a CORBA Component Model.

ORB (Object Request Broker). Usually refers to some vendor's implementation of the CORBA architecture.

OTM (Object Transaction Monitor).   Archaic term for COMWare derived from the term TPM.

point of instantiation (n).   The exact moment that a component instance is actually instantiated. Example: At the *point of instantiation*, we make empX an instance of a ParanoidEmployee.

point of interception (n, adj.). As a noun, this refers to the point at which a method request is intercepted by the COMWare runtime environment. As an adjective, this describes an algorithm that runs at the point of interception.

polling system (n).   A system that constantly checks to see if something has happened so that some action can be started. In contrast to an *event system*, in which the event itself will trigger the resulting action.

polymorphic (adj.).   Mainly used in geek-oriented singles bars to try to impress the opposite sex. Better to use *callee makes right*. Example: Because tellMeYourName is a *polymorphic* method, you can't be sure what code will actually be executed.

polymorphism (n).   Not recommended. Use *callee makes right*. Often used to describe the *polymorphic* methods of object-oriented programming languages. Example: Object-oriented programming languages support *polymorphism*.

proxy (n).   A synonym for an *instance surrogate*.

proxyless (adj.).   A component architecture based on the lack of an instance surrogate. Such an architecture would most likely be based on XML strings, in which the client would create an XML string representing a method invocation, and would pass that through to a generic distributed method system.

publish and subscribe (adj.).   A mode of communication based on *events*.

publisher (n).   The entity that raises an *event*.

proxy (n).   A synonym for the *instance surrogate* in the client process.

queued component (n).   The official Microsoft term for an *asynchronous component*.

raise (v).   The process of announcing that an *event* has occurred.

reference (n).   The EJB term for an *instance surrogate*, or *proxy*.

resource pooling (n).   An algorithm that allows expensive system resources (such as database connections) to be pooled so that they can be multiplexed among many clients.

rich client (n).   A client that is running a user side program, in contrast to a *thin client*.

role based security (n).   An authorization security model in which clients are assigned roles (similar to system level groups), and authorization to the middle tier is administered based on these roles.

rollback (v, n).   As a verb, a request to a database to terminate a transaction and undo all of the database updates that were part of the transaction. In contrast to *commit*. As a noun, the request itself. Synonym is *abort*. Verb example: Since there is not enough money in the savings account to cover the transfer, we requested that the transaction *rollback*.

RPC (Remote Procedure Call).   A technique for creating distributed systems based on the invocation of procedures. Example: Our old distributed banking system was based on the *RPC* model.

session bean (n).   A type of component defined by *EJB* that does not have a database ID associated with each instance. In contrast to an *entity bean*. Sessions beans are typically subdivided into *stateful session beans* and *stateless session beans*.

stateless (adj.).   A general description of a component implementation that does not have proxy-specific state that remains bound to an instance across method invocations.

stateful session bean (n).   A type of *session bean* defined by EJB that contains state, and whose state is managed automatically by the *container*. In contrast to a *stateless session bean*.

stateless session bean (n).   A type of *session bean* defined by *EJB* that does not have any state of which the container is involved in managing. Similar to a COM+ component. In contrast to a *stateful session bean*.

stub (n).   A synonym for an *instance surrogate*.

subscriber (n).   An entity that registers interest in an *event*.

surrogate (adj.).   An entity that lives in one process that takes the place of an entity in another process. Most commonly used for *instance surrogates* and *client surrogates*.

synchronous (adj.).   A work request that must be completed before the requestor can continue. In contrast to *asynchronous*.

thin client (n).   A client that is using a Web browser.

Three-phase commit protocol (n).   The algorithm that is used by a *Distributed Transaction Coordinator (DTC)* to control distributed transactions across multiple transactional resources (e.g., databases). The algorithm consists conceptually of a contemplative phase (in which DTC monitors the transactional resources being updated, a consensus phase (in which DTC asks each resource if it is willing to commit), and a final phase (in which DTC tells each resource to commit or rollback, depending on the outcome of the consensus phase).

transactional boundary management algorithm (n).   An algorithm that automatically manages the beginning and ending of transactions, based on the transactional needs of the components and the current transactional state of the client.

transactional flow (n).   The ability to invoke a method on a component (or other entity) and have the work done by that component (or entity) encompassed within the same transaction as the word done by the requestor.

transaction (n).   A collection of business logic that should be executed in its entirety if it all can be executed without errors; otherwise, it should not be executed at all.

TPM.   See *Transaction Processing Monitor*.

transactional integrity algorithm (n).   The algorithm used by business logic implementers to guarantee that the state inside their business logic is consistent with the state as stored on a database.

Transaction Processing Monitor (n).   A pre-COMWare middle tier infrastructure for managing business logic in large commerce systems.

two-phase commit protocol (n).   The common term used to describe the *three-phase commit protocol*.

type library (n).   In the Microsoft world, a machine-readable description of a component and its interface(s).

VTable (n).   A technique originally used by C++ to support *callee makes right* methods.

W3C (World Wide Web Consortium).   A software consortium that defines standards related to the Internet.

WLBS (Windows Load Balancing Service).   A Microsoft technology used for load balancing machines involved with responding to IP requests, most commonly used for load balancing Web servers.

XML (eXtensible Markup Language).   A neutral, self-describing format for data

Additional Resources

I f you are interested in following up on some of the issues raised in this book, here are some good starting places.

General COMWare Resources

If you enjoyed this book, you should definitely subscribe to *The Object-Watch Newsletter*, Roger Sessions' monthly e-mail newsletter on issues related to COMWare. You can read old issues at www.objectwatch.com. To subscribe, send e-mail to:

```
sub@objectwatch.com
```

with the message:

```
subscribe <yourName>,<yourEmail>
```

For example,

```
subscribe Roger Sessions,roger@objectwatch.com
```

For another perspective on the middle tier, see *Client/Server Survival Guide, Third Edition*, by Robert Orfali, Dan Harkey, and Jeri Edwards (John Wiley & Sons, Inc., New York, NY. 1999. ISBN 0-471-31615-6). I have always been a great fan of the Orfali and Harkey writing team. Although I rarely agree with what they say, they make their case with great style and an excellent understanding of distributed programming issues.

Transaction Processing Monitors

Probably the best single resources on TPM technology is the magnum opus *Transaction Processing: Concepts and Techniques* by Jim Gray and Andreas Reuter (Morgan Kaufmann Publishers, San Mateo, CA. 1992. ISBN 1-558-60190-2).

COM+

Mary Kirtland is a great writer and teacher, and has an excellent overview of Microsoft technologies. Although I generally do not like Microsoft Press, anything Mary writes is worth reading. Her latest book is about COM/DCOM/MTS, but is still highly relevant and well worth your investment. See *Designing Component-Based Applications*, by Mary Kirtland (Microsoft Press, Redmond, WA. 1998. ISBN 0-735-60523-8).

Don Box is planning an *Essential COM+, 2nd Edition* to be published by Addison-Wesley. It wasn't available as of press time, but if Don follows his usual form, this will be an indispensable guide for the serious programmer. Anything Don writes is an immediate classic.

David Platt has just come out with *Understanding COM+*. I have seen only one sample chapter, but David is a good writer and I have heard good things about the book from people who have seen the finished product. This book will probably fall somewhere between my book and Don Box's book in technical depth. Unfortunately, this is another Microsoft Press book, which means it can't be considered unbiased, but David is still worth reading. Look for *Understanding COM+*, by David Platt (Microsoft Press, Redmond, WA. 1999. ISBN 0-735-60666-8).

EJB

My favorite book on EJB is *Mastering Enterprise JavaBeans and the Java 2 Platform, Enterprise Edition*, by Ed Roman (John Wiley & Sons, Inc., New York, NY. 1999. ISBN 0-471-33229-1).

Another good overview of EJB is given by *Developing Java Enterprise Applications*, by Stephen Asbury and Scott R. Weiner (John Wiley & Sons, Inc., New York, NY. 1999. ISBN 0-471-32756-5).

For a pocket reference to EJB, see *Enterprise JavaBeans* by Richard Monson-Haefel (O'Reilly, Sebastopol, CA. 1999. ISBN 1-565-92605-6).

CORBA

If you are interested in a serious look at developing CORBA applications, check out *Enterprise CORBA* by Dirk Slama, Jason Garbis, and Perry Russell, all from IONA (Prentice Hall, Upper Saddle River, NJ. 1999. ISBN 0-130-83963-9).

A good book for comparing Microsoft and CORBA technologies is *COM and CORBA Side by Side: Architectures, Strategies, and Implementations*, by Jason Pritchard (Addison-Wesley, Reading, MA. 1999. ISBN 0-201-37945-7).